ANTHOLOGY
OF
AMERICAN
POETRY

ANTHOLOGY
OF
AMERICAN
POETRY

Edited by
GEORGE GESNER

GRAMERCY BOOKS
NEW YORK • AVENEL

Copyright © 1983 by Crown Publishers, Inc.
All rights reserved.

This 1994 edition is published by Gramercy Books,
distributed by Random House Value Publishing, Inc.,
40 Engelhard Avenue,
Avenel, New Jersey 07001

Random House
New York • Toronto • London • Sydney • Auckland

Manufactured in the United States of America

Library of Congress Cataloging-in-Publication Data
Main entry under title:
    Anthology of American poetry.
    1. American poetry. I. Gesner, George, 1954–
PS586.A57   1983   811′.008   82-20644

ISBN: 0-517-118904

8 7 6 5 4 3 2

Acknowledgments

Conrad Aiken   "All Lovely Things," "The Sounding," "The Nameless Ones," and "Music" from *Collected Poems* by Conrad Aiken. Copyright 1953, and © 1970 by Conrad Aiken; renewed © 1981 by Mary Aiken. Reprinted by permission of Oxford University Press, Inc.   •   Stephen Vincent Benét   "Days Pass: Men Pass" from *The Selected Works of Stephen Vincent Benét*. Copyright 1925 by Stephen Vincent Benét. Copyright renewed 1953 by Rosemary Carr Benét. Reprinted by permission of Brandt & Brandt Literary Agents, Inc. "Nomenclature" from *The Selected Works of Stephen Vincent Benét*. Copyright 1925 by Stephen Vincent Benét. Copyright renewed 1953 by Rosemary Carr Benét. Reprinted by permission of Brandt & Brandt Literary Agents, Inc. "Unfamiliar Quartet" by Stephen Vincent Benét, from *Ballads and Poems*, Doubleday & Co., Inc. Copyright 1918, 1920, 1923, 1929, 1930, 1931. Copyright renewed by Stephen Vincent Benét. Reprinted by permission of Brandt & Brandt Literary Agents, Inc. "Ghosts of a Lunatic Asylum" copyright 1918 by Stephen Vincent Benét. Copyright renewed 1946 by Rosemary Carr Benét. Reprinted by permission of Brandt & Brandt Literary Agents, Inc.   •   William Rose Benét   "Gate of Horn," "On a Dead Poet," "Vital Statistics," "The Stricken Average," and "Judgement" from *The Stairway of Surprise* by William Rose Benét. Copyright 1947 by William Rose Benét. Reprinted by permission of Harold Ober Associates, Incorporated.   •   E. E. Cummings   "my uncle daniel," "my sweet old etcetera," "it really must be nice," reprinted from *IS 5 Poems* by E. E. Cummings, by permission of Liveright Publishing Corporation. Copyright 1926 by Horace Liveright. Copyright renewed 1953 by E. E. Cummings. "my sweet old etcetera," "it really must be nice," "my uncle daniel" reprinted from *Complete Poems by E. E. Cummings* by permission of Granada Publishing Limited.   •   Hilda Doolittle   "Helen," "Flute Song," and "Lethe" by Hilda Doolittle, from *Collected Poems of H.D.* Copyright 1925, 1953 by Norman Holmes Pearson. Reprinted by permission of New Directions Publishing Corporation.   •   T. S. Eliot   "Sweeney Among the Nightingales," "Cousin Nancy," and "Aunt Helen" from *Collected Poems 1909–1962* by T. S. Eliot. Copyright 1936 by Harcourt Brace Jovanovich, Inc. Copyright © 1963, 1964 by T. S. Eliot. Reprinted by permission of the publisher. "Sweeney Among the Nightingales," "Cousin Nancy," and "Aunt Helen" from *Collected Poems 1909–1962* by T. S. Eliot. Reprinted by permission of Faber and Faber Ltd.   •   Amy Lowell   "A Gift," "A Lady," "Night Clouds," and "Nostalgia" from *The Complete Poetical Works of Amy Lowell*. Copyright © 1955 by Houghton Mifflin Company. Reprinted by permission of the Publisher.   •   Archibald MacLeish   "Mother Goose's Garland," "Grazing Locomotives," "Thunderhead," and "The Rape of the Swan" from *New and Collected Poems 1917–1976* by Archibald MacLeish. Copyright © 1976 by Archibald MacLeish. Reprinted by permission of Houghton Mifflin Company.   •   Edna St. Vincent Millay   "Afternoon on a Hill," "The Penitent," and "Feast" from *Collected Poems* by Edna St. Vincent Millay, Harper & Row. Copyright 1917, 1921, 1922, 1923, 1945, 1948, 1950, 1951, 1954 by Edna St. Vincent Millay and Norma Millay Ellis. Reprinted by permission of the publisher.   •   Marianne Moore   "No Swan So Fine," "To Military Progress," and "Silence" reprinted with permission of Macmillan Publishing Co., Inc. from *Collected Poems* by Marianne Moore. Copyright 1935 by Marianne Moore. Copyright © renewed 1963 by Marianne Moore and T. S. Eliot. "No Swan So Fine," "To Military Progress," and "Silence" reprinted by permission of Faber and Faber Ltd. from *The Complete Poems of Marianne Moore*.   •   Ogden Nash   "Old Men" copyright 1931 by Ogden Nash. "Song of the Open Road" copyright 1932 by Ogden Nash. First appeared in *The New Yorker*. "The Fish" copyright 1940 by Ogden Nash. All poems from *The Face is Familiar* copyright 1933, 1932, 1933, 1935, 1940 by Ogden Nash. Copyright 1933 by the Curtis Publishing Company. Reprinted by permission of Little, Brown and Company. "Song of the Open Road" copyright 1932 by Ogden Nash. "Old Men" copyright 1933 by Ogden Nash. "The Fish" copyright 1940 by Ogden Nash. Reprinted by permission of Curtis Brown, Ltd.   •   Dorothy Parker   "Comment," "Resume," and "Social Note" from *The Portable Dorothy Parker*, revised and enlarged edition, edited by Brendan Gill. Copyright 1926 by Dorothy Parker. Copyright renewed 1954 by Dorothy Parker. Reprinted by permission of Viking Penguin Inc. "Bohemia," and "On Being A Woman" from *The Portable Dorothy Parker*, revised and enlarged edition, edited by Brendan Gill. Copyright 1928 by Dorothy Parker. Copyright © renewed 1956 by Dorothy Parker. Reprinted by permission of Viking Penguin Inc. "On Being A Woman," "Bohemia,"

Contents

Miscellaneous

Foreword

"If I read a book," wrote Emily Dickinson, "and it makes my whole body so cold no fire can ever warm me, I know that is poetry. If I feel physically as if the top of my head were taken off, I know that is poetry. These are the only ways I know it. Is there any other way?"

Emily Dickinson sat in her house in Amherst, Massachusetts, composing her precisely felt poems, keenly aware of every element of life occurring around her. She sent her handwritten poems along with homemade biscuits to friends; only after her death was her work published. In anthologies like this one, readers can be exhilarated by her poetry; the great American poets represented here write so well that, like Dickinson, we can go cold and lightheaded with understanding.

Poems are important because they push beyond the simplifications we use every day. A man says to a woman, "I love you"—and what does he mean? He is using one simple phrase to label a thousand different sensations. Can the woman know exactly what he means? In poems, on the other hand, words like *love* come alive because the language of poetry is rich, specific, and evocative. Dickinson begins a poem, "My life has stood, a loaded gun": when a man uses that gun—a gun that is the speaker's *life*—we understand suddenly Dickinson's feelings about a kind of love that for her is very complicated.

Sometimes, in classrooms and in books, it is easy to forget that poems are written by real people with bills to pay. Poets are in no way different from their best readers: Walt Whitman was a reporter, William Carlos Williams a pediatrician, Marianne Moore a librarian, and Wallace Stevens an insurance executive. They all went to work every morning; they fell in love; they ate and drank, smiled and frowned, had aches and pains. Any reader of the *Anthology of American Poetry* encounters not only poems but poets. "I leap from the page to your arms," wrote Walt Whitman. He, like all the poets represented here, wrote poems not simply to get something off his chest but because he wanted to *communicate* with readers who were very important to him. "I considered long and seriously of you before you were born," Whitman announced in 1856. When we feel the tops of our heads taken off by a poem, we know the poet had cared long and hard enough to talk to us.

American writers have been writing for American readers for more than three centuries now. Poetry in the New World began to establish itself before the Constitution. Anne Bradstreet, emigrating from England with her Puritan husband, was one of the first in a long series of specifically American writers that continues vigorously into the present.

Bradstreet came to a wild country, but hardship, cold, and the deaths of her children never shook her faith in God, her love for her husband, or her belief that coming to the Massachusetts Bay Colony was the right choice to have made. American poets since Bradstreet have usually exhibited a persistent optimism about America even when the evidence pointed in the other direction. Centuries later, in the early 1800s, William Cullen Bryant and Ralph Waldo Emerson refined that optimism into a public poetry appropriate to stern, progressive New England, while Henry David Thoreau cut a path to a purer, more spartan life that embraced the independence and solitude of the individual living harmoniously with American nature. Likewise, Whitman turned American individualist aspirations into something of a religion—a religion that brought human beings together as one exuberant soul that was America, singing. Not even the Civil War could disturb his faith in his country's generative powers.

In the twentieth century, after the revolutionary precisions of the poems of Emily Dickinson, American poets expanded even further into an examination of all aspects of national life. Their styles became even more diverse—what poets could be more different than Robert Frost and Carl Sandburg? Paul Laurence Dunbar began chronicling the experience of black Americans, an activity continued by other black poets in the present day; Carl Sandburg took Whitman's long poetic line and explored the new industrial landscape, which still fascinates writers. Poets like T. S. Eliot, Wallace Stevens, Robert Frost, William Carlos Williams, Marianne Moore, and Ezra Pound remade the language of poetry to suit a complicated century. Free verse—that is, poetry that relies more on rhythm than on meter for its power—became one new way of communicating the American experience to reflect the strength and variety of the country. "Make it new," said Ezra Pound. America made it new, and so did its poets.

Although American poets became more and more diverse, they usually retained their fidelity to an important and lasting element of America: the home place, the land, the region. Who can think of

Robert Frost without thinking of New England? Frost is as much a part of his countryside as stone fences, maple syrup, and snow. Poets like Whitman bravely charted the westward path of the pioneers and the ever-changing urban landscape, and Native American poets both then and now created songs that reflected their tribal attachment to the soil and to nature. Edward Arlington Robinson wrote of small-town America, and Theodore Roethke embraced his native, damp Pacific Northwest. From Bradstreet to Updike, in one way or another, American poets long for solid ground beneath their feet.

Along with a sense of place came a poetic fascination with the idea of America as a nation—a country with a particular experience that set it apart from any place anywhere else in the world. A sense of America flourished not only among poets like Whitman and Williams but at the popular level as well, in ballads, in national hymns, and in folk stories told in verse—all feeding the American hunger to find out about itself. Side by side with a sense of country was a feeling for particularly American versions of religion, home, nature, and humor. Songs of the southern slaves and Native Americans gave a distinctly spiritual flavor to American poetry and to the American people as well.

"The United States themselves are essentially the greatest poem. . . . Here at last is something in the doings of men that corresponds with the broadcast doings of the day and night." In those words from the preface to his *Leaves of Grass*, Walt Whitman made it clear that American poetry is made of Americans. And it cannot do without American readers.

David Groff

New York

I
Poets of America

Anne Bradstreet

(1612?–1672)

Anne Bradstreet was born in England and sailed to America in 1630. She settled in the Massachusetts Bay Colony with her husband and father (who both became governors of the colony), where she lived a domestic Puritan lifestyle. Bradstreet's poetry reflected the family and religious concerns that shaped her life. She is now considered to be the first real American poet of consequence.

THE FLESH AND THE SPIRIT

In secret place where once I stood,
Close by the banks of lacrym flood,
I heard two sisters reason on
Things that are past and things to come.
One Flesh was called, who had her eye
On worldly wealth and vanity;
The other Spirit, who did rear
Her thoughts unto a higher sphere.
"Sister," quoth Flesh, "what livest thou on—
Nothing but meditation?
Doth contemplation feed thee, so
Regardlessly to let earth go?
Can speculation satisfy
Notion without reality?
Dost dream of things beyond the moon,
And dost thou hope to dwell there soon?
Hast treasures there laid up in store
That all in the world thou countest poor?
Art fancy sick, or turned a sot,

To catch at shadows which are not?
Come, come, I'll show unto thy sense
Industry hath its recompense.
What canst desire but thou mayst see
True substance in variety?
Dost honor like? Acquire the same,
As some to their immortal fame,
And trophies to thy name erect
Which wearing time shall ne'er deject.
For riches dost thou long full sore?
Behold enough of precious store;
Earth hath more silver, pearls, and gold
Than eyes can see or hands can hold.
Affectest thou pleasure? Take thy fill;
Earth hath enough of what you will.
Then let not go what thou mayst find
For things unknown, only in mind."

Spirit

"Be still, thou unregenerate part;
Disturb no more my settled heart,
For I have vowed, and so will do,
Thee as a foe still to pursue,
And combat with thee will and must
Until I see thee laid in the dust.
Sisters we are, yea, twins we be,
Yet deadly feud 'twixt thee and me;
For from one father are we not.
Thou by old Adam was begot,
But my arise is from above,
Whence my dear Father I do love.
Thou speakest me fair, but hatest me sore;
Thy flattering shows I'll trust no more.
How oft thy slave has thou me made
When I believed what thou has said,
And never had more cause of woe
Than when I did what thou bad'st do.
I'll stop mine ears at these thy charms,
And count them for my deadly harms.
Thy sinful pleasures I do hate,
Thy riches are to me no bait,
Thine honors do nor will I love,
For my ambition lies above.

My greatest honor it shall be
When I am victor over thee,
And triumph shall, with laurel head,
When thou my captive shalt be led.
How I do live thou needst not scoff,
For I have meat thou knowst not of:
The hidden manna I do eat,
The word of life it is my meat.
My thoughts do yield me more content
Than can thy hours in pleasure spent.
Nor are they shadows which I catch,
Nor fancies vain at which I snatch,
But reach at things that are so high
Beyond thy dull capacity.
Eternal substance I do see,
With which enrichéd I would be;
Mine eye doth pierce the heavens, and see
What is invisible to thee.
My garments are not silk or gold,
Nor such like trash which earth doth hold,
But royal robes I shall have on,
More glorious than the glistering sun.
My crown not diamonds, pearls, and gold,
But such as angels' heads enfold.
The city where I hope to dwell
There's none on earth can parallel:
The stately walls, both high and strong,
Are made of precious jasper stone;
The gates of pearl both rich and clear,
And angels are for porters there;
The streets thereof transparent gold,
Such as no eye did e'er behold;
A crystal river there doth run,
Which doth proceed from the Lamb's throne;
Of life there are the waters sure,
Which shall remain for ever pure;
Of sun or moon they have no need,
For glory doth from God proceed—
No candle there, nor yet torch-light,
For there shall be no darksome night.
From sickness and infirmity
For evermore they shall be free,
Nor withering age shall e'er come there,
But beauty shall be bright and clear.

This city pure is not for thee,
For things unclean there shall not be.
If I of Heaven may have my fill,
Take thou the world, and all that will."

A LETTER TO HER HUSBAND

Phœbus, make haste: the day 's too long; be gone;
The silent night 's the fittest time for moan.
But stay this once, unto my suit give ear,
And tell my griefs in either Hemisphere;
And if the whirling of thy wheels don't drown'd
The woful accents of my doleful sound,
If in thy swift Carrier thou canst make stay,
I crave this boon, this Errand by the way:
Commend me to the man more lov'd then life;
Shew him the sorrows of his widdowed wife,
My dumpish thoughts, my groans, my brakish tears,
My sobs, my longing hopes, my doubting fears;
And if he love, how can he there abide?
My interest 's more then all the world beside.
He that can tell the starrs or Ocean sand,
Or all the grass that in the Meads do stand,
The leaves in th' woods, the hail or drops of rain,
Or in a corn-field number every grain,
Or every mote that in the sun-shine hops,
May count my sighs and number all my drops.
Tell him the countless steps that thou dost trace
That once a day thy Spouse thou mayst imbrace;
And when thou canst not treat by loving mouth,
Thy rayes afar salute her from the south.
But for one moneth I see no day, poor soul,
Like those far scituate under the pole,
Which day by day long wait for thy arise:
O how they joy when thou dost light the skyes.
O *Phœbus*, hadst thou but thus long from thine
Restrain'd the beams of thy beloved shine,
At thy return, if so thou could'st or durst,
Behold a Chaos blacker then the first.
Tell him here 's worse then a confused matter—
His little world 's a fathom under water;
Nought but the fervor of his ardent beams
Hath power to dry the torrent of these streams.

Tell him I would say more, but cannot well:
Oppressed minds abruptest tales do tell.
Now post with double speed, mark what I say;
By all our loves conjure him not to stay.

LONGING FOR HEAVEN

As weary pilgrim now at rest
  Hugs with delight his silent nest,
His wasted limbes now lye full soft
  That myrie steps have troden oft,
Blesses himself to think upon
  his dangers past and travailes done;
The burning sun no more shall heat;
  Nor stormy raines on him shall beat;
The bryars and thornes no more shall scratch,
  nor hungry wolves at him shall catch;
He erring pathes no more shall tread,
  nor wild fruits eate in stead of bread;
For waters cold he doth not long,
  for thirst no more shall parch his tongue;
No rugged stones his feet shall gaule,
  nor stumps nor rocks cause him to fall;
All cares and feares he bids farwell,
  and meanes in safity now to dwell:
A pilgrim I on earth perplext,
  with sinns, with cares and sorrows vext,
By age and paines brought to decay,
  and my Clay house mouldring away,
Oh how I long to be at rest
  and soare on high among the blest!
This body shall in silence sleep,
  Mine eyes no more shall ever weep,
No fainting fits shall me assaile,
  nor grinding paines my body fraile,
With cares and fears ne'r cumbred be,
  Nor losses know nor sorrowes see.
What tho my flesh shall there consume?
  it is the bed Christ did perfume;
And when a few yeares shall be gone,
  this mortall shall be cloth'd upon:
A Corrupt Carcasse downe it lyes,
  a glorious body it shall rise;

In weaknes and dishonour sowne,
    in power 't is rais'd by Christ alone.
Then soule and body shall unite,
    and of their maker have the sight.
Such lasting joyes shall there behold
    as eare ne'r heard nor tongue e'er told.
Lord, make me ready for that day:
    then Come, deare bridgrome, Come away!

THE AUTHOR TO HER BOOK

Thou ill-form'd offspring of my feeble brain,
Who after birth didst by my side remain
Till snatcht from thence by friends less wise than true
Who thee abroad expos'd to publick view,
Made thee in raggs, halting to th'press to trudge
Where errors were not lessened (all may judge)
At thy return my blushing was not small,
My rambling brat (in print) should mother call.
I cast thee by as one unfit for light,
Thy Visage was so irksome in my sight;
Yet being mine own, at length affection would
Thy blemishes amend, if so I could:
I wash'd thy face, but more defects I saw,
And rubbing off a spot, still made a flaw.
I stretcht thy joints to make thee even feet,
Yet still thou run'st more hobling than is meet;
In better dress to trim thee was my mind,
But nought save home-spun Cloth i'th'house I find.
In this array 'mongst Vulgars mayst thou roam,
In Cricks hands beware thou dost not come,
And take thy way where yet thou art not known.
If for thy Father askt, say, thou hadst none:
And for thy Mother, she alas is poor,
Which caus'd her thus to send thee out of door.

TO MY DEAR AND LOVING HUSBAND

If ever two were one, then surely we.
If ever man were lov'd by wife, then thee.
If ever wife was happy in a man,
Compare with me, ye women, if you can.

I prize thy love more than whole Mines of gold,
Or all the riches that the East doth hold.
My love is such that Rivers cannot quench,
Nor ought but love from thee give recompence.
Thy love is such I can no way repay;
The heavens reward thee manifold I pray.
Then while we live, in love lets so persever,
That when we live no more, we may live ever.

UPON THE BURNING OF OUR HOUSE

July 10th, 1666

In silent night when rest I took,
For sorrow near I did not look,
I waken'd was with thundring noise
And piteous shreiks of dreadfull voice.
That fearfull sound of "Fire!" and "Fire!"
Let no man know is my Desire.

I, starting up, the light did spye,
And to my God my heart did cry
To strengthen me in my Distresse,
And not to leave me succourlesse.
Then coming out, beheld apace
The flame consume my dwelling place.

And when I could no longer look,
I blest his Name that gave and took,
That layd my goods now in the dust:
Yea so it was, and so 'twas just.
It was his own: it was not mine;
Far be it that I should repine.

He might of All justly bereft,
But yet sufficient for us left.
When by the Ruines oft I past,
My sorrowing eyes aside did cast,
And here and there the places spye
Where oft I sate, and long did lye.

Here stood that Trunk, and there that chest;
There lay that store I counted best:

My pleasant things in ashes lye,
And them behold no more shall I.
Under thy roof no guest shall sitt,
Nor at thy Table eat a bitt.

No pleasant tale shall e'er be told,
Nor things recounted done of old.
No Candle e'er shall shine in Thee,
Nor bridegroom's voice e'er heard shall bee.
In silence ever shalt thou lye;
Adeiu, Adeiu; All's vanity.

Then streight I 'gan my heart to chide:
And did thy wealth on earth abide?
Didst fix thy hope on mouldring dust,
The arm of flesh didst make thy trust?
Raise up thy thoughts above the skye,
That dunghill mists away may flie.

Thou hast an house on high erect,
Fram'd by that mighty Architect,
With glory richly furnished,
Stands permanent though this bee fled.
It's purchaséd, and paid for, too,
By Him who hath enough to doe.

A Prise so vast as is unknown,
Yet, by his Gift, is made thine own.
There's wealth enough, I need no more;
Farewell my Pelf, farewell my Store.
The world no longer let me Love,
My Hope and Treasure lyes Above.

Philip Freneau

(1752–1832)

Philip Freneau was born of French Huguenot parentage in New York City and grew up in New Jersey. He attended Princeton, where he met and befriended his classmate James Madison, who later became the fourth president of the United States. Freneau was known as the "Poet of the Revolution" and is considered to be the first real American-born poet. He studied law and became a journalist and navigator. Nevertheless, throughout his long and active life, Freneau battled sporadically with poverty and ill fortune. In 1815 Freneau's house burned down, which may have led him to drink. On a cold December night in 1832 Freneau was returning home from a gathering of friends when he slipped and fell in a swampy meadow, broke his hip, and died of exposure in the snow.

THE INDIAN BURYING GROUND

In spite of all the learned have said,
　I still my old opinion keep;
The posture, that we give the dead,
　Points out the soul's eternal sleep.

Not so the ancients of these lands—
　The Indian, when from life released,
Again is seated with his friends,
　And shares again the joyous feast.

His imaged birds, and painted bowl,
　And venison, for a journey dressed,

Bespeak the nature of the soul,
  Activity, that knows no rest.

His bow, for action ready bent,
  And arrows, with a head of stone,
Can only mean that life is spent,
  And not the old ideas gone.

Thou, stranger, that shalt come this way,
  No fraud upon the dead commit—
Observe the swelling turf, and say
  They do not lie, but here they sit.

Here still a lofty rock remains,
  On which the curious eye may trace
(Now wasted, half, by wearing rains)
  The fancies of a ruder race.

Here still an aged elm aspires,
  Beneath whose far-projecting shade
(And which the shepherd still admires)
  The children of the forest played!

There oft a restless Indian queen
  (Pale Shebah, with her braided hair)
And many a barbarous form is seen
  To chide the man that lingers there.

By midnight moons, o'er moistening dews;
  In habit for the chase arrayed,
The hunter still the deer pursues,
  The hunter and the deer, a shade!

All long shall timorous fancy see
  The painted chief, and pointed spear,
And Reason's self shall bow the knee
  To shadows and delusions here.

STANZAS

Occasioned by the Ruins of a Country Inn, Unroofed and
Blown Down in a Storm

Where now these mingled ruins lie
    A temple once to Bacchus rose,
Beneath whose roof, aspiring high,
    Full many a guest forgot his woes:

No more this dome, by tempests torn,
    Affords a social safe retreat;
But ravens here, with eye forlorn,
    And clustering bats henceforth will meet.

The Priestess of this ruined shrine,
    Unable to survive the stroke,
Presents no more the ruddy wine,
    Her glasses gone, her china broke.

The friendly Host, whose social hand
    Accosted strangers at the door,
Has left at length his wonted stand,
    And greets the weary guest no more.

Old creeping Time, that brings decay,
    Might yet have spared these mouldering walls,
Alike beneath whose potent sway
    A temple or a tavern falls.

Is this the place where mirth and joy,
    Coy nymphs and sprightly lads were found?
Indeed! no more the nymphs are coy,
    No more the flowing bowls go round.

Is this the place where festive song
    Deceived the wintry hours away?
No more the swains the tune prolong,
    No more the maidens join the lay:

Is this the place where Nancy slept
    In downy beds of blue and green?—
Dame Nature here no vigils kept,
    No cold unfeeling guards were seen.

'Tis gone!—and Nancy tempts no more,
    Deep, unrelenting silence reigns;
Of all that pleased, that charmed before,
    The tottering chimney scarce remains!

Ye tyrant winds, whose ruffian blast
    Through doors and windows blew too strong,
And all the roof to ruin cast,
    The roof that sheltered us so long.

Your wrath appeased, I pray be kind
    If Mopsus should the dome renew;
That we again may quaff his wine,
    Again collect our jovial crew.

THE WILD HONEY SUCKLE

Fair flower, that dost so comely grow,
Hid in this silent, dull retreat,
Untouched thy honied blossoms blow,
Unseen thy little branches greet:
    No roving foot shall crush thee here,
    No busy hand provoke a tear.

By Nature's self in white arrayed,
She bade thee shun the vulgar eye,
And planted here the guardian shade,
And sent soft waters murmuring by;
    Thus quietly thy summer goes,
    Thy days declining to repose.

Smit with those charms, that must decay,
I grieve to see your future doom;
They died—nor were those flowers more gay,
The flowers that did in Eden bloom;
    Unpitying frosts, and Autumn's power
    Shall leave no vestige of this flower.

From morning suns and evening dews
At first thy little being came:
If nothing once, you nothing lose,
For when you die you are the same;

The space between, is but an hour,
The frail duration of a flower.

THE INDIAN STUDENT

Or, Force of Nature

From Susquehanna's farthest springs
Where savage tribes pursue their game,
(His blanket tied with yellow strings,)
A shepherd of the forest came.

Not long before, a wandering priest
Expressed his wish, with visage sad—
"Ah, why (he cried) in Satan's waste,
"Ah, why detain so fine a lad?

"In white–man's land there stands a town
"Where learning may be purchased low—
"Exchange his blanket for a gown,
"And let the lad to college go."—

From long debate the council rose,
And viewing Shalum's tricks with joy
To Cambridge Hall, o'er waste of snows,
They sent the copper–coloured boy.

One generous chief a bow supplied,
This gave a shaft, and that a skin;
The feathers, in vermillion dyed,
Himself did from a turkey win:

Thus dressed so gay, he took his way
O'er barren hills, alone, alone!
His guide a star, he wandered far,
His pillow every night a stone.

At last he came, with foot so lame,
Where learned men talk heathen Greek,
And Hebrew lore is gabbled o'er,
To please the Muses,—twice a week.

Awhile he writ, awhile he read,
Awhile he conned their grammar rules—
(An Indian savage so well bred
Great credit promised to the schools.)

Some thought he would in law excel,
Some said in physic he would shine;
And one that knew him, passing well,
Beheld, in him, a sound Divine.

But those of more discerning eye
Even then could other prospects show,
And saw him lay his Virgil by
To wander with his dearer bow.

The tedious hours of study spent,
The heavy–moulded lecture done,
He to the woods a hunting went,
Through lonely wastes he walked, he run.

No mystic wonders fired his mind;
He sought to gain no learned degree,
But only sense enough to find
The squirrel in the hollow tree.

The shady bank, the purling stream,
The woody wild his heart possessed,
The dewy lawn, his morning dream
In fancy's gayest colours dressed.

"And why (he cried) did I forsake
"My native wood for gloomy walls;
"The silver stream, the limpid lake
"For musty books and college halls.

"A little could my wants supply—
"Can wealth and honour give me more;
"Or, will the sylvan god deny
"The humble treat he gave before?

"Let seraphs gain the bright abode,
"And heaven's sublimest mansions see—
"I only bow to Nature's God—
"The land of shades will do for me.

"These dreadful secrets of the sky
"Alarm my soul with chilling fear—
"Do planets in their orbits fly,
"And is the earth, indeed, a sphere?

"Let planets still their course pursue,
"And comets to the centre run—
"In Him my faithful friend I view,
"The image of my God—the Sun.

"Where Nature's ancient forests grow,
"And mingled laurel never fades,
"My heart is fixed;—and I must go
"To die among my native shades."

He spoke, and to the western springs,
(His gown discharged, his money spent,
His blanket tied with yellow strings,)
The shepherd of the forest went.

EUTAW SPRINGS

At Eutaw Springs the valiant died:
    Their limbs with dust are covered o'er;
Weep on, ye springs, your tearful tide;
    How many heroes are no more!

If in this wreck of ruin they
    Can yet be thought to claim a tear,
O smite thy gentle breast, and say
    The friends of freedom slumber here!

Thou, who shalt trace this bloody plain,
    If goodness rules thy generous breast,
Sigh for the wasted rural reign;
    Sigh for the shepherds sunk to rest!

Stranger, their humble groves adorn;
    You too may fall, and ask a tear:
'Tis not the beauty of the morn
    That proves the evening shall be clear.

They saw their injured country's woe,
  The flaming town, the wasted field;
Then rushed to meet the insulting foe;
  They took the spear—but left the shield.

Led by thy conquering standards, Greene,
  The Britons they compelled to fly:
None distant viewed the fatal plain,
  None grieved in such a cause to die—

But, like the Parthians famed of old,
  Who, flying, still their arrows threw,
These routed Britons, full as bold,
  Retreated, and retreating slew.

Now rest in peace our patriot band;
  Though far from nature's limits thrown,
We trust they find a happier land,
  A brighter Phœbus of their own.

TO A HONEY BEE

Thou, born to sip the lake or spring,
  Or quaff the waters of the stream,
Why hither come, on vagrant wing?
  Does Bacchus tempting seem—
    Did he for you this glass prepare?
    Will I admit you to a share?

Did storms harass or foes perplex,
  Did wasps or king-birds bring dismay—
Did wars distress, or labors vex,
  Or did you miss your way?
    A better seat you could not take
    Than on the margin of this lake.

Welcome!—I hail you to my glass:
  All welcome here you find;
Here let the cloud of trouble pass,
  Here be all care resigned.
    This fluid never fails to please,
    And drown the griefs of men or bees.

What forced you here we cannot know,
  And you will scarcely tell,
But cheery we would have you go
  And bid a glad farewell:
    On lighter wings we bid you fly—
    Your dart will now all foes defy.

Yet take not, oh! too deep a drink,
  And in this ocean die;
Here bigger bees than you might sink,
  Even bees full six feet high.
    Like Pharaoh, then, you would be said
    To perish in a sea of red.

Do as you please, your will is mine;
  Enjoy it without fear,
And your grave will be this glass of wine,
  Your epitaph—a tear;
    Go, take your seat in Charon's boat;
    We'll tell the hive, you died afloat.

Richard Henry Dana

(1787–1879)

Richard Henry Dana was born and raised in Boston, Massachusetts. He later became a member of the Anthology Club, which was, at the time, one of the city's prominent literary circles. In 1815 he helped found the *North American Review*, which became one of the great literary journals of the time. He also wrote for various other journals. His son, Richard Henry, Jr., was a well-known author and traveler.

THE LITTLE BEACH-BIRD

Thou little bird, thou dweller by the sea,
  Why takest thou its melancholy voice,
    And with that boding cry
    Why o'er the waves dost fly?
O, rather, bird, with me
  Through the fair land rejoice!

Thy flitting form comes ghostly dim and pale,
  As driven by a beating storm at sea;
    Thy cry is weak and scared,
    As if thy mates had shared
The doom of us. Thy wail,—
  What doth it bring to me?

Thou call'st along the sand, and haunt'st the surge
  Restless and sad; as if, in strange accord
    With the motion and the roar
    Of waves that drive to shore,

One spirit did ye urge—
 The Mystery—the Word.

Of thousands, thou, both sepulcher and pall,
 Old Ocean! A requiem o'er the dead,
  From out thy gloomy cells,
  A tale of mourning tells,—
Tells of man's woe and fall,
 His sinless glory fled.

Then turn thee, little bird, and take thy flight
 Where the complaining sea shall sadness bring
  Thy spirit nevermore.
  Come, quit with me the shore,
For gladness and the light,
 Where birds of summer sing.

MURDER OF A SPANISH LADY BY A PIRATE

A sound is in the Pyrenees!
Whirling and dark, comes roaring down
A tide, as of a thousand seas,
Sweeping both cowl and crown.
On field and vineyard thick and red it stood.
Spain's streets and palaces are full of blood;

And wrath and terror shake the land;
The peaks shine clear in watchfire lights;
Soon comes the tread of that stout band—
Bold Arthur and his knights.
Awake ye, Merlin!/Hear the shout from Spain!
The spell is broke!/Arthur is come again!

Too late for thee, thou young, fair bride;
The lips are cold, the brow is pale,
That thou didst kiss in love and pride.
He cannot hear thy wail,
Whom thou didst lull with fondly murmur'd sound—
His couch is cold and lonely in the ground.

He fell for Spain—her Spain no more;
For he was gone who made it dear;
And she would seek some distant shore,

At rest from strife and fear,
And wait amid her sorrows till the day
His voice of love should call her thence away.

Lee feign'd him grieved, and bow'd him low.
'Twould joy his heart could he but aid
So good a lady in her wo,
He meekly, smoothly said.
With wealth and servants she is soon aboard,
And that white steed she rode beside her lord.

The sun goes down upon the sea;
The shadows gather round her home.
"How like a pall are ye to me!
My home, how like a tomb!
Oh! blow, ye flowers of Spain, above his head:
Ye will not blow o'er me when I am dead."

And now the stars are burning bright;
Yet still she looks towards the shore,
Beyond the waters black in night.
"I ne'er shall see thee more!
Ye're many, waves, yet lonely seems your flow,
And I'm alone—scarce know I where I go."

Sleep, sleep, thou sad one, on the sea!
The wash of waters lulls thee now;
His arm no more will pillow thee,
Thy hand upon his brow.
He is not near, to hush thee or to save.
The ground is his, the sea must be thy grave.

The moon comes up, the night goes on.
Why in the shadow of the mast,
Stands that dark, thoughtful man alone?
Thy pledge, man; keep it fast!
Bethink thee of her youth and sorrows, Lee:
Helpless alone—and then her trust in thee!

When told the hardships thou hadst borne,
Her words were to thee like a charm.
With uncheer'd grief her heart is worn.
Thou wilt not do her harm!

He looks out on the sea that sleeps in light,
And growls an oath: "It is too still tonight!"

He sleeps; but dreams of massy gold,
And heaps of pearl. He stretch'd his hands.
He hears a voice: "Ill man, withhold."
     A pale one near him stands:
Her breath comes deathly cold upon his cheek;
Her touch is cold. He wakes with piercing shriek.

He wakes; but no relentings wake
Within his angry, restless soul.
"What, shall a dream Matt's purpose shake?
The gold will make all whole.
Thy merchant trade had nigh unmann'd thee, lad!
What, balk thy chance because a woman's sad?"

He cannot look on her mild eye—
Her patient words his spirit quell.
Within that evil heart there lie
The hates and fears of hell.
His speech is short; he wears a surly brow.
There's none will hear her shriek. What fear ye now?

The workings of the soul ye fear;
Ye fear the power that goodness hath;
Ye fear the Unseen One, ever near,
Walking his ocean path.
From out the silent void there comes a cry:
"Vengeance is mine! Lost man, thy doom is nigh!"

Nor dread of ever-during wo,
Nor the sea's awful solitude,
Can make thee, wretch, thy crime forego.
Then, bloody hand—to blood!
The scud is driving wildly over head;
The stars burn dim; the ocean moans its dead.

Moan for the living—moan our sins—
The wrath of man, more fierce than thine.
Hark! still thy waves! The work begins:
He makes the deadly sign.
The crew glide down like shadows. Eye and hand
Speak fearful meanings through that silent band.

They're gone. The helmsman stands alone,
And one leans idly o'er the bow.
Still as a tomb the ship keeps on;
Nor sound nor stirring now.
Hush, hark! as from the centre of the deep,
Shrieks! fiendish yells! They stab them in their sleep.

The scream of rage, the groan, the strife,
The blow, the gasp, the horrid cry,
The panting, stifled prayer for life,
The dying's heaving sigh,
The murderer's curse, the dead man's fix'd, still glare,
And Fear's, and Death's cold sweat—they all are there!

On pale, dead men, on burning cheek,
On quick, fierce eyes, brows hot and damp,
On hands that with the warm blood reek,
Shines the dim cabin lamp.
Leek look'd. "They sleep so sound," he laughing said,
"They'll scarcely wake for mistress or for maid."

A crash! They've forced the door; and then
One long, long, shrill, and piercing scream
Comes thrilling through the growl of men.
'Tis hers! Oh God, redeem
From worse than death thy suffering, helpless child!
That dreadful cry again—sharp, sharp, and wild!

It ceased. With speed o' th' lightning's flash,
A loose-robed form, with streaming hair,
Shoots by. A leap! a quick, short splash!
'Tis gone! There's nothing there!
The waves have swept away the bubbling tide.
Bright-crested waves, how proudly on ye ride!

She's sleeping in her silent cave,
Nor hears the stern, loud roar above,
Or strife of man on land or wave.
Young thing! thy home of love
Thou soon hast reach'd! Fair, unpolluted thing,
They harm'd thee not! Was dying suffering?

Oh, no! To live when joy was dead;
To go with one, lone, pining thought—

To mournful love thy being wed—
Feeling what death had wrought;
To live the child of wo, yet shed no tear,
Bear kindness, and yet share no joy nor fear;

To look on man, and deem it strange
That he on things of earth should brood,
When all its throng'd and busy range
To thee was solitude—
Oh, this was bitterness! Death came and press'd
Thy wearied lids, and brought thy sick heart rest.

THE SOUL

Come, Brother, turn with me from pining thought
And all the inward ills that sin has wrought;
Come, send abroad a love for all who live,
And feel the deep content in turn they give.
Kind wishes and good deeds,—they make not poor;
They'll home again, full laden, to thy door;
The streams of love flow back where they begin,
For springs of outward joys lie deep within.

Even let them flow, and make the places glad
Where dwell thy fellow–men. Shouldst thou be sad,
And earth seem bare, and hours, once happy, press
Upon thy thoughts, and make thy loneliness
More lonely for the past, thou then shalt hear
The music of those waters running near;
And thy faint spirit drink the cooling stream,
And thine eye gladden with the playing beam
That now upon the water dances, now
Leaps up and dances in the hanging bough.

Is it not lovely? Tell me, where doth dwell
The power that wrought so beautiful a spell?
In thine own bosom, Brother? Then as thine
Guard with a reverent fear this power divine.

And if, indeed, 't is not the outward state,
But temper of the soul by which we rate
Sadness or joy, even let thy bosom move
With noble thoughts and wake thee into love,

And let each feeling in thy breast be given
An honest aim, which, sanctified by Heaven,
And springing into act, new life imparts,
Till beats thy frame as with a thousand hearts.

Sin clouds the mind's clear vision,
Around the self-starved soul has spread a dearth.
The earth is full of life; the living Hand
Touched it with life; and all its forms expand
With principles of being made to suit
Man's varied powers and raise him from the brute.
And shall the earth of higher ends be full,—
Earth which thou tread'st,—and thy poor mind be dull?
Thou talk of life, with half thy soul asleep?
Thou "living dead man," let thy spirit leap
Forth to the day, and let the fresh air blow
Through thy soul's shut–up mansion. Wouldst thou know
Something of what is life, shake off this death;
Have thy soul feel the universal breath
With which all nature's quick, and learn to be
Sharer in all that thou dost touch or see;
Break from thy body's grasp, thy spirit's trance;
Give thy soul air, thy faculties expanse;
Love, joy, even sorrow,—yield thyself to all!
They make thy freedom, groveller, not thy thrall.
Knock off the shackles which thy spirit bind
To dust and sense, and set at large the mind!
Then move in sympathy with God's great whole,
And be like man at first, a *living soul.*

THE PLEASURE-BOAT

Come, hoist the sail, the fast let go!
    They're seated side by side;
Wave chases wave in pleasant flow;
    The bay is fair and wide.

The ripples lightly tap the boat,
    Loose! Give her to the wind!
She shoots ahead; they're all afloat;
    The strand is far behind.

No danger reach so fair a crew!
  Thou goddess of the foam,
I'll ever pay thee worship due,
  If thou wilt bring them home.

Fair ladies, fairer than the spray
  The prow is dashing wide,
Soft breezes take you on your way,
  Soft flow the blessèd tide.

O, might I like those breezes be,
  And touch that arching brow,
I'd dwell forever on the sea
  Where ye are floating now.

The boat goes tilting on the waves;
  The waves go tilting by;
There dips the duck,—her back she laves;
  O'erhead the sea–gulls fly.

Now, like the gulls that dart for prey,
  The little vessel stoops;
Now, rising, shoots along her way,
  Like them, in easy swoops.

The sunlight falling on her sheet,
  It glitters like the drift,
Sparkling, in scorn of summer's heat,
  High up some mountain rift.

The winds are fresh; she's driving fast
  Upon the bending tide;
The crinkling sail, and crinkling mast,
  Go with her side by side.

Why dies the breeze away so soon?
  Why hangs the pennant down?
The sea is glass; the sun at noon.—
  Nay, lady, do not frown;

For, see, the wingéd fisher's plume
  Is painted on the sea;
Below, a cheek of lovely bloom
  Whose eyes look up to thee.

She smiles; thou need'st must smile on her.
　And, see, beside her face
A rich, white cloud that doth not stir:
　What beauty, and what grace!

And pictured beach of yellow sand,
　And peakéd rock and hill,
Change the smooth sea to fairy–land;
　How lovely and how still!

From that far isle the thresher's flail
　Strikes close upon the ear;
The leaping fish, the swinging sail
　Of yonder sloop, sound near.

The parting sun sends out a glow
　Across the placid bay,
Touching with glory all the show,—
　A breeze! Up helm! Away!

Careening to the wind, they reach,
　With laugh and call, the shore.
They've left their footprints on the beach,
　But them I hear no more.

Fitz-Greene Halleck

(1790–1867)

Fitz-Greene Halleck, a native of Connecticut, was an active figure in the New York literary scene during its "Knickerbocker" period. His fame rests largely on a memorial poem to Joseph Rodman Drake and the popular "Croaker Pieces" on which he collaborated with Drake and contributed anonymously to the *Evening Post*. In fact, Halleck signed few of his poems and received no compensation for their publication. He made his living as an accountant and personal assistant to John Jacob Astor, a well-known patron of the arts. When Astor died, he left Halleck a yearly pension that provided a comfortable retirement. Halleck was influenced by such great poets as Lord Byron, Robert Burns, and Sir Walter Scott, particularly after a trip to Europe in 1822. "Burns" and "Alnwick Castle," which is an imitation of Scott, were written at that time.

ON THE DEATH OF
JOSEPH RODMAN DRAKE

Green be the turf above thee,
　Friend of my better days!
None knew thee but to love thee,
　Nor named thee but to praise.

Tears fell when thou wert dying,
　From eyes unused to weep,
And long, where thou art lying,
　Will tears the cold turf steep.

When hearts, whose truth was proven,
  Like thine, are laid in earth,
There should a wreath be woven
  To tell the world their worth;

And I who woke each morrow
  To clasp thy hand in mine,
Who shared thy joy and sorrow,
  Whose weal and woe were thine;

It should be mine to braid it
  Around thy faded brow,
But I've in vain essayed it,
  And feel I cannot now.

While memory bids me weep thee,
  Nor thoughts nor words are free,—
The grief is fixed too deeply
  That mourns a man like thee.

BURNS

To a Rose, Brought from Near Alloway
Kirk, in Ayrshire, in the Autumn of 1822

Wild Rose of Alloway! my thanks;
  Thou 'mindst me of that autumn noon
When first we met upon "the banks
  And braes of bonny Doon."

Like thine, beneath the thorn-tree's bough,
  My sunny hour was glad and brief;
We've crossed the winter sea, and thou
  Art withered—flower and leaf.

And will not thy death-doom be mine—
  The doom of all things wrought of clay—
And withered my life's leaf like thine,
  Wild rose of Alloway?

Not so his memory,—for his sake
  My bosom bore thee far and long,

His—who a humbler flower could make
　　Immortal as his song.

The memory of Burns—a name
　　That calls, when brimmed her festal cup,
A nation's glory and her shame,
　　In silent sadness up.

A nation's glory—be the rest
　　Forgot—she's canonized his mind;
And it is joy to speak the best
　　We may of human kind.

I've stood beside the cottage-bed
　　Where the Bard-peasant first drew breath;
A straw-thatched roof above his head,
　　A straw-wrought couch beneath.

And I have stood beside the pile,
　　His monument—that tells to Heaven
The homage of earth's proudest isle
　　To that Bard-peasant given!

Bid thy thoughts hover o'er that spot,
　　Boy-minstrel, in thy dreaming hour;
And know, however low his lot,
　　A Poet's pride and power:

The pride that lifted Burns from earth,
　　The power that gave a child of song
Ascendency o'er rank and birth,
　　The rich, the brave, the strong;

And if despondency weigh down
　　Thy spirit's fluttering pinions then,
Despair—thy name is written on
　　The roll of common men.

There have been loftier themes than his,
　　And longer scrolls, and louder lyres,
And lays lit up with Poesy's
　　Purer and holier fires;

Yet read the names that know not death;
  Few nobler ones than Burns are there;
And few have won a greener wreath
  Than that which binds his hair.

His is that language of the heart,
  In which the answering heart would speak,—
Thought, word, that bids the warm tear start,
  Or the smile light the cheek;

And his that music, to whose tone
  The common pulse of man keeps time,
In cot or castle's mirth or moan,
  In cold or sunny clime.

And who hath heard his song, nor knelt
  Before its spell with willing knee,
And listened, and believed, and felt
  The Poet's mastery

O'er the mind's sea, in calm and storm,
  O'er the heart's sunshine and its showers,
O'er Passion's moments bright and warm,
  O'er Reason's dark, cold hours;

On fields where brave men "die or do,"
  In halls where rings the banquet's mirth,
Where mourners weep, where lovers woo,
  From throne to cottage-hearth?

What sweet tears dim the eye unshed,
  What wild vows falter on the tongue,
When "Scots wha hae wi' Wallace bled,"
  Or "Auld Lang Syne" is sung!

Pure hopes, that lift the soul above,
  Come with his Cotter's hymn of praise,
And dreams of youth, and truth, and love,
  With "Logan's" banks and braes.

And when he breathes his master-lay
  Of Alloway's witch-haunted wall,
All passions in our frames of clay
  Come thronging at his call

Imagination's world of air,
  And our own world, its gloom and glee,
Wit, pathos, poetry, are there,
  And death's sublimity.

And Burns—though brief the race he ran,
  Though rough and dark the path he trod,
Lived—died—in form and soul a Man,
  The image of his God.

Through care, and pain, and want, and woe,
  With wounds that only death could heal,
Tortures—the poor alone can know,
  The proud alone can feel;

He kept his honesty and truth,
  His independent tongue and pen,
And moved, in manhood as in youth,
  Pride of his fellow-men.

Strong sense, deep feeling, passions strong,
  A hate of tyrant and of knave,
A love of right, a scorn of wrong,
  Of coward and of slave;

A kind, true heart, a spirit high,
  That could not fear and would not bow,
Were written in his manly eye
  And on his manly brow.

Praise to the bard! his words are driven,
  Like flower-seeds by the far winds sown,
Where'er, beneath the sky of heaven,
  The birds of fame have flown.

Praise to the man! a nation stood
  Beside his coffin with wet eyes,
Her brave, her beautiful, her good,
  As when a loved one dies.

And still, as on his funeral-day,
  Men stand his cold earth-couch around,
With the mute homage that we pay
  To consecrated ground.

And consecrated ground it is,
   The last, the hallowed home of one
Who lives upon all memories,
   Though with the buried gone.

Such graves as his are pilgrim-shrines,
   Shrines to no code nor creed confined—
The Delphian vales, the Palestines,
   The Meccas of the mind.

Sages with wisdom's garland wreathed,
   Crowned kings, and mitred priests of power,
And warriors with their bright swords sheathed,
   The mightiest of the hour;

And lowlier names, whose humble home
   Is lit by fortune's dimmer star,
Are there—o'er wave and mountain come,
   From countries near and far;

Pilgrims whose wandering feet have pressed
   The Switzer's snow, the Arab's sand,
Or trod the piled leaves of the West,
   My own green forest-land.

All ask the cottage of his birth,
   Gaze on the scenes he loved and sung,
And gather feelings not of earth
   His fields and streams among.

They linger by the Doon's low trees,
   And pastoral Nith, and wooded Ayr,
And round thy sepulchres, Dumfries!
   The poet's tomb is there.

But what to them the sculptor's art,
   His funeral columns, wreaths and urns?
Wear they not graven on the heart
   The name of Robert Burns?

MARCO BOZZARIS

At midnight, in his guarded tent,
   The Turk was dreaming of the hour
When Greece, her knee in suppliance bent,
   Should tremble at his power:
In dreams, through camp and court, he bore
The trophies of a conqueror;
   In dreams his song of triumph heard;
Then wore his monarch's signet ring:
Then pressed that monarch's throne—a king;
As wild his thoughts, and gay of wing,
   As Eden's garden bird.

At midnight, in the forest shades,
   Bozzaris ranged his Suliote band,
True as the steel of their tried blades,
   Heroes in heart and hand.
There had the Persian's thousands stood,
There had the glad earth drunk their blood
   On old Platæa's day;
And now there breathed that haunted air
The sons of sires who conquered there,
With arm to strike and soul to dare,
   As quick, as far as they.

An hour passed on—the Turk awoke;
   That bright dream was his last;
He woke—to hear his sentries shriek,
"To arms! they come! the Greek! the Greek!"
He woke—to die midst flame, and smoke,
And shout, and groan, and sabre-stroke,
   And death-shots falling thick and fast
As lightnings from the mountain-cloud;
And heard, with voice as trumpet loud,
   Bozzaris cheer his band;
"Strike—till the last armed foe expires;
Strike—for your altars and your fires;
Strike—for the green graves of your sires;
   Good—and your native land!"

They fought—like brave men, long and well;
   They piled that ground with Moslem slain,
They conquered—but Bozzaris fell,

Bleeding at every vein.
His few surviving comrades saw
His smile when rang their proud hurrah,
  And the red field was won;
Then saw in death his eyelids close
Calmly, as to a night's repose,
  Like flowers at set of sun.

Come to the bridal-chamber, Death!
  Come to the mother's, when she feels,
For the first time, her first-born's breath;
  Come when the blessed seals
That close the pestilence are broke,
And crowded cities wail its stroke;
Come in consumption's ghastly form,
The earthquake shock, the ocean storm;
Come when the heart beats high and warm
  With banquet-song, and dance, and wine;
And thou art terrible—the tear,
The groan, the knell, the pall, the bier,
And all we know, or dream, or fear
  Of agony, are thine.

But to the hero, when his sword
  Has won the battle for the free,
Thy voice sounds like a prophet's word;
And in its hollow tones are heard
  The thanks of millions yet to be.
Come, when his task of fame is wrought—
Come, with her laurel-leaf, blood-bought—
  Come in her crowning hour—and then
Thy sunken's eye's unearthly light
To him is welcome as the sight
  Of sky and stars to prisoned men;
Thy grasp is welcome as the hand
Of brother in a foreign land;
Thy summons welcome as the cry
That told the Indian isles were nigh
  To the world-seeking Genoese,
When the land wind, from woods of palm,
And orange-groves, and fields of balm,
  Blew o'er the Haytian seas.

Bozzaris! with the storied brave
    Greece nurtured in her glory's time,
Rest thee—there is no prouder grave,
    Even in her own proud clime.
She wore no funeral-weeds for thee,
    Nor bade the dark hearse wave its plume
Like torn branch from death's leafless tree
In sorrow's pomp and pageantry,
    The heartless luxury of the tomb;
But she remembers thee as one
Long loved and for a season gone;
For thee her poet's lyre is wreathed,
Her marble wrought, her music breathed;
For thee she rings the birthday bells;
Of thee her babe's first lisping tells;
For thine her evening prayer is said
At palace-couch and cottage-bed;
Her soldier, closing with the foe,
Gives for thy sake a deadlier blow;
His plighted maiden, when she fears
For him the joy of her young years,
Thinks of thy fate, and checks her tears;
    And she, the mother of thy boys,
Though in her eye and faded cheek
Is read the grief she will not speak,
    The memory of her buried joys,
And even she who gave thee birth,
Will, by their pilgrim-circled hearth,
    Talk of thy doom without a sigh;
For thou art Freedom's now, and Fame's:
One of the few, the immortal names,
    That were not born to die.

ALNWICK CASTLE

Home of the Percy's high-born race,
    Home of their beautiful and brave,
Alike their birth and burial place,
    Their cradle and their grave!
Still sternly o'er the castle gate
Their house's Lion stands in state,
    As in his proud departed hours;
And warriors frown in stone on high,

And feudal banners "flout the sky"
   Above his princely towers.

A gentle hill its side inclines,
   Lovely in England's fadeless green,
To meet the quiet stream which winds
   Through this romantic scene
As silently and sweetly still
As when, at evening, on that hill,
   While summer's wind blew soft and low,
Seated by gallant Hotspur's side,
His Katherine was a happy bride,
   A thousand years ago.

I wandered through the lofty halls
   Trod by the Percys of old fame,
And traced upon the chapel walls
   Each high, heroic name,
From him who once his standard set
Where now, o'er mosque and minaret,
   Glitter the Sultan's crescent moons,
To him who, when a younger son,
Fought for King George at Lexington,
   A major of dragoons.

That last half-stanza,—it has dashed
   From my warm lip the sparkling cup;
The light that o'er my eyebeam flashed,
   The power that bore my spirit up
Above this bank-note world, is gone;
And Alnwick's but a market town,
And this, alas! its market day,
And beasts and borderers throng the way;
Oxen and bleating lambs in lots,
Northumbrian boors and plaided Scots
   Men in the coal and cattle line;
From Teviot's bard and hero land,
From royal Berwick's beach of sand,
From Wooller, Morpeth, Hexham, and
   Newcastle-upon-Tyne.

These are not the romantic times
So beautiful in Spenser's rhymes,

So dazzling to the dreaming boy;
Ours are the days of fact, not fable,
Of knights, but not of the round table,
  Of Bailie Jarvie, not Rob Roy;
'Tis what "Our President," Monroe,
  Has called "the era of good feeling;"
The Highlander, the bitterest foe
To modern laws, has felt their blow,
Consented to be taxed, and vote,
And put on pantaloons and coat,
  And leave off cattle-stealing:
Lord Stafford mines for coal and salt,
The Duke of Norfolk deals in malt,
  The Douglas in red herrings;
And noble name and cultured land,
Palace, and park, and vassal band,
Are powerless to the notes of hand
  Of Rothschild or the Barings.

The age of bargaining, said Burke,
Has come: to-day the turbaned Turk
(Sleep, Richard of the lion heart!
Sleep on, nor from your cerements start)
  Is England's friend and fast ally;
The Moslem tramples on the Greek,
  And on the Cross and altar-stone,
  And Christendom looks tamely on,
And hears the Christian maiden shriek,
  And sees the Christian father die;
And not a sabre-blow is given
For Greece and fame, for faith and heaven,
  By Europe's craven chivalry.

You'll ask if yet the Percy lives
  In the armed pomp of feudal state.
The present representatives
  Of Hotspur and his "gentle Kate,"
Are some half-dozen serving-men
In the drab coat of William Penn;
  A chambermaid, whose lip and eye,
And cheek, and brown hair, bright and curling,
  Spoke nature's aristocracy;
And one, half groom, half seneschal,
Who bowed me through court, bower, and hall,

From donjon keep to turret wall,
For ten-and-sixpence sterling.

RED JACKET

A Chief of the Indian Tribes, the Tuscaroras

Cooper, whose name is with his country's woven,
  First in her files, her *Pioneer* of mind,
A wanderer now in other climes, has proven
  His love for the young land he left behind;

And throned her in the Senate Hall of Nations,
  Robed like the deluge rainbow, heaven–wrought,
Magnificent as his own mind's creations,
  And beautiful as its green world of thought.

And faithful to the Act of Congress, quoted
  As law-authority—it passed nem. con.—
He writes that we are, as ourselves have voted,
  The most enlighten'd people ever known.

That all our week is happy as a Sunday
  In Paris, full of song, and dance, and laugh;
And that, from Orleans to the Bay of Fundy,
  There's not a bailiff nor an epitaph

And, furthermore, in fifty years or sooner,
  We shall export our poetry and wine;
And our brave fleet, eight frigates and a schooner,
  Will sweep the seas from Zembla to the Line.

If he were with me, King of Tuscarora,
  Gazing as I, upon thy portrait now,
In all its medall'd, fringed, and beaded glory,
  Its eyes dark beauty, and its thoughtful brow—

Its brow, half martial and half diplomatic,
  Its eye, upsoaring like an eagle's wings;
Well might he boast that we, the Democratic,
  Outrival Europe—even in our kings.

For thou wert monarch born. Tradition's pages
   Tell not the planting of thy parent tree,
But that the forest tribes have bent for ages,
   To thee, and to thy sires, the subject knee.

Thy name is princely. Though no poet's magic
   Could make *Red Jacket* grace an English rhyme,
Unless he had a genius for the tragic,
   And introduced it in a pantomime;

Yet it is music in the language spoken
   Of thine own land; and on her herald-roll,
As nobly fought for, and as proud a token
   As *Cœur de Lion's*, of a warrior's soul.

Thy garb—though Austria's bosom-star would frighten
   That medal pale, as diamonds the dark mine,
And George the Fourth wore, in the dance at Brighton,
   A more becoming evening dress than thine;

Yet 'tis a brave one, scorning wind and weather,
   And fitted for thy couch on field and flood,
As Rob Roy's tartans for the Highland heather,
   Or forest green for England's Robin Hood.

Is strength a monarch's merit? (like a whaler's)
   Thou art as tall, as sinewy, and as strong
As earth's first kings—the Argo's gallant sailors,
   Heroes in history, and gods in song.

Is eloquence? Her spell is thine that reaches
   The heart, and makes the wisest head its sport;
And there's one rare, strange virtue in thy speeches,
   The secret of their mastery—they are short.

Is beauty? Thine has with thy youth departed,
   But the love-legends of thy manhood's years,
And she who perish'd, young and broken-hearted,
   Are—but I rhyme for smiles, and not for tears.

The monarch mind—the mystery of commanding,
   The godlike power, the art Napoleon,
Of winning, fettering, moulding, wielding, banding
   The hearts of millions till they move as one;

Thou hast it. At thy bidding men have crowded
   The road to death as to a festival;
And minstrel minds, without a blush, have shrouded
   With banner-folds of glory their dark pall.

Who will believe—not I—for in deceiving
   Lies the dear charm of life's delightful dream;
I cannot spare the luxury of believing
   That all things beautiful are what they seem.

Who will believe that, with a smile whose blessing
   Would, like the patriarch's, sooth a dying hour;
With voice as low, as gentle, and caressing
   As e'er won maiden's lip in moonlight bower;

With look, like patient Job's, eschewing evil;
   With motions graceful as a bird's in air;
Thou art, in sober truth, the veriest devil
   That e'er clinched fingers in a captive's hair?

That in thy veins there springs a poison fountain,
   Deadlier than that which bathes the Upas-tree;
And in thy wrath, a nursing Cat o' Mountain
   Is calm as her babe's sleep compared with thee?

And underneath that face like summer's ocean's,
   Its lip as moveless, and its cheek as clear,
Slumbers a whirlwind of the heart's emotions,
   Love, hatred, pride, hope, sorrow—all, save fear,

Love—for thy land, as if she were thy daughter,
   Her pipes in peace, her tomahawk in wars;
Hatred—of missionaries and cold water;
   Pride—in thy rifle trophies and thy scars;

Hope—that thy wrongs will be by the Great Spirit
   Remember'd and revenged when thou art gone;
Sorrow—that none are left thee to inherit
   Thy name, thy fame, thy passions, and thy throne.

William Cullen Bryant

(1794–1878)

William Cullen Bryant was born in Cummington, Massachusetts, to a father who was a physician and a mother who was descended from John and Priscilla Alden. Bryant was only a teenager when he penned his two greatest poems, "Thanatopsis" and "To a Waterfowl." In 1825 he moved to Manhattan to edit the *New York Review;* for the last fifty years of his life he edited the *Evening Post.* In 1878, after delivering an oration at the public unveiling of a statue in Central Park, Bryant died of sunstroke.

THANATOPSIS

To him who in the love of Nature holds
Communion with her visible forms, she speaks
A various language; for his gayer hours
She has a voice of gladness, and a smile
And eloquence of beauty, and she glides
Into his darker musings, with a mild
And healing sympathy, that steals away
Their sharpness, ere he is aware. When thoughts
Of the last bitter hour come like a blight
Over thy spirit, and sad images
Of the stern agony, and shroud, and pall,
And breathless darkness, and the narrow house,
Make thee to shudder, and grow sick at heart;—
Go forth, under the open sky, and list
To Nature's teachings, while from all around—
Earth and her waters, and the depths of air—
Comes a still voice—Yet a few days, and thee

The all-beholding sun shall see no more
In all his course; nor yet in the cold ground,
Where thy pale form was laid, with many tears,
Nor in the embrace of ocean, shall exist
Thy image. Earth, that nourished thee, shall claim
Thy growth, to be resolved to earth again,
And, lost each human trace, surrendering up
Thine individual being, shalt thou go
To mix for ever with the elements,
To be a brother to the insensible rock
And to the sluggish clod, which the rude swain
Turns with his share, and treads upon. The oak
Shall send his roots abroad, and pierce thy mould.

Yet not to thine eternal resting-place
Shalt thou retire alone, nor couldst thou wish
Couch more magnificent. Thou shalt lie down
With patriarchs of the infant world—with kings,
The powerful of the earth—the wise, the good,
Fair forms, and hoary seers of ages past,
All in one mighty sepulchre. The hills
Rock-ribbed and ancient as the sun,—the vales
Stretching in pensive quietness between;
The venerable woods—rivers that move
In majesty, and the complaining brooks
That make the meadows green; and, poured round all,
Old Ocean's gray and melancholy waste,—
Are but the solemn decorations all
Of the great tomb of man. The golden sun,
The planets, all the infinite host of heaven,
Are shining on the sad abodes of death,
Through the still lapse of ages. All that tread
The globe are but a handful to the tribes
That slumber in its bosom.—Take the wings
Of morning, pierce the Barcan wilderness,
Or lose thyself in the continuous woods
Where rolls the Oregon, and hears no sound,
Save his own dashings—yet the dead are there:
And millions in those solitudes, since first
The flight of years began, have laid them down
In their last sleep—the dead reign there alone.
So shalt thou rest, and what if thou withdraw
In silence from the living, and no friend
Take note of thy departure? All that breathe

Will share thy destiny. The gay will laugh
When thou art gone, the solemn brood of care
Plod on, and each one as before will chase
His favorite phantom; yet all these shall leave
Their mirth and their employments, and shall come
And make their bed with thee. As the long train
Of ages glide away, the sons of men,
The youth in life's green spring, and he who goes
In the full strength of years, matron and maid,
The speechless babe, and the gray-headed man—
Shall one by one be gathered to thy side,
By those, who in their turn shall follow them.

So live, that when thy summons comes to join
The innumerable caravan, which moves
To that mysterious realm, where each shall take
His chamber in the silent halls of death,
Thou go not, like the quarry-slave at night,
Scourged to his dungeon, but, sustained and soothed
By an unfaltering trust, approach thy grave,
Like one who wraps the drapery of his couch
About him, and lies down to pleasant dreams.

NOVEMBER

Yet one smile more, departing, distant sun!
   One mellow smile through the soft vapory air,
Ere, o'er the frozen earth, the loud winds run,
   Or snows are sifted o'er the meadows bare.
One smile on the brown hills and naked trees,
   And the dark rocks whose summer wreaths are cast,
And the blue gentian-flower, that, in the breeze,
   Nods lonely, of her beauteous race the last.
Yet a few sunny days, in which the bee
   Shall murmur by the hedge that skirts the way,
The cricket chirp upon the russet lea,
   And man delight to linger in thy ray.
Yet one rich smile, and we will try to bear
The piercing winter frost, and winds, and darkened air.

TO THE FRINGED GENTIAN

Thou blossom bright with autumn dew,
And colored with the heaven's own blue,
That openest when the quiet light
Succeeds the keen and frosty night.

Thou comest not when violets lean
O'er wandering brooks and springs unseen,
Or columbines, in purple dressed,
Nod o'er the ground-bird's hidden nest.

Thou waitest late and com'st alone,
When woods are bare and birds are flown,
And frosts and shortening days portend
The aged year is near his end.

Then doth thy sweet and quiet eye
Look through its fringes to the sky,
Blue—blue—as if that sky let fall
A flower from its cerulean wall.

I would that thus, when I shall see
The hour of death draw near to me,
Hope, blossoming within my heart,
May look to heaven as I depart.

"EARTH'S CHILDREN CLEAVE TO EARTH"

Earth's children cleave to Earth—her frail
   Decaying children dread decay.
Yon wreath of mist that leaves the vale
   And lessens in the morning ray—
Look, how, by mountain rivulet,
   It lingers as it upward creeps,
And clings to fern and copsewood set
   Along the green and dewy steeps:
Clings to the flowery kalmia, clings
   To precipices fringed with grass,
Dark maples where the wood-thrush sings,
   And bowers of fragrant sassafras.
Yet all in vain—it passes still
   From hold to hold, it cannot stay,
And in the very beams that fill

The world with glory, wastes away,
  Till, parting from the mountain's brow,
    It vanishes from human eye,
  And that which sprung of earth is now
    A portion of the glorious sky.

A PRESENTIMENT

"Oh father, let us hence—for hark,
  A fearful murmur shakes the air;
The clouds are coming swift and dark;—
  What horrid shapes they wear!
A wingèd giant sails the sky;
Oh father, father, let us fly!"

"Hush, child; it is a grateful sound,
  That beating of the summer shower;
Here, where the boughs hang close around,
  We'll pass a pleasant hour,
Till the fresh wind, that brings the rain,
Has swept the broad heaven clear again."

"Nay, father, let us haste—for see,
  That horrid thing with hornèd brow—
His wings o'erhang this very tree,
  He scowls upon us now;
His huge black arm is lifted high;
Oh father, father, let us fly!"

"Hush, child;" but, as the father spoke,
  Downward the livid firebolt came,
Close to his ear the thunder broke,
  And, blasted by the flame,
The child lay dead; while dark and still
Swept the grim cloud along the hill.

TO A WATERFOWL

Whither, midst falling dew,
While glow the heavens with the last steps of day,
Far, through their rosy depths, dost thou pursue
  Thy solitary way?

Vainly the fowler's eye
Might mark thy distant flight to do thee wrong,
As, darkly seen against the crimson sky,
   Thy figure floats along.

Seek'st thou the plashy brink
Of weedy lake, or marge of river wide,
Or where the rocking billows rise and sink
   On the chafed ocean-side?

There is a Power whose care
Teaches thy way along that pathless coast—
The desert and illimitable air—
   Lone wandering, but not lost.

All day thy wings have fanned,
At that far height, the cold, thin atmosphere,
Yet stoop not, weary, to the welcome land,
   Though the dark night is near.

And soon that toil shall end;
Soon shalt thou find a summer home, and rest,
And scream among thy fellows; reeds shall bend,
   Soon, o'er thy sheltered nest.

Thou'rt gone, the abyss of heaven
Hath swallowed up thy form; yet, on my heart
Deeply has sunk the lesson thou hast given,
   And shall not soon depart.

He who, from zone to zone,
Guides through the boundless sky thy certain flight,
In the long way that I must tread alone,
   Will lead my steps aright.

NO MAN KNOWETH HIS SEPULCHRE

When he, who, from the scourge of wrong,
   Aroused the Hebrew tribes to fly,
Saw the fair region, promised long,
   And bowed him on the hills to die;

God made his grave, to men unknown,
　　Where Moab's rocks a vale infold,
And laid the aged seer alone
　　To slumber while the world grows old.

Thus still, whene'er the good and just
　　Close the dim eye on life and pain,
Heaven watches o'er their sleeping dust
　　Till the pure spirit comes again.

Though nameless, trampled, and forgot,
　　His servant's humble ashes lie,
Yet God hath marked and sealed the spot,
　　To call its inmate to the sky.

GREEN RIVER

When breezes are soft and skies are fair,
I steal an hour from study and care,
And hie me away to the woodland scene,
Where wanders the stream with waters of green,
As if the bright fringe of herbs on its brink
Had given their stain to the waves they drink;
And they, whose meadows it murmurs through,
Have named the stream from its own fair hue.

Yet pure its waters—its shallows are bright
With colored pebbles and sparkles of light,
And clear the depths where its eddies play,
And dimples deepen and whirl away,
And the plane-tree's speckled arms o'ershoot
The swifter current that mines its root,
Through whose shifting leaves, as you walk the hill,
The quivering glimmer of sun and rill
With a sudden flash on the eye is thrown,
Like the ray that streams from the diamond-stone.
Oh, loveliest there the spring days come,
With blossoms, and birds, and wild-bees' hum;
The flowers of summer are fairest there,
And freshest the breath of the summer air;
And sweetest the golden autumn day
In silence and sunshine glides away.

Yet, fair as thou art, thou shunnest to glide,

Beautiful stream! by the village side;
But windest away from haunts of men,
To quiet valley and shaded glen;
And forest, and meadow, and slope of hill,
Around thee, are lonely, lovely, and still,
Lonely—save when, by thy rippling tides,
From thicket to thicket the angler glides;
Or the simpler comes, with basket and book,
For herbs of power on thy banks to look;
Or haply, some idle dreamer, like me,
To wander, and muse, and gaze on thee,
Still—save the chirp of birds that feed
On the river cherry and seedy reed,
And thy own wild music gushing out
With mellow murmur of fairy shout,
From dawn to the blush of another day,
Like traveller singing along his way.

That fairy music I never hear,
Nor gaze on those waters so green and clear,
And mark them winding away from sight,
Darkened with shade or flashing with light,
While o'er them the vine to its thicket clings,
And the zephyr stoops to freshen his wings,
But I wish that fate had left me free
To wander these quiet haunts with thee,
Till the eating cares of earth should depart,
And the peace of the scene pass into my heart;
And I envy thy stream, as it glides along
Through its beautiful banks in a trance of song.

Though forced to drudge for the dregs of men,
And scrawl strange words with the barbarous pen,
And mingle among the jostling crowd,
Where the sons of strife are subtle and loud—
I often come to this quiet place,
To breathe the airs that ruffle thy face,
And gaze upon thee in silent dream,
For in thy lonely and lovely stream
An image of that calm life appears
That won my heart in my greener years.

THE DEATH OF THE FLOWERS

The melancholy days are come, the saddest of the year,
Of wailing winds, and naked woods, and meadows brown and sere.
Heaped in the hollows of the grove, the autumn leaves lie dead;
They rustle to the eddying gust, and to the rabbit's tread;
The robin and the wren are flown, and from the shrubs the jay,
And from the wood-top calls the crow through all the gloomy day.

Where are the flowers, the fair young flowers, that lately sprang and
    stood
In brighter light and softer airs, a beauteous sisterhood?
Alas! they all are in their graves, the gentle race of flowers
Are lying in their lowly beds, with the fair and good of ours.
The rain is falling where they lie, but the cold November rain
Calls not from out the gloomy earth the lovely ones again.

The wind-flower and the violet, they perished long ago,
And the brier-rose and the orchis died amid the summer glow;
But on the hills the golden-rod, and the aster in the wood,
And the yellow sun-flower by the brook in autumn beauty stood,
Till fell the frost from the clear cold heaven, as fall as plague on
    men,
And the brightness of their smile was gone, from upland, glade, and
    glen.

And now, when comes the calm mild day, as still such days will
    come,
To call the squirrel and the bee from out their winter home;
When the sound of dropping nuts is heard, though all the trees are
    still,
And twinkle in the smoky light the waters of the rill,
The south wind searches for the flowers whose fragrance late he
    bore,

And sighs to find them in the wood and by the stream no more.
And then I think of one who in her youthful beauty died,
The fair meek blossom that grew up and faded by my side.
In the cold moist earth we laid her, when the forests cast the leaf,
And we wept that one so lovely should have a life so brief:
Yet not unmeet it was that one, like that young friend of ours,
So gentle and so beautiful, should perish with the flowers.

A SCENE ON THE BANKS OF THE HUDSON

Cool shades and dews are round my way,
And silence of the early day;
Mid the dark rocks that watch his bed,
Glitters the mighty Hudson spread,
Unrippled, save by drops that fall
From shrubs that fringe his mountain wall;
And o'er the clear still water swells
The music of the Sabbath bells.

All, save this little nook of land,
Circled with trees, on which I stand;
All, save that line of hills which lie
Suspended in the mimic sky—
Seems a blue void, above, below,
Through which the white clouds come and go;
And from the green world's farthest steep
I gaze into the airy deep.

Loveliest of lovely things are they,
On earth, that soonest pass away.
The rose that lives its little hour
Is prized beyond the sculptured flower.
Even love, long tried and cherished long,
Becomes more tender and more strong
At thought of that insatiate grave
From which its yearnings cannot save.

River! in this still hour thou hast
Too much of heaven on earth to last;
Nor long may thy still waters lie,
An image of the glorious sky.
Thy fate and mine are not repose,
And ere another evening close,
Thou to thy tides shalt turn again,
And I to seek the crowd of men.

THE BATTLE-FIELD

Once this soft turf, this rivulet's sands,
  Were trampled by a hurrying crowd,

And fiery hearts and armèd hands
  Encountered in the battle-cloud.

Ah! never shall the land forget
  How gushed the life-blood of her brave—
Gushed, warm with hope and courage yet,
  Upon the soil they fought to save.

Now all is calm, and fresh, and still;
  Alone the chirp of flitting bird,
And talk of children on the hill,
  And bell of wandering kine, are heard.

No solemn host goes trailing by
  The black-mouthed gun and staggering wain;
Men start not at the battle-cry,
  Oh, be it never heard again!

Soon rested those who fought; but thou
  Who minglest in the harder strife
For truths which men receive not now,
  Thy warfare only ends with life.

A friendless warfare! lingering long
  Through weary day and weary year,
A wild and many-weaponed throng
  Hang on thy front, and flank, and rear.

Yet nerve thy spirit to the proof,
  And blench not at thy chosen lot.
The timid good may stand aloof,
  The sage may frown—yet faint thou not.

Nor heed the shaft too surely cast,
  The foul and hissing bolt of scorn;
For with thy side shall dwell, at last,
  The victory of endurance born.

Truth, crushed to earth, shall rise again;
  Th' eternal years of God are hers;
But Error, wounded, writhes in pain,
  And dies among his worshippers.

Yea, though thou lie upon the dust,
    When they who helped thee flee in fear,
Die full of hope and manly trust,
    Like those who fell in battle here.

Another hand thy sword shall wield,
    Another hand the standard wave,
Till from the trumpet's mouth is pealed
    The blast of triumph o'er thy grave.

SONG OF MARION'S MEN

Our band is few but true and tried,
    Our leader frank and bold;
The British soldier trembles
    When Marion's name is told.
Our fortress is the good greenwood,
    Our tent the cypress-tree;
We know the forest round us,
    As seamen know the sea.
We know its walls of thorny vines,
    Its glades of reedy grass,
Its safe and silent islands
    Within the dark morass.

Woe to the English soldiery
    That little dread us near!
On them shall light at midnight
    A strange and sudden fear:
When, waking to their tents on fire,
    They grasp their arms in vain,
And they who stand to face us
    Are beat to earth again;
And they who fly in terror deem
    A mighty host behind,
And hear the tramp of thousands
    Upon the hollow wind.

Then sweet the hour that brings release
    From danger and from toil:
We talk the battle over,
    And share the battle's spoil.
The woodland rings with laugh and shout,

As if a hunt were up,
And woodland flowers are gathered
  To crown the soldier's cup.
With merry songs we mock the wind
  That in the pine-top grieves,
And slumber long and sweetly
  On beds of oaken leaves.

Well knows the fair and friendly moon
  The band that Marion leads—
The glitter of their rifles,
  The scampering of their steeds.
'Tis life to guide the fiery barb
  Across the moonlight plain;
'Tis life to feel the night-wind
  That lifts the tossing mane.
A moment in the British camp—
  A moment—and away
Back to the pathless forest,
  Before the peep of day.

Grave men there are by broad Santee,
  Grave men with hoary hairs;
Their hearts are all with Marion,
  For Marion are their prayers.
And lovely ladies greet our band
  With kindliest welcoming,
With smiles like those of summer,
  And tears like those of spring.
For them we wear these trusty arms,
  And lay them down no more
Till we have driven the Briton,
  Forever, from our shore.

Joseph Rodman Drake

(1795–1820)

Joseph Rodman Drake was born and bred in New York City. During his very short life he earned a medical degree, traveled abroad, married, and made a name for himself in the literary world. He is best remembered for his collaboration with Fitz-Greene Halleck on the "Croaker Pieces" and for his sensational patriotic piece, "The American Flag." Drake wrote a long fantastical poem, "The Culprit Fay," that was meant to romanticize the Hudson River—but the work was overshadowed by the Hudson River stories and sketches of Washington Irving.

THE AMERICAN FLAG

When Freedom from her mountain height
　Unfurled her standard to the air,
She tore the azure robe of night,
　And set the stars of glory there.
She mingled with its gorgeous dyes
The milky baldric of the skies,
And striped its pure celestial white
With streakings of the morning light;
Then from his mansion in the sun
She called her eagle bearer down,
And gave into his mighty hand
The symbol of her chosen land.

Majestic monarch of the cloud,
　Who rear'st aloft thy regal form,
To hear the tempest trumpings loud

And see the lightning lances driven,
   When strive the warriors of the storm,
And rolls the thunder drum of heaven,
Child of the sun! to thee 'tis given
   To guard the banner of the free,
To hover in the sulphur smoke,
To ward away the battle stroke,
And bid its blendings shine afar,
Like rainbows on the cloud of war,
   The harbingers of victory!

Flag of the brave! thy folds shall fly,
The sign of hope and triumph high,
When speaks the signal trumpet tone,
And the long line comes gleaming on.
Ere yet the life blood, warm and wet,
Has dimmed the glistening bayonet,
Each soldier eye shall brightly turn
To where thy sky-born glories burn,
And, as his springing steps advance,
Catch war and vengeance from the glance.
And when the cannon mouthings loud
Heave in wild wreaths the battle shroud,
And gory sabers rise and fall
Like shoots of flame on midnight's pall,
   Then shall thy meteor glances glow,
And cowering foes shall shrink beneath
   Each gallant arm that strikes below
That lovely messenger of death.

Flag of the seas! on ocean wave
Thy stars shall glitter o'er the brave;
When death, careering on the gale,
Sweeps darkly round the bellied sail,
And frighted waves rush wildly back
Before the broadside's reeling rack,
Each dying wanderer of the sea
Shall look at once to heaven and thee,
And smile to see thy splendors fly
In triumph o'er his closing eye.

Flag of the free heart's hope and home!
   By angel hands to valor given;
Thy stars have lit the welkin dome,

And all thy hues were born in heaven.
Forever float that standard sheet!
　　Where breathes the foe but falls before us,
With Freedom's soil beneath our feet,
　　And Freedom's banner streaming o'er us?

THE CULPRIT FAY

"My visual orbs are purged from film, and, lo!
　　Instead of Anster's turnip-bearing vales,
I see old fairy land's miraculous show!
　　Her trees of tinsel kissed by freakish gales,
Her ouphs that, cloaked in leaf-gold, skim the breeze,
　　And fairies, swarming ————————."

Tennant's Anster Fair

'Tis the middle watch of a summer's night,—
The earth is dark, but the heavens are bright;
Naught is seen in the vault on high
But the moon, and the stars, and the cloudless sky,
And the flood which rolls its milky hue,
A river of light on the welkin blue.
The moon looks down on old Cro'nest;
She mellows the shades on his shaggy breast,
And seems his huge gray form to throw
In a silver cone on the wave below.
His sides are broken by spots of shade,
By the walnut bough and the cedar made;
And through their clustering branches dark
Glimmers and dies the firefly's spark,—
Like starry twinkles that momently break
Through the rifts of the gathering tempest's rack.

The stars are on the moving stream,
　　And fling, as its ripples gently flow,
A burnished length of wavy beam
　　In an eel-like, spiral line below;
The winds are whist, and the owl is still;
　　The bat in the shelvy rock is hid;
And naught is heard on the lonely hill
But the cricket's chirp, and the answer shrill
　　Of the gauze-winged katydid;
And the plaint of the wailing whippoorwill,
　　Who moans unseen, and ceaseless sings

Ever a note of wail and woe,
    Till morning spreads her rosy wings,
And earth and sky in her glances glow.

'Tis the hour of fairy ban and spell:
The wood-tick has kept the minutes well;
He has counted them all with click and stroke
Deep in the heart of the mountain-oak,
And he has awakened the sentry elve
    Who sleeps with him in the haunted tree,
To bid him ring the hour of twelve,
    And call the fays to their revelry;
Twelve small strokes on his tinkling bell
('Twas made of the white snail's pearly shell):
"Midnight comes, and all is well!
Hither, hither wing your way!
'Tis is the dawn of the fairy-day."

They come from beds of lichen green,
They creep from the mullein's velvet screen;
    Some on the backs of beetles fly
From the silver tops of moon-touched trees,
    Where they swung in their cobweb hammocks high,
And rocked about in the evening breeze;
    Some from the hum-bird's downy nest,—
They had driven him out by elfin power,
    And, pillowed on plumes of his rainbow breast,
Had slumbered there till the charmèd hour;
    Some had lain in the scoop of the rock,
With glittering ising-stars inlaid;
    And some had opened the four-o'clock,
And stole within its purple shade.
    And now they throng the moonlight glade,
Above, below, on every side,—
    Their little minim forms arrayed
In the tricksy pomp of fairy pride!

They come not now to print the lea,
In freak and dance around the tree,
Or at the mushroom board to sup,
And drink the dew from the buttercup:
A scene of sorrow waits them now,
For an ouphe has broken his vestal vow;
He has loved an earthly maid,

And left for her his woodland shade;
He has lain upon her lip of dew,
And sunned him in her eye of blue,
Fanned her cheek with his wing of air,
Played in the ringlets of her hair,
And, nestling on her snowy breast,
Forgot the lily-king's behest.
For this the shadowy tribes of air
    To the elfin court must haste away:
And now they stand expectant there,
    To hear the doom of the culprit fay.

The throne was reared upon the grass,
Of spice-wood and of sassafras;
On pillars of mottled tortoise-shell
    Hung the burnished canopy,—
And o'er it gorgeous curtains fell
    Of the tulip's crimson drapery.
The monarch sat on his judgment-seat,
    On his brow the crown imperial shone,
The prisoner fay was at his feet,
    And his peers were ranged around the throne.
He waved his sceptre in the air,
    He looked around and calmly spoke;
His brow was grave and his eye severe,
    But his voice in a softened accent broke:
"Fairy! fairy! list and mark:
Thou hast broke thine elfin chain;
Thy flame-wood lamp is quenched and dark,
    And thy wings are dyed with a deadly stain,—
Thou hast sullied thine elfin purity
    In the glance of a mortal maiden's eye;
Thou hast scorned our dread decree,
    And thou shouldst pay the forfeit high.
But well I know her sinless mind
    Is pure as the angel forms above,
Gentle and meek, and chaste and kind,
    Such as a spirit well might love.
Fairy! had she spot or taint,
Bitter had been thy punishment:
Tied to the hornet's shardy wings;
Tossed on the pricks of nettles' stings;
Or seven long ages doomed to dwell
With the lazy worm in the walnut-shell

Or every night to writhe and bleed
Beneath the tread of the centipede;
Or bound in a cobweb-dungeon dim,
Your jailer a spider, huge and grim,
Amid the carrion bodies to lie
Of the worm, and the bug, and the murdered fly;
These it had been your lot to bear,
Had a stain been found on the earthly fair.
Now list, and mark our mild decree,—
Fairy, this your doom must be:

"Thou shalt seek the beach of sand
Where the water bounds the elfin land;
Thou shalt watch the oozy brine
Till the sturgeon leaps in the bright moonshine.
Then dart the glistening arch below,
And catch a drop from his silver bow.
The water-sprites will wield their arms
    And dash around, with roar and rave,
And vain are the woodland spirits' charms;
    They are the imps that rule the wave.
Yet trust thee in thy single might:
If thy heart be pure and thy spirit right,
Thou shalt win the warlock fight.

"If the spray-bead gem be won,
    The stain of thy wing is washed away;
But another errand must be done
    Ere thy crime be lost for aye:
Thy flame-wood lamp is quenched and dark,
Thou must re-illume its spark.
Mount thy steed, and spur him high
To the heaven's blue canopy;
And when thou seest a shooting star,
Follow it fast, and follow it far,—
The last faint spark of its burning train
Shall light the elfin lamp again.
Thou hast heard our sentence, fay;
Hence! to the water-side, away!"

The goblin marked his monarch well;
    He spake not, but he bowed him low,
Then plucked a crimson colen-bell,
    And turned him round in act to go.

The way is long, he cannot fly,
　His soilèd wing has lost its power,
And he winds adown the mountain high,
　For many a sore and weary hour.
Through dreary beds of tangled fern,
Through groves of nightshade dark and dern,
Over the grass and through the brake,
Where toils the ant and sleeps the snake;
　Now o'er the violet's azure flush
He skips along in lightsome mood;
　And now he thrids the bramble-bush,
Till its points are dyed in fairy blood.
He has leaped the bog, he has pierced the brier,
He has swum the brook, and waded the mire,
Till his spirits sank, and his limbs grew weak,
And the red waxed fainter in his cheek.
He had fallen to the ground outright,
　For rugged and dim was his onward track,
But there came a spotted toad in sight,
　And he laughed as he jumped upon her back;
He bridled her mouth with a silkweed twist,
　He lashed her sides with an osier thong;
And now, through evening's dewy mist,
　With leap and spring they bound along,
Till the mountain's magic verge is past,
And the beach of sand is reached at last.

Soft and pale is the moony beam,
Moveless still the glassy stream;
The wave is clear, the beach is bright
　With snowy shells and sparkling stones;
The shore-surge comes in ripples light,
　In murmurings faint and distant moans;
And ever afar in the silence deep
Is heard the splash of the sturgeon's leap,
And the bend of his graceful bow is seen,—
A glittering arch of silver sheen,
Spanning the wave of burnished blue,
And dripping with gems of the river-dew.

The elfin cast a glance around,
　As he lighted down from his courser toad,
Then round his breast his wings he wound,
　And close to the river's brink he strode;

He sprang on a rock, he breathed a prayer,
　Above his head his arms he threw,
Then tossed a tiny curve in air,
　And headlong plunged in the water blue.

Up sprung the spirits of the waves
From the sea-silk beds in their coral caves;
With snail-plate armor, snatched in haste,
They speed their way through the liquid waste;
Some are rapidly borne along
On the mailèd shrimp or the prickly prong;
Some on the blood-red leeches glide,
Some on the stony star-fish ride,
Some on the back of the lancing squab,
Some on the sideling soldier-crab;
And some on the jellied quarl, that flings
At once a thousand streamy stings;
They cut the wave with the living oar,
And hurry on to the moonlight shore,
To guard their realms and chase away
The footsteps of the invading fay.

Fearlessly he skims along,
His hope is high, and his limbs are strong;
He spreads his arms like the swallow's wing,
And throws his feet with a frog-like fling;
His locks of gold on the waters shine,
　At his breast the tiny foam-bees rise,
His back gleams bright above the brine,
　And the wake-line foam behind him lies.
But the water-sprites are gathering near
　To check his course along the tide;
Their warriors come in swift career
　And hem him round on every side;
On his thigh the leech has fixed his hold,
The quarl's long arms are round him rolled,
The prickly prong has pierced his skin,
And the squab has thrown his javelin;
The gritty star has rubbed him raw,
And the crab has struck with his giant claw;
He howls with rage, and he shrieks with pain
He strikes around, but his blows are vain;
Hopeless is the unequal fight,
Fairy! naught is left but flight.

He turned him round, and fled amain,
With hurry and dash, to the beach again;
He twisted over from side to side,
And laid his cheek to the cleaving tide;
The strokes of his plunging arms are fleet,
And with all his might he flings his feet,
But the water-sprites are round him still,
To cross his path and work him ill.
They bade the wave before him rise;
They flung the sea-fire in his eyes;
And they stunned his ears with the scallop-stroke,
With the porpoise heave and the drum-fish croak.
O, but a weary wight was he
When he reached the foot of the dogwood-tree.
Gashed and wounded, and stiff and sore,
He laid him down on the sandy shore;
He blessed the force of the charmèd line,
    And he banned the water-goblins' spite,
For he saw around in the sweet moonshine
Their little wee faces above the brine,
    Giggling and laughing with all their might
    At the piteous hap of the fairy wight.

Soon he gathered the balsam dew
    From the sorrel-leaf and the henbane bud;
Over each wound the balm he drew,
    And with cobweb lint he stanched the blood.
The mild west-wind was soft and low,
It cooled the heat of his burning brow;
And he felt new life in his sinews shoot,
As he drank the juice of the calamus-root;
And now he treads the fatal shore
As fresh and vigorous as before.

Wrapped in musing stands the sprite;
'T is the middle wane of night;
    His task is hard, his way is far,
But he must do his errand right
    Ere dawning mounts her beamy car,
And rolls her chariot wheels of light;
And vain are the spells of fairy-land,—
He must work with a human hand.

He cast a saddened look around;
   But he felt new joy his bosom swell,
When, glittering on the shadowed ground,
   He saw a purple muscle-shell;
Thither he ran, and he bent him low,
He heaved at the stern and he heaved at the bow,
And he pushed her over the yielding sand
Till he came to the verge of the haunted land.
She was as lovely a pleasure-boat
   As ever fairy had paddled in,
For she glowed with purple paint without,
   And shone with silvery pearl within;
A sculler's notch in the stern he made,
An oar he shaped of the bootle-blade;
Then sprung to his seat with a lightsome leap,
And launched afar on the calm, blue deep.

The imps of the river yell and rave.
They had no power above the wave;
But they heaved the billow before the prow,
   And they dashed the surge against her side,
And they struck her keel with jerk and blow,
   Till the gunwale bent to the rocking tide.
She wimpled about to the pale moonbeam,
Like a feather that floats on a wind-tossed stream;
And momently athwart her track
The quarl upreared his island back,
And the fluttering scallop behind would float,
And patter the water about the boat;
But he bailed her out with his colen-bell,
   And he kept her trimmed with a wary tread,
While on every side, like lightning, fell
   The heavy strokes of his bootle-blade.

Onward still he held his way,
Till he came where the column of moonshine lay,
And saw beneath the surface dim
The brown-backed sturgeon slowly swim;
Around him were the goblin train,—
But he sculled with all his might and main,
And followed wherever the sturgeon led,
Till he saw him upward point his head;
Then he dropped his paddle-blade,

And held his colen-goblet up
To catch the drop in its crimson cup.

With sweeping tail and quivering fin
   Through the wave the sturgeon flew,
And, like the heaven-shot javelin,
   He sprung above the waters blue.
Instant as the star-fall light
   He plunged him in the deep again.
But he left an arch of silver bright,
   The rainbow of the moony main.
It was a strange and lovely sight
   To see the puny goblin there;
He seemed an angel form of light,
   With azure wing and sunny hair,
   Throned on a cloud of purple fair,
Circled with blue and edged with white,
And sitting, at the fall of even,
Beneath the bow of summer heaven.

A moment, and its lustre fell;
   But ere it met the billow blue
He caught within his crimson bell
   A droplet of its sparkling dew!—
Joy to thee, fay! thy task is done,
Thy wings are pure, for the gem is won,—
Cheerly ply thy dripping oar,
And haste away to the elfin shore.

He turns, and, lo! on either side
The ripples on his path divide;
And the track o'er which his boat must pass
Is smooth as a sheet of polished glass.
Around, their limbs the sea–nymphs lave,
   With snowy arms half swelling out,
While on the glossed and gleamy wave
   Their sea-green ringlets loosely float.
They swim around with smile and song;
   They press the bark with pearly hand,
And gently urge her course along
   Toward the beach of speckled sand,
   And, as he lightly leaped to land,
They bade adieu with nod and bow;

Then gayly kissed each little hand,
And dropped in the crystal deep below.

A moment stayed the fairy there;
He kissed the beach and breathed a prayer;
Then spread his wings of gilded blue,
And on to the elfin court he flew.
As ever ye saw a bubble rise,
And shine with a thousand changing dyes,
Till, lessening far, through ether driven,
It mingles with the hues of heaven;
As, at the glimpse of morning pale,
The lance-fly spreads his silken sail,
And gleams with blendings soft and bright
Till lost in the shades of fading night,—
So rose from earth the lovely fay;
So vanished, far in heaven away!

*   *   *   *   *

Up, fairy! quit thy chickweed bower,
The cricket has called the second hour;
Twice again, and the lark will rise
To kiss the streaking of the skies,—
Up! thy charmèd armor don,
Thou 'lt need it ere the night be gone.

He put his acorn helmet on;
It was plumed of the silk of the thistle-down;
The corselet plate that guarded his breast
Was once the wild bee's golden vest;
His cloak, of a thousand mingled dyes,
Was formed of the wings of butterflies;
His shield was the shell of a lady-bug queen,
Studs of gold on a ground of green;
And the quivering lance which he brandished bright
Was the sting of a wasp he had slain in fight.
Swift he bestrode his firefly steed;
    He bared his blade of the bent-grass blue;
He drove his spurs of the cockle-seed,
    And away like a glance of thought he flew
To skim the heavens, and follow far
The fiery trail of the rocket-star.

The moth-fly, as he shot in air,
Crept under the leaf, and hid her there;
The katydid forgot its lay,
The prowling gnat fled fast away,
The fell mosquito checked his drone
And folded his wings till the fay was gone.
And the wily beetle dropped his head,
And fell on the ground as if he were dead;
They crouched them close in the darksome shade,
　　They quaked all o'er with awe and fear,
For they had felt the blue-bent blade,
　　And writhed at the prick of the elfin spear.
Many a time, on a summer's night,
When the sky was clear, and the moon was bright,
They had been roused from the haunted ground
By the yelp and bay of the fairy hound;
　　They had heard the tiny bugle-horn,
They had heard the twang of the maize-silk string,
When the vine-twig bows were tightly drawn,
　　And the needle-shaft through air was borne,
Feathered with down of the hum-bird's wing.
And now they deemed the courier ouphe
　　Some hunter-sprite of the elfin ground,
And they watched till they saw him mount the roof
　　That canopies the world around;
Then glad they left their covert lair,
And freaked about in the midnight air.

Up to the vaulted firmament
His path the firefly courser bent,
And at every gallop on the wind
He flung a glittering spark behind;
He flies like a feather in the blast
Till the first light cloud in heaven is past.
　　But the shapes of air have begun their work,
And a drizzly mist is round him cast;
　　He cannot see through the mantle murk;
He shivers with cold, but he urges fast;
　　Through storm and darkness, sleet and shade,
He lashes his steed, and spurs amain,—
For shadowy hands have twitched the rein,
　　And flame-shot tongues around him played,
And near him many a fiendish eye

Glared with a fell malignity,
And yells of rage, and shrieks of fear,
Came screaming on his startled ear.

His wings are wet around his breast,
The plume hangs dripping from his crest,
His eyes are blurred with the lightning's glare,
And his ears are stunned with the thunder's blare.
But he gave a shout, and his blade he drew,
    He thrust before and he struck behind,
Till he pierced their cloudy bodies through,
    And gashed their shadowy limbs of wind:
Howling the misty spectres flew,
    They rend the air with frightful cries;
For he has gained the welkin blue,
    And the land of clouds beneath him lies.

Up to the cope careering swift,
    In breathless motion fast,
Fleet as the swallow cuts the drift,
    Or the sea–roc rides the blast,
The sapphire sheet of eve is shot,
    The spherèd moon is past,
The earth but seems a tiny blot
    On a sheet of azure cast.
O, it was sweet, in the clear moonlight,
    To tread the starry plain of even!
To meet the thousand eyes of night,
    And feel the cooling breath of heaven!
But the elfin made no stop or stay
Till he came to the bank of the Milky Way;
Then he checked his courser's foot,
And watched for the glimpse of the planet–shoot.

Sudden along the snowy tide
    That swelled to meet their footsteps' fall,
The sylphs of heaven were seen to glide,
    Attired in sunset's crimson pall;
Around the fay they weave the dance,
    They skip before him on the plain,
And one has taken his wasp–sting lance,
    And one upholds his bridle–rein;
With warblings wild they lead him on
To where, through clouds of amber seen,

Studded with stars, resplendent shone
   The palace of the sylphid queen.
Its spiral columns, gleaming bright,
Were streamers of the northern light;
Its curtain's light and lovely flush
Was of the morning's rosy blush;
And the ceiling fair that rose aboon,
The white and feathery fleece of noon.

But, O, how fair the shape that lay
   Beneath a rainbow bending bright!
She seemed to the entrancèd fay
   The loveliest of the forms of light;
Her mantle was the purple rolled
   At twilight in the west afar;
'Twas tied with threads of dawning gold,
   And buttoned with a sparkling star.
Her face was like the lily roon
   That veils the vestal planet's hue;
Her eyes, two beamlets from the moon,
   Set floating in the welkin blue.
Her hair is like the sunny beam,
And the diamond gems which round it gleam
Are the pure drops of dewy even
That ne'er have left their native heaven.

She raised her eyes to the wondering sprite,
   And they leaped with smiles; for well I ween
Never before in the bowers of light
   Had the form of an earthly fay been seen.
Long she looked in his tiny face;
   Long with his butterfly cloak she played;
She smoothed his wings of azure lace,
   And handled the tassel of his blade;
And as he told, in accents low,
The story of his love and woe,
She felt new pains in her bosom rise,
And the tear–drop started in her eyes.
And "O, sweet spirit of earth," she cried,
   "Return no more to your woodland height,
But ever here with me abide
   In the land of everlasting light!
Within the fleecy drift we 'll lie,
   We'll hang upon the rainbow's rim;

And all the jewels of the sky
  Around thy brow shall brightly beam!
And thou shalt bathe thee in the stream
  That rolls its whitening foam aboon,
And ride upon the lightning's gleam,
  And dance upon the orbèd moon!
We 'll sit within the Pleiad ring,
  We 'll rest on Orion's starry belt,
And I will bid my sylphs to sing
  The song that makes the dew–mist melt;
Their harps are of the umber shade
  That hides the blush of waking day,
And every gleamy string is made
  Of silvery moonshine's lengthened ray;
And thou shalt pillow on my breast,
  While heavenly breathings float around,
And, with the sylphs of ether blest,
  Forget the joys of fairy ground."

She was lovely and fair to see,
And the elfin's heart beat fitfully;
But lovelier far, and still more fair,
The earthly form imprinted there;
Naught he saw in the heavens above
Was half so dear as his mortal love,
For he thought upon her looks so meek,
And he thought of the light flush on her cheek.
Never again might he bask and lie
On that sweet cheek and moonlight eye;
But in his dreams her form to see,
To clasp her in his revery,
To think upon his virgin bride,
Was worth all heaven, and earth beside.

"Lady," he cried, "I have sworn to-night,
On the word of a fairy knight,
To do my sentence–task aright;
My honor scarce is free from stain,—
I may not soil its snows again;
Betide me weal, betide me woe,
Its mandate must be answered now."
Her bosom heaved with many a sigh,
The tear was in her drooping eye;
But she led him to the palace gate,

And called the sylphs who hovered there,
And bade them fly and bring him straight,
  Of clouds condensed, a sable car.
With charm and spell she blessed it there,
From all the fiends of upper air;
Then round him cast the shadowy shroud,
And tied his steed behind the cloud;
And pressed his hand as she bade him fly
Far to the verge of the northern sky,
For by its wane and wavering light
There was a star would fall to–night.

Borne afar on the wings of the blast,
Northward away he speeds him fast,
And his courser follows the cloudy wain
Till the hoof–strokes fall like pattering rain.
The clouds roll backward as he flies,
Each flickering star behind him lies,
And he has reached the northern plain,
And backed his firefly steed again,
Ready to follow in its flight
The streaming of the rocket–light.

The star is yet in the vault of heaven,
  But it rocks in the summer gale;
And now 't is fitful and uneven,
  And now 't is deadly pale;
And now 't is wrapped in sulphur-smoke,
  And quenched is its rayless beam;
And now with a rattling thunder-stroke
  It bursts in flash and flame.
As swift as the glance of the arrowy lance
  That the storm-spirit flings from high,
The star-shot flew o'er the welkin blue,
  As it fell from the sheeted sky.
As swift as the wind in its train behind
  The elfin gallops along:
The fiends of the clouds are bellowing loud,
  But the sylphid charm is strong;
He gallops unhurt in the shower of fire,
  While the cloud-fiends fly from the blaze;
He watches each flake till its sparks expire,
  And rides in the light of its rays.
But he drove his steed to the lightning's speed,

And caught a glimmering spark;
Then wheeled around to the fairy ground,
    And sped through the midnight dark.

*   *   *   *   *

Ouphe and goblin! imp and sprite!
    Elf of eve! and starry fay!
Ye that love the moon's soft light,
    Hither,—hither wend your way;
Twine ye in a jocund ring,
    Sing and trip it merrily,
Hand to hand, and wing to wing,
    Round the wild witch-hazel tree.

Hail the wanderer again
    With dance and song, and lute and lyre;
Pure his wing and strong his chain,
    And doubly bright his fairy fire.
Twine ye in an airy round,
    Brush the dew and print the lea;
Skip and gambol, hop and bound,
    Round the wild witch-hazel tree.

The beetle guards our holy ground,
    He flies about the haunted place,
And if mortal there be found,
    He hums in his ears and flaps his face;
The leaf-harp sounds our roundelay,
    The owlet's eyes our lanterns be;
Thus we sing and dance and play
    Round the wild witch-hazel tree.

But hark! from tower to tree-top high,
    The sentry-elf his call has made;
A streak is in the eastern sky,
    Shapes of moonlight! flit and fade!
The hill-tops gleam in morning's spring,
The skylark shakes his dappled wing,
The day-glimpse glimmers on the lawn,
The cock has crowed, and the fays are gone.

BRONX

I sat me down upon a green bank–side,
  Skirting the smooth edge of a gentle river,
Whose waters seemed unwillingly to glide,
  Like parting friends who linger while they sever;
Enforced to go, yet seeming still unready,
Backward they wind their way in many a wistful eddy.

Gray o'er my head the yellow–vested willow
  Ruffled its hoary top in the fresh breezes,
Glancing in light, like spray on a green billow,
  Or the fine frostwork which young winter freezes;
When first his power in infant pastime trying,
Congeals sad autumn's tears on the dead branches lying.

From rocks around hung the loose ivy dangling,
  And in the clefts sumach of liveliest green,
Bright ising–stars the little beach was spangling,
  The gold–cup sorrel from his gauzy screen
Shone like a fairy crown, enchased and beaded,
Left on some morn, when light flashed in their eyes unheeded.

The humbird shook his sun–touch'd wings around,
  The bluefinch caroll'd in the still retreat;
The antic squirrel capered on the ground
  Where lichens made a carpet for his feet:
Through the transparent waves, the ruddy minkle
Shot up in glimmering sparks his red fin's tiny twinkle.

There were dark cedars with loose mossy tresses,
  White powdered dog–trees, and stiff hollies flaunting
Gaudy as rustics in their May–day dresses,
  Blue pelloret from purple leaves upslanting
A modest gaze, like eyes of a young maiden
Shining beneath dropp'd lids the evening of her wedding.

The breeze fresh springing from the lips of morn,
  Kissing the leaves, and sighing so to lose 'em,
The winding of the merry locust's horn,
  The glad spring gushing from the rock's bare bosom:
Sweet sights, sweet sounds, all sights, all sounds excelling,
Oh! 'twas a ravishing spot formed for a poet's dwelling.

And did I leave thy loveliness, to stand
   Again in the dull world of earthly blindness?
Pained with the pressure of unfriendly hands,
   Sick of smooth looks, agued with icy kindness?
Left I for this thy shades, where none intrude,
To prison wandering thought and mar sweet solitude?

Yet I will look upon thy face again,
   My own romantic Bronx, and it will be
A face more pleasant than the face of men.
   Thy waves are old companions, I shall see
A well–remembered form in each old tree,
And hear a voice long loved in thy wild minstrelsy.

Edward Coate Pinkney

(1802–1828)

Edward Coate Pinkney was born in London during his father's ten-
ure as United States Minister to Great Britain. Pinkney returned to
America, went to school in Baltimore, and joined the navy. He left
the navy to practice law but his health failed and he died at the
young age of twenty-six. While he left only a handful of verses,
these were good enough to have been praised by Edgar Allan Poe.

A HEALTH

I fill this cup to one made up
   Of loveliness alone,
A woman, of her gentle sex
   The seeming paragon;
To whom the better elements
   And kindly stars have given
A form so fair, that, like the air,
   'Tis less of earth than heaven.

Her every tone is music's own,
   Like those of morning birds,
And something more than melody
   Dwells ever in her words;
The coinage of her heart are they,
   And from her lips each flows
As one may see the burdened bee
   Forth issue from the rose.

Affections are as thoughts to her,
   The measures of her hours;
Her feelings have the fragrancy,
   The freshness of young flowers;
And lovely passions, changing oft,
   So fill her, she appears
The image of themselves by turns,—
   The idol of past years!

Of her bright face one glance will trace
   A picture on the brain,
And of her voice in echoing hearts
   A sound must long remain;
But memory, such as mine of her,
   So very much endears,
When death is nigh my latest sigh
   Will not be life's, but hers.

I fill this cup to one made up
   Of loveliness alone,
A woman, of her gentle sex
   The seeming paragon—
Her health! and would on earth there stood
   Some more of such a frame,
That life might be all poetry,
   And weariness a name.

A SERENADE

Look out upon the stars, my love,
   And shame them with thine eyes,
On which, than on the lights above,
   There hang more destinies.
Night's beauty is the harmony
   Of blending shades and light;
Then, lady, up,—look out, and be
   A sister to the night!

Sleep not! thine image wakes for aye
   Within my watching breast:
Sleep not! from her soft sleep should fly
   Who robs all hearts of rest.
Nay, lady, from thy slumbers break,

And make this darkness gay
With looks, whose brightness well might make
Of darker nights a day.

VOTIVE SONG

I burn no incense, hang no wreath,
   On this thine early tomb:
Such cannot cheer the place of death,
   But only mock its gloom.
Here odorous smoke and breathing flower
   No grateful influence shed;
They lose their perfume and their power,
   When offered to the dead.

And if, as is the Afghan's creed,
   The spirit may return,
A disembodied sense to feed,
   On fragrance, near its urn,—
It is enough that she, whom thou
   Didst love in living years,
Sits desolate beside it now,
   And fall these heavy tears.

THE INDIAN'S BRIDE

Why is that graceful female here,
With yon red hunter of the deer?
Of gentle mien and shape, she seems
   For civil halls design'd,
Yet with the stately savage walks
   As she were of his kind.
Look on her leafy diadem,
Enrich'd with many a floral gem:
Those simple ornaments about
   Her candid brow, disclose
The loitering Spring's last violet,
   And Summer's earliest rose;
But not a flower lies breathing there,
Sweet as herself, or half so fair.
Exchanging lustre with the sun,
   A part of day she strays;

A glancing, living, human smile,
  On nature's face she plays.
Can none instruct me what are these
Companions of the lofty trees?

Intent to blend with his her lot,
Fate form'd her all that he was not;
And as by mere unlikeness thoughts
  Associate we see,
Their hearts from very difference caught
  A perfect sympathy.
The household goddess here to be
Of that one dusky votary,
She left her pallid countrymen,
  An earthling most divine,
And sought in this sequester'd wood
  A solitary shrine.
Behold them roaming hand in hand,
Like night and sleep, along the land;
Observe their movements: he for her
  Restrains his active stride,
While she assumes a bolder gait
  To ramble at his side:
Thus, even as the steps they frame,
Their souls fast alter to the same.
The one forsakes ferocity,
  And momently grows mild;
The other tempers more and more
  The artful with the wild.
She humanizes him, and he
Educates her to liberty.

Oh, say not they must soon be old,
Their limbs prove faint, their breasts feel cold!
Yet envy I that sylvan pair
  More than my words express,
The singular beauty of their lot,
  And seeming happiness.
They have not been reduced to share
The painful pleasures of despair:
Their sun declines not in the sky,
  Nor are their wishes cast,
Like shadows of the afternoon,
  Repining towards the past:

With naught to dread or to repent,
The present yields them full content.
In solitude there is no crime;
    Their actions are all free,
And passion lends their way of life
    The only dignity;
And how should they have any cares?
Whose interest contends with theirs?

The world, or all they know of it,
Is theirs: for them the stars are lit;
For them the earth beneath is green,
    The heavens above are bright:
For them the moon doth wax and wane,
    And decorate the night;
For them the branches of those trees
Wave music in the vernal breeze;
For them upon that dancing spray
    The free bird sits and sings,
And glitt'ring insects flit about
    Upon delighted wings;
For them that brook, the brakes among,
Murmurs its small and drowsy song;
For them the many-colour'd clouds
    Their shapes diversify,
And change at once, like smiles and frowns,
    Th' expression of the sky.
For them and by them all is gay,
And fresh and beautiful as they:
The images their minds receive,
    Their minds assimilate,
To outward forms imparting thus
    The glory of their state.
Could aught be painted otherwise
Than fair, seen through her star-bright eyes?
He too, because she fills his sight,
    Each object falsely sees;
The pleasure that he has in her
    Makes all things seem to please.
And this is love; and it is life
They lead, that Indian and his wife.

MEMORY

How feels the guiltless dreamer, who
With idly curious gaze
Has let his mind's glance wander through
The relics of past days?
As feels the pilgrim that has scann'd,
Within their skirting wall,
The moonlit marbles of some grand
Disburied capital;
Masses of whiteness and of gloom,
The darkly bright remains
Of desolate palace, empty tomb,
And desecrated fanes:
For in the ruins of old hours,
Remembrance haply sees
Temples, and tombs, and palaces,
Not different from these.

George Pope Morris

(1802–1864)

George Pope Morris is probably known today solely for his poem "Woodman, Spare That Tree!" He was born in Philadelphia and spent most of his life in New York City working as a journalist. For twenty years he was editor of the *Mirror*, a journal he cofounded with Samuel Woodworth; he also founded the *Home Journal* with Nathaniel Parker Willis. These two literary magazines brought Morris much acclaim as an editor.

WOODMAN, SPARE THAT TREE!

Woodman, spare that tree!
   Touch not a single bough!
In youth it sheltered me,
   And I'll protect it now.
'Twas my forefather's hand
   That placed it near his cot;
There, woodman, let it stand,
   Thy ax shall harm it not.

That old familiar tree,
   Whose glory and renown
Are spread o'er land and sea—
   And wouldst thou hew it down?
Woodman, forbear thy stroke!
   Cut not its earth-bound ties;
Oh, spare that aged oak
   Now towering to the skies!

When but an idle boy,
   I sought its grateful shade;
In all their gushing joy
   Here, too, my sisters played.
My mother kissed me here;
   My father pressed my hand—
Forgive this foolish tear,
   But let that old oak stand.

My heartstrings round thee cling,
   Close as thy bark, old friend!
Here shall the wild bird sing,
   And still thy branches bend.
Old tree! the storm still brave!
   And, woodman, leave the spot;
While I've a hand to save,
   Thy ax shall harm it not.

THE RETORT

Old Nick, who taught the village school,
   Wedded a maid of homespun habit;
He was as stubborn as a mule,
   She was as playful as a rabbit.

Poor Jane had scarce become a wife,
   Before her husband sought to make her
The pink of country-polished life,
   And prim and formal as a Quaker.

One day the tutor went abroad,
   And simple Jenny sadly missed him;
When he returned, behind her lord
   She slyly stole, and fondly kissed him!

The husband's anger rose!—and red
   And white his face alternate grew!
"Less freedom, ma'am!" Jane sighed and said,
   "Oh, dear! I didn't know 'twas you!"

MY MOTHER'S BIBLE

This book is all that's left me now,—
   Tears will unbidden start,—
With faltering lip and throbbing brow
   I press it to my heart.
For many generations past
   Here is our family tree;
My mother's hands this Bible clasped,
   She, dying, gave it me.

Ah! well do I remember those
   Whose names these records bear;
Who round the hearthstone used to close,
   After the evening prayer,
And speak of what these pages said
   In tones my heart would thrill!
Though they are with the silent dead,
   Here are they living still!

My father read this holy book
   To brothers, sisters, dear;
How calm was my poor mother's look,
   Who loved God's word to hear!
Her angel face,—I see it yet!
   What thronging memories come!
Again that little group is met
   Within the halls of home!

Thou truest friend man ever knew,
   Thy constancy I've tried;
When all were false, I found thee true,
   My counsellor and guide.
The mines of earth no treasures give
   That could this volume buy;
In teaching me the way to live,
   It taught me how to die!

A LEAP FOR LIFE

Old Ironsides at anchor lay,
   In the harbor of Mahon;
A dead calm rested on the bay—

The waves to sleep had gone;
When little Jack, the captain's son,
    With gallant hardihood,
Climbed shroud and spar—and then upon
    The main-truck rose and stood!

A shudder ran through every vein—
    All eyes were turned on high!
There stood the boy, with dizzy brain,
    Between the sea and sky!
No hold had he above—below,
    Alone he stood in air!
At that far height none dared to go—
    No aid could reach him there.

We gazed—but not a man could speak!—
    With horror all aghast
In groups, with pallid brow and cheek,
    We watched the quivering mast.
The atmosphere grew thick and hot,
    And of a lurid hue,
As, riveted unto the spot,
    Stood officer and crew.

The father came on deck—He gasped,
    "O, God, Thy will be done!"
Then suddenly a rifle grasped,
    And aimed it at his son!
"Jump far out, boy! into the wave!
    Jump, or I fire!" he said:
"That only chance your life can save!
    Jump—jump, boy!"—He obeyed.

He sank—he rose—he lived—he moved—
    He for the ship struck out!
On board we hailed the lad beloved
    With many a manly shout.
His father drew, in silent joy,
    Those wet arms round his neck,
Then folded to his heart the boy,
    And fainted on the deck!

Ralph Waldo Emerson

(1803–1882)

Ralph Waldo Emerson, one of America's greatest and most original thinkers, was born in Boston, Massachusetts, the descendent of generations of New England ministers. He studied the classics as a youth and attended Harvard, graduating as the "class poet." He went on to become a minister and married, but tragedy struck a few months later when his wife died. Emerson became disenchanted with his work and traveled abroad in 1832. It was in his travels that he met and befriended Thomas Carlyle. On his return to America, Emerson settled on a farm in Concord and remarried. The poet Edwin Markham said of Emerson, "His poetry is only philosophy in verse, while his essays are only poetry in prose."

EACH AND ALL

Little thinks, in the field, yon red-cloaked clown,
Of thee from the hill-top looking down;
The heifer that lows in the upland farm,
Far-heard, lows not thine ear to charm;
The sexton, tolling his bell at noon,
Deems not that great Napoleon
Stops his horse, and lists with delight,
Whilst his files sweep round yon Alpine height;
Nor knowest thou what argument
Thy life to thy neighbor's creed has lent.
All are needed by each one;
Nothing is fair or good alone.
I thought the sparrow's note from heaven,
Singing at dawn on the alder bough;

I brought him home, in his nest, at even;
He sings the song, but it cheers not now,
For I did not bring home the river and sky;—
He sang to my ear,—they sang to my eye.
The delicate shells lay on the shore;
The bubbles of the latest wave
Fresh pearls to their enamel gave;
And the bellowing of the savage sea
Greeted their safe escape to me.
I wiped away the weeds and foam,
I fetched my sea-born treasures home;
But the poor, unsightly, noisome things
Had left their beauty on the shore,
With the sun and the sand and the wild uproar.
The lover watched his graceful maid,
As 'mid the virgin train she strayed,
Nor knew her beauty's best attire
Was woven still by the snow-white choir.
At last she came to his hermitage,
Like the bird from the woodlands to the cage;—
The gay enchantment was undone,
A gentle wife, but fairy none.
Then I said, "I covet truth;
Beauty is unripe childhood's cheat;
I leave it behind with the games of youth."—
As I spoke, beneath my feet
The ground-pine curled its pretty wreath,
Running over the club-moss burrs;
I inhaled the violet's breath;
Around me stood the oaks and firs;
Pine-cones and acorns lay on the ground;
Over me soared the eternal sky,
Full of light and of deity;
Again I saw, again I heard,
The rolling river, the morning bird;—
Beauty through my senses stole;
I yielded myself to the perfect whole.

THE PROBLEM

I like a church; I like a cowl;
I love a prophet of the soul;
And on my heart monastic aisles

Fall like sweet strains, or pensive smiles;
Yet not for all his faith can see
Would I that cowled churchman be.

Why should the vest on him allure,
Which I could not on me endure?

Not from a vain or shallow thought
His awful Jove young Phidias brought;
Never from lips of cunning fell
The thrilling Delphic oracle;
Out from the heart of nature rolled
The burdens of the Bible old;
The litanies of nations came,
Like the volcano's tongue of flame,
Up from the burning core below,—
The canticles of love and woe;
The hand that rounded Peter's dome,
And groined the aisles of Christian Rome,
Wrought in a sad sincerity;
Himself from God he could not free;
He builded better than he knew;—
The conscious stone to beauty grew.

Know'st thou what wove yon woodbird's nest
Of leaves, and feathers from her breast?
Or how the fish outbuilt her shell,
Painting with morn each annual cell?
Or how the sacred pine-tree adds
To her old leaves new myriads?

Such and so grew these holy piles,
Whilst love and terror laid the tiles.
Earth proudly wears the Parthenon,
As the best gem upon her zone;
And Morning opes with haste her lids,
To gaze upon the Pyramids;
O'er England's abbeys bends the sky,
As on its friends, with kindred eye;
For, out of Thought's interior sphere,
These wonders rose to upper air;
And Nature gladly gave them place,
Adopted them into her race,

And granted them an equal date
With Andes and with Ararat.

These temples grew as grows the grass:
Art might obey, but not surpass.
The passive Master lent his hand
To the vast soul that o'er him planned;
And the same power that reared the shrine,
Bestrode the tribes that knelt within.
Ever the fiery Pentecost
Girds with one flame the countless host,
Trances the heart through chanting choirs,
And through the priest the mind inspires.

The word unto the prophet spoken
Was writ on tables yet unbroken;
The word by seers or sibyls told,
In groves of oak, or fanes of gold,
Still floats upon the morning wind,
Still whispers to the willing mind.

One accent of the Holy Ghost
The heedless world hath never lost.
I know what say the fathers wise,—
The Book itself before me lies,
Old *Chrysostom*, best Augustine,
And he who blent both in his line,
The younger *Golden Lips* or mines,
Taylor, the Shakespeare of divines.
His words are music in my ear,
I see his cowled portrait dear;
And yet, for all his faith could see,
I would not the good bishop be.

THE VISIT

Askest, "How long thou shalt stay?"
Devastator of the day!
Know, each substance, and relation,
Thorough nature's operation,
Hath its unit, bound, and metre;
And every new compound
Is some product and repeater,—

Product of the earlier found.
But the unit of the visit,
The encounter of the wise,—
Say, what other metre is it
Than the meeting of the eyes?
Nature poureth into nature
Through the channels of that feature.
Riding on the ray of sight,
More fleet than waves or whirlwinds go,
Or for service, or delight,
Hearts to hearts their meaning show,
Sum their long experience,
And import intelligence.
Single look has drained the breast;
Single moment years confessed.
The duration of a glance
Is the term of convenance,
And, though thy rede be church or state,
Frugal multiples of that.
Speeding Saturn cannot halt;
Linger,—thou shalt rue the fault;
If Love his moment overstay,
Hatred's swift repulsions play.

MITHRIDATES

I cannot spare water or wine,
    Tobacco-leaf, or poppy, or rose;
From the earth-poles to the line,
    All between that works or grows,
Everything is kin of mine.

Give me agates for my meat;
Give me cantharids to eat;
From air and ocean bring me foods,
From all zones and altitudes;—

From all natures, sharp and slimy,
    Salt and basalt, wild and tame:
Tree and lichen, ape, sea-lion,
    Bird, and reptile, be my game.

Ivy for my fillet band;
Blinding dog-wood in my hand;
Hemlock for my sherbet cull me,
And the prussic juice to lull me;
Swing me in the upas boughs,
Vampyre-fanned, when I carouse.

Too long shut in strait and few,
Thinly dieted on dew,
I will use the world, and sift it,
To a thousand humors shift it,
As you spin a cherry.
O doleful ghosts, and goblins merry!
O all you virtues, methods, mights,
Means, appliances, delights,
Reputed wrongs and braggart rights,
Smug routine, and things allowed,
Minorities, things under cloud!
Hither! take me, use me, fill me,
Vein and artery, though ye kill me!
God! I will not be an owl,
But sun me in the Capitol.

TACT

What boots it, thy virtue,
  What profit thy parts,
While one thing thou lackest,—
  The art of all arts?

The only credentials,
  Passport to success:
Opens castle and parlor,—
  Address, man. Address.

The maiden in danger
  Was saved by the swain;
His stout arm restored her
  To Broadway again.

The maid would reward him,—
  Gay company come,—

They laugh, she laughs with them;
   He is moonstruck and dumb.

This clinches the bargain;
   Sails out of the bay;
Gets the vote in the senate,
   Spite of Webster and Clay.

Has for genius no mercy,
   For speeches no heed;
It lurks in the eyebeam,
   It leaps to its deed.

Church, market, and tavern,
   Bed and board, it will sway.
It has no to-morrow;
   It ends with to-day.

GOOD-BYE PROUD WORLD

Good-bye, proud world! I'm going home:
Thou art not my friend, and I'm not thine.
Long through thy weary crowds I roam;
A river-ark on the ocean brine,
Long I've been tossed like the driven foam;
But now, proud world! I'm going home.

Good-bye to Flattery's fawning face;
To Grandeur with his wise grimace;
To upstart Wealth's averted eye;
To supple Office, low and high;
To crowded halls, to court and street;
To frozen hearts and hasting feet;
To those who go, and those who come;
Good-bye, proud world! I'm going home.

I am going to my own hearth-stone,
Bosomed in yon green hills alone,—
A secret nook in a pleasant land,
Whose groves the frolic fairies planned;
Where arches green, the livelong day,
Echo the blackbird's roundelay,

And vulgar feet have never trod
A spot that is sacred to thought and God.

O, when I am safe in my sylvan home,
I tread on the pride of Greece and Rome;
And when I am stretched beneath the pines,
Where the evening star so holy shines,
I laugh at the lore and the pride of man,
At the sophist schools, and the learned clan;
For what are they all, in their high conceit,
When man in the bush with God may meet?

THE RHODORA

On Being Asked, Whence Is the Flower?

In May, when sea-winds pierced our solitudes,
I found the fresh Rhodora in the woods,
Spreading its leafless blooms in a damp nook,
To please the desert and the sluggish brook.
The purple petals, fallen in the pool,
Made the black water with their beauty gay;
Here might the red-bird come his plumes to cool,
And court the flower that cheapens his array.
Rhodora! if the sages ask thee why
This charm is wasted on the earth and sky,
Tell them, dear, that if eyes were made for seeing,
Then Beauty is its own excuse for being:
Why thou wert there, O rival of the rose!
I never thought to ask, I never knew;
But, in my simple ignorance, suppose
The self-same Power that brought me there brought you.

THE HUMBLE-BEE

Burly, dozing humble-bee,
Where thou art is clime for me.
Let them sail for Porto Rique,
Far-off heats through seas to seek;
I will follow thee alone,
Thou animated torrid-zone!

Zigzag steerer, desert cheerer,
Let me chase thy waving lines;
Keep me nearer, me thy hearer,
Singing over shrubs and vines.

Insect lover of the sun,
Joy of thy dominion!
Sailor of the atmosphere;
Swimmer through the waves of air,
Voyager of light and noon;
Epicurean of June;
Wait, I prithee, till I come
Within earshot of thy hum,—
All without is martyrdom.

When the south wind, in May days,
With a net of shining haze
Silvers the horizon wall,
And, with softness touching all,
Tints the human countenance
With a color of romance,
And, infusing subtle heats,
Turns the sod to violets,
Thou, in sunny solitudes,
Rover of the underwoods,
The green silence dost displace
With thy mellow, breezy bass.

Hot midsummer's petted crone,
Sweet to me thy drowsy tone
Tells of countless sunny hours,
Long days, and solid banks of flowers;
Of gulfs of sweetness without bound
In Indian wildernesses found;
Of Syrian peace, immortal leisure,
Firmest cheer, and bird-like pleasure.

Aught unsavory or unclean,
Hath my insect never seen;
But violets and bilberry bells,
Maple-sap, and daffodels,
Grass with green flag half-mast high.
Succory to match the sky,
Columbine with horn of honey,

Scented fern, and agrimony,
Clover, catchfly, adder's-tongue,
And brier-roses, dwelt among;
All besides was unknown waste,
All was picture as he passed.

Wiser far than human seer,
Yellow-breeched philosopher!
Seeing only what is fair,
Sipping only what is sweet,
Thou dost mock at fate and care,
Leave the chaff, and take the wheat.
When the fierce northwestern blast
Cools sea and land so far and fast,
Thou already slumberest deep;
Woe and want thou canst outsleep;
Want and woe, which torture us,
Thy sleep makes ridiculous.

THE SNOW-STORM

Announced by all the trumpets of the sky,
Arrives the snow, and, driving o'er the fields,
Seems nowhere to alight: the whited air
Hides hills and woods, the river, and the heaven,
And veils the farm-house at the garden's end.
The sled and traveller stopped, the courier's feet
Delayed, all friends shut out, the housemates sit
Around the radiant fireplace, enclosed
In a tumultuous privacy of storm.

Come see the north wind's masonry.
Out of an unseen quarry evermore
Furnished with tile, the fierce artificer
Curves his white bastions with projected roof
Round every windward stake, or tree, or door.
Speeding, the myriad-handed, his wild work
So fanciful, so savage, naught cares he
For number or proportion. Mockingly,
On coop or kennel he hangs Parian wreaths;
A swan-like form invests the hidden thorn;
Fills up the farmer's lane from wall to wall,
Maugre the farmer's sighs; and, at the gate,

A tapering turret overtops the work.
And when his hours are numbered, and the world
Is all his own, retiring, as he were not,
Leaves, when the sun appears, astonished Art
To mimic in slow structures, stone by stone,
Built in an age, the mad wind's nightwork,
The frolic architecture of the snow.

FABLE

The mountain and the squirrel
Had a quarrel;
And the former called the latter "Little Prig."
Bun replied,
"You are doubtless very big;
But all sorts of things and weather
Must be taken in together,
To make up a year
And a sphere.
And I think it no disgrace
To occupy my place.
If I'm not so large as you,
You are not so small as I,
And not half so spry.
I'll not deny you make
A very pretty squirrel track;
Talents differ; all is well and wisely put;
If I cannot carry forests on my back,
Neither can you crack a nut."

FORBEARANCE

Hast thou named all the birds without a gun?
Loved the wood-rose, and left it on its stalk?
At rich men's tables eaten bread and pulse?
Unarmed, faced danger with a heart of trust?
And loved so well a high behavior,
In man or maid, that thou from speech refrained,
Nobility more nobly to repay?
O, be my friend, and teach me to be thine!

GIVE ALL TO LOVE

Give all to love;
Obey thy heart;
Friends, kindred, days,
Estate, good-fame,
Plans, credit, and the Muse,—
Nothing refuse.

'Tis a brave master;
Let it have scope:
Follow it utterly,
Hope beyond hope:
High and more high
It dives into noon,
With wing unspent,
Untold intent;
But it is a god,
Knows its own path,
And the outlets of the sky.

It was not for the mean;
It requireth courage stout,
Souls above doubt,
Valor unbending;
It will reward,—
They shall return
More than they were,
And ever ascending.

Leave all for love;
Yet, hear me, yet,
One word more thy heart behoved,
One pulse more of firm endeavor,—
Keep thee today,
To-morrow, forever,
Free as an Arab
Of thy beloved.

Cling with life to the maid;
But when the surprise,
First vague shadow of surmise
Flits across her bosom young
Of a joy apart from thee,

Free be she, fancy-free;
Nor thou detain her vesture's hem,
Nor the palest rose she flung
From her summer diadem.

THE APOLOGY

Think me not unkind and rude
   That I walk alone in grove and glen;
I go to the god of the wood
   To fetch his word to men.

Tax not my sloth that I
   Fold my arms beside the brook;
Each cloud that floated in the sky
   Writes a letter in my book.

Chide me not, laborious band,
   For the idle flowers I brought;
Every aster in my hand
   Goes home loaded with a thought.

There was never mystery
   But 'tis figured in the flowers;
Was never secret history
   But birds tell it in the bowers.

One harvest from thy field
   Homeward brought the oxen strong;
A second crop thine acres yield,
   Which I gather in a song.

FAME

(Emerson's First Published Poem)

Ah, Fate! cannot a man
   Be wise without a beard?
From East to West, from Beersheba to Dan,
   Say, was it never heard,
That wisdom might in youth be gotten,
Or wit be ripe before 'twas rotten?

He pays too high a price
    For knowledge and for fame,
Who gives his sinews, to be wise,
    His teeth and bones, to buy a name,
And crawls through life a paralytic,
To earn the praise of bard and critic.

Is it not better done,
    To dine and sleep through forty years,
Be loved by few, be feared by none,
    Laugh life away, have wine for tears,
And take the mortal leap undaunted,
Content that all we asked was granted?

But Fate will not permit
    The seed of gods to die,
Nor suffer Sense to win from Wit
    Its guerdon in the sky,
Nor let us hide, whate'er our pleasure,
The world's light underneath a measure

Go then, sad youth, and shine!
    Go, sacrifice to fame;
Put love, joy, health, upon the shrine
    And life to fan the flame!
Thy hapless self for praises barter,
And die to Fame an honored martyr.

HYMN

Sung at the Completion of the
Concord Monument, April 19, 1836

By the rude bridge that arched the flood,
    Their flag to April's breeze unfurled,
Here once the embattled farmers stood,
    And fired the shot heard round the world.

The foe long since in silence slept;
    Alike the conqueror silent sleeps;
And Time the ruined bridge has swept
    Down the dark stream which seaward creeps.

On this green bank, by this soft stream,
  We set to-day a votive stone;
That memory may their deed redeem,
  When, like our sires, our sons are gone.

Spirit, that made those heroes dare
  To die, or leave their children free,
Bid Time and Nature gently spare
  The shaft we raise to them and thee.

BRAHMA

If the red slayer thinks he slays,
  Or if the slain think he is slain,
They know not well the subtle ways
  I keep, and pass, and turn again.

Far or forgot to me is near;
  Shadow and sunlight are the same;
The vanished gods to me appear;
  And one to me are shame and fame.

They reckon ill who leave me out;
  When me they fly, I am the wings;
I am the doubter and the doubt,
  And I the hymn the Brahmin sings.

The strong gods pine for my abode,
  And pine in vain the sacred Seven;
But thou, meek lover of the good!
  Find me, and turn thy back on heaven.

DAYS

Daughters of Time, the hypocritic Days,
Muffled and dumb like barefoot dervishes,
And marching single in an endless file,
Bring diadems and fagots in their hands.
To each they offer gifts after his will,
Bread, kingdoms, stars, and sky that holds them all.
I, in my pleached garden, watched the pomp,
Forgot my morning wishes, hastily

Took a few herbs and apples, and the Day
Turned and departed silent. I, too late,
Under her solemn fillet saw the scorn.

Nathaniel Parker Willis

(1806–1867)

Nathaniel Parker Willis was born in Portland, Maine, attended Yale, and inaugurated his writing career in Boston. He later moved to New York, where he became a distinguished and prominent man of letters. With George Pope Morris, he founded the *Home Journal* in 1846. In his day Willis earned himself a reputation as a man of social graces and a writer of clever verse and prose.

UNSEEN SPIRITS

The shadows lay along Broadway,
  'Twas near the twilight tide,
And slowly there a lady fair
  Was walking in her pride.
Along walked she; but, viewlessly,
  Walked spirits at her side.

Peace charmed the street beneath her feet
  And Honor charmed the air;
And all astir looked kind on her,
  And called her good as fair,
For all God ever gave to her
  She kept with chary care.

She kept with care her beauties rare
  From lovers warm and true,
For her heart was cold to all but gold,
  And the rich came not to woo—

But honored well are charms to sell
  If priests the selling do.

Now walking there was one more fair—
  A slight girl, lily pale;
And she had unseen company
  To make the spirit quail:
'Twixt Want and Scorn she walked forlorn,
  And nothing could avail.

No mercy now can clear her brow
  For this world's peace to pray;
For, as love's wild prayer dissolved in air,
  Her woman's heart gave way!—
But the sin forgiven by Christ in heaven
  By man is cursed alway!

SPRING

The Spring is here—the delicate-footed May,
With its slight fingers full of leaves and flowers,
And with it comes a thirst to be away,
In lovelier scenes to pass these sweeter hours,
A feeling like the worm's awakening wings,
Wild for companionship with swifter things.

We pass out from the city's feverish hum,
To find refreshment in the silent woods;
And nature that is beautiful and dumb,
Like a cool sleep upon the pulses broods—
Yet, even there a restless thought will steal,
To teach the indolent heart it still must feel.

Strange that the audible stillness of the noon,
The waters tripping with their silver feet,
The turning to the light of leaves in June,
And the light whisper as their edges meet—
Strange—that they fill not, with their tranquil tone,
The spirit, walking in their midst alone.

There's no contentment in a world like this,
Save in forgetting the immortal dream;

We may not gaze upon the stars of bliss,
That through the cloud rifts radiantly stream;
Birdlike, the prison'd soul will lift its eye
And pine till it is hooded from the sky.

TO HELEN IN A HUFF

Nay, lady, one frown is enough
    In a life as soon over as this—
And though minutes seem long in a huff,
    They're minutes 'tis pity to miss!
The smiles you imprison so lightly
    Are reckon'd, like days in eclipse;
And though you may smile again brightly,
    You've lost so much light from your lips!
        Pray, lady, smile!

The cup that is longest untasted
    May be with our bliss running o'er,
And, love when we will, we have wasted
    An age in not loving before!
Perchance Cupid's forging a fetter
    To tie us together some day,
And, just for the chance, we had better
    Be laying up love, I should say!
        Nay, lady, smile!

THE DECLARATION

'Twas late, and the gay company was gone,
And light lay soft on the deserted room
From alabaster vases, and a scent
Of orange leaves, and sweet verbena came
Through the unshutter'd window on the air,
And the rich pictures with their dark old tints
Hung like a twilight landscape, and all things
Seem'd hush'd into a slumber. Isabel,
The dark-eyed, spiritual Isabel
Was leaning on her harp, and I had stay'd
To whisper what I could not when the crowd
Hung on her look like worshippers. I knelt,
And with the fervor of a lip unused

To the cool breath of reason, told my love.
There was no answer, and I took the hand
That rested on the strings, and press'd a kiss
Upon it unforbidden—and again
Besought her, that this silent evidence
That I was not indifferent to her heart,
Might have the seal of one sweet syllable.
I kiss'd the small white fingers as I spoke,
And she withdrew them gently, and upraised
Her forehead from its resting place, and look'd
Earnestly on me—*She had been asleep!*

APRIL

"A violet by a mossy stone
Half hidden from the eye,
Fair as a star, when only one
Is shining in the sky."
Wordsworth

I have found violets. April hath come on,
And the cool winds feel softer, and the rain
Falls in the beaded drops of summer time.
You may hear birds at morning, and at eve
The tame dove lingers till the twilight falls,
Cooing upon the eaves, and drawing in
His beautiful bright neck, and, from the hills,
A murmur like the hoarseness of the sea
Tells the release of waters, and the earth
Sends up a pleasant smell, and the dry leaves
Are lifted by the grass; and so I know
That Nature, with her delicate ear, hath heard
The dropping of the velvet foot of Spring.
Take of my violets! I found them where
The liquid South stole o'er them, on a bank
That leaned to running water. There's to me
A daintiness about these early flowers
That touches me like poetry. They blow
With such a simple loveliness among
The common herbs of pasture, and breathe out
Their lives so unobtrusively, like hearts
Whose beatings are too gentle for the world.
I love to go in the capricious days
Of April and hung violets; when the rain

Is in the blue cups trembling, and they nod
So gracefully to the kisses of the wind.
It may be deem'd too idle, but the young
Read nature like the manuscript of heaven,
And call the flowers its poetry. Go out!
Ye spirits of habitual unrest,
And read it when the "fever of the world"
Hath made your hearts impatient, and, if life
Hath yet one spring unpoisoned, it will be
Like a beguiling music to its flow,
And you will no more wonder that I love
To hunt for violets in the April time.

Henry Wadsworth Longfellow

(1807–1882)

Henry Wadsworth Longfellow was born in Portland, Maine, a descendent on his mother's side of John and Priscilla Alden. He was educated at Bowdoin College in Maine, where he was a classmate of Nathaniel Hawthorne and future President Franklin Pierce. After graduation, he traveled abroad and upon his return became a professor of language at Bowdoin. Longfellow married in 1831 but lost his wife and child a few years later. In 1836 he took a Smith professorship at Harvard. Sixteen years later he resigned his post to James Russell Lowell in order to devote the rest of his life to his writing. Longfellow remarried in 1843, but in 1861 his second wife met a tragic death when her dress caught fire. Longfellow was badly burned in the accident. This episode brought to an end one of the most fruitful periods of Longfellow's career.

THE SKELETON IN ARMOR

"Speak! speak! thou fearful guest!
Who, with thy hollow breast
Still in rude armor drest,
   Comest to daunt me!
Wrapt not in Eastern balms,
But with thy fleshless palms
Stretched, as if asking alms,
   Why dost thou haunt me?"

Then from those cavernous eyes
Pale flashes seemed to rise,
As when the Northern skies

Gleam in December;
And, like the water's flow
Under December's snow,
Came a dull voice of woe
   From the heart's chamber.

"I was a Viking old!
My deeds, though manifold,
No Skald in song has told,
   No Saga taught thee!
Take heed that in thy verse
Thou dost the tale rehearse,
Else dread a dead man's curse;
   For this I sought thee.

"Far in the Northern Land,
By the wild Baltic's strand,
I, with my childish hand,
   Tamed the gerfalcon;
And, with my skates fast bound,
Skimmed the half-frozen Sound
That the poor whimpering hound
Trembled to walk on.

"Oft to his frozen lair
Tracked I the grisly bear,
While from my path the hare
   Fled like a shadow;
Oft through the forest dark
Followed the were-wolf's bark,
Until the soaring lark
   Sang from the meadow.

"But when I older grew,
Joining a corsair's crew,
O'er the dark sea I flew
   With the marauders.
Wild was the life we led;
Many the souls that sped,
Many the hearts that bled,
   By our stern orders.

"Many a wassail-bout
Wore the long Winter out;

Often our midnight shout
   Set the cocks crowing,
As we the Berserk's tale
Measured in cups of ale,
Draining the oaken pail
   Filled to o'erflowing.

"Once as I told in glee
Tales of the stormy sea,
Soft eyes did gaze on me,
   Burning yet tender;
And as the white stars shine
On the dark Norway pine,
On that dark heart of mine
   Fell their soft splendor.

"I wooed the blue-eyed maid,
Yielding, yet half afraid,
And in the forest's shade
   Our vows were plighted.
Under its loosened vest
Fluttered her little breast,
Like birds within their nest
   By the hawk frighted.

"Bright in her father's hall
Shields gleamed upon the wall,
Loud sang the minstrels all,
   Chanting his glory;
When of old Hildebrand
I asked his daughter's hand,
Mute did the minstrels stand
   To hear my story.

"While the brown ale he quaffed,
Loud then the champion laughed,
And as the wind gusts waft
   The sea foam brightly,
So the loud laugh of scorn,
Out of those lips unshorn,
From the deep drinking horn
   Blew the foam lightly.

"She was a Prince's child,
I but a Viking wild,
And though she blushed and smiled,
    I was discarded!
Should not the dove so white
Follow the sea mew's flight?
Why did they leave that night
    Her nest unguarded?

"Scarce had I put to sea,
Bearing the maid with me,—
Fairest of all was she
    Among the Norsemen!—
When on the white sea strand,
Waving his armëd hand,
Saw we old Hildebrand,
    With twenty horsemen.

"Then launched they to the blast,
Bent like a reed each mast,
Yet we were gaining fast,
    When the wind failed us;
And with a sudden flaw
Came round the gusty Skaw,
So that our foe we saw
    Laugh as he hailed us.

"And as to catch the gale
Round veered the flapping sail,
'Death!' was the helmsman's hail,
    'Death without quarter!'
Midships with iron keel
Struck we her ribs of steel;
Down her black hulk did reel
    Through the black water!

"As with his wings aslant,
Sails the fierce cormorant,
Seeking some rocky haunt,
    With his prey laden,
So toward the open main,
Beating to sea again,
Through the wild hurricane,
    Bore I the maiden.

"Three weeks we westward bore,
And when the storm was o'er,
Cloudlike we saw the shore
    Stretching to leeward;
There for my lady's bower
Built I the lofty tower,
Which, to this very hour,
    Stands looking seaward.

"There lived we many years;
Time dried the maiden's tears;
She had forgot her fears,
    She was a mother;
Death closed her mild blue eyes;
Under that tower she lies;
Ne'er shall the sun arise
    On such another.

"Still grew my bosom then,
Still as a stagnant fen!
Hateful to me were men,
    The sunlight hateful!
In the vast forest here,
Clad in my warlike gear,
Fell I upon my spear,
    Oh, death was grateful!

"Thus, seamed with many scars,
Bursting these prison bars,
Up to its native stars
    My soul ascended!
There from the flowing bowl
Deep drinks the warrior's soul,
Skoal! to the Northland! *skoal!*"
    Thus the tale ended.

THE WRECK OF THE HESPERUS

It was the schooner Hesperus,
    That sailed the wintry sea;
And the skipper had taken his little daughter,
    To bear him company.

Blue were her eyes as the fairy-flax,
  Her cheeks like the dawn of day,
And her bosom white as the hawthorn buds,
  That ope in the month of May.

The skipper he stood beside the helm,
  His pipe was in his mouth,
And he watched how the veering flaw did blow
  The smoke now West, now South.

Then up and spake an old sailor,
  Had sailed to the Spanish Main,
"I pray thee, put into yonder port,
  For I fear a hurricane.

"Last night, the moon had a golden ring,
  And to-night no moon we see!"
The skipper, he blew a whiff from his pipe,
  And a scornful laugh laughed he.

Colder and colder blew the wind,
  A gale from the Northeast,
The snow fell hissing in the brine,
  And the billows frothed like yeast.

Down came the storm, and smote amain
  The vessel in its strength;
She shuddered and paused, like a frighted steed,
  Then leaped her cable's length.

"Come hither! come hither! my little daughter,
  And do not tremble so;
For I can weather the roughest gale
  That ever wind did blow."

He wrapped her warm in his seaman's coat
  Against the stinging blast;
He cut a rope from a broken spar,
  And bound her to the mast.

"O father! I hear the church bells ring,
  Oh, say, what may it be?"
" 'Tis a fog bell on a rock-bound coast!"—
  And he steered for the open sea.

"O father! I hear the sound of guns,
  Oh, say, what may it be?"
"Some ship in distress, that cannot live
  In such an angry sea!"

"O father! I see the gleaming light,
  Oh, say, what may it be?"
But the father answered never a word,
  A frozen corpse was he.

Lashed to the helm, all stiff and stark,
  With his face turned to the skies,
The lantern gleamed through the gleaming snow
  On his fixed and glassy eyes.

Then the maiden clasped her hands and prayed
  That savëd she might be;
And she thought of Christ, who stilled the wave,
  On the Lake of Galilee.

And fast through the midnight dark and drear,
  Through the whistling sleet and snow,
Like a sheeted ghost, the vessel swept
  Tow'rds the reef of Norman's Woe.

And ever the fitful gusts between
  A sound came from the land;
It was the sound of the trampling surf
  On the rocks and the hard sea sand.

The breakers were right beneath her bows,
  She drifted a dreary wreck,
And a whooping billow swept the crew
  Like icicles from her deck.

She struck where the white and fleecy waves
  Looked soft as carded wool,
But the cruel rocks, they gored her side
  Like the horns of an angry bull.

Her rattling shrouds, all sheathed in ice,
  With the masts went by the board;
Like a vessel of glass, she strove and sank,
  Ho! ho! the breakers roared!

At daybreak, on the bleak sea beach,
　A fisherman stood aghast,
To see the form of a maiden fair,
　Lashed close to a drifting mast.

The salt sea was frozen on her breast
　The salt tears in her eyes;
And he saw her hair, like the brown seaweed,
　On the billows fall and rise.

Such was the wreck of the Hesperus,
　In the midnight and the snow!
Christ save us all from a death like this,
　On the reef of Norman's Woe!

THE VILLAGE BLACKSMITH

Under a spreading chestnut-tree
　The village smithy stands:
The smith, a mighty man is he,
　With large and sinewy hands;
And the muscles of his brawny arms
　Are strong as iron bands.

His hair is crisp, and black, and long,
　His face is like the tan;
His brow is wet with honest sweat,
　He earns whate'er he can,
And looks the whole world in the face,
　For he owes not any man.

Week in, week out, from morn till night,
　You can hear his bellows blow;
You can hear him swing his heavy sledge,
　With measured beat and slow,
Like a sexton ringing the village bell,
　When the evening sun is low.

And children coming home from school
　Look in at the open door;
They love to see the flaming forge,
　And hear the bellows roar,

And catch the burning sparks that fly
    Like chaff from a threshing-floor.

He goes on Sunday to the church,
    And sits among his boys;
He hears the parson pray and preach,
    He hears his daughter's voice,
Singing in the village choir,
    And it makes his heart rejoice.

It sounds to him like her mother's voice,
    Singing in Paradise!
He needs must think of her once more,
    How in the grave she lies;
And with his hard, rough hand he wipes
    A tear out of his eyes.

Toiling,—rejoicing,—sorrowing,
    Onward through life he goes;
Each morning sees some task begin,
    Each evening sees it close;
Something attempted, something done,
    Has earned a night's repose.

Thanks, thanks to thee, my worthy friend,
    For the lesson thou hast taught!
Thus at the flaming forge of life
    Our fortunes must be wrought;
Thus on its sounding anvil shaped
    Each burning deed and thought.

THE DAY IS DONE

The day is done, and the darkness
    Falls from the wings of Night,
As a feather is wafted downward
    From an eagle in his flight.

I see the lights of the village
    Gleam through the rain and the mist,
And a feeling of sadness comes o'er me
    That my soul cannot resist:

A feeling of sadness and longing
　　That is not akin to pain,
And resembles sorrow only
　　As the mist resembles rain.

Come, read to me some poem,
　　Some simple and heartfelt lay,
That shall soothe this restless feeling,
　　And banish the thoughts of day.

Not from the grand old masters,
　　Not from the bards sublime,
Whose distant footsteps echo
　　Through the corridors of Time.

For, like strains of martial music,
　　Their mighty thoughts suggest
Life's endless toil and endeavor;
　　And to-night I long for rest.

Read from some humbler poet,
　　Whose songs gushed from his heart,
As showers from the clouds of summer,
　　Or tears from the eyelids start;

Who through long days of labor,
　　And nights devoid of ease,
Still heard in his soul the music
　　Of wonderful melodies.

Such songs have power to quiet
　　The restless pulse of care,
And come like the benediction
　　That follows after prayer.

Then read from the treasured volume
　　The poem of thy choice,
And lend to the rhyme of the poet
　　The beauty of thy voice.

And the night shall be filled with music,
　　And the cares that infest the day
Shall fold their tents like the Arabs,
　　And as silently steal away.

MY LOST YOUTH

Often I think of the beautiful town
   That is seated by the sea;
Often in thought go up and down
The pleasant streets of that dear old town,
   And my youth comes back to me.
     And a verse of a Lapland song
     Is haunting my memory still:
     "A boy's will is the wind's will,
And the thoughts of youth are long, long thoughts."

I can see the shadowy lines of its trees,
   And catch, in sudden gleams,
The sheen of the far-surrounding seas,
And islands that were the Hersperides
   Of all my boyish dreams.
     And the burden of that old song,
     It murmurs and whispers still:
     "A boy's will is the wind's will,
And the thoughts of youth are long, long thoughts."

I remember the black wharves and the slips,
   And the sea-tides tossing free;
And Spanish sailors with bearded lips,
And the beauty and mystery of the ships,
   And the magic of the sea.
     And the voice of that wayward song
     Is singing and saying still:
     "A boy's will is the wind's will,
And the thoughts of youth are long, long thoughts."

I remember the bulwarks by the shore,
   And the fort upon the hill;
The sunrise gun, with its hollow roar,
The drum beat repeated o'er and o'er,
   And the bugle wild and shrill.
     And the music of that old song
     Throbs in my memory still:
     "A boy's will is the wind's will,
And the thoughts of youth are long, long thoughts."

I remember the sea fight far away,
   How it thundered o'er the tide!

And the dead captains as they lay
In their graves, o'erlooking the tranquil bay
  Where they in battle died.
    And the sound of that mournful song
    Goes through me with a thrill:
    "A boy's will is the wind's will,
And the thoughts of youth are long, long thoughts."

I can see the breezy dome of groves,
  The shadows of Deering's Woods;
And the friendships old and the early loves
Come back with a Sabbath sound, as of doves
  In quiet neighborhoods.
    And the verse of that sweet old song,
    It flutters and murmurs still:
    "A boy's will is the wind's will,
And the thoughts of youth are long, long thoughts."

I remember the gleams and glooms that dart
  Across the schoolboy's brain;
The song and the silence in the heart,
That in part are prophecies, and in part
  Are longings wild and vain.
    And the voice of that fitful song
    Sings on, and is never still:
    "A boy's will is the wind's will,
And the thoughts of youth are long, long thoughts."

There are things of which I may not speak;
  There are dreams that cannot die;
There are thoughts that make the strong heart weak,
And bring a pallor into the cheek,
  And a mist before the eye.
    And the words of that fatal song
    Come over me like a chill:
    "A boy's will is the wind's will,
And the thoughts of youth are long, long thoughts."

Strange to me now are the forms I meet
  When I visit the dear old town;
But the native air is pure and sweet,
And the trees that o'ershadow each well-known street,
  As they balance up and down,
    Are singing the beautiful song,

Are sighing and whispering still:
    "A boy's will is the wind's will,
And the thoughts of youth are long, long thoughts."

And Deering's Woods are fresh and fair,
    And with joy that is almost pain
My heart goes back to wander there,
And among the dreams of the days that were,
    I find my lost youth again.
        And the strange and beautiful song,
        The groves are repeating it still:
        "A boy's will is the wind's will,
And the thoughts of youth are long, long thoughts."

THE CHILDREN'S HOUR

Between the dark and the daylight,
    When the night is beginning to lower,
Comes a pause in the day's occupations,
    That is known as the Children's Hour.

I hear in the chamber above me
    The patter of little feet,
The sound of a door that is opened,
    And voices soft and sweet.

From my study I see in the lamplight,
    Descending the broad hall stair,
Grave Alice, and laughing Allegra,
    And Edith with golden hair.

A whisper, and then a silence:
    Yet I know by their merry eyes
They are plotting and planning together
    To take me by surprise.

A sudden rush from the stairway,
    A sudden raid from the hall!
By three doors left unguarded
    They enter my castle wall!

They climb up into my turret
  O'er the arms and back of my chair;
If I try to escape, they surround me;
  They seem to be everywhere.

They almost devour me with kisses,
  Their arms about me entwine,
Till I think of the Bishop of Bingen
  In his Mouse-Tower on the Rhine!

Do you think, O blue-eyed banditti,
  Because you have scaled the wall,
Such an old mustache as I am
  Is not a match for you all!

I have you fast in my fortress,
  And will not let you depart,
But put you down into the dungeon
  In the round-tower of my heart.

And there will I keep you forever,
  Yes, forever and a day.
Till the walls shall crumble to ruin,
  And moulder in dust away!

THE POET AND HIS SONGS

As the birds come in Spring,
  We know not from where;
As the stars come at evening
  From depths of the air;

As the rain comes from the cloud,
  And the brook from the ground;
As suddenly, low or loud,
  Out of silence a sound;

As the grape comes to the vine,
  The fruit to the tree;
As the wind comes to the pine,
  And the tide to the sea;

As come the white sails of ships
 O'er the ocean's verge;
As comes the smile to the lips,
 The foam to the surge;

So come to the Poet his songs,
 All hitherward blown
From the misty realm that belongs
 To the vast unknown.

His, and not his, are the lays
 He sings; and their fame
Is his, and not his; and the praise
 And the pride of a name.

For voices pursue him by day
 And haunt him by night,
And he listens and needs must obey,
 When the Angel says, "Write!"

PAUL REVERE'S RIDE

Listen, my children, and you shall hear
Of the midnight ride of Paul Revere,
On the eighteenth of April, in Seventy-five;
Hardly a man is now alive
Who remembers that famous day and year.

He said to his friend, "If the British march
By land or sea from the town tonight,
Hang a lantern aloft in the belfry arch
Of the North Church tower as a signal light,—
One, if by land, and two, if by sea;
And I on the opposite shore will be,
Ready to ride and spread the alarm
Through every Middlesex village and farm,
For the country folk to be up and to arm."

Then he said, "Good-night!" and with muffled oar
Silently rowed to the Charlestown shore.
Just as the moon rose over the bay,
Where swinging wide at her moorings lay
The Somerset, British man-of-war;

A phantom ship, with each mast and spar
Across the moon like a prison bar,
And a huge black hulk, that was magnified
By its own reflection in the tide.

Meanwhile, his friend, through alley and street,
Wanders and watches with eager ears.
Till in the silence around him he hears
The muster of men at the barrack door,
The sound of arms, and the tramp of feet,
And the measured tread of the grenadiers,
Marching down to their boats on the shore.

Then he climbed the tower of the Old North Church,
By the wooden stairs, with stealthy tread,
To the belfry-chamber overhead,
And startled the pigeons from their perch
On the sombre rafters, that round him made
Masses and moving shapes of shade,—
By the trembling ladder, steep and tall,
To the highest window in the wall,
Where he paused to listen and look down
A moment on the roofs of the town,
And the moonlight flowing over all.

Beneath, in the churchyard, lay the dead,
In their night-encampment on the hill,
Wrapped in silence so deep and still
That he could hear, like a sentinel's tread,
The watchful night-wind, as it went
Creeping along from tent to tent.
And seeming to whisper, "All is well!"
A moment only he feels the spell
Of the place and the hour, and the secret dread
Of the lonely belfry and the dead;
For suddenly all his thoughts are bent
On a shadowy something far away,
Where the river widens to meet the bay,—
A line of black that bends and floats
On the rising tide, like a bridge of boats.

Meanwhile, impatient to mount and ride,
Booted and spurred, with a heavy stride
On the opposite shore walked Paul Revere.

Now he patted his horse's side,
Now gazed at the landscape far and near,
Then, impetuous, stamped the earth,
And turned and tightened his saddle-girth;
But mostly he watched with eager search
The belfry-tower of the Old North Church,
As it rose above the graves on the hill,
Lonely and spectral and sombre and still.
And lo! as he looks, on the belfry's height
A glimmer, and then a gleam of light!
He springs to the saddle, the bridle he turns,
But lingers and gazes, till full on his sight
A second lamp in the belfry burns!

A hurry of hoofs in a village street,
A shape in the moonlight, a bulk in the dark,
And beneath, from the pebbles, in passing, a spark
Struck out by a steed flying fearless and fleet:
That was all! And yet, through the gloom and the light,
The fate of a nation was riding that night;
And the spark struck out by that steed in his flight,
Kindled the land into flame with its heat.

He has left the village and mounted the steep,
And beneath him, tranquil and broad and deep,
Is the Mystic, meeting the ocean tides;
And under the alders that skirt its edge,
Now soft on the sand, now loud on the ledge,
Is heard the tramp of his steed as he rides.

It was twelve by the village clock,
When he crossed the bridge into Medford town.
He heard the crowing of the cock,
And the barking of the farmer's dog,
And felt the damp of the river fog
That rises after the sun goes down.

It was one by the village clock,
When he galloped into Lexington.
He saw the gilded weathercock
Swim in the moonlight as he passed,
And the meeting-house windows, blank and bare,
Gaze at him with a spectral glare,

As if they already stood aghast
At the bloody work they would look upon.

It was two by the village clock,
When he came to the bridge in Concord town.
He heard the bleating of the flock,
And the twitter of birds among the trees,
And felt the breath of the morning breeze
Blowing over the meadows brown.
And one was safe and asleep in his bed
Who at the bridge would be first to fall,
Who that day would be lying dead,
Pierced by a British musket-ball.

You know the rest. In the books you have read,
How the British Regulars fired and fled,—
How the farmers gave them ball for ball,
From behind each fence and farm-yard wall,
Chasing the red-coats down the lane,
Then crossing the fields to emerge again
Under the trees at the turn of the road,
And only pausing to fire and load.

So through the night rode Paul Revere;
And so through the night went his cry of alarm
To every Middlesex village and farm,—
A cry of defiance and not of fear,
A voice in the darkness, a knock at the door,
And a word that shall echo forevermore!
For, borne on the night-wind of the Past,
Through all our history, to the last,
In the hour of darkness and peril and need,
The people will waken and listen to hear
The hurrying hoof-beats of that steed,
And the midnight message of Paul Revere.

CURFEW

I

Solemnly, mournfully,
Dealing its dole,

The Curfew Bell
  Is beginning to toll.

Cover the embers,
  And put out the light;
Toil comes with the morning,
  And rest with the night.

Dark grow the windows,
  And quenched is the fire;
Sound fades into silence,—
  All footsteps retire.

No voice in the chambers,
  No sound in the hall!
Sleep and oblivion
  Reign over all!

II

The book is completed,
  And closed, like the day;
And the hand that has written it
  Lays it away.

Dim grow its fancies;
  Forgotten they lie;
Like coals in the ashes,
  They darken and die.

Song sinks into silence,
  The story is told,
The windows are darkened,
  The hearth-stone is cold.

Darker and darker
  The black shadows fall;
Sleep and oblivion
  Reign over all.

CHRISTMAS BELLS

I heard the bells on Christmas Day
Their old, familiar carols play,
    And wild and sweet
    The words repeat
Of peace on earth, good-will to men!

And thought how, as the day had come,
The belfries of all Christendom
    Had rolled along
    The unbroken song
Of peace on earth, good-will to men!

Till, ringing, singing on its way,
The world revolved from night to day,
    A voice, a chime,
    A chant sublime
Of peace on earth, good-will to men!

Then from each black, accursed mouth
The cannon thundered in the South,
    And with the sound
    The carols drowned
Of peace on earth, good-will to men!

It was as if an earthquake rent
The hearth-stones of a continent,
    And made forlorn
    The household born
Of peace on earth, good-will to men!

And in despair I bowed my head;
"There is no peace on earth," I said;
    "For hate is strong,
    And mocks the song
Of peace on earth, good-will to men!"

Then pealed the bells more loud and deep:
"God is not dead; nor doth he sleep!
    The Wrong shall fail,
    The Right prevail,
With peace on earth, good-will to men!"

A PSALM OF LIFE

What the Heart of the Young Man Said to the Psalmist

Tell me not, in mournful numbers,
   "Life is but an empty dream!"
For the soul is dead that slumbers,
   And things are not what they seem.

Life is real! Life is earnest!
   And the grave is not its goal;
"Dust thou art, to dust returnest,"
   Was not spoken of the soul.

Not enjoyment, and not sorrow,
   Is our destined end or way;
But to act, that each to-morrow
   Finds us farther than to-day.

Art is long, and Time is fleeting,
   And our hearts, though stout and brave,
Still, like muffled drums, are beating
   Funeral marches to the grave.

In the world's broad field of battle,
   In the bivouac of Life,
Be not like dumb, driven cattle!
   Be a hero in the strife!

Trust no Future, howe'er pleasant!
   Let the dead Past bury its dead!
Act,—act in the living Present!
   Heart within, and God o'erhead!

Lives of great men all remind us
   We can make our lives sublime,
And, departing, leave behind us
   Footprints on the sands of time;

Footprints, that perhaps another,
   Sailing o'er life's solemn main,
A forlorn and shipwrecked brother,
   Seeing, shall take heart again.

Let us, then, be up and doing,
　With a heart for any fate;
Still achieving, still pursuing,
　Learn to labor and to wait.

FOOTSTEPS OF ANGELS

When the hours of Day are numbered,
　And the voices of the Night
Wake the better soul, that slumbered,
　To a holy, calm delight;

Ere the evening lamps are lighted,
　And, like phantoms grim and tall,
Shadows from the fitful fire-light
　Dance upon the parlor wall;

Then the forms of the departed
　Enter at the open door;
The beloved, the true-hearted,
　Come to visit me once more;

He, the young and strong, who cherished
　Noble longings for the strife,
By the roadside fell and perished,
　Weary with the march of life!

They, the holy ones and weakly,
　Who the cross of suffering bore,
Folded their pale hands so meekly,
　Spake with us on earth no more!

And with them the Being Beauteous,
　Who unto my youth was given,
More than all things else to love me,
　And is now a saint in heaven.

With a slow and noiseless footstep
　Comes that messenger divine,
Takes the vacant chair beside me,
　Lays her gentle hand in mine.

And she sits and gazes at me
  With those deep and tender eyes,
Like the stars, so still and saint-like,
  Looking downward from the skies.

Uttered not, yet comprehended,
  Is the spirit's voiceless prayer,
Soft rebukes, in blessings ended,
  Breathing from her lips of air.

O, though oft depressed and lonely,
  All my fears are laid aside,
If I but remember only
  Such as these have lived and died!

THE BELEAGUERED CITY

I have read, in some old marvellous tale,
  Some legend strange and vague,
That a midnight host of spectres pale
  Beleaguered the walls of Prague.

Beside the Moldau's rushing stream,
  With the wan moon overhead,
There stood, as in an awful dream,
  The army of the dead.

White as a sea-fog, landward bound,
  The spectral camp was seen,
And, with a sorrowful, deep sound,
  The river flowed between.

No other voice nor sound was there,
  No drum, nor sentry's pace;
The mist-like banners clasped the air,
  As clouds with clouds embrace.

But, when the old cathedral bell
  Proclaimed the morning prayer,
The white pavilions rose and fell
  On the alarmed air.

Down the broad valley fast and far
 The troubled army fled;
Up rose the glorious morning star,
 The ghastly host was dead.

I have read, in the marvellous heart of man,
 That strange and mystic scroll,
That an army of phantoms vast and wan
 Beleaguer the human soul.

Encamped beside Life's rushing stream,
 In Fancy's misty light,
Gigantic shapes and shadows gleam
 Portentous through the night.

Upon its midnight battle-ground
 The spectral camp is seen,
And, with a sorrowful, deep sound,
 Flows the River of Life between.

No other voice, nor sound is there,
 In the army of the grave;
No other challenge breaks the air,
 But the rushing of Life's wave.

And, when the solemn and deep church-bell
 Entreats the soul to pray,
The midnight phantoms feel the spell
 The shadows sweep away.

Down the broad Vale of Tears afar
 The spectral camp is fled;
Faith shineth as a morning star,
 Our ghastly fears are dead.

THE ARROW AND THE SONG

I shot an arrow into the air,
It fell to earth, I knew not where;
For, so swiftly it flew, the sight
Could not follow it in its flight.

I breathed a song into the air,
It fell to earth, I knew not where;
For who has sight so keen and strong,
That it can follow the flight of song?

Long, long afterward, in an oak
I found the arrow, still unbroke;
And the song, from beginning to end,
I found again in the heart of a friend.

THE BUILDERS

All are architects of Fate,
   Working in these walls of Time;
Some with massive deeds and great,
   Some with ornaments of rhyme.

Nothing useless is, or low;
   Each thing in its place is best;
And what seems but idle show
   Strengthens and supports the rest.

For the structure that we raise,
   Time is with materials filled;
Our to-days and yesterdays
   Are the blocks with which we build.

Truly shape and fashion these;
   Leave no yawning gaps between;
Think not, because no man sees,
   Such things will remain unseen.

In the elder days of Art,
   Builders wrought with greatest care
Each minute and unseen part;
   For the Gods see everywhere.

Let us do our work as well,
   Both the unseen and the seen!
Make the house, where Gods may dwell,
   Beautiful, entire, and clean.

Else our lives are incomplete,
   Standing in these walls of Time,
Broken stairways, where the feet
   Stumble as they seek to climb.

Build to-day, then, strong and sure,
   With a firm and ample base;
And ascending and secure
   Shall to-morrow find its place.

Thus alone can we attain
   To those turrets, where the eye
Sees the world as one vast plain,
   And one boundless reach of sky.

BIRDS OF PASSAGE

Black shadows fall
From the lindens tall,
That lift aloft their massive wall
   Against the southern sky;

And from the realms
Of the shadowy elms
A tide-like darkness overwhelms
   The fields that round us lie.

But the night is fair,
And everywhere
A warm, soft vapor fills the air,
   And distant sounds seem near;

And above, in the light
Of the star-lit night,
Swift birds of passage wing their flight
   Through the dewy atmosphere.

I hear the beat
Of their pinions fleet,
As from the land of snow and sleet
   They seek a southern lea.

I hear the cry
Of their voices high
Falling dreamily through the sky,
  But their forms I cannot see.

O, say not so!
Those sounds that flow
In murmurs of delight and woe
  Come not from wings of birds.

They are the throngs
Of the poet's songs,
Murmurs of pleasures, and pains, and wrongs,
  The sound of wingèd words.

This is the cry
Of souls, that high
On toiling, beating pinions, fly,
  Seeking a warmer clime.

From their distant flight
Through realms of light
It falls into our world of night,
  With the murmuring sound of rhyme.

John Greenleaf Whittier

(1807–1892)

John Greenleaf Whittier was born and raised as a Quaker on a farm near Haverhill, Massachusetts. He became familiar with Burns as a young teen and started writing poetry. He was a lover of nature and indeed epitomized the image of the "barefoot boy." Throughout his life, Whittier was an advocate of the lower classes and spoke out strongly against slavery. Unlike many of the American poets, Whittier did not go to college. In 1838 he moved to Philadelphia to edit the *Pennsylvania Freeman* and continued to make known his anti-slavery point of view. As a result the printing office was wrecked and burned. In 1840 Whittier returned to his home state and devoted the rest of his life to literary work. Whittier never married.

BARBARA FRIETCHIE

Up from the meadows rich with corn,
Clear in the cool September morn,
The clustered spires of Frederick stand
Green-walled by the hills of Maryland.

Round about them orchards sweep,
Apple and peach tree fruited deep,
Fair as the garden of the Lord
To the eyes of the famished rebel horde,

On that pleasant morn of the early fall
When Lee marched over the mountain-wall;
Over the mountains winding down,
Horse and foot, into Frederick town.

Forty flags with their silver stars,
Forty flags with their crimson bars,
Flapped in the morning wind: the sun
Of noon looked down, and saw not one.

Up rose old Barbara Frietchie then,
Bowed with her fourscore years and ten;
Bravest of all in Frederick town,
She took up the flag the men hauled down;

In her attic window the staff she set,
To show that one heart was loyal yet.
Up the street came the rebel tread,
Stonewall Jackson riding ahead.

Under his slouched hat left and right
He glanced; the old flag met his sight.
"Halt!"—the dust-brown ranks stood fast.
"Fire!"—out blazed the rifle-blast.

It shivered the window, pane and sash;
It rent the banner with seam and gash.
Quick, as it fell, from the broken staff
Dame Barbara snatched the silken scarf,

She leaned far out on the window-sill,
And shook it forth with a royal will.
"Shoot, if you must, this old gray head,
But spare your country's flag," she said.

A shade of sadness, a blush of shame,
Over the face of the leader came;
The nobler nature within him stirred
To life at that woman's deed and word;

"Who touches a hair of yon gray head
Dies like a dog! March on!" he said.
All day long through Frederick street
Sounded the tread of marching feet:

All day long that free flag tost
Over the heads of the rebel host.
Ever its torn folds rose and fell
On the loyal winds that loved it well;

And through the hill-gaps sunset light
Shone over it with a warm good-night.
Barbara Frietchie's work is o'er,
And the Rebel rides on his raids no more.

Honor to her! and let a tear
Fall, for her sake, on Stonewall's bier.
Over Barbara Frietchie's grave,
Flag of Freedom and Union, wave!

Peace and order and beauty draw
Round thy symbol of light and law;
And ever the stars above look down
On thy stars below in Frederick town!

THE BAREFOOT BOY

Blessings on thee, little man,
Barefoot boy, with cheek of tan!
With thy turned-up pantaloons,
And thy merry whistled tunes;
With thy red lip, redder still
Kissed by strawberries on the hill;
With the sunshine on thy face,
Through thy torn brim's jaunty grace;
From my heart I give thee joy,—
I was once a barefoot boy!
Prince thou art,—the grown-up man
Only is republican.
Let the million-dollared ride!
Barefoot, trudging at his side,
Thou hast more than he can buy
In the reach of ear and eye,—
Outward sunshine, inward joy:
Blessings on thee, barefoot boy!

Oh for boyhood's painless play,
Sleep that wakes in laughing day,
Health that mocks the doctor's rules,
Knowledge never learned of schools,
Of the wild bee's morning chase,
Of the wild-flower's time and place,
Flight of fowl and habitude

Of the tenants of the wood;
How the tortoise bears his shell,
How the woodchuck digs his cell,
And the ground-mole sinks his well;
How the robin feeds her young,
How the oriole's nest is hung;
Where the whitest lilies blow,
Where the freshest berries grow,
Where the ground-nut trails its vine,
Where the wood grape's clusters shine;
Of the black wasp's cunning way,
Mason of his walls of clay,
And the architectural plans
Of gray hornet artisans!
For, eschewing books and tasks,
Nature answers all he asks:
Hand in hand with her he walks,
Face to face with her he talks,
Part and parcel of her joy,—
Blessings on the barefoot boy!

Oh for boyhood's time of June,
Crowding years in one brief moon,
When all things I heard or saw,
Me, their master, waited for.
I was rich in flowers and trees,
Humming-birds and honey-bees;
For my sport the squirrel played,
Plied the snouted mole his spade;
For my taste the blackberry cone
Purpled over hedge and stone;
Laughed the brook for my delight
Through the day and through the night,
Whispering at the garden wall,
Talked with me from fall to fall;
Mine the sand-rimmed pickerel pond,
Mine the walnut slopes beyond,
Mine, on bending orchard trees,
Apples of Hesperides!
Still as my horizon grew,
Larger grew my riches too;
All the world I saw or knew
Seemed a complex Chinese toy,
Fashioned for a barefoot boy!

Oh for festal dainties spread,
Like my bowl of milk and bread;
Pewter spoon and bowl of wood,
On the door-stone, gray and rude!
O'er me, like a regal tent,
Cloudy-ribbed, the sunset bent,
Purple-curtained, fringed with gold,
Looped in many a wind-swung fold;
While for music came the play
Of the pied frogs' orchestra;
And, to light the noisy choir,
Lit the fly his lamp of fire.
I was monarch: pomp and joy
Waited on the barefoot boy!

Cheerily, then, my little man,
Live and laugh, as boyhood can!
Though the flinty slopes be hard,
Stubble-speared the new-mown sward,
Every morn shall lead thee through
Fresh baptisms of the dew;
Every evening from thy feet
Shall the cool wind kiss the heat:
All too soon these feet must hide
In the prison cells of pride,
Lose the freedom of the sod,
Like a colt's for work be shod,
Made to tread the mills of toil,
Up and down in ceaseless moil:
Happy if their track be found
Never on forbidden ground;
Happy if they sink not in
Quick and treacherous sands of sin.
Ah! that thou couldst know thy joy,
Ere it passes, barefoot boy!

SKIPPER IRESON'S RIDE

Of all the rides since the birth of time,
Told in story or sung in rhyme,—
On Apuleius's Golden Ass,
Or one-eyed Calender's horse of brass,
Witch astride of a human back,

Islam's prophet on Al-Borák,—
The strangest ride that ever was sped
Was Ireson's, out from Marblehead!
  Old Floyd Ireson, for his hard heart,
    Tarred and feathered and carried in a cart
      By the women of Marblehead!

Body of turkey, head of owl,
Wings a-droop like a rained-on fowl,
Feathered and ruffled in every part,
Skipper Ireson stood in the cart.
Scores of women, old and young,
Strong of muscle, and glib of tongue,
Pushed and pulled up the rocky lane,
Shouting and singing the shrill refrain:
  "Here's Flud Oirson, fur his horrd horrt,
    Torr'd an' futherr'd an' corr'd in a corrt
      By the women o' Morble'ead!"

Wrinkled scolds with hands on hips,
Girls in bloom of cheek and lips,
Wild-eyed, free-limbed, such as chase
Bacchus round some antique vase,
Brief of skirt, with ankles bare,
Loose of kerchief and loose of hair,
With conch-shells blowing and fish-horns' twang,
Over and over the Mænads sang:
  "Here's Flud Oirson, fur his horrd horrt,
    Torr'd an' futherr'd an' corr'd in a corrt
      By the women o' Morble'ead!"

Small pity for him!—He sailed away
From a leaking ship in Chaleur Bay,—
Sailed away from a sinking wreck,
With his own town's-people on her deck!
"Lay by! lay by!" they called to him.
Back he answered, "Sink or swim!
Brag of your catch of fish again!"
And off he sailed through the fog and rain!
  Old Floyd Ireson, for his hard heart,
    Tarred and feathered and carried in a cart
      By the women of Marblehead!

Fathoms deep in dark Chaleur
That wreck shall lie forevermore.
Mother and sister, wife and maid,
Looked from the rocks of Marblehead
Over the moaning and rainy sea,—
Looked for the coming that might not be!
What did the winds and the sea-birds say
Of the cruel captain who sailed away?—
  Old Floyd Ireson, for his hard heart,
   Tarred and feathered and carried in a cart
    By the women of Marblehead!

Through the street, on either side,
Up flew windows, doors swung wide;
Sharp-tongued spinsters, old wives gray,
Treble lent the fish-horn's bray.
Sea-worn grandsires, cripple-bound,
Hulks of old sailors run aground,
Shook head, and fist, and hat, and cane,
And cracked with curses the hoarse refrain:
  "Here's Flud Oirson, fur his horrd horrt,
   Torr'd an' futherr'd an' corr'd in a corrt
    By the women o' Morble'ead!"

Sweetly along the Salem road
Bloom of orchard and lilac showed.
Little the wicked skipper knew
Of the fields so green and the sky so blue.
Riding there in his sorry trim,
Like an Indian idol glum and grim,
Scarcely he seemed the sound to hear
Of voices shouting, far and near:
  "Here's Flud Oirson, fur his horrd horrt,
   Torr'd an' futherr'd an' corr'd in a corrt
    By the women o' Morble'ead!"

"Hear me, neighbors!" at last he cried,—
"What to me is this noisy ride?
What is the shame that clothes the skin
To the nameless horror that lives within?
Waking or sleeping, I see a wreck,
And hear a cry from a reeling deck!
Hate me and curse me,—I only dread
The hand of God and the face of the dead!"

Said old Floyd Ireson, for his hard heart,
Tarred and feathered and carried in a cart
    By the women of Marblehead!

Then the wife of the skipper lost at sea
Said, "God has touched him! why should we!"
Said an old wife mourning her only son,
"Cut the rogue's tether and let him run!"
So with soft relentings and rude excuse,
Half scorn, half pity, they cut him loose,
And gave him a cloak to hide him in,
And left him alone with his shame and sin.
    Poor Floyd Ireson, for his hard heart,
Tarred and feathered and carried in a cart
    By the women of Marblehead!

ICHABOD

So fallen! so lost! the light withdrawn
    Which once he wore!
The glory from his gray hairs gone
    Forevermore!

Revile him not, the Tempter hath
    A snare for all;
And pitying tears, not scorn and wrath,
    Befit his fall!

Oh, dumb be passion's stormy rage,
    When he who might
Have lighted up and led his age,
    Falls back in night.

Scorn! would the angels laugh, to mark
    A bright soul driven,
Fiend-goaded, down the endless dark,
    From hope and heaven!

Let not the land once proud of him
    Insult him now,
Nor brand with deeper shame his dim,
    Dishonored brow.

But let its humbled sons, instead,
    From sea to lake,
A long lament, as for the dead,
    In sadness make.

Of all we loved and honored, naught
    Save power remains;
A fallen angel's pride of thought,
    Still strong in chains.

All else is gone; from those great eyes
    The soul has fled:
When faith is lost, when honor dies,
    The man is dead!

Then, pay the reverence of old days
    To his dead fame;
Walk backward, with averted gaze,
    And hide the shame!

TELLING THE BEES

Here is the place; right over the hill
    Runs the path I took;
You can see the gap in the old wall still,
    And the stepping stones in the shallow brook.

There is the house, with the gate red-barred,
    And the poplars tall;
And the barn's brown length, and the cattle yard,
    And the white horns tossing above the wall.

There are the beehives ranged in the sun;
    And down by the brink
Of the brook are her poor flowers, weed-o'errun,
    Pansy and daffodil, rose and pink.

A year has gone, as the tortoise goes,
    Heavy and slow;
And the same rose blows, and the same sun glows,
    And the same brook sings of a year ago.

There's the same sweet clover smell in the breeze;
  And the June sun warm
Tangles his wings of fire in the trees,
  Setting, as then, over Fernside farm.

I mind me how, with a lover's care,
  From my Sunday coat
I brushed off the burs, and smoothed my hair,
  And cooled at the brookside my brow and throat.

Since we parted, a month has passed,—
  To love, a year;
Down through the beeches I looked at last
  On the little red gate and the well-sweep near.

I can see it all now,—the slantwise rain
  Of light through the leaves,
The sundown's blaze on her window-pane,
  The bloom of her roses under the eaves.

Just the same as a month before,—
  The house and the trees,
The barn's brown gable, the vine by the door,—
  Nothing changed but the hives of bees.

Before them, under the garden wall,
  Forward and back,
Went, drearily singing, the chore girl small,
  Draping each hive with a shred of black.

Trembling, I listened; the summer sun
  Had the chill of snow;
For I knew she was telling the bees of one
  Gone on the journey we all must go!

Then I said to myself, "My Mary weeps
  For the dead to-day;
Haply her blind old grandsire sleeps
  The fret and the pain of his age away."

But her dog whined low; on the doorway sill,
  With his cane to his chin,
The old man sat; and the chore girl still
  Sang to the bees stealing out and in.

And the song she was singing ever since
   In my ear sounds on:
"Stay at home, pretty bees, fly not hence!
   Mistress Mary is dead and gone!"

MY PLAYMATE

The pines were dark on Ramoth hill,
   Their song was soft and low;
The blossoms in the sweet May wind
   Were falling like the snow.

The blossoms drifted at our feet,
   The orchard birds sang clear;
The sweetest and the saddest day
   It seemed of all the year.

For, more to me than birds or flowers,
   My playmate left her home,
And took with her the laughing spring,
   The music and the bloom.

She kissed the lips of kith and kin,
   She laid her hand in mine:
What more could ask the bashful boy
   Who fed her father's kine?

She left us in the bloom of May:
   The constant years told o'er
Their seasons with as sweet May morns,
   But she came back no more.

I walk, with noiseless feet, the round
   Of uneventful years;
Still o'er and o'er I sow the spring
   And reap the autumn ears.

She lives where all the golden year
   Her summer roses blow;
The dusky children of the sun
   Before her come and go.

There haply with her jeweled hands
  She smooths her silken gown,—
No more the homespun lap wherein
  I shook the walnuts down.

The wild grapes wait us by the brook,
  The brown nuts on the hill,
And still the May-day flowers make sweet
  The woods of Follymill.

The lilies blossom in the pond,
  The bird builds in the tree,
The dark pines sing on Ramoth hill
  The slow song of the sea.

I wonder if she thinks of them,
  And how the old time seems,—
If ever the pines of Ramoth wood
  Are sounding in her dreams.

I see her face, I hear her voice:
  Does she remember mine?
And what to her is now the boy
  Who fed her father's kine?

What cares she that the orioles build
  For other eyes than ours,—
That other hands with nuts are filled,
  And other laps with flowers?

O playmate in the golden time!
  Our mossy seat is green,
Its fringing violets blossom yet,
  The old trees o'er it lean.

The winds so sweet with birch and fern
  A sweeter memory blow;
And there in spring the veeries sing
  The song of long ago.

And still the pines of Ramoth wood
  Are moaning like the sea,—
The moaning of the sea of change
  Between myself and thee!

AMY WENTWORTH

Her fingers shame the ivory keys
　　They dance so light along;
The bloom upon her parted lips
　　Is sweeter than the song.

O perfumed suitor, spare thy smiles!
　　Her thoughts are not of thee;
She better loves the salted wind,
　　The voices of the sea.

Her heart is like an outbound ship
　　That at its anchor swings;
The murmur of the stranded shell
　　Is in the song she sings.

She sings, and, smiling, hears her praise,
　　But dreams the while of one
Who watches from his sea-blown deck
　　The icebergs in the sun.

She questions all the winds that blow,
　　And every fog wreath dim,
And bids the sea birds flying north
　　Bear messages to him.

She speeds them with the thanks of men
　　He perilled life to save,
And grateful prayers like holy oil
　　To smooth for him the wave.

Brown Viking of the fishing smack!
　　Fair toast of all the town!
The skipper's jerkin ill beseems
　　The lady's silken gown!

But ne'er shall Amy Wentworth wear
　　For him the blush of shame
Who dares to set his manly gifts
　　Against her ancient name.

The stream is brightest at its spring,
　　And blood is not like wine;

Nor honored less than he who heirs
    Is he who founds a line.

Full lightly shall the prize be won,
    If love be fortune's spur;
And never maiden stoops to him
    Who lifts himself to her.

Her home is brave in Jaffrey Street,
    With stately stairways worn
By feet of old Colonial knights
    And ladies gentle born.

Still green about its ample porch
    The English ivy twines,
Trained back to show in English oak
    The herald's carven signs.

And on her, from the wainscot old,
    Ancestral faces frown,—
And this has worn the soldier's sword,
    And that the judge's gown.

But, strong of will and proud as they,
    She walks the gallery floor
As if she trod her sailor's deck
    By stormy Labrador!

The sweetbrier blooms on Kittery-side,
    And green are Eliot's bowers;
Her garden is the pebbled beach,
    The mosses are her flowers.

She looks across the harbor bar
    To see the white gulls fly;
His greeting from the Northern sea
    Is in their clanging cry.

She hums a song, and dreams that he,
    As in its romance old,
Shall homeward ride with silken sails
    And masts of beaten gold!

O, rank is good, and gold is fair,
  And high and low mate ill;
But love has never known a law
  Beyond its own sweet will!

PROEM

Written to Introduce the First General Collection
of His Poems

I love the old melodious lays
Which softly melt the ages through,
  The songs of Spenser's golden days,
  Arcadian Sidney's silvery phrase,
Sprinkling our noon of time with freshest morning dew.

Yet, vainly in my quiet hours
To breathe their marvelous notes I try;
  I feel them, as the leaves and flowers
  In silence feel the dewy showers,
And drink with glad, still lips the blessing of the sky.

The rigor of a frozen clime,
The harshness of an untaught ear,
  The jarring words of one whose rhyme
  Beat often Labor's hurried time,
Or Duty's rugged march through storm and strife, are here.

Of mystic beauty, dreamy grace,
No rounded art the lack supplies;
  Unskilled the subtle lines to trace,
  Or softer shades of Nature's face,
I view her common forms with unanointed eyes.

Nor mine the seerlike power to show
The secrets of the heart and mind;
  To drop the plummet line below
  Our common world of joy and woe,
A more intense despair or brighter hope to find.

Yet here at least an earnest sense
Of human right and weal is shown;
  A hate of tyranny intense,

And hearty in its vehemence,
As if my brother's pain and sorrow were my own.

O Freedom! if to me belong
Nor mighty Milton's gift divine,
   Nor Marvell's wit and graceful song,
   Still with a love as deep and strong
As theirs, I lay, like them, my best gifts on thy shrine!

THE HASCHISH

Of all that Orient lands can vaunt
   Of marvels with our own competing,
The strangest is the Haschist plant,
   And what will follow on its eating.

What pictures to the taster rise,
   Of Dervish or of Almeh dances!
Of Eblis, or of Paradise,
   Set all aglow with Houri glances!

The poppy visions of Cathay,
   The heavy beer-trance of the Suabian;
The wizard lights and demon play
   Of nights Walpurgis and Arabian!

The Mollah and the Christian dog
   Change place in mad metempsychosis;
The Muezzin climbs the synagogue,
   The Rabbi shakes his beard at Moses!

The Arab by his desert well
   Sits choosing from some Caliph's daughters,
And hears his single camel's bell
   Sound welcome to his regal quarters.

The Koran's reader makes complaint
   Of Shitan dancing on and off it;
The robber offers alms, the saint
   Drinks Tokay and blasphemes the Prophet.

Such scenes that Eastern plant awakes;
   But we have one ordained to beat it.

The Haschish of the West, which makes
  Or fools or knaves of all who eat it.

The preacher eats, and straight appears
  His Bible in a new translation;
Its angels negro overseers,
  And Heaven itself a snug plantation!

The man of peace, about whose dreams
  The sweet millennial angels cluster,
Tastes the mad weed, and plots and schemes,
  A raving Cuban filibuster!

The noisiest Democrat, with ease,
  It turns to Slavery's parish beadle;
The shrewdest statesman eats and sees
  Due southward point the polar needle.

The Judge partakes, and sits erelong
  Upon his bench a railing blackguard;
Decides off-hand that right is wrong,
  And reads the ten commandments backward.

O potent plant! so rare a taste
  Has never Turk or Gentoo gotten;
The hempen Haschish of the East
  Is powerless to our Western Cotton!

IN SCHOOL-DAYS

Still sits the school-house by the road,
  A ragged beggar sunning;
Around it still the sumachs grow
  And blackberry vines are running.

Within, the master's desk is seen,
  Deep scarred by raps official,
The warping floor, the battered seats,
  The jack-knife's carved initial;

The charcoal frescoes on its wall;
  Its door's worn sill, betraying

The feet that, creeping slow to school,
   Went storming out to playing!

Long years ago a winter sun
   Shone over it at setting;
Lit up its western window-panes,
   And low eaves' icy fretting.

It touched the tangled golden curls,
   And brown eyes full of grieving,
Of one who still her steps delayed
   When all the school were leaving.

For near her stood the little boy
   Her childish favor singled;
His cap pulled low upon a face
   Where pride and shame were mingled.

Pushing with restless feet the snow
   To right and left, he lingered;
As restlessly her tiny hands
   The blue-checked apron fingered.

He saw her lift her eyes; he felt
   The soft hand's light caressing,
And heard the tremble of her voice,
   As if a fault confessing.

"I'm sorry that I spelt the word;
   I hate to go above you,
Because,"—the brown eyes lower fell,—
   "Because, you see, I love you!"

Still memory to a gray-haired man
   That sweet child-face is showing.
Dear girl! the grasses on her grave
   Have forty years been growing!

He lives to learn, in life's hard school,
   How few who pass above him
Lament their triumph and his loss.
   Like her,—because they love him.

THE VANISHERS

Sweetest of all childlike dreams
   In the simple Indian lore
Still to me the legend seems
   Of the shapes who flit before.

Flitting, passing, seen and gone,
   Never reached nor found at rest,
Baffling search, but beckoning on
   To the Sunset of the Blest.

From the clefts of mountain rocks,
   Through the dark of lowland firs,
Flash the eyes and flow the locks
   Of the mystic Vanishers!

And the fisher in his skiff,
   And the hunter on the moss,
Hear their call from cape and cliff,
   See their hands the birch-leaves toss.

Wistful, longing, through the green
   Twilight of the clustered pines,
In their faces rarely seen
   Beauty more than mortal shines.

Fringed with gold their mantles flow
   On the slopes of westering knolls;
In the wind they whisper low
   Of the Sunset Land of Souls.

Doubt who may, O friend of mine!
   Thou and I have seen them too;
On before with beck and sign
   Still they glide, and we pursue.

More than clouds of purple trail
   In the gold of setting day;
More than gleams of wing or sail
   Beckon from the sea-mist gray.

Glimpses of immortal youth,
   Gleams and glories seen and flown,

Far-heard voices sweet with truth,
    Airs from viewless Edens blown;

Beauty that eludes our grasp,
    Sweetness that transcends our taste,
Loving hands we may not clasp,
    Shining feet that mock our haste;

Gentle eyes we closed below,
    Tender voices heard once more,
Smile and call us, as they go
    On and onward, still before.

Guided thus, O friend of mine!
    Let us walk our little way,
Knowing by each beckoning sign
    That we are not quite astray.

Chase we still, with baffled feet,
    Smiling eye and waving hand,
Sought and seeker soon shall meet,
    Lost and found, in Sunset Land!

CASSANDRA SOUTHWICK

1658

To the God of all sure mercies let my blessing rise today,
From the scoffer and the cruel He hath plucked the spoil away;
Yea, He who cooled the furnace around the faithful three,
And tamed the Chaldean lions, hath set His handmaid free!

Last night I saw the sunset melt through my prison bars,
Last night across my damp earth-floor fell the pale gleam of stars;
In the coldness and the darkness all through the long night-time,
My grated casement whitened with autumn's early rime.

Alone, in that dark sorrow, hour after hour crept by;
Star after star looked palely in and sank adown the sky;
No sound amid night's stillness, save that which seemed to be
The dull and heavy beating of the pulses of the sea;

All night I sat unsleeping, for I knew that on the morrow
The ruler and the cruel priest would mock me in my sorrow,
Dragged to their place of market, and bargained for and sold,
Like a lamb before the shambles, like a heifer from the fold!

Oh, the weakness of the flesh was there,—the shrinking and the
    shame;
And the low voice of the Tempter like whispers to me came:
"Why sit'st thou thus forlornly," the wicked murmur said,
"Damp walls thy bower of beauty, cold earth thy maiden bed?

"Where be the smiling faces, and voices soft and sweet,
Seen in thy father's dwelling, heard in the pleasant street?
Where be the youths whose glances, the summer Sabbath through,
Turned tenderly and timidly unto thy father's pew?

"Why sit'st thou here, Cassandra?—Bethink thee with what mirth
Thy happy schoolmates gather around the warm, bright hearth;
How the crimson shadows tremble on foreheads white and fair,
On eyes of merry girlhood, half hid in golden hair.

"Not for thee the hearth fire brightens, not for thee kind words are
    spoken,
Not for thee the nuts of Wenham woods by laughing boys are
    broken;
No first-fruits of the orchard within thy lap are laid,
For thee no flowers of autumn the youthful hunters braid.

"O weak, deluded maiden!—by crazy fancies led,
With wild and raving railers an evil path to tread;
To leave a wholesome worship, and teaching pure and sound,
And mate with maniac women, loose-haired and sackcloth bound,—

"Mad scoffers of the priesthood, who mock at things divine,
Who rail against the pulpit, and holy bread and wine;
Sore from their cart-tail scourgings, and from the pillory lame,
Rejoicing in their wretchedness, and glorying in their shame.

"And what a fate awaits thee!—a sadly toiling slave,
Dragging the slowly lengthening chain of bondage to the grave!
Think of thy woman's nature, subdued in hopeless thrall,
The easy prey of any, the scoff and scorn of all!"

Oh, ever as the Tempter spoke, and feeble Nature's fears
Wrung drop by drop the scalding flow of unavailing tears,
I wrestled down the evil thoughts, and strove in silent prayer,
To feel, O Helper of the weak! that Thou indeed wert there!

I thought of Paul and Silas, within Philippi's cell,
And how from Peter's sleeping limbs the prison shackles fell,
Till I seemed to hear the trailing of an angel's robe of white,
And to feel a blessed presence invisible to sight.

Bless the Lord for all his mercies!—for the peace and love I felt,
Like dew of Hermon's holy hill, upon my spirit melt;
When "Get behind me, Satan!" was the language of my heart,
And I felt the Evil Tempter with all his doubts depart.

Slow broke the gray cold morning; again the sunshine fell,
Flecked with the shade of bar and grate within my lonely cell;
The hoar-frost melted on the wall, and upward from the street
Came careless laugh and idle word, and tread of passing feet.

At length the heavy bolts fell back, my door was open cast,
And slowly at the sheriff's side, up the long street I passed;
I heard the murmur round me, and felt, but dared not see,
How, from every door and window, the people gazed on me.

And doubt and fear fell on me, shame burned upon my cheek,
Swam earth and sky around me, my trembling limbs grew weak:
"O Lord! support thy handmaid; and from her soul cast out
The fear of man, which brings a snare, the weakness and the
    doubt."

Then the dreary shadows scattered, like a cloud in morning's
    breeze,
And a low deep voice within me seemed whispering words like
    these:
"Though thy earth be as the iron, and thy heaven a brazen wall,
Trust still His loving-kindness whose power is over all."

We paused at length, where at my feet the sunlit waters broke
On glaring reach of shining beach, and shingly wall of rock;
The merchant-ships lay idly there, in hard clear lines on high,
Tracing with rope and slender spar their network on the sky.

And there were ancient citizens, cloak-wrapped and grave and cold,
And grim and stout sea-captains with faces bronzed and old,
And on his horse, with Rawson, his cruel clerk at hand,
Sat dark and haughty Endicott, the ruler of the land.

And poisoning with his evil words the ruler's ready ear,
The priest leaned o'er his saddle, with laugh and scoff and jeer;
It stirred my soul, and from my lips the seal of silence broke,
As if through woman's weakness a warning spirit spoke.

I cried, "The Lord rebuke thee, thou smiter of the meek,
Thou robber of the righteous, thou trampler of the weak!
Go light the dark, cold hearth-stones,—go turn the prison lock
Of the poor hearts thou hast hunted, thou wolf amid the flock!"

Dark lowered the brows of Endicott, and with a deeper red
O'er Rawson's wine-empurpled cheek the flush of anger spread;
"Good people," quoth the white-lipped priest, "heed not her words
    so wild,
Her Master speaks within her,—the Devil owns his child!"

But gray heads shook, and young brows knit, the while the sheriff
    read
That law the wicked rulers against the poor have made,
Who to their house of Rimmon and idol priesthood bring
No bended knee of worship, nor gainful offering.

Then to the stout sea-captains the sheriff, turning, said,—
"Which of ye, worthy seamen, will take this Quaker maid?
In the Isle of fair Barbadoes, or on Virginia's shore,
You may hold her at a higher price than Indian girl or Moor."

Grim and silent stood the captains; and when again he cried,
"Speak out, my worthy seamen!"—no voice, no sign replied;
But I felt a hard hand press my own, and kind words met my ear,—
"God bless thee, and preserve thee, my gentle girl and dear!"

A weight seemed lifted from my heart, a pitying friend was nigh,—
I felt it in his hard, rough hand, and saw it in his eye;
And when again the sheriff spoke, that voice, so kind to me,
Growled back its stormy answer like the roaring of the sea,—

"Pile my ship with bars of silver, pack with coins of Spanish gold,
From keel-piece up to deck-plank, the roomage of her hold,

By the living God who made me!—I would sooner in your bay
Sink ship and crew and cargo, than bear this child away!"

"Well answered, worthy captain, shame on their cruel laws!"
Ran through the crowd in murmurs loud the people's just applause.
"Like the herdsman of Tekoa, in Israel of old,
Shall we see the poor and righteous again for silver sold?"

I looked on haughty Endicott; with weapon half-way drawn,
Swept round the throng his lion glare of bitter hate and scorn;
Fiercely he drew his bridle-rein, and turned in silence back,
And sneering priest and baffled clerk rode murmuring in his track.

Hard after them the sheriff looked, in bitterness of soul;
Thrice smote his staff upon the ground, and crushed his parchment
    roll.
"Good friends," he said, "since both have fled, the ruler and the
    priest,
Judge ye, if from their further work I be not well released."

Loud was the cheer which, full and clear, swept round the silent
    bay,
As, with kind words and kinder looks, he bade me go my way;
For He who turns the courses of the streamlet of the glen,
And the river of great waters, had turned the hearts of men.

Oh, at that hour the very earth seemed changed beneath my eye,
A holier wonder round me rose the blue walls of the sky,
A lovelier light on rock and hill and stream and woodland lay,
And softer lapsed on sunnier sands the waters of the bay.

Thanksgiving to the Lord of life! to Him all praises be,
Who from the hands of evil men hath set his handmaid free;
All praise to Him before whose power the mighty are afraid,
Who takes the crafty in the snare which for the poor is laid!

Sing, O my soul, rejoicingly, on evening's twilight calm
Uplift the loud thanksgiving, pour forth the grateful psalm;
Let all dear hearts with me rejoice, as did the saints of old,
When of the Lord's good angel the rescued Peter told.

And weep and howl, ye evil priests and mighty men of wrong,
The Lord shall smite the proud, and lay His hand upon the strong.

Woe to the wicked rulers in His avenging hour!
Woe to the wolves who seek the flocks to raven and devour!

But let the humble ones arise, the poor in heart be glad,
And let the mourning ones again with robes of praise be clad.
For He who cooled the furnace, and smoothed the stormy wave,
And tamed the Chaldean lions, is mighty still to save!

MAUD MULLER

Maud Muller on a summer's day
Raked the meadow sweet with hay.
Beneath her torn hat glowed the wealth
Of simple beauty and rustic health.

Singing, she wrought, and her merry glee
The mock-bird echoed from his tree.
But when she glanced to the far-off town,
White from its hill-slope looking down,

The sweet song died, and a vague unrest
And a nameless longing filled her breast,—
A wish that she hardly dared to own,
For something better than she had known.

The Judge rode slowly down the lane,
Smoothing his horse's chestnut mane.
He drew his bridle in the shade
Of the apple-trees, to greet the maid,

And asked a draught from the spring that flowed
Through the meadow across the road.
She stooped where the cool spring bubbled up,
And filled for him her small tin cup,

And blushed as she gave it, looking down
On her feet so bare, and her tattered gown.
"Thanks!" said the Judge; "a sweeter draught
From a fairer hand was never quaffed."

He spoke of the grass and flowers and trees,
Of the singing birds and the humming bees;

Then talked of the haying, and wondered whether
The cloud in the west would bring foul weather.

And Maud forgot her brier-torn gown,
And her graceful ankles bare and brown;
And listened, while a pleased surprise
Looked from her long-lashed hazel eyes.

At last, like one who for delay
Seeks a vain excuse, he rode away.
Maud Muller looked and sighed: "Ah me!
That I the Judge's bride might be!

"He would dress me up in silks so fine,
And praise and toast me at his wine.
My father should wear a broadcloth coat;
My brother should sail a painted boat.

"I'd dress my mother so grand and gay,
And the baby should have a new toy each day.
And I'd feed the hungry and clothe the poor,
And all should bless me who left our door."

The Judge looked back as he climbed the hill,
And saw Maud Muller standing still.
"A form more fair, a face more sweet,
Ne'er hath it been my lot to meet.

"And her modest answer and graceful air
Show her wise and good as she is fair.
Would she were mine, and I to-day,
Like her, a harvester of hay;

"No doubtful balance of rights and wrongs,
Nor weary lawyers with endless tongues,
But low of cattle and song of birds,
And health and quiet and loving words."

But he thought of his sisters, proud and cold,
And his mother, vain of her rank and gold.
So, closing his heart, the Judge rode on,
And Maud was left in the field alone.

But the lawyers smiled that afternoon,
When he hummed in court an old love-tune;
And the young girl mused beside the well
Till the rain on the unraked clover fell.

He wedded a wife of richest dower,
Who lived for fashion, as he for power.
Yet oft, in his marble hearth's bright glow,
He watched a picture come and go;

And sweet Maud Muller's hazel eyes
Looked out in their innocent surprise.

Oft, when the wine in his glass was red,
He longed for the wayside well instead;
And closed his eyes on his garnished rooms
To dream of meadows and clover-blooms.

And the proud man sighed, with a secret pain,
"Ah, that I were free again!
Free as when I rode that day,
Where the barefoot maiden raked her hay."

She wedded a man unlearned and poor,
And many children played round he' door.
But care and sorrow, and childbirth pain,
Left their traces on heart and brain.

And oft, when the summer sun shone hot
On the new-mown hay in the meadow lot,
And she heard the little spring brook fall
Over the roadside, through the wall,

In the shade of the apple-tree again
She saw a rider draw his rein;
And, gazing down with timid grace,
She felt his pleased eyes read her face.

Sometimes her narrow kitchen walls
Stretched away into stately halls;
The weary wheel to a spinnet turned,
The tallow candle an astral burned,

And for him who sat by the chimney lug,
Dozing and grumbling o'er pipe and mug,
A manly form at her side she saw,
And joy was duty and love was law.

Then she took up her burden of life again,
Saying only, "It might have been."
Alas for maiden, alas for Judge,
For rich repiner and household drudge!

God pity them both! and pity us all,
Who vainly the dreams of youth recall.
For of all sad words of tongue or pen,
The saddest are these: "It might have been!"

Ah, well! for us all some sweet hope lies
Deeply buried from human eyes;
And, in the hereafter, angels may
Roll the stone from its grave away!

THE HUNTERS OF MEN

Have ye heard of our hunting, o'er mountain and glen,
Through cane-brake and forest,—the hunting of men?
The lords of our land to this hunting have gone,
As the fox-hunter follows the sound of the horn;
Hark! the cheer and the hallo! the crack of the whip,
And the yell of the hound as he fastens his grip!
All blithe are our hunters, and noble their match,
Though hundreds are caught, there are millions to catch.
So speed to their hunting, o'er mountain and glen,
Through cane-brake and forest,—the hunting of men!

Gay luck to our hunters! how nobly they ride
In the glow of their zeal, and the strength of their pride!
The priest with his cassock flung back on the wind,
Just screening the politic statesman behind;
The saint and the sinner, with cursing and prayer,
The drunk and the sober, ride merrily there.
And woman, kind woman, wife, widow, and maid,
For the good of the hunted, is lending her aid:
Her foot's in the stirrup, her hand on the rein,
How blithely she rides to the hunting of men!

Oh, goodly and grand is our hunting to see,
In this "land of the brave and this home of the free."
Priest, warrior, and statesman, from Georgia to Maine,
All mounting the saddle, all grasping the rein;
Right merrily hunting the black man, whose sin
Is the curl of his hair and the hue of his skin!

Woe, now, to the hunted who turns him at bay!
Will our hunters be turned from their purpose and prey?
Will their hearts fail within them? their nerves tremble, when
All roughly they ride to the hunting of men?

Ho! alms for our hunters! all weary and faint,
Wax the curse of the sinner and prayer of the saint.
The horn is wound faintly, the echoes are still,
Over cane-brake and river, and forest and hill.

Haste, alms for our hunters! the hunted once more
Have turned from their flight with their backs to the shore:
What right have they here in the home of the white,
Shadowed o'er by our banner of Freedom and Right?
Ho! alms for the hunters! or never again
Will they ride in their pomp to the hunting of men!

Alms, alms for our hunters! why will ye delay,
When their pride and their glory are melting away?
The parson has turned; for, on charge of his own,
Who goeth a warfare, or hunting, alone?
The politic statesman looks back with a sigh,
There is doubt in his heart, there is fear in his eye.
Oh, haste, lest that doubting and fear shall prevail,
And the head of his steed take the place of the tail.
Oh, haste, ere he leave us! for who will ride then,
For pleasure or gain, to the hunting of men?

Edgar Allan Poe

(1809–1849)

Edgar Allan Poe was born in Boston and was orphaned by the time he was two years old. He was soon adopted by a well-to-do merchant named John Allan. In 1815 the Allans moved to England, where the young Poe went to school, excelling in athletics, writing and debate. Several years later he returned to America and for one year attended the University of Virginia. He went on to enlist in the army and then attended West Point. As Poe became more involved with his writing he grew restless, and finally he was asked to leave the Academy. Later he became an editor with the *Southern Literary Messenger,* which was a vehicle for many southern writers, including Poe himself. At the age of twenty-seven Poe married his 14-year-old cousin, Virginia Clemm, and continued working in various editorial capacities. His wife died in 1847 and just a few days before he was to remarry, Poe died. Today he is known as an originator of the detective story, a great poet, a master prose writer, and respected literary critic.

TO HELEN

Helen, thy beauty is to me
  Like those Nicæan barks of yore
That gently, o'er a perfumed sea,
  The weary, wayworn wanderer bore
To his own native shore.

On desperate seas long wont to roam,
  Thy hyacinth hair, thy classic face,
Thy Naiad airs have brought me home

To the glory that was Greece
And the grandeur that was Rome.

Lo! in yon brilliant window niche
    How statue-like I see thee stand,
The agate lamp within thy hand!
    Ah, Psyche, from the regions which
    Are Holy Land!

THE HAUNTED PALACE

In the greenest of our valleys
    By good angels tenanted,
Once a fair and stately palace—
    Radiant palace—reared its head.
In the monarch Thought's dominion,
    It stood there;
Never seraph spread a pinion
    Over fabric half so fair.

Banners yellow, glorious, golden,
    On its roof did float and flow
(This—all this—was in the olden
    Time long ago),
And every gentle air that dallied,
    In that sweet day,
Along the ramparts plumed and pallid,
    A wingèd odor went away.

Wanderers in that happy valley
    Through two luminous windows saw
Spirits moving musically,
    To a lute's well-tunèd law,
Round about a throne where, sitting,
    Porphyrogene,
In state his glory well befitting,
    The ruler of the realm was seen.

And all with pearl and ruby glowing
    Was the fair palace door,
Through which came flowing, flowing, flowing,
    And sparkling evermore,

A troop of Echoes, whose sweet duty
  Was but to sing,
In voices of surpassing beauty,
  The wit and wisdom of their king.

But evil things, in robes of sorrow,
  Assailed the monarch's high estate;
(Ah, let us mourn, for never morrow
  Shall dawn upon him desolate!)
And round about his home the glory
  That blushed and bloomed,
Is but a dim-remembered story
  Of the old time entombed.

And travelers now within that valley
  Through the red-litten windows see
Vast forms that move fantastically
  To a discordant melody;
While, like a ghastly rapid river,
  Through the pale door
A hideous throng rush out forever,
  And laugh—but smile no more.

THE CITY IN THE SEA

Lo! Death has reared himself a throne
In a strange city lying alone
Far down within the dim West,
Where the good and the bad and the worst and the best
Have gone to their eternal rest.
There shrines and palaces and towers
(Time-eaten towers that tremble not)
Resemble nothing that is ours.
Around, by lifting winds forgot,
Resignedly beneath the sky
The melancholy waters lie.

No rays from the holy heaven come down
On the long night-time of that town;
But light from out the lurid sea
Streams up the turrets silently,
Gleams up the pinnacles far and free:
Up domes, up spires, up kingly halls,

Up fanes, up Babylon-like walls,
Up shadowy long-forgotten bowers
Of sculptured ivy and stone flowers,
Up many and many a marvelous shrine
Whose wreathèd friezes intertwine
The viol, the violet, and the vine.

Resignedly beneath the sky
The melancholy waters lie.
So blend the turrets and shadows there
That all seem pendulous in air,
While from a proud tower in the town
Death looks gigantically down.

There open fanes and gaping graves
Yawn level with the luminous waves;
But not the riches there that lie
In each idol's diamond eye,—
Not the gayly jeweled dead,
Tempt the waters from their bed;
For no ripples curl, alas,
Along that wilderness of glass;
No swellings tell that winds may be
Upon some far-off happier sea;
No heavings hint that winds have been
On seas less hideously serene!

But lo, a stir is in the air!
The wave—there is a movement there!
As if the towers had thrust aside,
In slightly sinking, the dull tide;
As if their tops had feebly given
A void within the filmy Heaven!
The waves have now a redder glow,
The hours are breathing faint and low;
And when, amid no earthly moans,
Down, down that town shall settle hence,
Hell, rising from a thousand thrones,
Shall do it reverence.

THE SLEEPER

At midnight, in the month of June,
I stand beneath the mystic moon.
An opiate vapor, dewy, dim,
Exhales from out her golden rim,
And, softly dripping, drop by drop,
Upon the quiet mountain top,
Steals drowsily and musically
Into the universal valley.
The rosemary nods upon the grave;
The lily lolls upon the wave;
Wrapping the fog about its breast,
The ruin molders into rest;
Looking like Lethe, see! the lake
A conscious slumber seems to take,
And would not, for the world, awake.
All beauty sleeps!—and lo! where lies
Irene, with her destinies!

O lady bright! can it be right,
This window open to the night?
The wanton airs, from the tree top,
Laughingly through the lattice drop;
The bodiless airs, a wizard rout,
Flit through thy chamber in and out,
And wave the curtain canopy
So fitfully, so fearfully,
Above the closed and fringëd lid
'Neath which thy slumb'ring soul lies hid,
That, o'er the floor and down the wall,
Like ghosts the shadows rise and fall.
O lady dear, hast thou no fear?
Why and what art thou dreaming here?
Sure thou art come o'er far-off seas,
A wonder to these garden trees!
Strange is thy pallor: strange thy dress:
Strange, above all, thy length of tress,
And this all solemn silentness!

The lady sleeps. Oh, may her sleep,
Which is enduring, so be deep!
Heaven have her in its sacred keep!
This chamber changed for one more holy,

This bed for one more melancholy,
I pray to God that she may lie
Forever with unopened eye,
While the pale sheeted ghosts go by.

My love, she sleeps. Oh, may her sleep,
As it is lasting, so be deep!
Soft may the worms about her creep!
Far in the forest, dim and old,
For her may some tall vault unfold:
Some vault that oft hath flung its black
And wingèd panels fluttering back,
Triumphant, o'er the crested palls
Of her grand family funerals:
Some sepulcher, remote, alone,
Against whose portal she hath thrown,
In childhood, many an idle stone:
Some tomb from out whose sounding door
She ne'er shall force an echo more,
Thrilling to think, poor child of sin,
It was the dead who groaned within!

ULALUME

The skies they were ashen and sober;
    The leaves they were crispèd and sear,
    The leaves they were withering and sear;
It was night in the lonesome October
    Of my most immemorial year;
It was hard by the dim lake of Auber,
    In the misty mid region of Weir:
It was down by the dank tarn of Auber,
    In the ghoul-haunted woodland of Weir.

Here once, through an alley Titanic
    Of cypress I roamed with my Soul—
    Of cypress, with Psyche, my Soul.
They were days when my heart was volcanic
    As the scoriac rivers that roll,
    As the lavas that restlessly roll
Their sulphurous currents down Yaanek
    In the ultimate climes of the pole,

That groan as they roll down Mount Yaanek
    In the realms of the boreal pole.

Our talk had been serious and sober,
    But our thoughts they were palsied and sear,
    Our memories were treacherous and sear,
For we knew not the month was October,
    And we marked not the night of the year,
    (Ah, night of all nights in the year!)
We noted not the dim lake of Auber
    (Though once we had journeyed down here),
Remembered not the dank tarn of Auber
    Nor the ghoul-haunted woodland of Weir.

And now, as the night was senescent
    And star-dials pointed to morn,
    As the star-dials hinted of morn,
At the end of our path a liquescent
    And nebulous luster was born,
Out of which a miraculous crescent
    Arose with a duplicate horn,
Astarte's bediamonded crescent
    Distinct with its duplicate horn.

And I said—"She is warmer than Dian:
    She rolls through an ether of sighs,
    She revels in a region of sighs:
She has seen that the tears are not dry on
    These cheeks, where the worm never dies,
And has come past the stars of the Lion
    To point us the path to the skies,
    To the Lethean peace of the skies:
Come up, in despite of the Lion,
    To shine on us with her bright eyes:
Come up through the lair of the Lion,
    With love in her luminous eyes."

But Psyche, uplifting the finger,
    Said—"Sadly this star I mistrust,
    Her pallor I strangely mistrust:
Oh, hasten!—oh, let us not linger!
    Oh, fly!—let us fly!—for we must."
In terror she spoke, letting sink her
    Wings until they trailed in the dust;

In agony sobbed, letting sink her
    Plumes till they trailed in the dust,
    Till they sorrowfully trailed in the dust.

I replied—"This is nothing but dreaming:
    Let us on by this tremulous light!
    Let us bathe in this crystalline light!
Its sibyllic splendor is beaming
    With hope and in beauty to-night:
    See, it flickers up the sky through the night!
Ah, we safely may trust to its gleaming,
    And be sure it will lead us aright:
We safely may trust to a gleaming
    That cannot but guide us aright,
    Since it flickers up to Heaven through the night."

Thus I pacified Psyche and kissed her,
    And tempted her out of her gloom,
    And conquered her scruples and gloom;
And we passed to the end of the vista,
    But were stopped by the door of a tomb,
    By the door of a legended tomb;
And I said—"What is written, sweet sister,
    On the door of this legended tomb?"
    She replied—"Ulalume—Ulalume—
    'Tis the vault of thy lost Ulalume!"

Then my heart it grew ashen and sober
    As the leaves that were crispéd and sear,
    As the leaves that were withering and sear,
And I cried—"It was surely October
    On this very night of last year
    That I journeyed—I journeyed down here,
    That I brought a dread burden down here:
    On this night of all nights in the year,
    Ah, what demon has tempted me here?
Well I know, now, this dim lake of Auber,
    This misty mid region of Weir:
Well, I know, now, this dank tarn of Auber,
    This ghoul-haunted woodland of Weir."

ANNABEL LEE

It was many and many a year ago,
   In a kingdom by the sea,
That a maiden there lived whom you may know
   By the name of Annabel Lee;
And this maiden she lived with no other thought
   Than to love and be loved by me.

I was a child and she was a child,
   In this kingdom by the sea,
But we loved with a love that was more than love,
   I and my Annabel Lee;
With a love that the wingëd seraphs of heaven
   Coveted her and me.

And this was the reason that, long ago,
   In this kingdom by the sea,
A wind blew out of a cloud, chilling
   My beautiful Annabel Lee;

So that her highborn kinsman came
   And bore her away from me,
To shut her up in a sepulcher
   In this kingdom by the sea.

The angels, not half so happy in heaven,
   Went envying her and me;
Yes! that was the reason (as all men know,
   In this kingdom by the sea)
That the wind came out of the cloud by night,
   Chilling and killing my Annabel Lee.

But our love it was stronger by far than the love
   Of those who were older than we,
   Of many far wiser than we;
And neither the angels in heaven above,
   Nor the demons down under the sea,
Can ever dissever my soul from the soul
   Of the beautiful Annabel Lee:

For the moon never beams, without bringing me dreams
   Of the beautiful Annabel Lee;
And the stars never rise, but I feel the bright eyes

Of the beautiful Annabel Lee;
And so, all the night-tide, I lie down by the side
Of my darling—my darling—my life and my bride,
　In her sepulcher there by the sea,
　In her tomb by the sounding sea.

TO ONE IN PARADISE

Thou wast all that to me, love,
　For which my soul did pine:
A green isle in the sea, love,
　A fountain and a shrine
All wreathed with fairy fruits and flowers,
　And all the flowers were mine.

Ah, dream too bright to last!
　Ah, starry Hope, that didst arise
But to be overcast!
　A voice from out the Future cries,
"On! on!"—but o'er the Past
　(Dim gulf) my spirit hovering lies
Mute, motionless, aghast.

For, alas! alas! with me
　The light of Life is o'er!
No more—no more—no more—
(Such language holds the solemn sea
　To the sands upon the shore!)
Shall bloom the thunder-blasted tree,
　Or the stricken eagle soar.

And all my days are trances,
　And all my nightly dreams
Are where thy gray eye glances,
　And where thy footstep gleams—
In what ethereal dances,
　By what eternal streams.

THE BELLS

I

Hear the sledges with the bells,
      Silver bells!
What a world of merriment their melody foretells!
   How they tinkle, tinkle, tinkle,
     In the icy air of night!
  While the stars, that oversprinkle
  All the heavens, seem to twinkle
    With a crystalline delight;
   Keeping time, time, time,
    In a sort of Runic rhyme,
To the tintinnabulation that so musically wells
 From the bells, bells, bells, bells,
    Bells, bells, bells—
  From the jingling and the tinkling of the bells.

II

Hear the mellow wedding bells,
     Golden bells!
What a world of happiness their harmony fortells!
  Through the balmy air of night
  How they ring out their delight!
    From the molten-golden notes,
     And all in tune,
    What a liquid ditty floats
To the turtle-dove that listens, while she gloats
     On the moon!
 Oh, from out the sounding cells,
What a gush of euphony voluminously wells!
    How it swells!
    How it dwells
   On the Future! how it tells
   Of the rapture that impels
  To the swinging and the ringing
   Of the bells, bells, bells,
  Of the bells, bells, bells, bells,
    Bells, bells, bells—
To the rhyming and the chiming of the bells!

Hear the loud alarum bells,
  Brazen bells!
What a tale of terror, now, their turbulency tells!
  In the startled ear of night
  How they scream out their affright!
   Too much horrified to speak,
   They can only shriek, shriek,
    Out of tune,
In a clamorous appealing to the mercy of the fire,
In a mad expostulation with the deaf and frantic fire,
   Leaping higher, higher, higher,
   With a desperate desire,
  And a resolute endeavor
  Now—now to sit or never,
 By the side of the pale-faced moon.
   Oh, the bells, bells, bells!
   What a tale their terror tells
    Of Despair!
  How they clang, and clash, and roar!
  What a horror they outpour
On the bosom of the palpitating air!
  Yet the ear it fully knows,
    By the twanging
    And the clanging,
  How the danger ebbs and flows;
 Yet the ear distinctly tells,
    In the jangling
    And the wrangling,
 How the danger sinks and swells,—
By the sinking or the swelling in the anger of the bells,
   Of the bells,
  Of the bells, bells, bells, bells,
   Bells, bells, bells—
In the clamor and the clangor of the bells!

IV

  Hear the tolling of the bells,
   Iron bells!
What a world of solemn thought their monody compels!
  In the silence of the night
  How we shiver with affright

At the melancholy menace of their tone!
  For every sound that floats
  From the rust with their throats
        Is a groan.
  And the people—ah, the people,
  They that dwell up in the steeple,
        All alone,
  And who tolling, tolling, tolling,
    In that muffled monotone,
  Feel a glory in so rolling
    On the human heart a stone—
They are neither man nor woman,
They are neither brute nor human,
    They are Ghouls:
  And their king it is who tolls;
  And he rolls, rolls, rolls,
        Rolls
    A pæan from the bells;
  And his merry bosom swells
    With the pæan of the bells,
  And he dances, and he yells:
  Keeping time, time, time,
  In a sort of Runic rhyme,
    To the pæan of the bells,
        Of the bells,
  Keeping time, time, time,
  In a sort of Runic rhyme,
    To the throbbing of the bells,
  Of the bells, bells, bells—
    To the sobbing of the bells;
  Keeping time, time, time,
    As he knells, knells, knells,
  In a happy Runic Rhyme,
    To the rolling of the bells,
  Of the bells, bells, bells:
    To the tolling of the bells,
Of the bells, bells, bells, bells,
        Bells, bells, bells—
To the moaning and the groaning of the bells.

THE RAVEN

Once upon a midnight dreary, while I pondered, weak and weary,
Over many a quaint and curious volume of forgotten lore,—
While I nodded, nearly napping, suddenly there came a tapping,
As of some one gently rapping, rapping at my chamber door.
" 'Tis some visitor," I muttered, "tapping at my chamber door:
    Only this and nothing more."

Ah, distinctly I remember it was in the bleak December,
And each separate dying ember wrought its ghost upon the floor.
Eagerly I wished the morrow;—vainly I had sought to borrow
From my books surcease of sorrow—sorrow for the lost Lenore,
For the rare and radiant maiden whom the angels name Lenore:
    Nameless here for evermore.

And the silken sad uncertain rustling of each purple curtain
Thrilled me—filled me with fantastic terrors never felt before;
So that now, to still the beating of my heart, I stood repeating
" 'Tis some visitor entreating entrance at my chamber door,
Some late visitor entreating entrance at my chamber door:
    This it is and nothing more."

Presently my soul grew stronger; hesitating then no longer,
"Sir," said I, "or Madam, truly your forgiveness I implore;
But the fact is I was napping, and so gently you came rapping,
And so faintly you came tapping, tapping at my chamber door,
That I scarce was sure I heard you"—here I opened wide the
    door:—
    Darkness there and nothing more.

Deep into that darkness peering, long I stood there wondering,
    fearing,
Doubting, dreaming dreams no mortals ever dared to dream before;
But the silence was unbroken, and the stillness gave no token,
And the only word there spoken was the whispered word "Lenore":
This I whispered, and an echo murmured back the word, "Lenore":
    Merely this and nothing more.

Back into the chamber turning, all my soul within me burning,
Soon again I heard a tapping somewhat louder than before.
"Surely," said I, "surely that is something at my window lattice;
Let me see, then, what thereat is, and this mystery explore;

Let my heart be still a moment and this mystery explore:
    'Tis the wind and nothing more."

Open here I flung the shutter, when, with many a flirt and flutter,
In there stepped a stately Raven of the saintly days of yore.
Not the least obeisance made he; not a minute stopped or stayed he;
But, with mien of lord or lady, perched above my chamber door,
Perched upon a bust of Pallas just above my chamber door:
    Perched, and sat, and nothing more.

Then this ebony bird beguiling my sad fancy into smiling
By the grave and stern decorum of the countenance it wore,—
"Though thy crest be shorn and shaven, thou," I said, "art sure no
        craven,
Ghastly grim and ancient Raven wandering from the Nightly shore:
Tell me what thy lordly name is on the Night's Plutonian shore!"
    Quoth the Raven, "Nevermore."

Much I marveled this ungainly fowl to hear discourse so plainly,
Though it answers little meaning—little relevancy bore;
For we cannot help agreeing that no living human being
Ever yet was blessed with seeing bird above his chamber door,
Bird or beast upon the sculptured bust above his chamber door,
    With such name as "Nevermore."

But the Raven, sitting lonely on the placid bust, spoke only
That one word, as if his soul in that one word he did outpour.
Nothing further then he uttered, not a feather then he fluttered,
Till I scarcely more than muttered,—"Other friends have flown
        before;
On the morrow *he* will leave me, as my Hopes have flown before."
    Then the bird said, "Nevermore."

Startled at the stillness broken by reply so aptly spoken,
"Doubtless," said I, "what it utters is its only stock and store,
Caught from some unhappy master whom unmerciful Disaster
Followed fast and followed faster, till his songs one burden bore:
Till the dirges of his Hope that melancholy burden bore
    Of 'Never—nevermore.' "

But the Raven still beguiling all my fancy into smiling,
Straight I wheeled a cushioned seat in front of bird and bust and
        door;
Then, upon the velvet sinking, I betook myself to linking

Fancy unto fancy, thinking what this ominous bird of yore,
What this grim, ungainly, ghastly, gaunt, and ominous bird of yore
    Meant in croaking "Nevermore."

This I sat engaged in guessing, but no syllable expressing
To the fowl whose fiery eyes now burned into my bosom's core;
This and more I sat divining, with my head at ease reclining
On the cushion's velvet lining that the lamplight gloated o'er,
But whose velvet violet lining with the lamplight gloating o'er
    She shall press, ah, nevermore!

Then, methought, the air grew denser, perfumed from an unseen
    censer
Swung by seraphim whose foot-falls tinkled on the tufted floor.
"Wretch," I cried, "thy god hath lent thee—by these angels he hath
    sent thee
Respite—respite and nepenthe from thy memories of Lenore!
Quaff, oh quaff this kind nepenthe, and forget this lost Lenore!"
    Quoth the raven, "Nevermore."

"Prophet!" said I, "thing of evil! prophet still, if bird or devil!
Whether Tempter sent, or whether tempest tossed thee here ashore,
Desolate yet all undaunted, on this desert land enchanted—
On this home by Horror haunted—tell me truly, I implore:
Is there—*is* there balm in Gilead?—tell me—tell me, I implore!"
    Quoth the Raven, "Nevermore."

"Prophet!" said I, "thing of evil—prophet still, if bird or devil!
By that Heaven that bends above us, by that God we both adore,
Tell this soul with sorrow laden if, within the distant Aidenn,
It shall clasp a sainted maiden whom the angels name Lenore:
Clasp a rare and radiant maiden whom the angels name Lenore!"
    Quoth the Raven, "Nevermore."

"Be that word our sign of parting, bird or fiend!" I shrieked, up-
    starting:
"Get thee back into the tempest and the Night's Plutonian shore!
Leave no black plume as a token of that lie thy soul hath spoken!
Leave my loneliness unbroken! quit the bust above my door!
Take thy beak from out my heart, and take thy form from off my
    door!"
    Quoth the Raven, "Nevermore."

And the Raven, never flitting, still is sitting, still is sitting
On the pallid bust of Pallas just above my chamber door;
And his eyes have all the seeming of a demon's that is dreaming,
And the lamplight o'er him streaming throws his shadow on the
     floor:
And my soul from out that shadow that lies floating on the floor
     Shall be lifted—nevermore!

SONNET—TO SCIENCE

Science, true daughter of Old Time thou art!
Who alterest all things with thy peering eyes.
Why preyest thou thus upon the poet's heart,
    Vulture, whose wings are dull realities?
How should he love thee, or how deem thee wise,
    Who wouldst not leave him in his wandering
To seek for treasure in the jewelled skies,
    Albeit he soared with an undaunted wing?
Hast thou not dragged Diana from her car,
    And driven the Hamadryad from the wood
To seek a shelter in some happier star?
    Hast thou not torn the Naiad from her flood,
The Elfin from the green grass, and from me
The summer dream beneath the tamarind tree?

SONG FROM "AL AARAAF"

Neath blue-bell or streamer,
    Or tufted wild spray
That keeps from the dreamer
    The moonbeam away,
Bright beings that ponder,
    With half-closing eyes,
On the stars which your wonder
    Hath drawn from the skies,
'Till they glance thro' the shade and
    Come down to your brow
Like eyes of the maiden
    Who calls on you now,—
Arise from your dreaming
    In violet bowers,
To duty beseeming

These star-litten hours,
    And shake from your tresses
        Encumber'd with dew
The breath of those kisses
    That cumber them too
(Oh, how, without you, Love,
    Could angels be blest?)—
Those kisses of true love
    That lull'd ye to rest!
Up! shake from your wing
    Each hindering thing:
The dew of the night—
    It would weigh down your flight;
And true-love caresses—
    O, leave them apart;
They are light on the tresses,
    But lead on the heart.
Ligeia! Ligeia!
    My beautiful one!
Whose harshest idea
    Will to melody run,
O, is it thy will
    On the breezes to toss?
Or, capriciously still,
    Like the lone Albatross,
Incumbent on night
    (As she on the air)
To keep watch with delight
    On the harmony there?
Ligeia, wherever
    Thy image may be,
No magic shall sever
    Thy music from thee!
Thou hast bound many eyes
    In a dreamy sleep;
But the strains still arise
    Which *thy* vigilance keep:
The sound of the rain
    Which leaps down to the flower,
And dances again
    In the rhythm of the shower,
The murmur that springs
    From the growing of grass
Are the music of things—

But are modell'd, alas!
Away, then, my dearest,
   O, hie thee away
To springs that lie clearest
   Beneath the moon-ray;
To lone lake that smiles,
   In its dream of deep rest,
At the many star-isles
   That enjewel its breast.
Where wild flowers, creeping,
   Have mingled their shade,
On its margin is sleeping
   Full many a maid;
Some have left the cool glade, and
   Have slept with the bee:
Arouse them, my maiden,
   On the moorland and lea;
Go, breathe on their slumber,
   All softly in ear,
The musical number
   They slumber'd to hear;
For what can awaken
   An angel so soon,
Whose sleep hath been taken
   Beneath the cold moon,
As the spell which no slumber
   Of witchery may test,
The rhythmical number
   Which lull'd him to rest?

THE CONQUEROR WORM

Lo, 'tis a gala night
   Within the lonesome latter years;
An angel throng, bewinged, bedight
   In veils, and drowned in tears,
Sit in a theater, to see
   A play of hopes and fears,
While the orchestra breathes fitfully
   The music of the spheres.

Mimes, in the form of God on high,
   Mutter and mumble low,

And hither and thither fly—
   Mere puppets they, who come and go
At bidding of vast formless things
   That shift the scenery to and fro,
Flapping from out their Condor wings,
   Invisible wo!

That motley drama, oh, be sure
   It shall not be forgot!
With its Phantom chased for evermore
   By a crowd that seize it not,
Through a circle that ever returneth in
   To the self-same spot,
And much of Madness, and more of Sin,
   And Horror the soul of the plot.

But see, amid the mimic rout
   A crawling shape intrude!
A blood-red thing that writhes from out
   The scenic solitude!
It writhes! it writhes! with mortal pangs
   The mimes become its food,
And seraphs sob at vermin fangs
   In human gore imbued.

Out, out are the lights—out all!
   And over each quivering form
The curtain, a funeral pall,
   Comes down with the rush of a storm;
While the angels, all pallid and wan,
   Uprising, unveiling, affirm
That the play is the tragedy "Man,"
   And its hero the Conqueror Worm.

ELDORADO

   Gaily bedight,
     A gallant knight,
In sunshine and in shadow,
     Had journeyed long,
     Singing a song,
In search of Eldorado.

But he grew old—
This knight so bold,—
And o'er his heart a shadow
Fell as he found
No spot of ground
That looked like Eldorado.

And, as his strength
Failed him at length,
He met a pilgrim shadow.
"Shadow," said he.
"Where can it be—
This land of Eldorado?"

"Over the Mountains
Of the Moon,
Down the Valley of the Shadow,
Ride, boldly ride,"
The shade replied,
"If you seek for Eldorado!"

A DREAM WITHIN A DREAM

Take this kiss upon the brow!
And, in parting from you now,
Thus much let me avow—
You are not wrong, who deem
That my days have been a dream;
Yet if hope has flown away
In a night, or in a day,
In a vision, or in none,
Is it therefore the less *gone?*
All that we see or seem
Is but a dream within a dream.

I stand amid the roar
Of a surf-tormented shore,
And I hold within my hand
Grains of the golden sand—
How few! yet how they creep
Through my fingers to the deep,
While I weep—while I weep!
O God! can I not grasp

Them with a tighter clasp?
O God! can I not save
One from the pitiless wave?
Is *all* that we see or seem
But a dream within a dream?

LENORE

Ah, broken is the golden bowl! the spirit flown forever!
Let the bell toll!—a saintly soul floats on the Stygian river;
And, Guy De Vere, hast *thou* no tear?—weep now or never more!
See! on yon drear and rigid bier low lies thy love, Lenore!
Come! let the burial rite be read—the funeral song be sung!—
An anthem for the queenliest dead that ever died so young—
A dirge for her the doubly dead in that she died so young.

"Wretches! ye loved her for her wealth and hated her for her pride,
"And when she fell in feeble health, ye blessed her—that she died!
"How *shall* the ritual, then, be read?—the requiem how be sung
"By you—by yours, the evil eye,—by yours, the slanderous tongue
"That did to death the innocence that died, and died so young?"

Peccavimus; but rave not thus! and let a Sabbath song
Go up to god so solemnly the dead may feel no wrong!
The sweet Lenore hath "gone before," with Hope, that flew beside,
Leaving thee wild for the dear child that should have been thy
         bride—
For her, the fair and *debonair*, that now so lowly lies,
The life upon her yellow hair but not within her eyes—
The life still there, upon her hair—the death upon her eyes.

"Avaunt! to-night my heart is light. No dirge will I upraise.
"But waft the angel on her flight with a pæan of old days!
"Let *no* bell toll!—lest her sweet soul, amid its hallowed mirth,
"Should catch the note, as it doth float up from the damnèd Earth.
"To friends above, from fiends below, the indignant ghost is riven—
"From Hell unto a high estate far up within the Heaven—
"From grief and groan, to a golden throne, beside the King of
         Heaven."

ROMANCE

Romance, who loves to nod and sing,
With drowsy head and folded wing,
Among the green leaves as they shake
Far down within some shadowy lake,
To me a painted paroquet
Hath been—a most familiar bird—
Taught me my alphabet to say—
To lisp my very earliest word
While in the wood I did lie,
A child—with a most knowing eye.

Of late, eternal Condor years
So shake the very Heaven on high
With tumult as they thunder by,
I have no time for idle cares
Through gazing on the unquiet sky.
And when an hour with calmer wings
Its down upon my spirit flings—
That little time, with lyre and rhyme
To while away—forbidden things!
My heart would feel to be a crime
Unless it trembled with the strings.

DREAM-LAND

By a route obscure and lonely,
Haunted by ill angels only,
Where an Eidolon, named NIGHT,
On a black throne reigns upright,
I have reached these lands but newly
From an ultimate dim Thule—
From a wild weird clime that lieth, sublime,
    Out of SPACE—out of TIME.

Bottomless vales and boundless floods,
And chasms, and caves, and Titan woods,
With forms that no man can discover
For the tears that drip all over;
Mountains toppling evermore
Into seas without a shore;
Seas that restlessly aspire,

Surging, unto skies of fire;
Lakes that endlessly outspread
Their lone waters—lone and dead,—
Their still waters—still and chilly
With the snows of the lolling lily.

By the lakes that thus outspread
Their lone waters, lone and dead,—
Their sad waters, sad and chilly
With the snows of the lolling lily,—
By the mountains—near the river
Murmuring lowly, murmuring ever,—
By the grey woods,—by the swamp
Where the toad and the newt encamp,—
By the dismal tarns and pools
   Where dwell the Ghouls,—
By each spot the most unholy—
In each nook most melancholy,—
There the traveller meets, aghast,
Sheeted Memories of the Past—
Shrouded forms that start and sigh
As they pass the wanderer by—
White-robed forms of friends long given,
In agony, to the Earth—and Heaven.

For the heart whose woes are legion
'Tis a peaceful, soothing region—
For the spirit that walks in shadow
'Tis—oh 'tis an Eldorado!
But the traveller, travelling through it,
May not—dare not openly view it;
Never its mysteries are exposed
To the weak human eye unclosed;
So wills its King, who hath forbid
The uplifting of the fringèd lid;
And thus the sad Soul that here passes
Beholds it but through darkened glasses.

By a route obscure and lonely,
Haunted by ill angels only,
Where an Eidolon, named NIGHT,
On a black throne reigns upright,
I have wandered home but newly
From this ultimate dim Thule.

FOR ANNIE

Thank Heaven! the crisis—
    The danger is past,
And the lingering illness
    Is over at last—
And the fever called "Living"
    Is conquered at last.

Sadly, I know
    I am shorn of my strength,
And no muscle I move
    As I lie at full length—
But no matter!—I feel
    I am better at length.

And I rest so composedly
    Now, in my bed,
That any beholder
    Might fancy me dead—
Might start at beholding me,
    Thinking me dead.

The moaning and groaning,
    The sighing and sobbing,
Are quieted now,
    With that horrible throbbing
At heart:—ah that horrible,
    Horrible throbbing!

The sickness—the nausea—
    The pitiless pain—
Have ceased with the fever
    That maddened my brain—
With the fever called "Living"
    That burned in my brain.

And oh! of all tortures
    That torture the worst
Has abated—the terrible
    Torture of thirst
For the napthaline river
    Of Passion accurst:—

I have drank of a water
  That quenches all thirst:—

Of a water that flows,
  With a lullaby sound,
From a spring but a very few
  Feet under ground—
From a cavern not very far
  Down under ground.

And ah! let it never
  Be foolishly said
That my room it is gloomy
  And narrow my bed;
For a man never slept
  In a different bed—
And, to sleep, you must slumber
  In just such a bed.

My tantalized spirit
  Here blandly reposes,
Forgetting, or never
  Regretting, its roses—
Its old agitations
  Of myrtles and roses:

For now, while so quietly
  Lying, it fancies
A holier odor
  About it, of pansies—
A rosemary odor,
  Commingled with pansies—
With rue and the beautiful
  Puritan pansies.

And so it lies happily,
  Bathing in many
A dream of the truth
  And the beauty of Annie—
Drowned in a bath
  Of the tresses of Annie.

She tenderly kissed me,
  She fondly caressed,

And then I fell gently
  To sleep on her breast—
Deeply to sleep
  From the heaven of her breast.

When the light was extinguished,
  She covered me warm,
And she prayed to the angels
  To keep me from harm—
To the queen of the angels
  To shield me from harm.

And I lie so composedly,
  Now, in my bed,
(Knowing her love)
  That you fancy me dead—
And I rest so contendedly,
  Now, in my bed,
(With her love at my breast)
  That you fancy me dead—
That you shudder to look at me,
  Thinking me dead:—

But my heart it is brighter
  Than all of the many
Stars of the sky,
  For it sparkles with Annie—
It glows with the light
  Of the love of my Annie—
With the thought of the light
  Of the eyes of my Annie.

Oliver Wendell Holmes

(1809–1894)

Oliver Wendell Holmes, a native of Cambridge, Massachusetts, was a descendant of Anne Bradstreet and an inheritor of a respected poetic legacy. He graduated from Harvard in 1829, set out to study law, but switched to medicine, earning his M.D. from Harvard in 1836. Eleven years later he became a chairman of anatomy and physiology at the Harvard Medical School. Holmes practiced many trades during his lifetime: novelist, scientist, teacher, poet, lecturer, essayist, and humorist. Holmes's only son and namesake went on to become a justice of the Supreme Court of the United States.

THE BALLAD OF THE OYSTERMAN

It was a tall young oysterman lived by the river-side,
His shop was just upon the bank, his boat was on the tide;
The daughter of a fisherman, that was so straight and slim,
Lived over on the other bank, right opposite to him.

It was the pensive oysterman that saw a lovely maid,
Upon a moonlight evening, a sitting in the shade;
He saw her wave her handkerchief, as much as if to say,
"I'm wide awake, young oysterman, and all the folks away."

Then up arose the oysterman, and to himself said he,
"I guess I'll leave the skiff at home, for fear that folks should see;
I read it in the story-book, that, for to kiss his dear,
Leander swam the Hellespont,—and I will swim this here."

And he has leaped into the waves, and crossed the shining stream,
And he has clambered up the bank, all in the moonlight gleam;
O there were kisses sweet as dew, and words as soft as rain,—
But they have heard her father's step, and in he leaps again!

Out spoke the ancient fisherman,—"O what was that, my
      daughter?"
" 'T was nothing but a pebble, sir, I threw into the water."
"And what is that, pray tell me, love, that paddles off so fast?"
"It's nothing but a porpoise, sir, that's been a swimming past."

Out spoke the ancient fisherman,—"Now bring me my harpoon!
I'll get into my fishing-boat, and fix the fellow soon."
Down fell that pretty innocent, as falls a snow-white lamb,
Her hair drooped round her pallid cheeks, like seaweed on a clam.

Alas for those two loving ones! she waked not from her swound,
And he was taken with the cramp, and in the waves was drowned;
But Fate has metamorphosed them, in pity of their woe,
And now they keep an oyster-shop for mermaids down below.

THE CHAMBERED NAUTILUS

This is the ship of pearl, which, poets feign,
    Sail the unshadowed main,—
    The venturous bark that flings
On the sweet summer wind its purpled wings
In gulfs enchanted, where the Siren sings,
    And coral reefs lie bare,
Where the cold sea-maids rise to sun their streaming hair.

Its webs of living gauze no more unfurl;
    Wrecked is the ship of pearl!
    And every chambered cell,
Where its dim dreaming life was wont to dwell,
As the frail tenant shaped his growing shell,
    Before thee lies revealed,—
Its irised ceiling rent, its sunless crypt unsealed!

Year after year beheld the silent toil
    That spread his lustrous coil;
    Still, as the spiral grew,
He left the past year's dwelling for the new,

Stole with soft step its shining archway through,
  Built up its idle door,
Stretched in his last-found home, and knew the old no more.

Thanks for the heavenly message brought by thee,
  Child of the wandering sea,
  Cast from her lap, forlorn!
From thy dead lips a clearer note is born
Than ever Triton blew from wreathéd horn!
  While on mine ear it rings,
Through the deep caves of thought I hear a voice that sings:—

Build thee more stately mansions, O my soul,
  As the swift seasons roll!
  Leave thy low-vaulted past!
Let each new temple, nobler than the last,
Shut thee from heaven with a dome more vast,
  Till thou at length art free,
Leaving thine outgrown shell by life's unresting sea!

OLD IRONSIDES

Ay, tear her tattered ensign down!
  Long has it waved on high,
And many an eye has danced to see
  That banner in the sky;
Beneath it rung the battle shout,
  And burst the cannon's roar;—
The meteor of the ocean air
  Shall sweep the clouds no more!

Her deck, once red with heroes' blood,
  Where knelt the vanquished foe,
When winds were hurrying o'er the flood,
  And waves were white below,
No more shall feel the victor's tread,
  Or know the conquered knee;—
The harpies of the shore shall pluck
  The eagle of the sea!

O better that her shattered hulk
  Should sink beneath the wave;

Her thunders shook the mighty deep,
　And there should be her grave;
Nail to the mast her holy flag,
　Set every threadbare sail,
And give her to the god of storms,
　The lightning and the gale!

THE LAST LEAF

I saw him once before,
As he passed by the door,
　And again
The pavement stones resound,
As he totters o'er the ground
　With his cane.

They say that in his prime,
Ere the pruning-knife of Time
　Cut him down,
Not a better man was found
By the Crier on his round
　Through the town.

But now he walks the streets,
And he looks at all he meets
　Sad and wan,
And he shakes his feeble head,
That it seems as if he said,
　"They are gone."

The mossy marbles rest
On the lips that he has prest
　In their bloom,
And the names he loved to hear
Have been carved for many a year
　On the tomb.

My grandmamma has said—
Poor old lady, she is dead
　Long ago—
That he had a Roman nose,
And his cheek was like a rose
　In the snow.

But now his nose is thin,
And it rests upon his chin
　　Like a staff,
And a crook is in his back,
And a melancholy crack
　　In his laugh.

I know it is a sin
For me to sit and grin
　　At him here;
But the old three-cornered hat,
And the breeches, and all that,
　　Are so queer!

And if I should live to be
The last leaf upon the tree
　　In the spring,
Let them smile, as I do now,
At the old forsaken bough
　　Where I cling.

TO AN INSECT

I love to hear thine earnest voice,
　　Wherever thou art hid,
Thou testy little dogmatist,
　　Thou pretty Katydid!
Thou mindest me of gentlefolks,—
　　Old gentlefolks are they,—
Thou say'st an undisputed thing
　　In such a solemn way.

Thou art a female, Katydid!
　　I know it by the trill
That quivers through thy piercing notes,
　　So petulant and shrill;
I think there is a knot of you
　　Beneath the hollow tree,—
A knot of spinster Katydids,—
　　Do Katydids drink tea?

O tell me where did Katy live,
　　And what did Katy do?

And was she very fair and young,
  And yet so wicked, too?
Did Katy love a naughty man,
  Or kiss more cheeks than one?
I warrant Katy did no more
  Than many a Kate has done.

Dear me! I'll tell you all about
  My fuss with little Jane,
And Ann, with whom I used to walk
  So often down the lane,
And all that tore their locks of black,
  Or wet their eyes of blue,—
Pray tell me, sweetest Katydid,
  What did poor Katy do?

Ah no! the living oak shall crash,
  That stood for ages still,
The rock shall rend its mossy base
  And thunder down the hill,
Before the little Katydid
  Shall add one word, to tell
The mystic story of the maid
  Whose name she knows so well.

Peace to the ever-murmuring race!
  And when the latest one
Shall fold in death her feeble wings
  Beneath the autumn sun,
Then shall she raise her fainting voice,
  And lift her drooping lid,
And then the child of future years
  Shall hear what Katy did.

REFLECTIONS OF A PROUD PEDESTRIAN

I saw the curl of his waving lash,
  And the glance of his knowing eye,
And I knew that he thought he was cutting a dash,
  As his steed went thundering by.

And he may ride in the rattling gig,
  Or flourish the Stanhope gay,

And dream that he looks exceeding big
  To the people that walk in the way;

But he shall think, when the night is still,
  On the stable-boy's gathering numbers,
And the ghost of many a veteran bill
  Shall hover around his slumbers;

The ghastly dun shall worry his sleep,
  And constables cluster around him,
And he shall creep from the wood-hole deep
  Where their spectre eyes have found him!

Ay! gather your reins, and crack your thong,
  And bid your steed go faster;
He does not know, as he scrambles along,
  That he has a fool for his master;

And hurry away on your lonely ride,
  Nor deign from the mire to save me;
I will paddle it stoutly at your side
  With the tandem that nature gave me!

THE DEACON'S MASTERPIECE

Or, the Wonderful "One-Hoss Shay"

A Logical Story

Have you heard of the wonderful one-hoss shay,
That was built in such a logical way
It ran a hundred years to a day,
And then, of a sudden, it——ah, but stay,
I'll tell you what happened without delay,
Scaring the parson into fits,
Frightening people out of their wits,—
Have you ever heard of that, I say?
Seventeen hundred and fifty-five.
Georgius Secundus was then alive,—
Snuffy old drone from the German hive.
That was the year when Lisbon-town
Saw the earth open and gulp her down,
And Braddock's army was done so brown,

Left without a scalp to its crown.
It was on the terrible Earthquake-day
That the Deacon finished the one-hoss shay.

Now in building of chaises, I tell you what,
There is always *somewhere* a weakest spot,—
In hub, tire, felloe, in spring or thill,
In panel, or crossbar, or floor, or sill,
In screw, bolt, thoroughbrace,—lurking still,
Find it somewhere you must and will,—
Above or below, or within or without,—
And that's the reason, beyond a doubt,
That a chaise *breaks down*, but doesn't *wear out*.

But the Deacon swore, (as Deacons do,
With an "I dew vum," or an "I tell *yeou*,")
He would build one shay to beat the taown
'n' the keounty 'n' all the kentry raoun';
It should be so built that it *couldn'* break daown:
—"Fur," said the Deacon, "'t's mighty plain
Thut the weakes' place mus' stan' the strain;
'n' the way t' fix it, uz I maintain, Is only jest
T' make that place uz strong uz the rest."

So the Deacon inquired of the village folk
Where he could find the strongest oak,
That couldn't be split nor bent nor broke,—
That was for spokes and floor and sills;
He sent for lancewood to make the thills;
The crossbars were ash, from the straightest trees,
The panels of white-wood, that cuts like cheese,
But lasts like iron for things like these;
The hubs of logs from the "Settler's ellum,"—
Last of its timber,—they could n't sell 'em,
Never an axe had seen their chips,
And the wedges flew from between their lips,
Their blunt ends frizzled like celery-tips;
Step and prop-iron, bolt and screw,
Spring, tire, axle, and linchpin too,
Steel of the finest, bright and blue;
Thoroughbrace bison-skin, thick and wide;
Boot, top, dasher, from tough old hide
Found in the pit when the tanner died.

That was the way he "put her through."—
"There!" said the Deacon, "naow she'll dew!"

Do! I tell you, I rather guess
She was a wonder, and nothing less!
Colts grew horses, beards turned gray,
Deacon and deaconess dropped away,
Children and grandchildren—where were they?
But there stood the stout old one-hoss shay
As fresh as on Lisbon-earthquake-day!

EIGHTEEN HUNDRED;—it came and found
The Deacon's masterpiece strong and sound.
Eighteen hundred increased by ten;—
"Hahnsum kerridge" they called it then.
Eighteen hundred and twenty came;—
Running as usual; much the same.
Thirty and forty at last arrive,
And then come fifty, and FIFTY-FIVE.

Little of all we value here
Wakes on the morn of its hundredth year
Without both feeling and looking queer.
In fact, there's nothing that keeps its youth,
So far as I know, but a tree and truth.
(This is a moral that runs at large;
Take it.—You're welcome.—No extra charge.)

FIRST OF NOVEMBER,—the Earthquake-day—
There are traces of age in the one-hoss shay,
A general flavor of mild decay,
But nothing local, as one may say.
There could n't be,—for the Deacon's art
Had made it so like in every part
That there was n't a chance for one to start.
For the wheels were just as strong as the thills,
And the floor was just as strong as the sills,
And the panels just as strong as the floor,
And the whipple-tree neither less nor more,
And the back-crossbar as strong as the fore,
And spring and axle and hub *encore*.
And yet, *as a whole*, it is past a doubt
In another hour it will be *worn out!*

First of November, 'Fifty-five!
This morning the parson takes a drive.
Now, small boys, get out of the way!
Here comes the wonderful one-hoss shay,
Drawn by a rat-tailed, ewe-necked bay.
"Huddup!" said the parson.—Off went they.
The parson was working his Sunday's text,—
Had got to *fifthly*, and stopped perplexed
At what the—Moses—was coming next.
All at once the horse stood still,
Close by the meet'n'-house on the hill.
—First a shiver, and then a thrill,
Then something decidedly like a spill,—
And the parson was sitting upon a rock,
At half past nine by the meet'n'-house clock,—
Just the hour of the Earthquake shock!

—What do you think the parson found,
When he got up and stared around?
The poor old chaise in a heap or mound,
As if it had been to the mill and ground!
You see, of course, if you're not a dunce,
How it went to pieces all at once,—
All at once, and nothing first,—
Just as bubbles do when they burst.

End of the wonderful one-hoss shay.
Logic is logic. That's all I say.

CONTENTMENT

"Man wants but little here below."

Little I ask; my wants are few;
   I only wish a hut of stone,
(A *very plain* brown stone will do,)
    That I may call my own;—
And close at hand is such a one,
In yonder street that fronts the sun.

Plain food is quite enough for me;
   Three courses are as good as ten;—
If Nature can subsist on three,

Thank Heaven for three. Amen!
I always thought cold victual nice;—
My *choice* would be vanilla-ice.

I care not much for gold or land;—
   Give me a mortgage here and there,—
Some good bank-stock, some note of hand,
   Or trifling railroad share,—
I only ask that Fortune send
A *little* more than I shall spend.

Honors are silly toys, I know,
   And titles are but empty names;
I would, *perhaps*, be Plenipo,—
   But only near St. James;
I'm very sure I should not care
To fill our Gubernator's chair.

Jewels are bawbles; 't is a sin
   To care for such unfruitful things;—
One good-sized diamond in a pin,—
   Some, *not so large*, in rings,—
A ruby, and a pearl, or so,
Will do for me;—I laugh at show.

My dame should dress in cheap attire;
   (Good, heavy silks are never dear;)—
I own perhaps I *might* desire
   Some shawls of true Cashmere,—
Some marrowy crapes of China silk,
Like wrinkled skins on scalded milk.

I would not have the horse I drive
   So fast that folks must stop and stare;
An easy gait—two, forty-five—
   Suits me; I do not care;—
Perhaps, for just a *single spurt*,
Some seconds less would do no hurt.

Of pictures, I should like to own
   Titians and Raphaels three or four,—
I love so much their style and tone,—
   One Turner, and no more,

(A landscape,—foreground golden dirt,—
The sunshine painted with a squirt.)

Of books but few,—some fifty score
    For daily use, and bound for wear;
The rest upon an upper floor;—
    Some *little* luxury *there*
Of red morocco's gilded gleam,
And vellum rich as country cream.

Busts, cameos, gems,—such things as these,
    Which others often show for pride,
I value for their power to please,
    And selfish churls deride;—
One Stradivarius, I confess,
Two Meerschaums, I would fain possess.

Wealth's wasteful tricks I will not learn
    Nor ape the glittering upstart fool;—
Shall not carved tables serve my turn,
    But *all* must be of buhl?
Give grasping pomp its double share,—
I ask but *one* recumbent chair.

Thus humble let me live and die,
    Nor long for Midas' golden touch;
If Heaven more generous gifts deny,
    I shall not miss them *much*,—
Too grateful for the blessing lent
Of simple tastes and mind content!

SUN AND SHADOW

As I look from the isle, o'er its billows of green,
    To the billows of foam-crested blue,
Yon bark, that afar in the distance is seen,
    Half dreaming, my eyes will pursue:
Now dark in the shadow, she scatters the spray
    As the chaff in the stroke of the flail;
Now white as the sea-gull, she flies on her way,
    The sun gleaming bright on her sail.

Yet her pilot is thinking of dangers to shun,—
    Of breakers that whiten and roar;
How little he cares, if in shadow or sun
    They see him who gaze from the shore!
He looks to the beacon that looms from the reef,
    To the rock that is under his lee,
As he drifts on the blast, like a wind-wafted leaf,
    O'er the gulfs of the desolate sea.

Thus drifting afar to the dim-vaulted caves
    Where life and its ventures are laid,
The dreamers who gaze while we battle the waves
    May see us in sunshine or shade;
Yet true to our course, though the shadows grow dark,
    We'll trim our broad sail as before,
And stand by the rudder that governs the bark,
    Nor ask how we look from the shore!

THE ANGEL-THIEF

1829–1888

Time is a thief who leaves his tools behind him;
    He comes by night, he vanishes at dawn;
We track his footsteps, but we never find him:
    Strong locks are broken, massive bolts are drawn,

And all around are left the bars and borers,
    The splitting wedges and the prying keys,
Such aids as serve the soft-shod vault explorers
    To crack, wrench open, rifle as they please.

Ah, these are tools which Heaven in mercy lends us!
    When gathering rust has clenched our shackles fast,
Time is the angel-thief that Nature sends us
    To break the cramping fetters of our past.

Mourn as we may for treasures he has taken,
    Poor as we feel of hoarded wealth bereft,
More precious are those implements forsaken,
    Found in the wreck his ruthless hands have left.

Some lever that a casket's hinge has broken
    Pries off a bolt, and lo! our souls are free;
Each year some Open Sesame is spoken,
    And every decade drops its master-key.

So as from year to year we count our treasure,
    Our loss seems less, and larger look our gains;
Time's wrongs repaid in more than even measure,—
    We lose our jewels, but we break our chains.

THE OLD MAN DREAMS

O for one hour of youthful joy!
    Give back my twentieth spring!
I'd rather laugh, a bright-haired boy,
    Than reign, a gray-beard king.

Off with the spoils of wrinkled age!
    Away with Learning's crown!
Tear out life's Wisdom-written page,
    And dash its trophies down!

One moment let my life-blood stream
    From boyhood's fount of flame!
Give me one giddy, reeling dream
    Of life all love and fame!

My listening angel heard the prayer,
    And, calmly smiling, said,
"If I but touch thy silvered hair
    They hasty wish hath sped.

"But is there nothing in thy track,
    To bid thee fondly stay,
While the swift seasons hurry back
    To find the wished-for day?"

"Ah, truest soul of womankind!
    Without thee what were life?
One bliss I cannot leave behind:
    I'll take—my—precious—wife!"

—The angel took a sapphire pen
  And wrote in rainbow dew,
The man would be a boy again,
  And be a husband too!

"And is there nothing yet unsaid,
  Before the change appears?
Remember, all their gifts have fled
  With those dissolving years."

"Why yes"; for memory would recall
  My fond paternal joys;
"I could not bear to leave them all—
  I'll take—my—girl—and—boys."

The smiling angel dropped his pen,—
  "Why this will never do;
The man would be a boy again,
  And be a father too!"

And so I laughed,—my laughter woke
  The household with its noise,—
And wrote my dream, when morning broke,
  To please the gray-haired boys.

Jones Very

(1813–1880)

Jones Very was born in Salem, Massachusetts, and spent much of his early life at sea with his sea-captain father. He graduated from Harvard in 1836, became a tutor in Greek, and entered divinity school. His poems are deeply religious.

TO THE CANARY-BIRD

I cannot hear thy voice with others' ears,
Who make of thy lost liberty a gain;
And in thy tale of blighted hopes and fears
Feel not that every note is born with pain.
Alas! that with thy music's gentle swell
Past days of joy should through thy memory throng,
And each to thee their words of sorrow tell,
While ravish'd sense forgets thee in thy song.
The heart that on the past and future feeds,
And pours in human words its thoughts divine,
Though at each birth the spirit inly bleeds,
Its song may charm the listening ear like thine,
And men with gilded cage and praise will try
To make the bard, like thee, forget his native sky.

THE EARTH

I would lie low—the ground on which men tread—
Swept by thy Spirit like the wind of heaven;
An earth, where gushing springs and corn for bread

By me at every season should be given;
Yet not the water or the bread that now
Supplies their tables with its daily food,
But they should gather fruit from every bough,
Such as Thou givest me, and call it good;
And water from the stream of life should flow,
By every dwelling that thy love has built,
Whose taste the ransomed of thy Son shall know,
Whose robes are washed from every stain of guilt;
And men would own it was thy hand that blest,
And from my bosom find a surer rest.

THE LATTER RAIN

The latter rain,—it falls in anxious haste
Upon the sun-dried fields and branches bare,
Loosening with searching drops the rigid waste,
As if it would each root's lost strength repair;
But not a blade grows green as in the spring,
No swelling twig puts forth its thickening leaves;
The robins only mid the harvests sing,
Pecking the grain that scatters from the sheaves:
The rain falls still,—the fruit all ripened drops,
It pierces chestnut burr and walnut shell,
The furrowed fields disclose the yellow crops,
Each bursting pod of talents used can tell,
And all that once received the early rain
Declare to man it was not sent in vain.

THE LAMENT OF THE FLOWERS

I looked to find Spring's early flowers,
    In spots where they were wont to bloom;
But they had perished in their bowers;
    The haunts they loved had proved their tomb!

The alder, and the laurel green,
    Which sheltered them, had shared their fate;
And but the blackened ground was seen,
    Where hid their swelling buds of late.

From the bewildered, homeless bird,
  Whose half-built nest the flame destroys,
A low complaint of wrong I heard,
  Against the thoughtless, ruthless boys.

Sadly I heard its notes complain,
  And ask the young its haunts to spare;
Prophetic seemed the sorrowing strain,
  Sung o'er its home, but late so fair!

'No more with hues like ocean shell
  The delicate wind-flower here shall blow;
The spot that loved its form so well
  Shall ne'er again its beauty know.

'Or, if it bloom, like some pale ghost
  'T will haunt the black and shadeless dell,
Where once it bloomed a numerous host,
  Of its once pleasant bowers to tell.

'And coming years no more shall find
  The laurel green upon the hills;
The frequent fire leaves naught behind,
  But e'en the very roots it kills.

'No more upon the turnpike's side
  The rose shall shed its sweet perfume;
The traveler's joy, the summer's pride,
  Will share with them a common doom.

'No more shall these returning fling
  Round childhood's home a heavenly charm,
With song of bird in early spring,
  To glad the heart and save from harm.'

THE STRANGERS

Each care-worn face is but a book
  To tell of houses bought or sold;
Or filled with words that mankind took
  From those who lived and spoke of old.

I see none whom I know, for they
　　See other things than him they meet;
And though they stop me by the way,
　　'T is still some other one to greet.

There are no words that reach my ear
　　Those speak who tell of other things
Than what they mean for me to hear,
　　For in their speech the counter rings.

I would be where each word is true,
　　Each eye sees what it looks upon;
For here my eye has seen but few,
　　Who in each act that act have done.

THE DEAD

I see them,—crowd on crowd they walk the earth,
Dry leafless trees no autumn wind laid bare;
And in their nakedness find cause for mirth,
And all unclad would winter's rudeness dare;
No sap doth through their clattering branches flow,
Whence springing leaves and blossoms bright appear;
Their hearts the living God have ceased to know
Who gives the spring-time to th' expectant year.
They mimic life, as if from Him to steal
His glow of health to paint the livid cheek;
They borrow words for thoughts they cannot feel,
That with a seeming heart their tongue may speak;
And in their show of life more dead they live
Than those that to the earth with many tears they give.

John Godfrey Saxe

(1816–1887)

John Godfrey Saxe was born in Highgate, Vermont. He graduated from Middlebury College in 1839, went on to study law, was admitted to the bar, and became a prominent lawyer. In 1850 he became the editor of the *Burlington Sentinel,* a job that proved to be a stepping stone to a political career. Saxe served as the attorney general of Vermont and ran unsuccessfully as the Democratic candidate for governor. He devoted the latter part of his life to writing. In 1874 Saxe was injured in a railway accident and never fully recovered. In the next few years his wife, three daughters, and eldest son all died, and he lived the remainder of his life as a recluse.

HOW CYRUS LAID THE CABLE

A Ballad

Come, listen all unto my song;
   It is no silly fable;
'T is all about the mighty cord
   They call the Atlantic Cable.

Bold Cyrus Field he said, says he,
   I have a pretty notion
That I can run a telegraph
   Across the Atlantic Ocean.

Then all the people laughed, and said,
   They'd like to see him do it;

He might get half-seas-over, but
   He never could go through it.

To carry out his foolish plan
   He never would be able;
He might as well go hang himself
   With his Atlantic Cable.

But Cyrus was a valiant man,
   A fellow of decision;
And heeded not their mocking words,
   Their laughter and derision.

Twice did his bravest efforts fail,
   And yet his mind was stable;
He wa'n't the man to break his heart
   Because he broke his cable.

"Once more, my gallant boys!" he cried:
   "Three times!—you know the fable,—
(I'll make it *thirty*," muttered he,
   "But I will lay the cable!")

Once more they tried,—hurrah! hurrah!
   What means this great commotion?
The Lord be praised! the cable's laid
   Across the Atlantic Ocean!

Loud ring the bells,—for, flashing through
   Six hundred leagues of water,
Old Mother England's benison
   Salutes her eldest daughter!

O'er all the land the tidings speed,
   And soon, in every nation,
They'll hear about the cable with
   Profoundest admiration!

Now, long live President and Queen;
   And long live gallant Cyrus;
And may his courage, faith, and zeal
   With emulation fire us;

And may we honor evermore
The manly, bold, and stable;
And tell our sons, to make them brave,
How Cyrus laid the cable!

RHYME OF THE RAIL

Singing through the forests,
Rattling over ridges,
Shooting under arches,
Rumbling over bridges,
Whizzing through the mountains,
Buzzing o'er the vale,—
Bless me! this is pleasant,
Riding on the Rail!

Men of different "stations"
In the eye of Fame
Here are very quickly
Coming to the same.
High and lowly people,
Birds of every feather,
On a common level
Traveling together!

Gentleman in shorts,
Looming very tall;
Gentleman at large,
Talking very small;
Gentleman in tights,
With a loose-ish mien;
Gentleman in gray,
Looking rather green.

Gentleman quite old,
Asking for the news;
Gentleman in black,
In a fit of blues;
Gentleman in claret,
Sober as a vicar;
Gentleman in Tweed,
Dreadfully in liquor!

Stranger on the right,
   Looking very sunny,
Obviously reading
   Something rather funny.
Now the smiles are thicker,
   Wonder what they mean?
Faith he's got the KNICKER-
   BOCKER Magazine!

Stranger on the left,
   Closing up his peepers;
Now he snores amain,
   Like the Seven Sleepers;
At his feet a volume
   Gives the explanation,
How the man grew stupid
   From "Association"!

Ancient maiden lady
   Anxiously remarks,
That there must be peril
   'Mong so many sparks!
Roguish-looking fellow,
   Turning to the stranger,
Says it's his opinion
   She is out of danger!

Woman with her baby,
   Sitting *vis-à-vis;*
Baby keeps a squalling;
   Woman looks at me;
Asks about the distance,
   Says it's tiresome talking,
Noises of the cars
   Are so very shocking!

Market-woman careful
   Of the precious casket,
Knowing eggs are eggs,
   Tightly holds her basket;
Feeling that a smash,
   If it came, would surely
Send her eggs to pot
   Rather prematurely!

Singing through the forests,
    Rattling over ridges,
Shooting under arches,
    Rumbling over bridges,
Whizzing through the mountains,
    Buzzing o'er the vale,—
Bless me! this is pleasant,
    Riding on the Rail!

MY FAMILIAR

Ecce iterum crispinus!

I

Again I hear that creaking step!—
    He's rapping at the door!—
Too well I know the boding sound
    That ushers in a bore.
I do not tremble when I meet
    The stoutest of my foes,
But Heaven defend me from the friend
    Who comes—but never goes!

II

He drops into my easy-chair,
    And asks about the news;
He peers into my manuscript,
    And gives his candid views;
He tells me where he likes the line,
    And where he's forced to grieve;
He takes the strangest liberties,—
    But never takes his leave!

III

He reads my daily paper through
    Before I've seen a word;
He scans the lyric (that I wrote)
    And thinks it quite absurd;
He calmly smokes my last cigar,

And coolly asks for more;
He opens everything he sees—
   Except the entry door!

IV

He talks about his fragile health,
   And tells me of the pains
He suffers from a score of ills
   Of which he ne'er complains;
And how he struggled once with death
   To keep the fiend at bay;
On themes like those away he goes,—
   But never goes away!

V

He tells me of the carping words
   Some shallow critic wrote;
And every precious paragraph
   Familiarly can quote;
He thinks the writer did me wrong;
   He'd like to run him through!
He says a thousand pleasant things,—
   But never says, "Adieu!"

VI

Whene'er he comes,—that dreadful man,—
   Disguise it as I may,
I know that, like an Autumn rain,
   He'll last throughout the day.
In vain I speak of urgent tasks;
   In vain I scowl and pout;
A frown is no extinguisher,—
   It does not put him out!

VII

I mean to take the knocker off,
   Put crape upon the door,
Or hint to John that I am gone
   To stay a month or more.
I do not tremble when I meet

The stoutest of my foes,
But Heaven defend me from the friend
Who never, never goes!

THE EXPECTED SHIP

Thus I heard a poet say,
  As he sang in merry glee,
"Ah! 't will be a golden day,
  When my ship comes o'er the sea!

"I do know a cottage fine,
  As a poet's house should be,
And the cottage shall be mine,
  When my ship comes o'er the sea!

"I do know a maiden fair,
  Fair, and fond, and dear to me,
And we'll be a wedded pair,
  When my ship comes o'er the sea!

"And within that cottage fine,
  Blest as any king may be,
Every pleasure shall be mine,
  When my ship comes o'er the sea!

"To be rich is to be great;
  Love is only for the free;
Grant me patience, while I wait
  Till my ship comes o'er the sea!"

Months and years have come and gone
  Since the poet sang to me,
Yet he still keeps hoping on
  For the ship from o'er the sea!

Thus the siren voice of Hope
  Whispers still to you and me
Of something in the future's scope,
  Some golden ship from o'er the sea!

Never sailor yet hath found,
  Looking windward or to lee,

Any vessel homeward bound,
　　Like that ship from o'er the sea!

Never comes the shining deck;
　　But that tiny cloud may be—
Though it seems the merest speck—
　　The promised ship from o'er the sea!

Never looms the swelling sail,
　　But the wind is blowing free,
And *that* may be the precious gale
　　That brings the ship from o'er the sea!

THE HEAD AND THE HEART

The head is stately, calm, and wise,
　　And bears a princely part;
And down below in secret lies
　　The warm, impulsive heart.

The lordly head that sits above,
　　The heart that beats below,
Their several office plainly prove,
　　Their true relation show.

The head, erect, serene, and cool,
　　Endowed with Reason's art,
Was set aloft to guide and rule
　　The throbbing, wayward heart.

And from the head, as from the higher,
　　Comes every glorious thought;
And in the heart's transforming fire
　　All noble deeds are wrought.

Yet each is best when both unite
　　To make the man complete;
What were the heat without the light?
　　The light, without the heat?

WHERE THERE'S A WILL THERE'S A WAY

"Aut viam inveniam, aut faciam."

It was a noble Roman,
   In Rome's imperial day,
Who heard a coward croaker,
   Before the Castle, say:
"They're safe in such a fortress;
   There is no way to shake it!"
"On—on!" exclaimed the hero,
   "I'll find a way, or make it!"

Is *Fame* your aspiration?
   Her path is steep and high;
In vain he seeks her temple,
   Contents to gaze and sigh:
The shining throne is waiting,
   But he alone can take it
Who says, with Roman firmness
   "I'll find a way, or make it!"

Is *Learning* your ambition?
   There is no royal road;
Alike the peer and peasant
   Must climb to her abode:
Who feels the thirst of knowledge
   In Helicon may slake it,
If he has still the Roman will
   "To find a way, or make it!"

Are *Riches* worth the getting?
   They must be bravely sought;
With wishing and with fretting
   The boom cannot be bought:
To all the prize is open,
   But only he can take it
Who says, with Roman courage,
   "I'll find a way, or make it!"

In *Love's* impassioned warfare
   The tale has ever been,
That victory crowns the valiant,—
   The brave are they who win:

Though strong is Beauty's castle,
  A lover still may take it,
Who says, with Roman daring,
  "I'll find a way, or make it!"

COMIC MISERIES

I

My dear young friend, whose shining wit
  Sets all the room ablaze,
Don't think yourself "a happy dog,"
  For all your merry ways;
But learn to wear a sober phiz,
  Be stupid, if you can,
It's such a very serious thing
  To be a funny man!

II

You're at an evening party, with
  A group of pleasant folks,—
You venture quietly to crack
  The least of little jokes:
A lady doesn't catch the point,
  And begs you to explain,—
Alas for one who drops a jest
  And takes it up again!

III

You're talking deep philosophy
  With very special force,
To edify a clergyman
  With suitable discourse:
You think you've got him,—when he calls
  A friend across the way,
And begs you'll say that funny thing
  You said the other day!

IV

You drop a pretty *jeu-de-mot*
  Into a neighbor's ears,
Who likes to give you credit for
  The clever thing he hears,
 And so he hawks your jest about,
  The old, authentic one,
Just breaking off the point of it,
  And leaving out the pun!

V

By sudden change in politics,
  Or sadder change in Polly,
You lose your love, or loaves, and fall
  A prey to melancholy,
While everybody marvels why
  Your mirth is under ban,
They think your very grief "a joke,"
  You're such a funny man!

VI

You follow up a stylish card
  That bids you come and dine,
And bring along your freshest wit
  (To pay for musty wine);
You're looking very dismal, when
  My lady bounces in,
And wonders what you're thinking of,
  And why you don't begin!

VII

You're telling to a knot of friends
  A fancy-tale of woes
That cloud your matrimonial sky,
  And banish all repose,—
A solemn lady overhears
  The story of your strife,
And tells the town the pleasant news:—
  You quarrel with your wife!

VIII

My dear young friend, whose shining wit
   Sets all the room ablaze,
Don't think yourself "a happy dog,"
   For all your merry ways;
But learn to wear a sober phiz,
   Be stupid, if you can,
It's such a very serious thing
   To be a funny man!

WISHING

Of all amusements for the mind,
   From logic down to fishing,
There is n't one that you can find
   So very cheap as "wishing."
A very choice diversion too,
   If we but rightly use it,
And not, as we are apt to do,
   Pervert it, and abuse it.

I wish,—a common wish, indeed,—
   My purse were somewhat fatter,
That I might cheer the child of need,
   And not my pride to flatter;
That I might make Oppression reel,
   As only gold can make it,
And break the Tyrant's rod of steel,
   As only gold can break it.

I wish—that Sympathy and Love,
   And every human passion
That has its origin above,
   Would come and keep in fashion;
That Scorn, and Jealousy, and Hate,
   And every base emotion,
Were buried fifty fathom deep
   Beneath the waves of Ocean!

I wish—that friends were always true,
   And motives always pure;
I wish the good were not so few,

I wish the bad were fewer;
  I wish that parsons ne'er forgot
    To heed their pious teaching;
  I wish that practicing was not
    So different from preaching!

I wish—that modest worth might be
    Appraised with truth and candor;
  I wish that innocence were free
    From treachery and slander;
  I wish that men their vows would mind;
    That women ne'er were rovers;
  I wish that wives were always kind,
    And husbands always lovers!

I wish—in fine—that Joy and Mirth,
    And every good Ideal,
  May come erewhile, throughout the earth,
    To be the glorious Real;
  Till God shall every creature bless
    With his supremest blessing,
  And Hope be lost in Happiness,
    And wishing in Possessing!

EARLY RISING

"God bless the man who first invented sleep!"
  So Sancho Panza said, and so say I:
And bless him, also, that he didn't keep
  His great discovery to himself; nor try
To make it—as the lucky fellow might—
A close monopoly by patent-right!

Yes; bless the man who first invented sleep
  (I really can't avoid the iteration);
But blast the man, with curses loud and deep,
  Whate'er the rascal's name, or age, or station,
Who first invented, and went round advising,
That artificial cut-off,—Early Rising!

"Rise with the lark, and with the lark to bed,"
  Observes some solemn, sentimental owl;
Maxims like these are very cheaply said;

But, ere you make yourself a fool or fowl,
Pray just inquire about his rise and fall,
And whether larks have any beds at all!

The time for honest folks to be abed
    Is in the morning, if I reason right;
And he who cannot keep his precious head
    Upon his pillow till it's fairly light,
And so enjoy his forty morning winks,
Is up to knavery; or else—he drinks!

Thomson, who sung about the "Seasons," said
    It was a glorious thing to *rise* in season;
But then he said it—lying—in his bed,
    At ten o'clock, A.M.,—the very reason
He wrote so charmingly. The simple fact is,
His preaching wasn't sanctioned by his practice.

'T is, doubtless, well to be sometimes awake,—
    Awake to duty, and awake to truth,—
But when, alas! a nice review we take
    Of our best deeds and days, we find, in sooth,
The hours that leave the slightest cause to weep
Are those we passed in childhood or asleep!

'T is beautiful to leave the world awhile
    For the soft visions of the gentle night;
And free, at last, from mortal care or guile,
    To live as only in the angels' sight,
In sleep's sweet realm so cosily shut in,
Where, at the worst, we only *dream* of sin!

So let us sleep, and give the Maker praise.
    I like the lad who, when his father thought
To clip his morning nap by hackneyed phrase
    Of vagrant worm by early songster caught,
Cried, "Served him right!—it's not at all surprising;
The worm was punished, sir, for early rising!"

ECHO

I asked of Echo, t'other day
    (Whose words are often few and funny),

What to a novice she could say
   Of courtship, love, and matrimony.
   Quoth Echo plainly,—"Matter-o'-money!"

Whom should I marry? Should it be
   A dashing damsel, gay and pert,
A pattern of inconstancy;
   Or selfish, mercenary flirt?
   Quoth Echo, sharply,—"Nary flirt!"

What if, aweary of the strife
   That long has lured the dear deceiver,
She promise to amend her life,
   And sin no more; can I believe her?
   Quoth Echo, very promptly,—"Leave her!"

But if some maiden with a heart
   On me should venture to bestow it,
Pray, should I act the wiser part
   To take the treasure or forego it?
   Quoth Echo, with decision,—"Go it!"

But what if, seemingly afraid
   To bind her fate in Hymen's fetter,
She vow she means to die a maid,
   In answer to my loving letter?
   Quoth Echo, rather coolly,—"Let her!"

What if, in spite of her disdain,
   I find my heart intwined about
With Cupid's dear delicious chain
   So closely that I can't get out?
   Quoth Echo, laughingly,—"Get out!"

But if some maid with beauty blest,
   As pure and fair as Heaven can make her,
Will share my labor and my rest
   Till envious Death shall overtake her?
   Quoth Echo (sotto voce),—"Take her!"

SONNET TO A CLAM

Dum tacent claimant

Inglorious friend! most confident I am
    Thy life is one of very little ease;
    Albeit men mock thee with their similes
And prate of being "happy as a clam!"
What though thy shell protects thy fragile head
    From the sharp bailiffs of the briny sea?
    Thy valves are, sure, no safety-valves to thee,
While rakes are free to desecrate thy bed,
And bear thee off—as foemen take their spoil—
    Far from thy friends and family to roam;
    Forced, like a Hessian, from thy native home,
To meet destruction in a foreign broil!
    Though thou art tender yet thy humble bard
    Declares, O clam! thy case is shocking hard!

Henry David Thoreau

(1817–1862)

Henry David Thoreau was born and raised in Concord, Massachusetts. He was given a particularly well-rounded education, especially in languages. He played the flute and became an enthusiastic naturalist early in life. He opened a private school with his brother, but in 1841 the school closed and he went to work for Ralph Waldo Emerson as a tutor in the family. However, being a naturalist at heart, as well as a professional surveyor, Thoreau eventually went to live in the woods in search of a more primitive life-style. Thoreau was indeed a man with a mission, advocating such causes as conservation, antislavery, and the concept of living simply. He was a man of great energy and lived an active life until he died.

SIC VITA

I am a parcel of vain strivings tied
　　By a chance bond together,
　Dangling this way and that, their links
　　Were made so loose and wide,
　　　　Methinks,
　　　For milder weather.

A bunch of violets without their roots,
　　And sorrel intermixed,
　Encircled by a wisp of straw
　　Once coiled about their shoots,
　　　　The law
　　　By which I'm fixed.

A nosegay which Time clutched from out
    Those fair Elysian fields,
With weeds and broken stems, in haste,
    Doth make the rabble rout
       That waste
    The day he yields.

And here I bloom for a short hour unseen,
    Drinking my juices up,
With no root in the land
    To keep my branches green,
       But stand
    In a bare cup.

Some tender buds were left upon my stem
    In mimicry of life,
But ah! the children will not know,
    Till time has withered them,
       The woe
    With which they're rife.

But now I see I was not plucked for naught,
    And after in life's vase
Of glass set while I might survive,
    But by a kind hand brought
       Alive
    To a strange place.

That stock thus thinned will soon redeem its hours,
    And by another year,
Such as God knows, with freer air,
    More fruits and fairer flowers
       Will bear,
    While I droop here.

SMOKE

Light-winged Smoke! Icarian bird,
Melting thy pinions in thy upward flight,
Lark without song, and messenger of dawn,
Circling above the hamlets as thy nest;
Or else, departing dream, and shadowy form
Of midnight vision, gathering up thy skirts;

By night star-veiling, and by day
Darkening the light and blotting out the sun;
Go thou my incense upward from this hearth,
And ask the gods to pardon this clear flame.

MIST

Low-anchored cloud,
Newfoundland air,
Fountain-head and source of rivers,
Dew-cloth, dream drapery,
And napkin spread by fays;
Drifting meadow of the air,
Where bloom the daisied banks and violets,
And in whose fenny labyrinth
The bittern booms and heron wades;
Spirit of lakes and seas and rivers,
Bear only perfumes and the scent
Of healing herbs to just men's fields!

INSPIRATION

Whate'er we leave to God, God does,
　And blesses us;
The work we choose should be our own,
　God lets alone.

If with light head erect I sing,
　Though all the muses lend their force,
From my poor love of anything,
　The verse is weak and shallow as its source.

But if with bended neck I grope,
　Listening behind me for my wit,
With faith superior to hope,
　More anxious to keep back than forward it,

Making my soul accomplice there
　Unto the flame my heart hath lit,
Then will the verse forever wear,—
　Time cannot bend the line which God hath writ.

Always the general show of things
  Floats in review before my mind,
And such true love and reverence brings,
  That sometimes I forget that I am blind.

But now there comes unsought, unseen,
  Some clear, divine electuary,
And I who had but sensual been,
  Grow sensible, and as God is, am wary.

I hearing get who had but ears,
  And sight, who had but eyes before,
I moments live who lived but years,
  And truth discern who knew but learning's lore.

I hear beyond the range of sound,
  I see beyond the range of sight,
New earths and skies and seas around,
  And in my day the sun doth pale his light.

A clear and ancient harmony
  Pierces my soul through all its din,
As through its utmost melody,—
  Farther behind than they—farther within.

More swift its bolt than lightning is,
  Its voice than thunder is more loud,
It doth expand my privacies
  To all, and leave me single in the crowd.

It speaks with such authority,
  With so serene and lofty tone,
That idle Time runs gadding by,
  And leaves me with Eternity alone.

Then chiefly is my natal hour,
  And only then my prime of life,
Of manhood's strength it is the flower,
  'Tis peace's end and war's beginning strife.

'T 'hath come in summer's broadest noon,
  By a grey wall or some chance place,
Unseasoned time, insulted June,
  And vexed the day with its presuming face.

Such fragrance round my couch it makes,
   More rich than are Arabian drugs,
That my soul scents its life and wakes
   The body up beneath its perfumed rugs.

Such is the Muse—the heavenly maid,
   The star that guides our mortal course,
Which shows where life's true kernel's laid,
   Its wheat's fine flower, and its undying force.

She with one breath attunes the spheres,
   And also my poor human heart,
With one impulse propels the years
   Around, and gives my throbbing pulse its start.

I will no doubt forever more,
   Nor falter from a steadfast faith,
For though the system be turned o'er,
   God takes not back the word which once he saith.

I will then trust the love untold
   Which not my worth nor want has bought,
Which wooed me young and woos me old,
   And to this evening hath me brought.

My memory I'll educate
   To know the one historic truth,
Remembering to the latest date
   The only true and sole immortal youth.

Be but thy inspiration given,
   No matter through what danger sought,
I'll fathom hell or climb to heaven,
   And yet esteem that cheap which love has bought.

WINTER MEMORIES

Within the circuit of this plodding life
There enter moments of an azure hue,
Untarnished fair as is the violet
Or anemone, when the spring strews them
By some meandering rivulet, which make
The best philosophy untrue that aims

But to console man for his grievances.
I have remembered when the winter came,
High in my chamber in the frosty nights,
When in the still light of the cheerful moon,
On every twig and rail and jutting spout,
The icy spears were adding to their length
Against the arrows of the coming sun,
How in the shimmering noon of summer past
Some unrecorded beam slanted across
The upland pastures where the Johnswort grew;
Or heard, amid the verdure of my mind,
The bee's long smothered hum, on the blue flag
Loitering amidst the mead; or busy rill,
Which now through all its course stands still and dumb
Its own memorial,—purling at its play
Along the slopes, and through the meadows next,
Until its youthful sound was hushed at last
In the staid current of the lowland stream;
Or seen the furrows shine but late upturned,
And where the fieldfare followed in the rear,
When all the fields around lay bound and hoar
Beneath a thick integument of snow.
So by God's cheap economy made rich
To go upon my winter's task again.

TO THE MAIDEN IN THE EAST

Low in the eastern sky
Is set thy glancing eye;
And though its gracious light
Ne'er riseth to my sight,
Yet every star that climbs
Above the gnarled limbs
  Of yonder hill,
Conveys thy gentle will.

Believe I knew thy thought,
And that the zephyrs brought
Thy kindest wishes through,
As mine they bear to you,
That some attentive cloud
Did pause amid the crowd

Over my head,
While gentle things were said.

Believe the thrushes sung,
And that the flower-bells rung,
That herbs exhaled their scent,
And beasts knew what was meant,
The trees a welcome waved,
And lakes their margins laved,
　　When thy free mind
To my retreat did wind.

It was a summer eve,
The air did gently heave
While yet a low-hung cloud
Thy eastern skies did shroud;
The lightning's silent gleam,
Startling my drowsy dream,
　　Seemed like the flash
Under thy dark eyelash.

Still will I strive to be
As if thou wert with me;
Whatever path I take,
It shall be for thy sake,
Of gentle slope and wide,
As thou wert by my side,
　　Without a root
To trip thy gentle foot.

I'll walk with gentle pace,
And choose the smoothest place,
And careful dip the oar,
And shun the winding shore,
And gently steer my boat
Where water-lilies float,
　　And cardinal flowers
Stand in their sylvan bowers.

James T. Fields

(1817–1881)

James Thomas Fields was born in Portsmouth, New Hampshire. In 1838 he became a book publisher with the firm of Ticknor & Fields, where he remained until 1870. He wrote several books, including at least two volumes of poetry. His best-known poem is "Ballad of the Tempest." Fields also served as editor of the *Atlantic Monthly* from 1861 to 1870.

THE OWL CRITIC

"Who stuffed that white owl?" No one spoke in the shop:
The barber was busy, and he couldn't stop;
The customers, waiting their turns, were all reading
The "Daily," the "Herald," the "Post," little heeding
The young man who blurted out such a blunt question;
Not one raised a head, or even made a suggestion;
      And the barber kept on shaving.

"Don't you see, Mister Brown,"
Cried the youth, with a frown,
"How wrong the whole thing is,
How preposterous each wing is,
How flattened the head is, how jammed down the neck is—
In short, the whole owl, what an ignorant wreck 't is!
I make no apology;
I've learned owl-ecology.
I've passed days and nights in a hundred collections,
And cannot be blinded to any deflections
Arising from unskilful fingers that fail

To stuff a bird right, from his beak to his tail.
Mister Brown! Mister Brown!
Do take that bird down,
Or you'll soon be the laughing-stock all over town!"
    And the barber kept on shaving.

"I've *studied* owls,
And other night fowls,
And I tell you
What I know to be true:
An owl cannot roost
With his limbs so unloosed;
No owl in this world
Ever had his claws curled,
Ever had his legs slanted,
Ever had his bill canted,
Ever had his neck screwed
Into that attitude.
He can't *do* it, because
'T is against all bird-laws.
Anatomy teaches,
Ornithology preaches
An owl has a toe
That *can't* turn out so!
I've made the white owl my study for years,
And to see such a job almost moves me to tears!
Mister Brown, I'm amazed
You should be so gone crazed
As to put up a bird
In that posture absurd!
To *look* at that owl really brings on a dizziness;
The man who stuffed *him* don't half know his business!"
    And the barber kept on shaving.

"Examine those eyes.
I'm filled with surprise
Taxidermists should pass
Off on you such poor glass;
So unnatural they seem
They'd make Audubon scream,
And John Burroughs laugh
To encounter such chaff.
Do take that bird down;

Have him stuffed again, Brown!"
                    And the barber kept on shaving.

"With some sawdust and bark
I could stuff in the dark
An owl better than that.
I could make an old hat
Look more like an owl
Than that horrid fowl,
Stuck up there so stiff like a side of coarse leather.
In fact, about *him* there's not one natural feather."

Just then, with a wink and a sly normal lurch,
The owl, very gravely, got down from his perch,
Walked round, and regarded his fault-finding critic
(Who thought he was stuffed) with a glance analytic,
And then fairly hooted, as if he should say:
"Your learning's at fault *this* time, any way;
Don't waste it again on a live bird, I pray.
I'm an owl; you're another. Sir Critic, good-day!"
                    And the barber kept on shaving.

JUPITER AND TEN

Mrs. Chub was rich and portly,
    Mrs. Chub was very grand,
Mrs. Chub was always reckoned
    A lady in the land.

You shall see her marble mansion
    In a very stately square,—
Mr. C. knows what it cost him,
    But that's neither here nor there.

Mrs. Chub was so sagacious,
    Such a patron of the arts,
And she gave such foreign orders,
    That she won all foreign hearts.

Mrs. Chub was always talking,
    When she went away from home,
Of a prodigious painting
    Which had just arrived from Rome.

"Such a treasure," she insisted,
    "One might never see again!"
"What's the subject?" we inquired.
    "It is Jupiter and Ten!"

"Ten *what?*" we blandly asked her,
    For the knowledge we did lack.
"Ah! that I cannot tell you,
    But the name is on the back.

"There it stands in printed letters.
    Come tomorrow, gentlemen,
Come and see our splendid painting,
    Our fine *Jupiter and Ten.*"

When Mrs. Chub departed,
    Our brains we all did rack,—
She could not be mistaken,
    For the name was on the back.

So we begged a great Professor
    To lay aside his pen,
And give some information
    Touching "Jupiter and Ten."

And we pondered well the subject,
    And our Lemprière we turned,
To discover what the *Ten* were;
    But we could not, though we burned!

But when we saw the picture,—
    Oh, Mrs. Chub! Oh, fie! Oh!
We perused the printed label,
    And 'twas *Jupiter and Io!*

THE ALARMED SKIPPER

"It was an Ancient Mariner."

Many a long, long year ago,
    Nantucket skippers had a plan
Of finding out, though "lying low,"
    How near New York their schooners ran.

They greased the lead before it fell,
  And then, by sounding through the night,
Knowing the soil that stuck, so well,
  They always guessed their reckoning right.

A skipper gray, whose eyes were dim,
  Could tell, by *tasting,* just the spot,
And so below he'd "dowse the glim,"—
  After, of course, his "something hot."

Snug in his berth, at eight o'clock,
  This ancient skipper might be found;
No matter how his craft would rock,
  He slept,—for skippers' naps are sound!

The watch on deck would now and then
  Run down and wake him, with the lead;
He'd up, and taste, and tell the men
  How many miles they went ahead.

One night, 't was Jotham Marden's watch,
  A curious wag,—the peddler's son,—
And so he mused (the wanton wretch),
  "To-night I'll have a grain of fun.

"We're all a set of stupid fools
  To think the skipper knows by *tasting*
What ground he's on,—Nantucket schools
  Don't teach such stuff, with all their basting!"

And so he took the well-greased lead
  And rubbed it o'er a box of earth
That stood on deck,—a parsnip-bed,—
  And then he sought the skipper's berth.

"Where are we now, sir? Please to taste."
  The skipper yawned, put out his tongue,
Then oped his eyes in wondrous haste,
  And then upon the floor he sprung!

The skipper stormed and tore his hair,
  Thrust on his boots, and roared to Marden,
"Nantucket's sunk, and here we are
  Right over old Marm Hackett's garden!"

THE TURTLE AND FLAMINGO

A Song for My Little Friends

A lively young turtle lived down by the banks
    Of a dark-rolling stream called the Jingo,
And one summer day, as he went out to play,
    Fell in love with a charming flamingo,—
        An enormously genteel flamingo!
        An expansively crimson flamingo!
        A beautiful, bouncing flamingo!

Spake the turtle in tones like a delicate wheeze:
    "To the water I've oft seen you in go,
And your form has impressed itself deep on my shell,
    You perfectly modeled flamingo!
        You uncommonly brilliant flamingo!
        You tremendously scorching flamingo!
        You inexpres-*si*-ble flamingo!

"To be sure, I'm a turtle and you are a belle,
    And *my* language is not your fine lingo;
But smile on me, tall one, and be my bright flame,
    You miraculous, wondrous flamingo!
        You blazingly beauteous flamingo!
        You turtle-absorbing flamingo!
        You inflammably gorgeous flamingo!"

Then the proud bird blushed redder than ever before,
    And that was quite un-nec-ces-*sa*-ry,
And she stood on one leg and looked out of one eye,
    The position of things for to vary,—
        This aquatical, musing flamingo!
        This dreamy, uncertain flamingo!
        This embarrassing, harassing flamingo!

Then she cried to the quadruped, greatly amazed,
    "Why your passion toward *me* do you hurtle?
I'm an ornithological wonder of grace,
    And you're an illogical turtle,—
        A waddling, impossible turtle!
        A low-minded, grass-eating turtle!
        A highly improbable turtle!

"I measure four feet from my nose to my toes—
    Just observe the flamboyant spec-*tacle!*
Do you think a flamingo like me would stoop down
    Her fortune with yours, sir, to shackle?
        I *can't,* you pre-*pos*-terous turtle!
        You aldermaniculous turtle!
        You damp and ridiculous turtle!"

Then the turtle sneaked off with his nose to the ground,
    And never more looked at the lasses;
And falling asleep, while indulging his grief,
    Was gobbled up whole by Agassiz,—
        The peripatetic Agassiz!
        The turtle-dissecting Agassiz!
        The illustrious, industrious Agassiz.

Go with me to Cambridge some cool pleasant day,
    And the skeleton lover I'll show you;
He's in a hard case, but he'll look in your face,
    Pretending (the rogue!) he don't know you!
        Oh, the deeply deceptive young turtle!
        The double-faced, glassy-cased turtle!
        The *green,* but a very *mock* turtle!

BALLAD OF THE TEMPEST

We were crowded in the cabin,
    Not a soul would dare to sleep,—
It was midnight on the waters,
    And a storm was on the deep.

'Tis a fearful thing in winter
    To be shattered by the blast,
And to hear the rattling trumpet
    Thunder, "Cut away the mast!"

So we shuddered there in silence,—
    For the stoutest held his breath,
While the hungry sea was roaring
    And the breakers talked with death.

As thus we sat in darkness
    Each one busy with his prayers,

"We are lost!" the captain shouted,
　　As he staggered down the stairs.

But his little daughter whispered,
　　As she took his icy hand,
"Isn't God upon the ocean,
　　Just the same as on the land?"

Then we kissed the little maiden,
　　And we spake in better cheer,
And we anchored safe in harbor
　　When the morn was shining clear.

James Russell Lowell

(1819–1891)

James Russell Lowell was born in Cambridge, Massachusetts, into one of New England's most distinguished families. He graduated from Harvard in 1838 and went on to study law, but gave up his practice to pursue literature. In 1844 he married Maria White, a poet in her own right. Sadly, three of his four children did not survive past infancy, and his wife died in 1853. Two years later, Lowell succeeded Longfellow as the chairman of the modern languages department at Harvard. In 1857 he married his daughter's governess and also took on the editorial responsibilities of the *Atlantic Monthly*. In 1867 he published the second series of his famous *Biglow Papers*, a satire against slavery written in a New England Yankee dialect. He also served as a United States minister to Spain and continued his diplomatic service in England where he was a public speaker of record. He returned to America in 1885.

TO THE DANDELION

Dear common flower, that grow'st beside the way,
Fringing the dusty road with harmless gold!
First pledge of blithesome May,
Which children pluck, and, full of pride, uphold—
High-hearted buccaneers, o'erjoyed that they
An Eldorado in the grass have found,
Which not the rich earth's ample round
May match in wealth!—thou art more dear to me
Than all the prouder summer-blooms may be.

Gold such as thine ne'er drew the Spanish prow
Through the primeval hush of Indian seas;
    Nor wrinkled the lean brow
Of age, to rob the lover's heart of ease.
'Tis the Spring's largess, which she scatters now
To rich and poor alike, with lavish hand;
    Though most hearts never understand
    To take it at God's value, but pass by
    The offered wealth with unrewarded eye.

Thou art my tropics and mine Italy;
To look at thee unlocks a warmer clime;
    The eyes thou givest me
Are in the heart, and heed not space or time:
    Not in mid June the golden-cuirassed bee
Feels a more summer-like, warm ravishment
    In the white lily's breezy tent,
    His conquered Sybaris, than I, when first
From the dark green thy yellow circles burst.

Then think I of deep shadows on the grass;
Of meadows where in sun the cattle graze,
    Where, as the breezes pass,
The gleaming rushes lean a thousand ways;
    Of leaves that slumber in a cloudy mass,
Or whiten in the wind; of waters blue,
    That from the distance sparkle through
    Some woodland gap; and of a sky above,
Where one white cloud like a stray lamb doth move.

My childhood's earliest thoughts are linked with thee;
The sight of thee calls back the robin's song,
    Who, from the dark old tree
Beside the door, sang clearly all day long;
    And I, secure in childish piety,
Listened as if I heard an angel sing
    With news from heaven, which he did bring
    Fresh every day to my untainted ears,
    When birds and flowers and I were happy peers.

How like a prodigal doth nature seem,
When thou, for all thy gold, so common art!
    Thou teachest me to deem
More sacredly of every human heart,

Since each reflects in joy its scanty gleam
Of heaven, and could some wondrous secret show,
   Did we but pay the love we owe,
  And with a child's undoubting wisdom look
  On all these living pages of God's book.

THE FIRST SNOW-FALL

The snow had begun in the gloaming,
   And busily all the night
Had been heaping field and highway
   With a silence deep and white.

Every pine and fir and hemlock
   Wore ermine too dear for an earl,
And the poorest twig on the elm-tree
   Was ridged inch deep with pearl.

From sheds new-roofed with Carrara
   Came Chanticleer's muffled crow,
The stiff rails softened to swan's-down,
   And still fluttered down the snow.

I stood and watched by the window
   The noiseless work of the sky,
And the sudden flurries of snow-birds,
   Like brown leaves whirling by.

I thought of a mound in sweet Auburn
   Where a little headstone stood;
How the flakes were folding it gently,
   As did robins the babes in the wood.

Up spoke our own little Mabel,
   Saying, "Father, who makes it snow?"
And I told of the good All-father
   Who cares for us here below.

Again I looked at the snow-fall
   And thought of the leaden sky
That arched o'er our first great sorrow,
   When that mound was heaped so high.

I remembered the gradual patience
　That fell from that cloud like snow,
Flake by flake, healing and hiding
　The scar that renewed our woe.

And again to the child I whispered,
　"The snow that husheth all,
Darling, the merciful Father
　Alone can make it fall!"

Then, with eyes that saw not, I kissed her;
　And she, kissing back, could not know
That *my* kiss was given to her sister,
　Folded close under deepening snow.

THE COURTIN'

from *The Biglow Papers*

God makes sech nights, all white an' still
　Fur'z you can look or listen,
Moonshine an' snow on field an' hill,
　All silence an' all glisten.

Zekle crep' up quite unbeknown
　An' peeked in thru' the winder,
An' there sot Huldy all alone,
　'Ith no one nigh to hender.

A fireplace filled the room's one side
　With half a cord o' wood in—
There warn't no stoves (tell comfort died)
　To bake ye to a puddin'.

The wa'nut logs shot sparkles out
　Towards the pootiest, bless her,
An' leetle flames danced all about
　The chiny on the dresser.

Agin the chimbley crook-necks hung,
　An' in amongst 'em rusted
The ole queen's-arm thet gran'ther Young
　Fetched back f'om Concord busted.

The very room, coz she was in,
    Seemed warm f'om floor to ceilin',
An' she looked full ez rosy agin
    Ez the apples she was peelin'.

'T was kin' o' kingdom-come to look
    On sech a blessed cretur,
A dogrose blushin' to a brook
    Ain't modester nor sweeter.

He was six foot o' man, A 1,
    Clear grit an' human natur',
None couldn't quicker pitch a ton
    Nor dror a furrer straighter.

He'd sparked it with full twenty gals,
    He'd squired 'em, danced 'em, druv 'em,
Fust this one, an' then thet, by spells—
    All is, he could n't love 'em.

But long o' her his veins 'ould run
    All crinkly like curled maple,
The side she breshed felt full o' sun
    Ez a south slope in Ap'il.

She thought no v'ice hed sech a swing
    Ez hisn in the choir;
My! when he made Ole Hundred ring,
    She *knowed* the Lord was nigher.

An' she'd blush scarlit, right in prayer,
    When her new meetin'-bunnet
Felt somehow thru' its crown a pair
    O' blue eyes sot upon it.

Thet night, I tell ye, she looked *some!*
    She seemed to 've gut a new soul,
For she felt sartin-sure he'd come,
    Down to her very shoe-sole.

She heered a foot, an' knowed it tu,
    A-raspin' on the scraper,—
All ways to once her feelins flew
    Like sparks in burnt-up paper.

He kin' o' l'itered on the mat
  Some doubtfle o' the sekle,
His heart kep' goin' pity-pat,
  But hern went pity Zekle.

An' yit she gin her cheer a jerk
  Ez though she wished him furder,
An' on her apples kep' to work,
  Parin' away like murder.

"You want to see my Pa, I s'pose?"
  "Wal . . . no . . . I come dasignin' "—
"To see my Ma? She's sprinklin' clo'es
  Agin to-morrer's i'nin'."

To say why gals act so or so,
  Or don't, 'ould be persumin';
Mebby to mean *yes* an' say *no*
  Comes nateral to women.

He stood a spell on one foot fust,
  Then stood a spell on t' other,
An' on which one he felt the wust
  He could n't ha' told ye nuther.

Says he, "I'd better call agin;"
  Says she, "Think likely, Mister."
Thet last word pricked him like a pin,
  An' . . . Wal, he up an' kist her.

When Ma bimeby upon 'em slips,
  Huldy sot pale ez ashes,
All kin' o' smily roun' the lips
  An' teary roun' the lashes.

For she was jes' the quiet kind
  Whose naturs never vary,
Like streams that keep a summer mind
  Snowhid in Jenooary.

The blood clost roun' her heart felt glued
  Too tight for all expressin',
Tell mother see how metters stood,
  An' gin 'em both her blessin'.

Then her red come back like the tide
  Down to the Bay o' Fundy,
An' all I know is they was cried
  In meetin' come nex' Sunday.

FORGETFULNESS

There's a haven of sure rest
    From the loud world's bewildering stress
As a bird dreaming on her nest,
As dew hid in a rose's breast,
As Hesper in the glowing West;
        So the heart sleeps
        In thy calm deeps,
Serene Forgetfulness!

No sorrow in that place may be,
  The noise of life grows less and less:
As moss far down within the sea,
As, in white lily caves, a bee,
As life in a hazy reverie;
        So the heart's wave
        In thy dim cave,
Hushes, Forgetfulness!

Duty and care fade far away
  What toil may be we cannot guess:
As a ship anchored in the bay,
As a cloud a summer-noon astray,
As water-blooms in a breezeless day;
        So, 'neath thine eyes,
        The full heart lies,
And dreams, Forgetfulness!

WITH A PRESSED FLOWER

This little flower from afar
Hath come from other lands to thine;
For, once, its white and drooping star
Could see its shadow in the Rhine.

Perchance some fair-haired German maid
Hath plucked one from the self-same stalk,
And numbered over, half afraid,
Its petals in her evening walk.

"He loves me, loves me not," she cries;
"He loves me more than earth or heaven!"
And then glad tears have filled her eyes
To find the number was uneven.

And thou must count its petals well,
Because it is a gift from me;
And the last one of all shall tell
Something I've often told to thee.

But here at home, where we were born,
Thou wilt find flowers just as true,
Down-bending every summer morn
With freshness of New-England dew.

For Nature, ever kind to love,
Hath granted them the same sweet tongue,
Whether with German skies above,
Or here our granite rocks among.

THE FOUNTAIN

Into the sunshine,
    Full of the light,
Leaping and flashing
    From morn till night!

Into the moonlight,
    Whiter than snow,
Waving so flower-like
    When the winds blow!

Into the starlight,
    Rushing in spray,
Happy at midnight,
    Happy by day!

Ever in motion,
  Blithesome and cheery.
Still climbing heavenward,
  Never aweary;—

Glad of all weathers,
  Still seeming best,
Upward or downward,
  Motion thy rest;—

Full of a nature
  Nothing can tame,
Changed every moment,
  Ever the same;—

Ceaseless aspiring,
  Ceaseless content,
Darkness or sunshine
  Thy element;—

Glorious fountain!
  Let my heart be
Fresh, changeful, constant,
  Upward, like thee!

LONGING

Of all the myriad moods of mind
  That through the soul come thronging,
Which one was e'er so dear, so kind,
  So beautiful as Longing?
The thing we long for, that we are
  For one transcendent moment,
Before the Present poor and bare
  Can make its sneering comment.

Still, through our paltry stir and strife,
  Glows down the wished Ideal,
And Longing moulds in clay what Life
  Carves in the marble Real;
To let the new life in, we know,
  Desire must ope the portal;—

Perhaps the longing to be so
　　Helps make the soul immortal.

Longing is God's fresh heavenward will
　　With our poor earthward striving;
We quench it that we may be still
　　Content with merely living;
But, would we learn that heart's full scope
　　Which we are hourly wronging,
Our lives must climb from hope to hope
　　And realize our longing.

Ah! let us hope that to our praise
　　Good God not only reckons
The moments when we tread his ways,
　　But when the spirit beckons,—
That some slight good is also wrought
　　Beyond self-satisfaction,
When we are simply good in thought,
　　Howe'er we fail in action.

IN AN ALBUM

The misspelt scrawl, upon the wall
By some Pompeian idler traced,
In ashes packed (ironic fact!)
Lies eighteen centuries uneffaced,
While many a page of bard and sage,
Deemed once mankind's immortal gain,
Lost from Time's ark, leaves no more mark
Than a keel's furrow through the main.

O Chance and Change! our buzz's range
Is scarcely wider than a fly's;
Then let us play at fame to-day,
To-morrow be unknown and wise;
And while the fair beg locks of hair,
And autographs, and Lord knows what,
Quick! let us scratch our moment's match,
Make our brief blaze, and be forgot!

Too pressed to wait, upon her slate
Fame writes a name or two in doubt;

Scarce written, these no longer please,
And her own finger rubs them out:
It may ensue, fair girl, that you
Years hence this yellowing leaf may see,
And put to task, your memory ask
In vain, "This Lowell, who was he?"

SHE CAME AND WENT

As a twig trembles, which a bird
   Lights on to sing, then leaves unbent,
So is my memory thrilled and stirred;—
   I only know she came and went.

As clasps some lake, by gusts unriven,
   The blue dome's measureless content,
So my soul held that moment's heaven;—
   I only know she came and went.

As, at one bound, our swift spring heaps
   The orchards full of bloom and scent,
So clove her May my wintry sleeps;—
   I only know she came and went.

An angel stood and met my gaze,
   Through the low doorway of my tent;
The tent is struck, the vision stays;—
   I only know she came and went.

O, when the room grows slowly dim,
   And life's last oil is nearly spent,
One gush of light these eyes will brim,
   Only to think she came and went.

THE STREET

They pass me by like shadows, crowds on crowds,
Dim ghosts of men, that hover to and fro,
Hugging their bodies round them, like thin shrouds
Wherein their souls were buried long ago:
They trampled on their youth, and faith, and love,
They cast their hope of human-kind away,

With Heaven's clear messages they madly strove,
And conquered,—and their spirits turned to clay:
Lo! how they wander round the world, their grave,
Whose ever-gaping maw by such is fed,
Gibbering at living men, and idly rave,
"We, only, truly live, but ye are dead."
Alas! poor fools, the anointed eye may trace
A dead soul's epitaph in every face!

WITHOUT AND WITHIN

My coachman, in the moonlight there,
   Looks through the side-light of the door;
I hear him with his brethren swear,
   As I could do,—but only more.

Flattening his nose against the pane,
   He envies me my brilliant lot,
Breathes on his aching fist in vain,
   And dooms me to a place more hot.

He sees me in to supper go,
   A silken wonder by my side,
Bare arms, bare shoulders, and a row
   Of flounces, for the door too wide.

He thinks how happy is my arm,
   'Neath its white-gloved and jewelled load;
And wishes me some dreadful harm,
   Hearing the merry corks explode.

Meanwhile I inly curse the bore
   Of hunting still the same old coon,
And envy him, outside the door,
   The golden quiet of the moon.

The winter wind is not so cold
   As the bright smile he sees me win,
Nor the host's oldest wine so old
   As our poor gabble, sour and thin.

I envy him the rugged prance
   By which his freezing feet he warms,

And drag my lady's chains, and dance,
  The galley-slave of dreary forms.

Oh, could he have my share of din,
  And I his quiet—past a doubt
'Twould still be one man bored within,
  And just another bored without.

Walt Whitman

(1819–1892)

Walt Whitman, America's great national poet, was born in West Hills, Long Island, New York. When he was a young boy his family moved to Brooklyn where he went to school, afterward earning his living as a printer, reporter, and teacher. Whitman loved to travel and eventually left his work to take up a Bohemian life-style. He presented *Leaves of Grass* in 1855. By 1861 it was in its third edition. Whitman spent three years of the Civil War volunteering as an army nurse. In 1865 he took a position in the Department of the Interior, but after reading some of his poetry the secretary dismissed him. Whitman's health, which had been deteriorating since his Civil War service, continued to worsen, and he suffered a paralyzing stroke in 1873. He retired to Camden, New Jersey, in 1884.

O CAPTAIN! MY CAPTAIN!

O Captain! my Captain, our fearful trip is done,
The ship has weather'd every rack, the prize we sought is won,
The port is near, the bells I hear, the people all exulting,
While follow eyes the steady keel, the vessel grim and daring;
    But O heart! heart! heart!
      O the bleeding drops of red,
        Where on the deck my Captain lies,
          Fallen cold and dead.

O Captain! my Captain! rise up and hear the bells;
Rise up—for you the flag is flung—for you the bugle trills,
For you bouquets and ribbon'd wreaths—for you the shores
    a-crowding,

For you they call, the swaying mass, their eager faces turning;
　　　Here Captain! dear father!
　　　　The arm beneath your head!
　　　　　It is some dream that on the deck,
　　　　　　You've fallen cold and dead.

My Captain does not answer, his lips are pale and still,
My father does not feel my arm, he has no pulse nor will,
The ship is anchor'd safe and sound, its voyage closed and done,
From fearful trip the victor ship comes in with object won;
　　　Exult O shores, and ring O bells!
　　　　But I with mournful tread,
　　　　　Walk the deck my Captain lies,
　　　　　　Fallen cold and dead.

OLD WAR-DREAMS

In midnight sleep of many a face of anguish,
Of the look at first of the mortally wounded (of that indescribable
　　　look),
Of the dead on their backs with arms extended wide,
　　　　I dream, I dream, I dream.

Of scenes of Nature, fields and mountains,
Of skies so beauteous after a storm, and at night the moon so unearthly
　　　bright,
Shining sweetly, shining down, where we dig the trenches and
　　　gather the heaps,
　　　　I dream, I dream, I dream.

Long have they pass'd, faces and trenches and fields,
Where through the carnage I moved with a callous composure, or
　　　away from the fallen,
Onward I sped at the time—but now of their forms at night,
　　　　I dream, I dream, I dream.

WHEN LILACS LAST IN THE DOORYARD BLOOM'D

1

When lilacs last in the dooryard bloom'd,
And the great star early droop'd in the western sky in the night,
I mourn'd, and yet shall mourn with ever-returning spring.

Ever-returning spring, trinity sure to me you bring,
Lilac blooming perennial and drooping star in the west,
And thought of him I love.

2

O powerful western fallen star!
O shades of night—O moody, tearful night!
O great star disappear'd—O the black murk that hides the star!
O cruel hands that hold me powerless—O helpless soul of me!
O harsh surrounding cloud that will not free my soul.

3

In the dooryard fronting an old farm-house near the white-wash'd
        palings,
Stands the lilac-bush tall-growing with heart-shaped leaves of rich
        green,
With many a pointed blossom rising delicate, with the perfume
        strong I love,
With every leaf a miracle—and from this bush in the door-yard,
With delicate-colour'd blossoms and heart-shaped leaves of rich
        green,
A sprig with its flower I break.

4

In the swamp in secluded recesses,
A shy and hidden bird is warbling a song.

Solitary the thrush,
The hermit withdrawn to himself, avoiding the settlements,
Sings by himself a song.

Song of the bleeding throat,
Death's outlet song of life (for well dear brother I know,
If thou wast not granted to sing thou would'st surely die).

5

Over the breast of the spring, the land, amid cities,
Amid lanes and through old woods, where lately the violets peep'd
    from the ground, spotting the gray débris,
Amid the grass in the fields each side of the lanes, passing the endless
    grass,
Passing the yellow-spear'd wheat, every grain from its shroud in the
    dark-brown fields uprisen,
Passing the apple-tree blows of white and pink in the orchards,
Carrying a corpse to where it shall rest in the grave,
Night and day journeys a coffin.

6

Coffin that passes through lanes and streets,
Through day and night with the great cloud darkening the land,
With the pomp of the inloop'd flags with the cities draped in black,
With the show of the States themselves as of crape-veil'd women
    standing,
With processions long and winding and the flambeaus of the night,
With the countless torches lit, with the silent sea of faces and the
    unbared heads,
With the waiting depot, the arriving coffin, and the sombre faces,
With dirges through the night, with the thousand voices rising
    strong and solemn,
With all the mournful voices of the dirges pour'd around the coffin,
The dim-lit churches and the shuddering organs—where amid these
    you journey,
With the tolling tolling bells' perpetual clang,
Here, coffin that slowly passes,
I give you my sprig of lilac.

7

(Nor for you, for one alone,
Blossoms and branches green to coffins all I bring,
For fresh as the morning, thus would I chant a song for you O sane
    and sacred death.

All over bouquets of roses,
O death, I cover you over with roses and early lilies,
But mostly and now the lilac that blooms the first,
Copious I break, I break the sprigs from the bushes,
With loaded arms I come, pouring for you,
For you and the coffins all of you O death.)

8

O western orb sailing the heaven,
Now I know what you must have meant as a month since I walk'd,
As I walk'd in silence the transparent shadowy night,
As I saw you had something to tell as you bent to me night after
    night,
As you dropp'd from the sky low down as if to my side (while the
    other stars all look'd on),
As we wander'd together the solemn night (for something I know
    not what kept me from sleep),
As the night advanced, and I saw on the rim of the west how full
    you were of woe,
As I stood on the rising ground in the breeze in the cool transparent
    night,
As I watch'd where you pass'd and was lost in the netherward black
    of the night,
As my soul in its trouble dissatisfied sank, as where you sad orb,
Concluded, dropt in the night, and was gone.

9

Sing on there in the swamp,
O singer bashful and tender, I hear your notes, I hear your call,
I hear, I come presently, I understand you,
But a moment I linger, for the lustrous star has detain'd me,
The star my departing comrade holds and detains me.

10

O how shall I warble myself for the dead one there I loved?
And how shall I deck my song for the large sweet soul that has
    gone?
And what shall my perfume be for the grave of him I love?

Sea-winds blown from east and west,
Blown from the Eastern sea and blown from the Western sea, till

· 257 ·

there on the prairies meeting,
These and with these and the breath of my chant,
I'll perfume the grave of him I love.

11

O what shall I hang on the chamber walls?
And what shall the pictures be that I hang on the walls,
To adorn the burial-house of him I love?

Pictures of growing spring and farms and homes,
With the Fourth-month eve at sundown, and the gray smoke lucid
    and bright,
With floods of the yellow gold of the gorgeous, indolent, sinking
    sun, burning, expanding the air,
With the fresh sweet herbage under foot, and the pale green leaves
    of the trees prolific,
In the distance the flowing glaze, the breast of the river, with a
    wind-dapple here and there,
With ranging hills on the banks, with many a line against the sky,
    and shadows,
And the city at hand with dwellings so dense, and stacks of chimneys,
And all the scenes of life and the workshops, and the workmen
    homeward returning.

12

Lo, body and soul—this land,
My own Manhattan with spires, and the sparkling and hurrying
    tides, and the ships,
The varied and ample land, the South and the North in the light,
    Ohio's shores and flashing Missouri,
And ever the far-spreading prairies cover'd with grass and corn.

Lo, the most excellent sun so calm and haughty,
The violet and purple morn with just-felt breezes,
The gentle soft-born measureless light,
The miracle spreading bathing all, the fulfill'd noon,
The coming eve delicious, the welcome night and the stars,
Over my cities shining all, enveloping man and land.

Sing on, sing on you gray-brown bird,
Sing from the swamps, the recesses, pour your chant from the
    bushes,
Limitless out of the dusk, out of the cedars and pines.
Sing on dearest brother, warble your reedy song,
Loud human song, with voice of uttermost woe.

O liquid and free and tender!
O wild and loose to my soul—O wondrous singer!
You only I hear—yet the star holds me (but will soon depart),
Yet the lilac with mastering odour holds me.

14

Now while I sat in the day and look'd forth,
In the close of the day with its light and the fields of spring, and the
    farmers preparing their crops,
In the large unconscious scenery of my land with its lakes and
    forests,
In the heavenly aerial beauty (after the perturb'd winds and the
    storms),
Under the arching heavens of the afternoon swift passing, and the
    voices of children and women,
The many-moving sea-tides, and I saw the ships how they sail'd,
And the summer approaching with richness, and the fields all busy
    with labour,
And the infinite separate houses, how they all went on, each with its
    meals and minutia of daily usages,
And the streets how their throbbings throbb'd, and the cities
    pent—lo, then and there,
Falling upon them all and among them all, enveloping me with the
    rest,
Appear'd the cloud, appear'd the long black trail,
And I knew death, its thought, and the sacred knowledge of death.

Then with the knowledge of death as walking one side of me,
And the thought of death close-walking the other side of me,
And I in the middle as with companions, and as holding the hands
    of companions,
I fled forth to the hiding receiving night that talks not,

Down to the shores of the water, the path by the swamp in the
  dimness,
To the solemn shadowy cedars and ghostly pines so still.

And the singer so shy to the rest receiv'd me,
The gray-brown bird I know receiv'd us comrades three,
And he sang the carol of death, and a verse for him I love.

From deep secluded recesses,
From the fragrant cedars and the ghostly pines so still,
Came the carol of the bird.

And the charm of the carol rapt me,
As I held as if by their hands my comrades in the night,
And the voice of my spirit tallied the song of the bird.

Come lovely and soothing death,
Undulate round the world, serenely arriving, arriving,
In the day, in the night, to all, to each,
Sooner or later delicate death.

Prais'd be the fathomless universe,
For life and joy, and for objects and knowledge curious,
And for love, sweet love—but praise! praise! praise!
For the sure-enwinding arms of cool-enfolding death.

Dark mother always gliding near with soft feet,
Have none chanted for thee a chant of fullest welcome?
Then I chant it for thee, I glorify thee above all,
I bring thee a song that when thou must indeed come, come
  unfalteringly.

Approach strong deliveress,
When it is so, when thou hast taken them I joyously sing the dead,
Lost in the loving floating ocean of thee,
Laved in the flood of thy bliss O death.

From me to thee glad serenades,
Dances for thee I propose saluting thee, adornments and feastings
  for thee,
And the sights of the open landscape and the high-spread sky are
  fitting,
And life and the fields, and the huge and thoughtful night.

The night in silence under many a star,
The ocean shore and the husky whispering wave whose voice I
  know,
And the soul turning to thee O vast and well-veil'd death,
And the body gratefully nestling close to thee.

Over the tree-tops I float thee a song,
Over the rising and sinking waves, over the myriad fields and the
  prairies wide,
Over the dense-pack'd cities all and the teeming wharves and ways,
I float this carol with joy, with joy to thee O death.

15

To the tally of my soul,
Loud and strong kept up the gray-brown bird,
With pure deliberate notes spreading filling the night.
Loud in the pines and cedars dim,
Clear in the freshness moist and the swamp-perfume,
And I with my comrades there in the night.

While my sight that was bound in my eyes unclosed,
As to long panoramas of visions.

And I saw askant the armies,
I saw as in noiseless dreams hundreds of battle-flags,
Borne through the smoke of the battles and pierc'd with missiles I
  saw them,
And carried hither and yon through the smoke, and torn and
  bloody,
And at last but a few shreds left on the staffs (and all in silence),
And the staffs all splinter'd and broken.

I saw battle-corpses, myriads of them,
And the white skeletons of young men, I saw them,
I saw the débris and débris of all the slain soldiers of the war,
But I saw they were not as was thought,
They themselves were fully at rest, they suffer'd not,
The living remain'd and suffer'd, the mother suffer'd,
And the wife and the child and the musing comrade suffer'd,
And the armies that remain'd suffer'd.

Passing the visions, passing the night,
Passing, unloosing the hold of my comrades' hands,
Passing the song of the hermit bird and the tallying song of my soul,
Victorious song, death's outlet song, yet varying ever-altering song,
As low and wailing, yet clear the notes, rising and falling, flooding
    the night,
Sadly sinking and fainting, as warning and warning, and yet again
    bursting with joy,
Covering the earth and filling the spread of the heaven,
As that powerful psalm in the night I heard from recesses,
Passing, I leave thee lilac with heart-shaped leaves,
I leave thee there in the dooryard, blooming, returning with spring.

I cease from my song for thee,
From my gaze on thee in the west, fronting the west, cummuning
    with thee,
O comrade lustrous with silver face in the night.

Yet each to keep and all, retrievements out of the night,
The song, the wondrous chant of the gray-brown bird,
And the tallying chant, the echo arous'd in my soul,
With the lustrous and drooping star with the countenance full of
    woe,
With the holders holding my hand nearing the call of the bird,
Comrades mine and I in the midst, and their menory ever to keep,
    for the dead I loved so well,
For the sweetest, wisest soul of all my days and lands—and this for
    his dear sake,
Lilac and star and bird twined with the chant of my soul,
There in the fragrant pines and the cedars dusk and dim.

I HEAR AMERICA SINGING

I hear America singing, the varied carols I hear,
Those of mechanics, each one singing his as it should be blithe and
    strong,
The carpenter singing his as he measures his plank or beam,
The mason singing his as he makes ready for work, or leaves off
    work,
The boatman singing what belongs to him in his boat, the deckhand
    singing on the steamboat deck,

The shoemaker singing as he sits on his bench, the hatter singing as he stands,
The wood-cutter's song, the ploughboy's on his way in the morning, or at noon intermission or at sundown,
The delicious singing of the mother, or of the young wife at work, or of the girl sewing or washing,
Each singing what belongs to him or her and to none else,
The day what belongs to the day—at night the party of young fellows, robust, friendly,
Singing with open mouths their strong melodious songs.

A NOISELESS, PATIENT SPIDER

A noiseless, patient spider,
I marked, where, on a little promontory, it stood isolated;
Marked how, to explore the vacant, vast surrounding,
It launched forth filament, filament, filament, out of itself;
Ever unreeling them—ever tirelessly speeding them.

And you, O my Soul, where you stand,
Surrounded, surrounded, in measureless oceans of space,
Ceaselessly musing, venturing, throwing,—seeking the spheres, to connect them;
Till the bridge you will need, be formed—till the ductile anchor hold;
Till the gossamer thread you fling, catch somewhere, O my Soul.

ONCE I PASS'D THROUGH A POPULOUS CITY

Once I pass'd through a populous city imprinting my brain for future use with its shows, architecture, customs, traditions,
Yet now of all that city I remember only a woman I casually met there who detain'd me for love of me,
Day by day and night by night we were together—all else has long been forgotten by me,
I remember I say only that woman who passionately clung to me,
Again we wander, we love, we separate again,
Again she holds me by the hand, I must not go,
I see her close beside me with silent lips sad and tremulous.

A GLIMPSE

A glimpse through an interstice caught,
Of a crowd of workmen and drivers in a bar-room around the stove
    late of a winter night, and I unremark'd seated in a corner,
Of a youth who loves me and whom I love, silently approaching and
    seating himself near, that he may hold me by the hand,
A long while amid the noises of coming and going, of drinking and
    oath and smutty jest,
There we two, content, happy in being together, speaking little,
    perhaps not a word.

WHEN I HEARD THE LEARN'D ASTRONOMER

When I heard the learn'd astronomer,
When the proofs, the figures, were ranged in columns before me,
When I was shown the charts and diagrams, to add, divide, and
    measure them,
When I sitting heard the astronomer where he lectured with much
    applause in the lecture-room,
How soon unaccountable I became tired and sick,
Till rising and gliding out I wander'd off by myself,
In the mystical moist night-air, and from time to time,
Look'd up in perfect silence at the stars.

AS I LAY WITH MY HEAD IN YOUR LAP CAMERADO

As I lay with my head in your lap camerado,
The confession I made I resume, what I said to you and the open air
    I resume,
I know I am restless and make others so,
I know my words are weapons full of danger, full of death,
For I confront peace, security, and all the settled laws, to unsettle
    them,
I am more resolute because all have denied me than I could ever
    have been had all accepted me,
I heed not and have never heeded either experience, cautions,
    majorities, nor ridicule,
And the threat of what is call'd hell is little or nothing to me,

And the lure of what is call'd heaven is little or nothing to me;
Dear camerado! I confess I have urged you onward with me, and
    still urge you, without the least idea what is our destination,
Or whether we shall be victorious, or utterly quell'd and defeated.

I SIT AND LOOK OUT

I sit and look out upon all the sorrows of the world, and upon all
    oppression and shame,
I hear secret convulsive sobs from young men at anguish with
    themselves, remorseful after deeds done,
I see in low life the mother misused by her children, dying, neglected,
    gaunt, desperate,
I see the wife misused by her husband, I see the treacherous seducer
    of young women,
I mark the ranklings of jealousy and unrequited love attempted to be
    hid, I see these sights on the earth,
I see the workings of battle, pestilence, tyranny, I see martyrs and
    prisoners,
I observe a famine at sea, I observe the sailors casting lots who shall
    be kill'd to preserve the lives of the rest,
I observe the slights and degradations cast by arrogant persons upon
    laborers, the poor, and upon negroes, and the like;
All these—all the meanness and agony without end I sitting look out
    upon,
See, hear, and am silent.

OUT OF THE CRADLE ENDLESSLY ROCKING

Out of the cradle endlessly rocking,
Out of the mocking-bird's throat, the musical shuttle,
Out of the Ninth-month midnight,
Over the sterile sands and the fields beyond, where the child leaving
    his bed wandered alone, bareheaded, barefoot,
Down from the showered halo,
Up from the mystic play of shadows twining and twisting as if they
    were alive,
Out from the patches of briers and blackberries,
From the memories of the bird that chanted to me,
From your memories, sad brother, from the fitful risings and fallings
    I heard,

From under that yellow half-moon late-risen and swollen as if with
 tears,
From those beginning notes of yearning and love there in the mist,
From the thousand responses of my heart never to cease.
From the myriad thence-aroused words,
From the word stronger and more delicious than any,
From such as now they start the scene revisiting,
As a flock, twittering, rising, or overhead passing,
Borne hither, ere all eludes me, hurriedly,
A man, yet by these tears a little boy again,
Throwing myself on the sand, confronting the waves,
I, chanter of pains and joys, uniter of here and hereafter,
Taking all hints to use them, but swiftly leaping beyond them,
A reminiscence sing.
Once Paumanok,
When the lilac-scent was in the air and Fifth-month grass was
 growing,
Up this seashore in some briers,
Two feathered guests from Alabama, two together,
And their nest, and four light-green eggs spotted with brown,
And every day the he-bird to and fro near at hand,
And every day the she-bird crouched on her nest, silent, with bright
 eyes,
And every day I, a curious boy, never too close, never disturbing
 them,
Cautiously peering, absorbing, translating.

Shine! shine! shine!
Pour down your warmth, great sun!
While we bask, we two together.

Two together!
Winds blow south, or winds blow north,
Day come white, or night come black,
Home, or rivers and mountains from home,
Singing all time, minding no time,
While we two keep together.

Till of a sudden,
Maybe killed, unknown to her mate,
One forenoon the she-bird crouched not on the nest,
Nor returned that afternoon, nor the next,
Nor ever appeared again.

And thenceforward all summer in the sound of the sea,
And at night under the full of the moon in calmer weather,
Over the hoarse surging of the sea,
Or flitting from brier to brier by day,
I saw, I heard at intervals the remaining one, the he-bird,
The solitary guest from Alabama.

Blow! blow! blow!
Blow up sea-winds along Paumanok's shore;
I wait and I wait till you blow my mate to me.

Yes, when the stars glistened,
All night long on the prong of a moss-scalloped stake,
Down almost amid the slapping waves,
Sat the lone singer, wonderful, causing tears.

He called on his mate,
He poured forth the meanings which I of all men know.

Yes, my brother, I know,—
The rest might not, but I have treasured every note,
For more than once dimly down to the beach gliding,
Silent, avoiding the moonbeams, blending myself with the shadows,
Recalling now the obscure shapes, the echoes, the sounds and sights
     after their sorts,
The white arms out in the breakers tirelessly tossing,
I, with bare feet, a child, the wind wafting my hair,
Listened long and long.

Listened to keep, to sing, now translating the notes,
Following you, my brother.

Soothe! soothe! soothe!
Close on its wave soothes the wave behind,
And again another behind embracing and lapping, every one close,
But my love soothes not me, not me.

Low hangs the moon, it rose late,
It is lagging—O I think it is heavy with love, with love.

O madly the sea pushes upon the land,
With love, with love.

O night! do I not see my love fluttering out among the breakers?
What is that little black thing I see there in the white?

Loud! loud! loud!
Loud I call to you, my love!

High and clear I shoot my voice over the waves,
Surely you must know who is here, is here,
You must know who I am, my love.
Low-hanging moon!
What is that dusky spot in your brown yellow?
O it is the shape, the shape of my mate!
O moon, do not keep her from me any longer.

Land! land! O land!
Whichever way I turn, O, I think you could give me my mate back
    again if you only would,
For I am almost sure I see her dimly whichever way I look.

O rising stars!
Perhaps the one I want so much will rise, will rise with some of
    you.

O throat! O trembling throat!
Sound clearer through the atmosphere!
Pierce the woods, the earth,
Somewhere listening to catch you must be the one I want.

Shake out carols!
Solitary here, the night's carols!
Carols of lonesome love! death's carols!
Carols under that lagging, yellow, waning moon!
O under that moon where she droops almost down into the sea!
O reckless despairing carols!

But soft! sink low!
Soft! let me just murmur,
And do you wait a moment, you husky-noised sea,
For somewhere I believe I heard my mate responding to me,
So faint, I must be still, be still to listen,
But not altogether still, for then she might not come immediately to
    me.

Hither, my love!
Here I am! here!
With this just-sustained note I announce myself to you,
This gentle call is for you, my love, for you.

Do not be decoyed elsewhere:
That is the whistle of the wind, it is not my voice,
That is the fluttering, the fluttering of the spray,
Those are the shadows of leaves.

A darkness! O in vain!
O I am very sick and sorrowful.
O brown halo in the sky near the moon, drooping upon the sea!
O troubled reflection in the sea!
O throat! O throbbing heart!
And I singing uselessly! uselessly all the night.

O past! O happy life! O songs of joy!
In the air, in the woods, over fields,
Loved! loved! loved! loved! loved!
But my mate no more, no more with me!
We two together no more.

The aria sinking,
All else continuing, the stars shining,
The winds blowing, the notes of the bird continuous echoing,
With angry moans the fierce old mother incessantly moaning,
On the sands of Paumanok's shore gray and rustling,
The yellow half-moon enlarged, sagging down, drooping, the face of
      the sea almost touching,
The boy ecstatic, with his bare feet the waves, with his hair the
      atmosphere dallying,
The love in the heart long pent, now loose, now at last tumultuously
      bursting,
The aria's meaning, the ears, the soul, swiftly depositing,
The strange tears down the cheeks coursing,
The colloquy there, the trio, each uttering,
The undertone, the savage old mother incessantly crying,
To the boy's soul's questions sullenly timing, some drown'd secret
      hissing,
To the outsetting bard.
Demon or bird! (said the boy's soul)
Is it indeed toward your mate you sing? or is it really to me?

For I, that was a child, my tongue's use sleeping, now I have heard
    you,
Now in a moment I know what I am for, I awake,
And already a thousand singers, a thousand songs, clearer, louder
    and more sorrowful than yours,
A thousand warbling echoes have started to life within me, never to
    die.

O you singers solitary, singing by yourself, projecting me,
O solitary me listening, never more shall I cease perpetuating you,
Never more shall I escape, never more the reverberations,
Never more the cries of unsatisfied love be absent from me,
Never again leave me to be the peaceful child I was before what
    there in the night,
By the sea under the yellow and sagging moon,
The messenger there aroused, the fire, the sweet hell within,
The unknown want, the destiny of me.
O give me the clew! (it lurks in the night here somewhere)
O if I am to have so much, let me have more!

A word then, (for I will conquer it)
The word final, superior to all,
Subtle, sent up—what is it?—I listen;
Are you whispering it, and have been all the time, you sea-waves?
Is that it from your liquid rims and wet sands?
Whereto answering, the sea,
Delaying not, hurrying not,
Whispered me through the night, and very plainly before daybreak,
Lisped to me the low and delicious word death,
And again death, death, death, death,
Hissing melodious, neither like the bird nor like my aroused child's
    heart,
But edging near as privately for me, rustling at my feet,
Creeping thence steadily up to my ears and laving me softly all over,
Death, death, death, death, death.

Which I do not forget,
But fuse the song of my dusky demon and brother,
That he sang to me in the moonlight on Paumanok's gray beach,
With the thousand responsive songs at random,
My own songs awakened from that hour,
And with them the key, the word up from the waves,
The word of the sweetest song and all songs,
That strong and delicious word which, creeping to my feet,

(Or like some old crone rocking the cradle, swathed in sweet
    garments, bending aside)
The sea whispered me.

MIRACLES

Why, who makes much of a miracle?
As to me I know of nothing else but miracles,
Whether I walk the streets of Manhattan,
Or dart my sight over the roofs of houses toward the sky,
Or wade with naked feet along the beach just in the edge of the
    water,
Or stand under trees in the woods,
Or talk by day with any one I love,
Or sit at table at dinner with the rest,
Or look at strangers opposite me riding in the car,
Or watch honey-bees busy around the hive of a summer forenoon,
Or animals feeding in the fields,
Or the wonderfulness of the sundown, or of stars shining so quiet
    and bright,
Or the exquisite delicate thin curve of the new moon in spring;
These with the rest, one and all, are to me miracles,
The whole referring, yet each distinct and in its place.
To me every hour of the light and dark is a miracle,
Every cubic inch of space is a miracle,
Every square yard of the surface of the earth is spread with the
    same,
Every foot of the interior swarms with the same.

To me the sea is a continual miracle,
The fishes that swim—the rocks—the motion of the waves—the
    ships with men in them,
What stranger miracles are there?

DIRGE FOR TWO VETERANS

The last sunbeam
Lightly falls from the finished Sabbath,
On the pavement here, and there beyond it is looking,
    Down a new-made double grave,

Lo, the moon ascending,
Up from the east the silvery round moon,
Beautiful over the house-tops ghastly, phantom moon,
   Immense and silent moon.

I see a sad procession,
And I hear the sound of coming full-key'd bugles,
All the channels of the city streets they're flooding,
   As with voices and with tears.

I hear the great drums pounding,
And the small drums steady whirring,
And every blow of the great convulsive drums,
   Strikes me through and through.

For the son is brought with the father,
(On the foremost ranks of the fierce assault they fell,
Two veterans son and father dropt together,
   And the double grave awaits them).

Now nearer blow the bugles,
And the drums strike more convulsive,
And the daylight o'er the pavement quite has faded,
   And the strong dead-march enwraps me.

In the eastern sky up-buoying,
The sorrowful vast phantom moves illumin'd,
('Tis some mother's large transparent face,
   In heaven brighter growing).

O strong dead-march, you please me!
O moon immense with your silvery face, you soothe me!
O my soldiers twain! O my veterans passing to burial!
   What I have I also give you.

The moon gives you light,
And the bugles and the drums give you music,
And my heart, O my soldiers, my veterans,
   My heart gives you love.

COME UP FROM THE FIELDS, FATHER

Come up from the fields, father, here's a letter from our Pete,
And come to the front door, mother, here's a letter from thy dear
    son.

Lo, 'tis autumn,
Lo, where the trees, deeper green, yellower and redder,
Cool and sweeten Ohio's villages with leaves fluttering in the
    moderate wind,
Where apples ripe in the orchards hang and grapes on the trellis'd
    vines,
(Smell you the smell of the grapes on the vines?
Smell you the buckwheat where the bees were lately buzzing?)
Above all, lo, the sky so calm, so transparent after the rain and with
    wondrous clouds,
Below too, all calm, all vital and beautiful, and the farm prospers
    well.

Down in the fields all prospers well,
But now from the fields come father, come at the daughter's call,
And come to the entry mother, to the front door come right away.
Fast as she can she hurries, something ominous, her steps trembling,
She does not tarry to smooth her hair nor adjust her cap.

Open the envelope quickly,
O this is not our son's writing, yet his name is sign'd,
O a strange hand writes for our dear son, O stricken mother's soul!

All swims before her eyes, flashes with black, she catches the main
    words only,
Sentences broken, *gunshot wound in the breast, cavalry skirmish,
taken to hospital,*
At present low, but will soon be better.

Ah now the single figure to me,
Amid all teeming and wealthy Ohio with all its cities and farms,
Sickly white in the face and dull in the head, very faint,
By the jamb of a door leans.

Grieve not so, dear mother, (the just-grown daughter speaks
    through her sobs,
The little sisters huddle around speechless and dismay'd,)
See dearest mother, the letter says Pete will soon be better.

Alas poor boy, he will never be better, (nor may-be needs to be better that brave and simple soul,)
While they stand at home at the door he is dead already,
The only son is dead.

But the mother needs to be better,
She with thin form presently drest in black,
By day her meals untouch'd, then at night fitfully sleeping, often waking,
In the midnight waking, weeping, longing with one deep longing,
O that she might withdraw unnoticed, silent from life escape and withdraw,
To follow, to seek, to be with her dear dead son.

BEAT! BEAT! DRUMS!

Beat! beat! drums!—blow! bugles! blow!
Through the windows—through doors—burst like a ruthless force,
Into the solemn church, and scatter the congregation,
Into the school where the scholar is studying;
Leave not the bridegroom quiet—no happiness must he have now with his bride,
Not the peaceful farmer any peace, ploughing his field or gathering his grain,
So fierce you whirr and pound you drums—so shrill you bugles blow.

Beat! beat! drums!—blow! bugles! blow!
Over the traffic of cities—over the rumble of wheels in the streets;
Are beds prepared for sleepers at night in the houses? no sleepers must sleep in those beds,
No bargainers' bargains by day—no brokers or speculators—would they continue?
Would the talkers be talking? would the singer attempt to sing?
Would the lawyer rise in the court to state his case before the judge?
Then rattle quicker, heavier drums—you bugles wilder blow.

Beat! beat! drums!—blow! bugles! blow!
Make no parley—stop for no expostulation,
Mind not the timid—mind not the weeper or prayer,
Mind not the old man beseeching the young man,
Let not the child's voice be heard, nor the mother's entreaties,

Make even the trestles to shake the dead where they lie awaiting the
hearses,
So strong you thump O terrible drums—so loud you bugles blow.

Herman Melville

(1819–1891)

Herman Melville was one of America's greatest writers, although he was never able to savor that reputation during his lifetime. In 1830 his father went bankrupt, a state of affairs that probably hastened his death. In order to support his family Melville worked as a clerk, salesman, and teacher before signing on for a short stint as a cabin boy in 1839. Following that job he traveled through the middle states and then, in 1841, signed on as a seaman on a whaler. Eventually he deserted, but ended up on another ship whose crew mutinied. After a short imprisonment in Tahiti, he moved to Hawaii, and in 1844 returned to Boston. During the next twenty years he wrote more than a dozen books—novels, including *Typee, Mardi,* and, of course, *Moby-Dick;* a volume of short stories; and at least one travel journal. But Melville's work was not well received, and he failed to gain the readership he truly deserved. During the latter years of his life Melville's writing was restricted mainly to poetry.

THE MALDIVE SHARK

About the Shark, phlegmatical one,
Pale sot of the Maldive sea,
The sleek little pilot-fish, azure and slim,
How alert in attendance be.
From his saw-pit of mouth, from his charnel of maw
They have nothing of harm to dread,
But liquidly glide on his ghastly flank
Or before his Gorgonian head;
Or lurk in the port of serrated teeth
In white triple tiers of glittering gates,

And there find a haven when peril's abroad,
An asylum in jaws of the Fates!
They are friends; and friendly they guide him to prey,
Yet never partake of the treat—
Eyes and brains to the dotard lethargic and dull,
Pale ravener of horrible meat.

L'ENVOI

The Return of the Sire De Nesle
A.D. 16—

My towers at last! These rovings end,
Their thirst is slaked in larger dearth:
The yearning infinite recoils,
    For terrible is earth.

Kaf thrusts his snouted crags through fog:
Araxes swells beyond his span,
And knowledge poured by pilgrimage
    Overflows the banks of man.

But thou, my stay, thy lasting love
One lonely good, let this but be!
Weary to view the wide world's swarm,
    But blest to fold but thee.

IN A GARRET

Gems and jewels let them heap—
    Wax sumptuous as the Sophi:
For me, to grapple from Art's deep
    One dripping trophy!

THE BENCH OF BOORS

In bed I muse on Tenier's boors,
Embrowned and beery losels all:
    A wakeful brain
    Elaborates pain:

Within low doors the slugs of boors
Laze and yawn and doze again.

In dreams they doze, the drowsy boors,
Their hazy hovel warm and small:
   Thought's ampler bound
   But chill is found:
Within low doors the basking boors
Snugly hug the ember-mound.

Sleepless, I see the slumberous boors
Their blurred eyes blink, their eyelids fall:
   Thought's eager sight
   Aches—overbright!
Within low doors the boozy boors
Cat-naps take in pipe-bowl light.

THE PORTENT

1859

Hanging from the beam,
   Slowly swaying (such the law),
Gaunt the shadow on your green, Shenandoah!
The cut is on the crown
(Lo, John Brown),
And the stabs shall heal no more.

Hidden in the cap
   Is the anguish none can draw;
So your future veils its face, Shenandoah!
But the streaming beard is shown
(Weird John Brown),
The meteor of the war.

SHILOH
A REQUIEM

April, 1862

Skimming lightly, wheeling still,
   The swallows fly low

Over the fields in clouded days,
　　The forest-field of Shiloh—
Over the field where April rain
Solaced the parched one stretched in pain
Through the pause of night
That followed the Sunday fight
　　Around the church of Shiloh—
The church so lone, the log-built one,
That echoed to many a parting groan
　　　And natural prayer
　　Of dying foemen mingled there—
Foemen at morn, but friends at eve—
　　Fame or country least their care:
(What like a bullet can undeceive!)
　　But now they lie low,
While over them the swallows skim,
　　And all is hushed at Shiloh.

THE ATTIC LANDSCAPE

Tourist, spare the avid glance
　　That greedy roves the sight to see:
Little here of "Old Romance,"
　　Or Picturesque of Tivoli.

No flushful tint the sense to warm—
Pure outline pale, a linear charm.
The clear-cut hills carved temples face,
Respond, and share their sculptural grace.

THE LOVER AND THE SYRINGA-BUSH

Like a lit-up Christmas Tree,
　　Like a grotto pranked with spars,
Like white corals in green sea,
　　Like night's sky of crowded stars—
To me like these you show, Syringa
　　Such heightening power has love, believe,
While here by Eden's gate I linger
　　Love's tryst to keep, with truant Eve.

Thomas Buchanan Read

(1822–1872)

Born in Guthriesville, Pennsylvania, Thomas Buchanan Read was a portrait painter by trade. He wrote a few volumes of poetry and also edited a collection called *The Female Poets of America*. "Sheridan's Ride" is his best-known poem.

DRIFTING

My soul to-day
Is far away,
Sailing the Vesuvian Bay;
My wingèd boat,
A bird afloat,
Swings round the purple peaks remote:—

Round purple peaks
It sails, and seeks
Blue inlets and their crystal creeks,
Where high rocks throw,
Through deeps below,
A duplicated golden glow.

Far, vague, and dim,
The mountains swim;
While on Vesuvius' misty brim,
With outstretched hands,
The gray smoke stands
O'erlooking the volcanic lands.

Here Ischia smiles
O'er liquid miles;
And yonder, bluest of the isles,
Calm Capri waits,
Her sapphire gates
Beguiling to her bright estates.

I heed not, if
My rippling skiff
Float swift or slow from cliff to cliff;
With dreamful eyes
My spirit lies
Under the walls of Paradise.

Under the walls
Where swells and falls
The Bay's deep breast at intervals,
At peace I lie,
Blown softly by
A cloud upon this liquid sky.

The day, so mild,
Is Heaven's own child,
With Earth and Ocean reconciled;
The airs I feel
Around me steal
Are murmuring to the murmuring keel.

Over the rail
My hand I trail
Within the shadow of the sail,
A joy intense,
The cooling sense
Glides down my drowsy indolence.

With dreamful eyes
My spirit lies
Where Summer sings and never dies,—
O'erveiled with vines
She glows and shines
Among her future oil and wines.

Her children, hid
The cliffs amid,

Are gamboling with the gamboling kid;
  Or down the walls,
  With tipsy calls,
Laugh on the rocks like waterfalls.

  The fisher's child,
  With tresses wild,
Under the smooth, bright sand beguiled,
  With glowing lips,
  Sings as she skips,
Or gazes at the far-off ships.

  Yon deep bark goes
  Where traffic blows,
From lands of sun to lands of snows;
  This happier one,—
  Its course is run
From lands of snow to lands of sun.

  O happy ship,
  To rise and dip,
With the blue crystal at your lip!
  O happy crew,
  My heart with you
Sails, and sails, and sings anew!

  No more, no more
  The worldly shore
 Upbraids me with its loud uproar:
  With dreamful eyes
  My spirit lies
Under the walls of Paradise!

SHERIDAN'S RIDE

Up from the South at break of day,
Bringing to Winchester fresh dismay,
The affrighted air with a shudder bore,
Like a herald in haste, to the chieftain's door,
The terrible grumble and rumble and roar,
Telling the battle was on once more,
And Sheridan twenty miles away.

And wider still those billows of war
Thundered along the horizon's bar,
And louder yet into Winchester rolled
The roar of that red sea uncontrolled,
Making the blood of the listener cold
As he thought of the stake in that fiery fray,
With Sheridan twenty miles away.

But there is a road from Winchester town,
A good, broad highway leading down;
And there through the flash of the morning light,
A steed as black as the steeds of night,
Was seen to pass as with eagle flight.
As if he knew the terrible need,
He stretched away with the utmost speed;
Hills rose and fell,—but his heart was gay,
With Sheridan fifteen miles away.

Under his spurning feet the road
Like an arrowy Alpine river flowed,
And the landscape sped away behind
Like an ocean flying before the wind;
And the steed, like a bark fed with furnace ire,
Swept on with his wild eyes full of fire;
But, lo! he is nearing his heart's desire,
He is snuffing the smoke of the roaring fray,
With Sheridan only five miles away.

The first that the General saw were the groups
Of stragglers, and then the retreating troops;
What was done,—what to do,—a glance told him both,
And, striking his spurs with a terrible oath,
He dashed down the line mid a storm of huzzas,
And the wave of retreat checked its course there because
The sight of the master compelled it to pause.
With foam and with dust the black charger was gray,
By the flash of his eye, and his nostril's play
He seemed to the whole great army to say,
"I have brought you Sheridan all the way
From Winchester, down to save the day!"

Hurrah, hurrah for Sheridan!
Hurrah, hurrah for horse and man!
And when their statues are placed on high,

Under the dome of the Union sky,—
The American soldier's Temple of Fame,—
There with the glorious General's name
Be it said in letters both bold and bright:
"Here is the steed that saved the day
By carrying Sheridan into the fight,
From Winchester,—twenty miles away!"

THE ANGLER

But look! o'er the fall see the angler stand,
Swinging his rod with skilful hand;
The fly at the end of his gossamer line
    Swims through the sun like a summer moth,
Till, dropt with a careful precision fine,
    It touches the pool beyond the froth.
A-sudden, the speckled hawk of the brook
Darts from his covert and seizes the hook.
Swift spins the reel; with easy slip
The line pays out, and the rod like a whip,
Lithe and arrowy, tapering, slim,
Is bent to a bow o'er the brooklet's brim,
Till the trout leaps up in the sun, and flings
The spray from the flash of his finny wings;
Then falls on his side, and, drunken with fright,
    Is towed to the shore like a staggering barge,
    Till beached at last on the sandy marge,
Where he dies with the hues of the morning light,
While his sides with a cluster of stars are bright.
The angler in his basket lays
The constellation, and goes his ways.

THE CLOSING SCENE

Within the sober realm of leafless trees,
    The russet year inhaled the dreamy air;
Like some tanned reaper, in his hour of ease,
    When all the fields are lying brown and bare.

The gray barns looking from their hazy hills,
    O'er the dun waters widening in the vales,

Sent down the air a greeting to the mills,
    On the dull thunder of alternate flails.

All sights were mellowed and all sounds subdued,
    The hills seemed further and the stream sang low,
As in a dream the distant woodman hewed
    His winter log with many a muffled blow.

The embattled forests, erewhile armed with gold,
    Their banners bright with every martial hue,
Now stood like some sad, beaten host of old,
    Withdrawn afar in Time's remotest blue.

On sombre wings the vulture tried his flight;
    The dove scarce heard his sighing mate's complaint;
And, like a star slow drowning in the light,
    The village church vane seemed to pale and faint.

The sentinel cock upon the hillside crew,—
    Crew thrice,—and all was stiller than before;
Silent, till some replying warden blew
    His alien horn, and then was heard no more.

Where erst the jay, within the elm's tall crest,
    Made garrulous trouble round her unfledged young;
And where the oriole hung her swaying nest,
    By every light wind like a censer swung;

Where sang the noisy martens of the eves,
    The busy swallows circling ever near,—
Foreboding, as the rustic mind believes,
    An early harvest and a plenteous year;

Where every bird that waked the vernal feast
    Shook the sweet slumber from its wings at morn,
To warn the reaper of the rosy east;—
    All now was sunless, empty, and forlorn.

Alone, from out the stubble, piped the quail;
    And croaked the crow through all the dreary gloom;
Alone, the pheasant, drumming in the vale,
    Made echo in the distance to the cottage-loom.

There was no bud, no bloom upon the bowers;
  The spiders moved their thin shrouds night by night,
The thistle-down, the only ghost of flowers,
  Sailed slowly by,—passed noiseless out of sight.

Amid all this—in this most dreary air,
  And where the woodbine shed upon the porch
Its crimson leaves, as if the year stood there,
  Firing the floor with its inverted torch,—

Amid all this, the centre of the scene,
  The white-haired matron, with monotonous tread,
Plied the swift wheel, and with her joyless mien
  Sat like a fate, and watched the flying thread.

She had known Sorrow. He had walked with her,
  Oft supped, and broke with her the ashen crust,
And in the dead leaves still she heard the stir
  Of his thick mantle trailing in the dust.

While yet her cheek was bright with summer bloom,
  Her country summoned and she gave her all;
And twice War bowed to her his sable plume,—
  Re-gave the sword to rust upon the wall.

Re-gave the sword, but not the hand that drew
  And struck for liberty the dying blow;
Nor him who, to his sire and country true,
  Fell 'mid the ranks of the invading foe.

Long, but not loud, the droning wheel went on,
  Like the low murmur of a hive at noon;
Long, but not loud, the memory of the gone
  Breathed through her lips a sad and tremulous tune.

At last the thread was snapped,—her head was bowed;
  Life dropped the distaff through her hands serene;
And loving neighbors smoothed her careful shroud,
  While death and winter closed the autumn scene.

THE BRAVE AT HOME

I

The maid who binds her warrior's sash
   With smile that well her pain dissembles,
The while beneath her drooping lash
   One starry tear-drop hangs and trembles,
Though Heaven alone records the tear,
   And Fame shall never know her story,
Her heart has shed a drop as dear
   As e'er bedewed the field of glory!

II

The wife who girds her husband's sword,
   Mid little ones who weep or wonder,
And bravely speaks the cheering word,
   What though her heart be rent asunder,
Doomed nightly in her dreams to hear
   The bolts of death around him rattle,
Hath shed as sacred blood as e'er
   Was poured upon the field of battle!

III

The mother who conceals her grief
   While to her breast her son she presses,
Then breathes a few brave words and brief,
   Kissing the patriot brow she blesses,
With no one but her secret God
   To know the pain that weighs upon her,
Sheds holy blood as e'er the sod
   Received on Freedom's field of honor!

George Henry Boker

(1823–1890)

George Henry Boker was born in Philadelphia, Pennsylvania, into a fairly wealthy family. He graduated from Princeton and traveled abroad. In 1871 he was appointed United States Minister to Turkey and later was appointed a minister to Russia. Boker is mostly known for his verse dramas.

A BALLAD OF SIR JOHN FRANKLIN

O, whither sail you, Sir John Franklin?
　　Cried a whaler in Baffin's Bay.
To know if between the land and the pole
　　I may find a broad sea way.

I charge you back, Sir John Franklin,
　　As you would live and thrive;
For between the land and the frozen pole
　　No man may sail alive.

But lightly laughed the stout Sir John,
　　And spoke unto his men:
Half England is wrong, if he be right;
　　Bear off to westward then.

O, whither sail you, brave Englishman?
　　Cried the little Esquimau.
Between your land and the polar star
　　My goodly vessels go.

Come down, if you would journey there,
　The little Indian said;
And change your cloth for fur clothing,
　Your vessel for a sled.

But lightly laughed the stout Sir John,
　And the crew laughed with him too:—
A sailor to change from ship to sled,
　I ween, were something new.

All through the long, long polar day,
　The vessels westward sped;
And wherever the sail of Sir John was blown,
　The ice gave way and fled:—

Gave way with many a hollow groan,
　And with many a surly roar,
But it murmured and threatened on every side,
　And closed where he sailed before.

Ho! see ye not, my merry men,
　The broad and open sea?
Bethink ye what the whaler said,
Think of the little Indian's sled!
　The crew laughed out in glee.

Sir John, Sir John, 'tis bitter cold,
　The scud drives on the breeze,
The ice comes looming from the north,
　The very sunbeams freeze.

Bright summer goes, dark winter comes,—
　We cannot rule the year;
But long ere summer's sun goes down,
　On yonder sea we'll steer.

The dripping icebergs dipped and rose,
　And floundered down the gale;
The ships were stayed, the yards were manned,
　And furled the useless sail.

The summer's gone, the winter's come,—
　We sail not on yonder sea:

Why sail we not, Sir John Franklin?—
   A silent man was he.

The summer goes, the winter comes,—
   We cannot rule the year:
I ween we cannot rule the ways,
   Sir John, wherein we'd steer.

The cruel ice came floating on,
   And closed beneath the lee,
Till the thickening waters dashed no more:
'Twas ice around, behind, before—
   My God! there is no sea!

What think you of the whaler now?
   What of the Esquimau?
A sled were better than a ship,
   To cruise through ice and snow.

Down sank the baleful crimson sun,
   The northern light came out,
And glared upon the ice-bound ships,
   And shook its spears about.

The snow came down, storm breeding storm,
   And on the decks was laid,
Till the weary sailor, sick at heart,
   Sank down beside his spade.

Sir John, the night is black and long,
   The hissing wind is bleak,
The hard, green ice as strong as death:—
   I prithee, Captain, speak!

The night is neither bright nor short,
   The singing breeze is cold,—
The ice is not so strong as hope,
   The heart of man is bold!

What hope can scale this icy wall,
   High over the main flagstaff?
Above the ridges the wolf and bear
Look down, with a patient, settled stare,
   Look down on us and laugh.

The summer went, the winter came,—
    We could not rule the year;
But summer will melt the ice again,
And open a path to the sunny main,
    Whereon our ships shall steer.

The winter went, the summer went,
    The winter came around;
But the hard, green ice was strong as death,
And the voice of hope sank to a breath,
    Yet caught at every sound.

Hark! heard you not the noise of guns?—
    And there, and there, again?
'Tis some uneasy iceberg's roar,
    As he turns in the frozen main.

Hurra! Hurra! the Esquimaux
    Across the ice fields steal:
God give them grace for their charity!—
    Ye pray for the silly seal.

Sir John, where are the English fields,
    And where are the English trees,
And where are the little English flowers
    That open in the breeze?

Be still, be still, my brave sailors!
    You shall see the fields again,
And smell the scent of the opening flowers,
    The grass, and the waving grain.

Oh! when shall I see my orphan child?
    My Mary waits for me.
Oh! when shall I see my old mother,
    And pray at her trembling knee?

Be still, be still, my brave sailors!
    Think not such thoughts again.
But a tear froze slowly on his cheek:
    He thought of Lady Jane.

Ah! bitter, bitter grows the cold,
    The ice grows more and more;

More settled stare the wolf and bear,
   More patient than before.

O, think you, good Sir John Franklin,
   We'll ever see the land?
'Twas cruel to send us here to starve,
   Without a helping hand.

'Twas cruel, Sir John, to send us here,
   So far from help or home,
To starve and freeze on this lonely sea
I ween the lords of the Admiralty
   Would rather send than come.

Oh! whether we starve to death alone,
   Or sail to our own country,
We have done what man has never done—
The truth is founded, the secret won—
   We passed the Northern Sea!

DIRGE FOR A SOLDIER

Close his eyes; his work is done!
   What to him is friend or foeman,
Rise of moon, or set of sun,
   Hand of man, or kiss of woman?
     Lay him low, lay him low,
     In the clover or the snow!
     What cares he? he cannot know:
     Lay him low!

As man may, he fought his fight,
   Proved his truth by his endeavor;
Let him sleep in solemn night,
   Sleep forever and forever.
     Lay him low, lay him low,
     In the clover or the snow!
     What cares he? he cannot know:
     Lay him low!

Fold him in his country's stars,
   Roll the drum and fire the volley!
What to him are all our wars,

What but death bemocking folly?
  Lay him low, lay him low,
  In the clover or the snow!
What cares he? he cannot know:
  Lay him low!

Leave him to God's watching eye,
  Trust him to the hand that made him.
Mortal love weeps idly by:
  God alone has power to aid him.
  Lay him low, lay him low,
  In the clover or the snow!
What cares he? he cannot know:
  Lay him low!

THE BLACK REGIMENT

May 27, 1863

Dark as the clouds of even,
Ranked in the western heaven,
Waiting the breath that lifts
All the dead mass, and drifts
Tempest and falling brand
Over a ruined land,—
So still and orderly,
Arm to arm, knee to knee,
Waiting the great event,
Stands the black regiment.

Down the long dusky line
Teeth gleam and eyeballs shine;
And the bright bayonet,
Bristling and firmly set,
Flashed with a purpose grand,
Long ere the sharp command
Of the fierce rolling drum
Told them their time had come,
Told them what work was sent
For the black regiment.

"Now," the flag-sergeant cried,
"Though death and hell betide,

Let the whole nation see
If we are fit to be
Free in this land; or bound
Down, like the whining hound,—
Bound with red stripes of pain
In our cold chains again!"
O, what a shout there went
From the black regiment!

"Charge!" Trump and drum awoke;
Onward the bondmen broke;
Bayonet and sabre-stroke
Vainly opposed their rush.
Through the wild battle's crush,
With but one thought aflush,
Driving their lords like chaff,
In the guns' mouths they laugh;
Or at the slippery brands
Leaping with open hands,
Down they tear man and horse,
Down in their awful course;
Trampling with bloody heel
Over the crashing steel,—
All their eyes forward bent,
Rushed the black regiment.

"Freedom!" their battle-cry,—
"Freedom! or leave to die!"
Ah! and they meant the word,
Not as with us 't is heard,
Not a mere party shout;
They gave their spirits out,
Trusted the end to God,
And on the gory sod
Rolled in triumphant blood,
Glad to strike one free blow,
Whether for weal or woe;
Glad to breathe one free breath,
Though on the lips of death;
Praying,—alas! in vain!—
That they might fall again,
So they could once more see
That burst to liberty!

This was what "freedom" lent
To the black regiment.

Hundreds on hundreds fell;
But they are resting well;
Scourges and shackles strong
Never shall do them wrong.
O, to the living few,
Soldiers, be just and true!
Hail them as comrades tried;
Fight with them side by side;
Never, in field or tent,
Scorn the black regiment!

Bayard Taylor

(1825–1878)

Bayard Taylor was born in Kennett Square, a small Quaker town in Pennsylvania, and was only a teenager when his first poetry was published. Taylor combined his extensive travel experiences with his writing. He lived the life of a vagabond in Europe for two years and was a gold digger in California. He reported on the historic gold rush of 1849. He worked for the U.S. diplomatic service in St. Petersburg, Russia, and in 1878 was appointed Minister to Berlin, but he died shortly after his arrival there. Taylor is best remembered for his translation of Goethe's *Faust*.

BEDOUIN SONG

From the Desert I come to thee
   On a stallion shod with fire;
And the winds are left behind
   In the speed of my desire.
Under thy window I stand,
   And the midnight hears my cry:
I love thee, I love but thee,
   With a love that shall not die
     Till the sun grows cold,
     And the stars are old,
     And the leaves of the Judgment
     Book unfold!

Look from thy window and see
   My passion and my pain;
I lie on the sands below,

And I faint in thy disdain.
Let the night winds touch thy brow
　With the heat of my burning sigh,
And melt thee to hear the vow
　Of a love that shall not die
　　Till the sun grows cold,
　　And the stars are old,
　　And the leaves of the Judgment
　　Book unfold!

My steps are nightly driven,
　By the fever in my breast,
To hear from thy lattice breathed
　The word that shall give me rest.
Open the door of thy heart,
　And open thy chamber door,
And my kisses shall teach thy lips
　The love that shall fade no more
　　Till the sun grows cold,
　　And the stars are old,
　　And the leaves of the Judgment
　　Book unfold!

AMERICA

From the National Ode, July 4, 1876

Foreseen in the vision of sages,
　Foretold when martyrs bled,
She was born on the longing of ages,
　By the truth of the noble dead
　And the faith of the living fed!
No blood in her lightest veins
Frets at remembered chains,
Nor shame of bondage has bowed her head.
　In her form and features still
　The unblenching Puritan will,
　Cavalier honor, Huguenot grace,
　The Quaker truth and sweetness,
And the strength of the danger-girdled race
Of Holland, blend in a proud completeness.
From the homes of all, where her being began,
　She took what she gave to Man;

Justice, that knew no station,
　　Belief, as soul decreed,
Free air for aspiration,
　Free force for independent deed!
　She takes, but to give again,
As the sea returns the rivers in rain;
And gathers the chosen of her seed
From the hunted of every crown and creed.
　Her Germany dwells by a gentler Rhine;
　Her Ireland sees the old sunburst shine;
　Her France pursues some stream divine;
　Her Norway keeps his mountain pine;
　Her Italy waits by the western brine;
　　And, broad-based under all,
Is planted England's oaken-hearted mood,
　　As rich in fortitude
As e'er went worldward from the island-wall!
　　Fused in her candid light,
To one strong race all races here unite;
Tongues melt in hers, hereditary foemen
Forget their sword and slogan, kith and clan.
　　'Twas glory, once, to be a Roman:
She makes it glory, now, to be a man!

THE BALLAD OF HIRAM HOVER

Where the Moosatockmaguntic
Pours its waters in the Skuntic,
　Met, along the forest side
　Hiram Hover, Huldah Hyde.

She, a maiden fair and dapper,
He, a red-haired, stalwart trapper,
　Hunting beaver, mink, and skunk
　In the woodlands of Squeedunk.

She, Pentucket's pensive daughter,
Walked beside the Skuntic water
　Gathering, in her apron wet,
　Snake-root, mint, and bouncing-bet.

"Why," he murmured, loth to leave her,
"Gather yarbs for chills and fever,

When a lovyer bold and true,
Only waits to gather you?"

"Go," she answered, "I'm not hasty,
I prefer a man more tasty;
    Leastways, one to please me well
    Should not have a beasty smell."

"Haughty Huldah!" Hiram answered,
"Mind and heart alike are cancered;
    Jest look here! these peltries give
    Cash, wherefrom a pair may live.

"I, you think, am but a vagrant,
Trapping beasts by no means fragrant;
    Yet, I'm sure it's worth a thank—
    I've a handsome sum in bank."

Turned and vanished Hiram Hover,
And, before the year was over,
    Huldah, with the yarbs she sold,
    Bought a cape, against the cold.

Black and thick the furry cape was,
Of a stylish cut the shape was;
    And the girls, in all the town,
    Envied Huldah up and down.

Then at last, one winter morning,
Hiram came without a warning.
    "Either," said he, "you are blind,
    Huldah, or you've changed your mind.

"Me you snub for trapping varmints,
Yet you take the skins for garments;
    Since you wear the skunk and mink,
    There's no harm in me, I think."

"Well," said she, "we will not quarrel,
Hiram; I accept the moral,
    Now the fashion's so I guess
    I can't hardly do no less."

Thus the trouble all was over
Of the love of Hiram Hover.
    Thus he made sweet Huldah Hyde
    Huldah Hover as his bride.

Love employs, with equal favor,
Things of good and evil savor;
    That which first appeared to part,
    Warmed, at last, the maiden's heart.

Under one impartial banner,
Life, the hunter, Love the tanner,
    Draw, from every beast they snare,
    Comfort for a wedded pair!

PALABRAS GRANDIOSAS

After T—B—A—

I lay i' the bosom of the sun,
Under the roses dappled and dun.
I thought of the Sultan Gingerbeer,
In his palace beside the Bendemeer,
With his Afghan guards and his eunuchs blind,
And the harem that stretched for a league behind.

The tulips bent i' the summer breeze,
Under the broad chrysanthemum-trees,
And the minstrel, playing his culverin,
Made for mine ears a merry din.
If I were the Sultan, and he were I,
Here i' the grass he should loafing lie,
And I should bestride my zebra steed,
And ride to the hunt of the centipede:
While the pet of the harem, Dandeline,
Should fill me a crystal bucket of wine,
And the kislar aga, Up-to-Snuff,
Should wipe my mouth when I sighed, "Enough!"
And the gay court poet, Fearfulbore,
Should sit in the hall when the hunt was o'er,
And chant me songs of silvery tone,
Not from Hafiz, but—mine own!

Ah, wee sweet love, beside me here,
I am not the Sultan Gingerbeer,
Nor you the odalisque Dandeline,
Yet I am yourn, and you are mine!

ANGELO ORDERS HIS DINNER

I, Angelo, obese, black-garmented,
Respectable, much in demand, well fed
With mine own larder's dainties, where, indeed,
Such cakes of myrrh or fine alyssum seed,
Thin as a mallow-leaf, embrowned o' the top.
Which, cracking, lets the ropy, trickling drop
Of sweetness touch your tongue, or potted nests
Which my recondite recipe invests
With cold conglomerate tidbits—ah, the bill!
(You say), but given it were mine to fill
My chests, the case so put were yours, we'll say
(This counter, here, your post, as mine to-day),
And you've an eye to luxuries, what harm
In smoothing down your palate with the charm
Yourself concocted? There we issue take;
And see! as thus across the rim I break
This puffy paunch of glazed embroidered cake,
So breaks, through use, the lust of watering chaps
And craveth plainness: do I so? Perhaps;
But that's my secret. Find me such a man
As Lippo yonder, built upon the plan
Of heavy storage, double-navelled, fat
From his own giblet's oils, an Ararat
Uplift o'er water, sucking rosy draughts
From Noah's vineyard,—crisp, enticing wafts
Yon kitchen now emits, which to your sense
Somewhat abate the fear of old events,
Qualms to the stomach,—I, you see, am slow
Unnecessary duties to forego,—
You understand? A venison haunch, *haut gout*.
Ducks that in Cimbrian olives mildly stew.
And sprigs of anise, might one's teeth provoke
To taste, and so we wear the complex yoke
Just as it suits,—my liking, I confess,
More to receive, and to partake no less,
Still more obese, while through thick adipose

Sensation shoots, from testing tongue to toes
Far off, dim-conscious, at the body's verge,
Where the froth-whispers of its waves emerge
On the untasting sand. Stay, now! a seat
Is bare: I, Angelo, will sit and eat.

THE CANTELOPE

Side by side in the crowded streets,
    Amid its ebb and flow,
We walked together one autumn morn;
    ('Twas many years ago!)

The markets blushed with fruits and flowers;
    (Both Memory and Hope!)
You stopped and bought me at the stall,
    A spicy cantelope.

We drained together its honeyed wine,
    We cast the seeds away;
I slipped and fell on the moony rinds,
    And you took me home on a dray!

The honeyed wine of your love is drained;
    I limp from the fall I had;
The snow-flakes muffle the empty stall,
    And everything is sad.

The sky is an inkstand, upside down,
    It splashes the world with gloom;
The earth is full of skeleton bones,
    And the sea is a wobbling tomb!

THE PROMISSORY NOTE

In the lonesome latter years
    (Fatal years!)
To the dropping of my tears
Danced the mad and mystic spheres
In a rounded, reeling rune,
    'Neath the moon,
To the dripping and the dropping of my tears.

Ah, my soul is swathed in gloom,
        (Ulalume!)
In a dim Titanic tomb,
For my gaunt and gloomy soul
Ponders o'er the penal scroll,
O'er the parchment (not a rhyme),
Out of place,—out of time,—
I am shredded, shorn, unshifty,
        (Oh, the fifty!)
And the days have passed, the three,
        Over me!
And the debit and the credit are as one to him and me!

        'Twas the random runes I wrote
At the bottom of the note,
        (Wrote and freely
        Gave to Greeley)
In the middle of the night,
In the mellow, moonless night,
When the stars were out of sight,
When my pulses, like a knell,
        (Israfel!)
Danced with dim and dying fays
O'er the ruins of my days,
O'er the dimeless, timeless days,
When the fifty, drawn at thirty,
Seeming thrifty, yet the dirty
Lucre of the market, was the most that I could raise!

        Fiends controlled it,
        (Let him hold it!)
Devils held for me the inkstand and the pen;
        Now the days of grace are o'er,
        (Ah, Lenore!)
I am but as other men;
What is time, time, time,
To my rare and runic rhyme,
To my random, reeling rhyme,
By the sands along the shore,
Where the tempest whispers, "Pay him!" and I answer,
    "Nevermore!"

CAMERADOS

Everywhere, everywhere, following me;
Taking me by the buttonhole, pulling off my boots, hustling me
    with the elbows;
Sitting down with me to clams and the chowder-kettle;
Plunging naked at my side into the sleek, irascible surges;
Soothing me with the strain that I neither permit nor prohibit;
Flocking this way and that, reverent, eager, orotund, irrepressible;
Denser than sycamore leaves when the north-winds are scouring
    Paumanok;
What can I do to restrain them? Nothing, verily nothing.
Everywhere, everywhere, crying aloud for me;
Crying, I hear; and I satisfy them out of my nature;
And he that comes at the end of the feast shall find something over.
Whatever they want I give; though it be something else, they shall
    have it.
Drunkard, leper, Tammanyite, small-pox and cholera patient,
    shoddy and codfish millionnaire,
And the beautiful young men, and the beautiful young women, all
    the same,
Crowding, hundreds of thousands, cosmical multitudes,
Buss me and hang on my hips and lean up to my shoulders,
Everywhere listening to my yawp and glad whenever they hear it;
Everywhere saying, say it, Walt, we believe it:
Everywhere, everywhere.

THE SONG OF THE CAMP

"Give us a song!" the soldiers cried,
    The outer trenches guarding,
When the heated guns of the camps allied,
    Grew weary of bombarding.

The dark Redan, in silent scoff,
    Lay, grim and threatening, under;
And the tawny mound of the Malakoff
    No longer belched its thunder.

There was a pause. A guardsman said,
    "We storm the forts to-morrow;
Sing while we may, another day
    Will bring enough of sorrow."

They lay along the battery's side,
  Below the smoking cannon:
Brave hearts, from Severn and from Clyde,
  And from the banks of Shannon.

They sang of love, and not of fame;
  Forgot was Britain's glory:
Each heart recalled a different name,
  But all sang "Annie Laurie."

Voice after voice caught up the song,
  Until its tender passion
Rose like an anthem, rich and strong,—
  Their battle-eve confession.

Dear girl, her name he dared not speak,
  But, as the song grew louder,
Something upon the soldier's cheek
  Washed off the stains of powder.

Beyond the darkening ocean burned
  The bloody sunset's embers,
While the Crimean valleys learned
  How English love remembers.

And once again a fire of hell
  Rained on the Russian quarters,
With scream of shot, and burst of shell,
  And bellowing of the mortars!

And Irish Nora's eyes are dim
  For a singer, dumb and gory;
And English Mary mourns for him
  Who sang of "Annie Laurie."

Sleep, soldiers! still in honored rest
  Your truth and valor wearing:
The bravest are the tenderest,—
  The loving are the daring.

Richard Henry Stoddard

(1825–1903)

Richard Henry Stoddard was born in Hingham, Massachusetts, and moved with his family to New York in 1835, after his father, a sea captain, was lost at sea. Stoddard's reputation rests on his illustrious career as a literary reviewer for the *New York World* from 1860 to 1870 and the *New York Mail and Express* from 1880 to 1903.

"THERE ARE GAINS FOR ALL OUR LOSSES"

There are gains for all our losses,
    There are balms for all our pain:
But when youth, the dream, departs,
It takes something from our hearts,
    And it never comes again.

We are stronger, and are better,
    Under manhood's sterner reign:
Still we feel that something sweet
Followed youth, with flying feet,
    And will never come again.

Something beautiful is vanished,
    And we sigh for it in vain:
We behold it everywhere,
On the earth, and in the air,
    But it never comes again.

THE DYING LOVER

The grass that is under me now
  Will soon be over me, Sweet:
When you walk this way again,
  I shall not hear your feet.

You may walk this way again
  And shed your tears like dew:
They will be no more to me then
  Than mine are now to you.

ABRAHAM LINCOLN

Not as when some great Captain falls
In battle, where his Country calls,
  Beyond the struggling lines
  That push his dread designs

To doom, by some stray ball struck dead:
Or, in the last charge, at the head
  Of his determined men,
  Who *must* be victors then.

Nor as when sink the civic great,
The safer pillars of the State,
  Whose calm, mature, wise words
  Suppress the need of swords.

With no such tears as e'er were shed
Above the noblest of our dead
  Do we to-day deplore
  The Man that is no more.

Our sorrow hath a wider scope,
Too strange for fear, too vast for hope,
  A wonder, blind and dumb,
  That waits—what is to come!

Not more astounded had we been
If Madness, that dark night, unseen,
  Had in our chambers crept,
  And murdered while we slept!

We woke to find a mourning earth,
Our Lares shivered on the hearth,
   The roof-tree fallen, all
   That could affright, appall!

Such thunderbolts, in other lands,
Have smitten the rod from royal hands,
   But spared, with us, till now,
   Each laureled Cæsar's brow.

No Cæsar he whom we lament,
A Man without a precedent,
   Sent, it would seem, to do
   His work, and perish, too.

Not by the weary cares of State,
The endless tasks, which will not wait,
   Which, often done in vain,
   Must yet be done again:

Not in the dark, wild tide of war,
Which rose so high, and rolled so far,
   Sweeping from sea to sea
   In awful anarchy:

Four fateful years of mortal strife,
Which slowly drained the nation's life,
   (Yet for each drop that ran
   There sprang an armëd man!)

Not then; but when, by measures meet,
By victory, and by defeat,
   By courage, patience, skill,
   The people's fixed *"We will!"*

Had pierced, had crushed Rebellion dead,
Without a hand, without a head,
   At last, when all was well,
   He fell, O how he fell!

The time, the place, the stealing shape,
The coward shot, the swift escape,
   The wife—the widow's scream,—
   It is a hideous Dream!

A dream? What means this pageant, then?
These multitudes of solemn men,
   Who speak not when they meet,
   But throng the silent street?

The flags half-mast that late so high
Flaunted at each new victory?
   (The stars no brightness shed,
   But bloody looks the red!)

The black festoons that stretch for miles,
And turn the streets to funeral aisles?
   (No house too poor to show
   The nation's badge of woe.)

The cannon's sudden, sullen boom,
The bells that toll of death and doom,
   The rolling of the drums,
   The dreadful car that comes?

Cursed be the hand that fired the shot,
The frenzied brain that hatched the plot,
   Thy country's Father slain
   By thee, thou worse than Cain!

Tyrants have fallen by such as thou,
And good hath followed—may it now!
   (God lets bad instruments
   Produce the best events.)

But he, the man we mourn to-day,
No tyrant was: so mild a sway
   In one such weight who bore
   Was never known before.

Cool should he be, of balanced powers,
The ruler of a race like ours,
   Impatient, headstrong, wild,
   The Man to guide the Child.

And this *he* was, who most unfit
(So hard the sense of God to hit),
   Did seem to fill his place;
   With such a homely face,

Such rustic manners, speech uncouth,
(That somehow blundered out the truth),
   Untried, untrained to bear
   The more than kingly care.

Ah! And his genius put to scorn
The proudest in the purple born,
   Whose wisdom never grew
   To what, untaught, he knew,

The People, of whom he was one:
No gentleman, like Washington,
   (Whose bones, methinks, make room,
   To have him in their tomb!)

A laboring man, with horny hands,
Who swung the ax, who tilled his lands,
   Who shrank from nothing new,
   But did as poor men do.

One of the People! Born to be
Their curious epitome;
   To share yet rise above
   Their shifting hate and love.

O honest face, which all men knew!
O tender heart, but known to few!
   O wonder of the age,
   Cut off by tragic rage!

Peace! Let the long procession come,
For hark, the mournful, muffled drum,
   The trumpet's wail afar,
   And see, the awful car!

Peace! Let the sad procession go,
While cannon boom and bells toll slow.
   And go, thou sacred car,
   Bearing our woe afar!

Go, darkly borne, from State to State,
Whose loyal, sorrowing cities wait
   To honor all they can
   The dust of that good man.

Go, grandly borne, with such a train
As greatest kings might die to gain.
    The just, the wise, the brave,
    Attend thee to the grave.

And you, the soldiers of our wars,
Bronzed veterans, grim with noble scars,
    Salute him once again,
    Your late commander—slain!

So sweetly, sadly, sternly goes
The Fallen to his last repose.
    Beneath no mighty dome,
    But in his modest home;

The churchyard where his children rest,
The quiet spot that suits him best,
    There shall his grave be made,
    And there his bones be laid.

And there his countrymen shall come,
With memory proud, with pity dumb,
    And strangers far and near,
    For many and many a year.

For many a year and many an age,
While History on her ample page
    The virtues shall enroll
    Of that Paternal Soul.

THE ABDICATION OF NOMAN

Noman, the King of Hira, sat one day
In his pavilion, pitched at Karwanak,
With Bahram Gour, the son of Yezdejird,
And Adi Ibn Zeid, the Persian bard.
Cross-legged on scarlet cushions stuffed with down
They sat and smoked; the bubbling of their pipes
Was like a river in the land of sleep.
The curtain of the tent was drawn aside,
Looped up with golden cords; a twinkling gleam
Glanced from the tassels, smote the water-bowls,
And perished in the great sea-emerald

On Noman's turban: other light was none;
They lolled away the hours in purple dusk.

Before the doorway of the tent they saw
The palace park and garden bright with spring.
A pillared avenue of stately palms
Slept in the sun; a fountain rose and fell,
Breaking the silver surface at its base;
Gold-fish like sunken ingots lay in heaps
Beneath the fountain's rain; beside its rim,
Dipping his long bill in a lotus cup,
A black crane stooped; between the silent palms
A length of silken carpet was unrolled:
A white gazelle dangled a silver chain,
Picking its way through tufts of broidered flowers.
Flowers of all hues and odors streaked the ground,
Roses, fire-red, large tulips, cups of flame,
Banks of snow lilies turning dew to pearls,
And rolling rivers of anemonies,
The flowers that Noman loved; their crimson leaves
Were rubies set on stalks of emerald.
Broad meadows stretched afar wherein, dim-seen
Through winking haze, the still Euphrates lay—
The great Euphrates fresh from Babylon.

Between their whiffs of smoke with happy eyes
They drank the landscape in; to Bahram Gour
It grew his father's garden at Madain—
Save that the Emir's daughter was not there,
Whereat he sighed: his long beard Adi stroked,
And thrummed his idle fingers in the air,
Turning a couplet in his tuneful brain,
Noman alone was sad, for he nor had
The poet's idleness, nor prince's youth;
Grown gray in troubled rule he longed for rest,
But found it never: fair things made him grieve,
Because their lives are short. He saw the end.

"Why grasp at wealth and power? Why hoard up gold?
Or make our whims a law for other men?
Earth hides her gold in veinèd rocks and hills,
Packs it in river sands: we dig it out,
And stamp our Kingly faces in its light,
And call it ours. Does Earth give up her claim?

Not she, she calmly waits, and takes it back.
We sift the sands, dive down into the waves,
Ransack the caves for gems; Earth gives them up.
I have a hundred caskets full of pearls,
Ten chests of chrysolites, a turquoise plate
That holds a maund of corn, a chandelier,
The chains whereof are beryls linked with gold,
Its flame a ruby, found in Balashan.
Not mine, but Earth's; for I shall pass away,
I, and my race, but Earth will still remain,
And keep my gems; in palaces like mine,
To swell the treasury of future Kings,
Or, haply, in the caverns where they grew.

We build rich palaces, and wall them in,
Make parks and gardens near, plant trees, sow flowers,
And say, 'All this is ours!' But what says Earth?
She only smiles her still cold smile of scorn.
Forests a thousand parasangs in length
Are hers, and hers the tropic's zone of bloom,
And when we die our marble palaces—
She lets the jackal prowl about their courts.

My days have numbered five and sixty years,
Twenty and eight were passed upon the throne:
I count them lost. I may have gained some power,
Added a few wild tribes to those I rule,
And treasures to my treasure, but my life
(I had so little time to think of that)
Is not a whit the richer, save in cares.
Ah, who that knows himself would be a King?"

So spake the King the secret of his heart,
Like one who babbles to himself alone.
His head dropped on his bosom, and his beard
Hung in his lap: the shadow of his words
Drifted across the stream of Adi's thought,
And when the King had ended he began:

"Name me the King whose power was vast enough
To cope with Death, or cheat the Sepulchre.
Whither is Chosroes gone, the mightiest, he,
Of Persian Kings? Whither did Sapor go?

And they, the fair-haired race, the Romans lords—
Tell me why no memorial lives of them.
And he, the nameless King, who Hadhr built,
Where Khabur and the lordly Tigris flow.
He faced his palace walks with marble slabs,
Polished and white, and raised his roof so high,
His ridgy roofs, the birds made nests thereon,
The thought of dying never crossed his mind,
But not the less he died, and died alone;
For when Death came to that unhappy King
The very sentinels had fled his gates."

    "The end of all things must be near at hand,"
Said Bahram Gour, half earnest, half in jest,
"For lo, the world hath now two Solomons,
Whose wisdom is compressed in three small words,
The knell of Folly, 'All is Vanity!'
It may be so, my dear philosophers,
But are you free from blame? What says the song?
'It is my sight that fails me, not the rose
That waxes pale; my scent that is too coarse,
No lack of odor in the heavenly musk,'
Cry down the world who will, but Bahram Gour
Will love it still." "And I," the poet said,
His fancied sadness dying with the words
That gave it birth, "and never more than now,
When to the quiet tent and drowsy pipe
Succeeds the eager life on flying steeds."

    From out their marble stalls the dusky grooms
Led forth the royal stud of milk-white mares.
The falconers came next with hooded birds,
Each with a silver label on its leg;
And then the keepers with the beasts of chase
In chains, lithe panthers, and keen-scented dogs,
Tigers, whose tawny hides are mapped with black,
And lions trained to hunt,—the white gazelle
Fled from their cruel eyes to Noman's tent.
Slowly like one who wills away a dream,
Lifting his head the King called home his thoughts.
He saw the trembling creature at his feet,
And fondled it; the voice of Adi's lute,
Wooing a song, brought Adi to his mind,
The jingling of a scabbard Bahram Gour;

Adi still sat and smoked, but Bahram Gour
Had risen, and was girding on his sword.
"My sombre fancies led me from the chase;
But now that I have found myself once more
Let us depart at once. They wait for us."
He beckoned, and the grooms led up their steeds.

But the palms whose shadows struck their brows,
Launching across the carpet's bed of flowers,
Around the fountain's glittering mist they rode.
The fretful panthers snuffed, and tugged their chains,
The calmer lions, quiet in their strength,
Strode on, and dragged their keepers after them.

Not far from Hira by the river's side,
Where stood a ruined city was a tomb,
Between the river and the tomb were trees
Whose twinkling leaves were shaken by the wind.
Dropping the hunt before the game was roused
Thither the King and poet rode alone;
They saw the shaken boughs, but felt no wind.
"The leaves are tongues," said Noman, "and they speak,
With some grave message charged, or prophecy.
You read the hidden meaning of the flowers,
Can you expound the language of the trees?"

"Many have here dismounted from their steeds
And kneeling camels in the days of old;
Have slaked their thirst with wine beneath our shade,
And led their camels to the limpid tide.
They strained their shining wine from precious flasks,
They tossed the splendid trappings of their steeds;
Gayly they lived, the pensioners of Time:
But ere life's noon they died, cut off by Fate.
Their ashes drift and waste like withered leaves,
Blown by the east wind now, now by the west."
So spake the trees of Adi. So he spake.

"All things are in a league with my grave thoughts
To make me think of death," replied the King.
"If leaves whose little lives of sun and dew
Last not the year out say that man is dust,
What must the dust, where men by millions sleep,
The dead of ages, say?" The poet stooped,

And scooped his two hands full of dry white dust,
And held it to his ear. "Interpret it."
"Know that the dust was once a man like thee,
Know, too, that thou wilt one day be but dust."
So spake the dust to Adi. So he spake.

"The words are changed," said Noman, "not the tune,
For that still urges man's mortality.
When man forgets his end, nor earth nor heaven
Can hold their peace. The tomb remains to speak.
I go to question that. Wait for me here.
Fear not to see me enter its dark walls;
The time will come when they will shut me in
Forever: now I shall return again."
He waved the poet back, and throwing wide
Its mouldering doors went down into the tomb.

Before the place a watchful sentinel
The poet paced his beat with noiseless steps,
Hearkening the while to catch the King's least call.
He heard the talking leaves above his head,
The river rippling on the sandy shore,
But not the King; the grass was growing thick
Around the tomb, but where the mares were hitched
It grew not; cutting with his sword a swath,
He bore an armful to the hungry mares:
But still the King nor called to him, nor came.

At last the fiery arrows of the noon
Drove back the lessening shadows of the trees,
And hemmed them in a circle round their trunks;
To this the bard retreated from the heat.
The happy light came down upon his heart,
And stretched at ease he sang a summer song.

"The morning moon is set, the stars are gone;
Beside the palace gate the peacocks strut,
And in the tank the early lotus wakes.

The dew fell all night long, and drenched my robe,
The nightingale complained to me, in vain:
I waited for the dawn to meet my love.
She stands before me in the garden walk,

Her blue robe bordered with a fringe of pearls;
She offers me a rose; I kneel to her.

'Nay, speak not yet, though all your words are pearls;
Your smiles outrun your speech, and greet me first:
But when you smile not, speak, or I shall die!
I kiss the rose,—I would it were your lips!
But wherefore? Such a kiss would end my days.
Pity me, Sweet, my heart is at your feet!'

My long black hair is streaked with silver threads,
Tears dim my eyes; yet still in thought I see
The Rose of Beauty in the garden walk.

She sleeps the long, long sleep; disturb her not.
O nightingales, be silent, or depart:
And thou, my heart, be still, or moan and break."

The river rippled louder, but the leaves
Crowding together whispered, and the clash
Shook one at Adi's feet: the dust was stirred.
He raised his eyes, and lo, a cloud of dust
Blown from the clattering hoofs of flying steeds,
He knew the milk-white mares, and knew the troop
That rode them—Noman's huntsmen; Bahram Gour
Trailing his spear rode wildly at their head.
"The King is lost," he shouted as he came:
"Not so," said Adi, pointing to the tomb,
"The King is there. He muses in the tomb,
Perchance he sleeps. I would have shared his dreams,
But he forbade, and made me wait him here."
Then Bahram Gour went down into the tomb,
To wake the King, and many of the lords
Went with him; those who stayed behind were hushed.
They heard the talking leaves above their heads,
The river rippling on the sandy shore,
But not the King. At length a voice was heard—
The King is dead!" and Bahram Gour came out
Bearing a lifeless body in his arms.

BIRDS

Birds are singing round my window,
   Tunes the sweetest ever heard,
And I hang my cage there daily,
   But I never catch a bird.

So with thoughts my brain is peopled,
   And they sing there all day long:
But they will not fold their pinions
   In the little cage of Song!

John Townsend Trowbridge

(1827–1916)

John Townsend Trowbridge was born on a farm in Ogden, New York. He was a popular writer of juvenile fiction and used the pen name "Paul Creyton." Trowbridge was a contributing and managing editor for *Our Young Folks*. He pursued his long journalistic career in New York and Boston.

MIDWINTER

The speckled sky is dim with snow,
The light flakes falter and fall slow;
Athwart the hill-top, rapt and pale,
Silently drops a silvery veil;
And all the valley is shut in
By flickering curtains gray and thin.

But cheerily the chickadee
Singeth to me on fence and tree;
The snow sails round him as he swings,
White as the down of angels' wings.

I watch the slow flakes as they fall
On bank and brier and broken wall;
Over the orchard, waste and brown,
All noiselessly they settle down,
Tipping the apple-boughs, and each
Light quivering twig of plum and peach.

On turf and curb and bower-roof
The snow-storm spreads its ivory woof;
It paves with pearl the garden-walk;
And lovingly round tattered stalk
And shivering stem its magic weaves
A mantle fair as lily-leaves.

The hooded beehive, small and low,
Stands like a maiden in the snow;
And the old door-slab is half-hid
Under an alabaster lid.

All day it snows: the sheeted post
Gleams in the dimness like a ghost;
All day the blasted oak has stood
A muffled wizard of the wood;
Garland and airy cap adorn
The sumach and the wayside thorn,
And clustering spangles lodge and shine
In the dark tresses of the pine.

The ragged bramble, dwarfed and old,
Shrinks like a beggar in the cold;
In surplice white the cedar stands,
And blesses him with priestly hands.

Still cheerily the chickadee
Singeth to me on fence and tree:
But in my inmost ear is heard
The music of a holier bird;
And heavenly thoughts as soft and white
As snow-flakes, on my soul alight,
Clothing with love my lonely heart,
Healing with peace each bruisèd part,
Till all my being seems to be
Transfigured by their purity.

DARIUS GREENE AND HIS
FLYING-MACHINE

If ever there lived a Yankee lad,
Wise or otherwise, good or bad,

Who, seeing the birds fly, didn't jump
With flapping arms from stake or stump,
    Or, spreading the tail
    Of his coat for a sail,
Take a soaring leap from post or rail,
    And wonder why
    He couldn't fly,
And flap and flutter and wish and try—
If ever you knew a country dunce
Who didn't try that as often as once,
All I can say is, that's a sign
He never would do for a hero of mine.

An aspiring genius was D. Green:
The son of a farmer, age fourteen;
His body was long and lank and lean—
Just right for flying, as will be seen;
He had two eyes as bright as a bean,
And a freckled nose that grew between,
A little awry—for I must mention
That he had riveted his attention
Upon his wonderful invention,
Twisting his tongue as he twisted the strings,
And working his face as he worked the wings,
And with every turn of gimlet and screw
Turning and screwing his mouth round too,
    Till his nose seemed bent
    To catch the scent,
Around some corner, of new-baked pies,
And his wrinkled cheeks and his squinting eyes
Grew puckered into a queer grimace,
That made him look very droll in the face,
    And also very wise.

And wise he must have been, to do more
Than ever a genius did before,
Excepting Dædalus of yore
And his son Icarus, who wore
    Upon their backs
    Those wings of wax
He had read of in the old almanacs.
Darius was clearly of the opinion
That the air is also man's dominion,
And that, with paddle or fin or pinion,

We soon or late shall navigate
The azure as now we sail the sea.
The thing looks simple enough to me;
   And if you doubt it,
Hear how Darius reasoned about it.
   "The birds can fly an' why can't I?
   Must we give in," says he with a grin,
   "That the bluebird an' phœbe
   Are smarter'n we be?
Jest fold our hands an' see the swaller
An' blackbird an' catbird beat us holler?
Doos the little chatterin', sassy wren,
No bigger'n my thumb, know more than men?
   Just show me that!
   Ur prove 't the bat
Hez got more brains than's in my hat.
An' I'll back down, an' not till then!"
He argued further: "Nur I can't see
What's th' use o' wings to a bumble-bee,
Fur to git a livin' with, more'n to me;—
   Ain't my business
   Important's his'n is?
   That Icarus
   Made a perty muss—
Him an' his daddy Dædalus
They might 'a' knowed wings made o' wax
Wouldn't stand sun-heat an' hard whacks.
   I'll make mine o' luther,
   Ur suthin' ur other."

And he said to himself, as he tinkered and planned:
"But I ain't goin' to show my hand
To mummies that never can understand
The fust idee that's big an' grand."
So he kept his secret from all the rest,
Safely buttoned within his vest;
And in the loft above the shed
Himself he locks, with thimble and thread
And wax and hammer and buckles and screws
And all such things as geniuses use;—
Two bats for patterns, curious fellows!
A charcoal-pot and a pair of bellows;
Some wire, and several old umbrellas;
A carriage-cover, for tail and wings;

A piece of harness; and straps and strings;
   And a big strong box,
   In which he locks
These and a hundred other things.
His grinning brothers, Reuben and Burke
And Nathan and Jotham and Solomon, lurk
Around the corner to see him work—
Sitting cross-legged, like a Turk,
Drawing the waxed-end through with a jerk,
And boring the holes with a comical quirk
Of his wise old head, and a knowing smirk.
But vainly they mounted each other's backs,
And poked through knot-holes and pried through cracks;
With wood from the pile and straw from the stacks
He plugged the knot-holes and caulked the cracks;
And a dipper of water, which one would think
He had brought up into the loft to drink
   When he chanced to be dry,
   Stood always nigh,
   For Darius was sly!
And whenever at work he happened to spy
At chink or crevice a blinking eye.
He let the dipper of water fly.
"Take that! an' ef ever ye git a peep,
Guess ye'll ketch a weasel asleep!"
   And he sings as he locks
   His big strong box:—

"The weasel's head is small an' trim,
An' he is little an' long an' slim,
An' quick of motion an' nimble of limb
   An' ef you'll be
   Advised by me
Keep wide awake when ye're ketchin' him!"

So day after day
He stitched and tinkered and hammered away,
   Till at last 'twas done—
The greatest invention under the sun!
"An' now," says Darius, "horray fur some fun!"

   'Twas the Fourth of July,
   And the weather was dry,
And not a cloud was on all the sky,

Save a few light fleeces, which here and there,
    Half mist, half air,
Like foam on the ocean went floating by—
Just as lovely a morning as ever was seen
For a nice little trip in a flying machine.
Thought cunning Darius: "Now I shan't go
Along 'ith the fellers to see the show.
I'll say I've got sich a terrible cough!
An' then, when the folks 'ave all gone off,
I'll hev full swing fur to try the thing,
An' practise a little on the wing."
"Ain't goin' to see the celebration?"
Says brother Nate. "No; botheration!
I've got sich a cold—a toothache—I—
My gracious!—feel's though I should fly!"
    Said Jotham, "Sho!
    Guess ye better go."
    But Darius said, "No!
Shouldn't wonder 'f you might see me, though,
'Long 'bout noon, ef I git red
O' this jumpin', thumpin' pain 'n my head."
For all the while to himself he said:—
    "I tell ye what!
I'll fly a few times around the lot,
To see how 't seems, then soon's I've got
The hang o' the thing, ez likely's not,
    I'll astonish the nation,
    An' all creation,
By flyin' over the celebration!
Over their heads I'll sail like an eagle;
I'll balance myself on my wings like a sea-gull:
I'll dance on the chimbleys; I'll stand on the steeple;
I'll flop up to winders an' scare the people!
I'll light on the liberty-pole, an' crow;
An' I'll say to the gawpin' fools below,
    'What world's this 'ere
    That I've come near?'
Fur I'll make 'em b'lieve I'm a chap f'm the moon;
An' I'll try to race 'ith their ol' balloon!"
    He crept from his bed;
And, seeing the others were gone, he said,
"I'm gittin' over the cold 'n my head."
    And away he sped.
To open the wonderful box in the shed.

His brothers had walked but a little way,
When Jotham to Nathan chanced to say,
"What is the feller up to, hey!"
"Don'o'—the 's suthin' ur other to pay,
Ur he wouldn't 'a' stayed tu hum to-day."
Says Burke, "His toothache's all 'n his eye!
He never 'd missed a Fo'th-o'-July,
Ef he hedn't got some machine to try."
Then Sol, the little one, spoke: "By darn!
Le's hurry back an' hide 'n the barn,
An' pay him fur tellin' us that yarn!"
"Agreed!" Through the orchard they creep back
Along by the fences, behind the stack,
And one by one, through a hole in the wall,
In under the dusty barn they crawl,
Dressed in their Sunday garments all;
And a very astonishing sight was that,
When each in his cobwebbed coat and hat
Came up through the floor like an ancient rat
    And there they hid;
    And Reuben slid
The fastenings back, and the door undid.
    "Keep dark!" said he,
"While I squint an' see what the' is to see."

As knights of old put on their mail—
    From head to foot an iron suit
Iron jacket and iron boot,
Iron breeches, and on the head
No hat, but an iron pot instead,
    And under the chin the bail,
(I believe they called the thing a helm,)
Then sallied forth to overwhelm
The dragons and pagans that plagued the earth
    So this *modern* knight
    Prepared for flight,
Put on his wings and strapped them tight
Jointed and jaunty, strong and light—
Buckled them fast to shoulder and hip;
Ten feet they measured from tip to tip
And a helm had he, but that he wore,
Not on his head, like those of yore,
    But more like the helm of a ship.

"Hush!" Reuben said,
　"He's up in the shed!
He's opened the winder—I see his head!
He stretches it out, an' pokes it about,
Lookin' to see 'f the coast is clear,
　An' nobody near;—
Guess he don' o' who's hid in here!
He's riggin' a spring board over the sill!
Stop laffin', Solomon! Burke, keep still!
He's a climbin' out now—Of all the things!
What's he got on? I vum, it's wings!
An' that 'tother thing? I vum, it's a tail!
An' there he sits like a hawk on a rail!
Steppin' careful, he travels the length
Of his spring-board, and teeters to try its strength.
Now he stretches his wings, like a monstrous bat;
Peeks over his shoulder; this way an' that,
Fur to see 'f the' 's any one passin' by;
But the' 's on'y a caf an' goslin nigh.
They turn up at him a wonderin' eye,
To see— The dragon! he's goin' to fly!
Away he goes! Jimminy! what a jump!
　Flop—flop—an' plump
　To the ground with a thump!
Flutt'rin' an' flound'rin' all 'n a lump!"

As a demon is hurled by an angel's spear,
Heels over head, to his proper sphere—
Heels over head, and head over heels,
Dizzily down the abyss he wheels—
So fell Darius. Upon his crown,
In the midst of the barn-yard, he came down,
In a wonderful whirl of tangled strings,
Broken braces and broken springs,
Broken tail and broken wings,
Shooting-stars, and various things;
Barn-yard litter of straw and chaff,
And much that wasn't so sweet by half.
Away with a bellow fled the calf,
And what was that? Did the gosling laugh?
'Tis a merry roar from the old barn-door.
And he hears the voice of Jotham crying,
"Say, D'rius! how do you like flyin'?"
Slowly, ruefully, where he lay,

Darius just turned and looked that way,
As he stanched his sorrowful nose with his cuff.
"Wal, I like flyin' well enough,"
He said; "but the' ain't such a thunderin' sight
O' fun in 't when ye come to light."

I just have room for the MORAL here:
And this is the moral—Stick to your sphere.
Or if you insist, as you have the right,
On spreading your wings for a loftier flight,
The moral is—Take care how you light.

THE VAGABONDS

We are two travelers, Roger and I.
   Roger's my dog.—Come here, you scamp!
Jump for the gentleman,—mind your eye!
   Over the table,—look out for the lamp!
The rogue is growing a little old;
   Five years we've tramped through wind and weather,
And slept outdoors when nights were cold,
   And ate and drank—and starved—together.

We've learned what comfort is, I tell you!
   A bed on the floor, a bit of rosin,
A fire to thaw our thumbs (poor fellow!
   The paw he holds up there's been frozen),
Plenty of catgut for my fiddle
   (This outdoor business is bad for strings),
Then a few nice buckwheats hot from the griddle,
   And Roger and I set up for kings!

No, thank ye, Sir,—I never drink;
   Roger and I are exceedingly moral,—
Aren't we, Roger?—See him wink!—
   Well, something hot, then,—we won't quarrel.
He's thirsty, too,—see him nod his head?
   What a pity, Sir, that dogs can't talk!
He understands every word that's said,—
   And he knows good milk from water-and-chalk.

The truth is, Sir, now I reflect,
   I've been so sadly given to grog,

I wonder I've not lost the respect
    (Here's to you, Sir!) even of my dog.
But he sticks by, through thick and thin;
    And this old coat, with its empty pockets,
And rags that smell of tobacco and gin,
    He'll follow while he has eyes in his sockets.

There isn't another creature living
    Would do it, and prove, through every disaster,
So fond, so faithful, and so forgiving,
    To such a miserable, thankless master!
No, Sir!—see him wag his tail and grin!
    By George! it makes my old eyes water!
That is, there's something in this gin
    That chokes a fellow. But no matter!

We'll have some music, if you're willing,
    And Roger (hem! what plague a cough is, Sir!)
Shall march a little— Start, you villain!
    Paws up! Eyes front! Salute your officer!
'Bout face! Attention! Take your rifle!
    (Some dogs have arms, you see!) Now hold your
Cap while the gentlemen give a trifle,
    To aid a poor old patriot soldier!

March! Halt! Now show how the rebel shakes
    When he stands up to hear his sentence.
Now tell us how many drams it takes
    To honor a jolly new acquaintance.
Five yelps,—that's five; he's mighty knowing!
    The night's before us, fill the glasses!—
Quick, Sir! I'm ill,—my brain is going!—
    Some brandy,—thank you,—there!—it passes!

Why not reform? That's easily said;
    But I've gone through such wretched treatment,
Sometimes forgetting the taste of bread,
    And scarce remembering what meat meant,
That my poor stomach's past reform;
    And there are times when, mad with thinking,
I'd sell out heaven for something warm
    To prop a horrible inward sinking.

Is there a way to forget to think?
  At your age, Sir, home, fortune, friends,
A dear girl's love,—but I took to drink,—
  The same old story; you know how it ends.
If you could have seen these classic features,—
  You needn't laugh, Sir; they were not then
Such a burning libel on God's creatures:
  I was one of your handsome men!

If you had seen *her*, so fair and young,
  Whose head was happy on this breast!
If you could have heard the songs I sung
  When the wine went round, you wouldn't have guessed
That ever I, Sir, should be straying
  From door to door, with fiddle and dog,
Ragged and penniless, and playing
  To you to-night for a glass of grog!

She's married since,—a parson's wife:
  'Twas better for her that we should part,
Better the soberest, prosiest life
  Than a blasted home and a broken heart.
I have seen her? Once: I was weak and spent
  On the dusty road: a carriage stopped:
But little she dreamed, as on she went,
  Who kissed the coin that her fingers dropped!

You've set me talking, Sir; I'm sorry;
  It makes me wild to think of the change!
What do you care for a beggar's story?
  Is it amusing? you find it strange?
I had a mother so proud of me!
  'Twas well she died before.—Do you know
If the happy spirits in heaven can see
  The ruin and wretchedness here below?

Another glass, and strong, to deaden
  This pain; then Roger and I will start.
I wonder, has he such a lumpish, leaden,
  Aching thing in place of a heart?
He is sad sometimes, and would weep, if he could,
  No doubt remembering things that were,—
A virtuous kennel, with plenty of food,
  And himself a sober, respectable cur.

I'm better now; that glass was warming.—
　　You rascal! limber your lazy feet!
We must be fiddling and performing
　　For supper and bed, or starve in the street.—
Not a very gay life to lead, you think?
　　But soon we shall go where lodgings are free,
And the sleepers need neither victuals nor drink:—
　　The sooner, the better for Roger and me!

FILLING AN ORDER

Read at the Holmes Breakfast, Boston, Dec. 3, 1879

To Nature, in her shop one day, at work compounding simples,
Studying fresh tints for Beauty's cheeks, or new effects in dimples,
An order came: she wiped in haste her fingers and unfolded
The scribbled scrap, put on her specs, and read it, while she scolded.

"From Miss Columbia! I declare! of all the upstart misses!
What will the jade be asking next? Now what an order this is!
Where's Boston? Oh, that one-horse town out there beside the
　　ocean!
She wants—of course, she always wants—another little notion!

"This time, three geniuses, A 1, to grace her favorite city:
The first a bard; the second wise; the third supremely witty;
None of the staid and hackneyed sort, but some peculiar flavor,
Something unique and fresh for each, will be esteemed a favor!
Modest demands! as if my hands had but to turn and toss over
A Poet veined with dew and fire, a Wit, and a Philosopher!

"But now let's see!" She put aside her old, outworn expedients,
And in a quite unusual way began to mix ingredients,—
Some in the fierce retort distilled, some pounded by the pestle,—
And set the simmering souls to steep, each in its glowing vessel.
In each, by turns, she poured, she stirred, she skimmed the shining
　　liquor,
Threw laughter in, to make it thin, or thought, to make it thicker.
But when she came to choose the clay, she found, to her vexation,
That, with a stock on hand to fill an order for a nation,
Of that more finely tempered stuff, electric and ethereal,
Of which a genius must be formed, she had but scant material—

For three? For one! What should be done? A bright idea struck her;
Her old witch-eyes began to shine, her mouth began to pucker.

Says she, "The fault, I'm well aware, with genius is the presence
Of altogether too much clay, with quite too little essence,
And sluggish atoms that obstruct the spiritual solution;
So now, instead of spoiling these by over-much dilution,
With their fine elements I'll make a single, rare phenomenon,
And of three common geniuses concoct a most uncommon one,
So that the world shall smile to see a soul so universal,
Such poesy and pleasantry, packed in so small a parcel."

So said, so done; the three in one she wrapped, and stuck the label:
Poet, Professor, Autocrat of Wit's own Breakfast-Table.

THE CHARCOALMAN

Though rudely blows the wintry blast,
And sifting snows fall white and fast,
Mark Haley drives along the street,
Perched high upon his wagon seat;
His sombre face the storm defies,
And thus from morn till eve he cries,
    "Charco'! charco'!"
While echo faint and far replies,
    "Hark, oh! hark, oh!"
"Charco'!"—"Hark, oh!"—Such cherry sounds
Attend him on his daily rounds.

The dust begrimes his ancient hat;
His coat is darker far than that;
'T is odd to see his sooty form
All speckled with the feathery storm;
Yet in his honest bosom lies
Nor spot nor speck, though still he cries,
    "Charco'! charco'!"
While many a roguish lad replies,
    "Ark, ho! ark, ho!"
"Charco'!"—"Ark, ho!"—Such various sounds
Announce Mark Haley's morning rounds.

Thus all the cold and wintery day
He labors much for little pay;

Yet feels no less of happiness
Than many a richer man, I guess,
When through the shades of eve he spies
The light of his own home, and cries,
    "Charco'! charco'!"
And Martha from the door replies,
    "Mark, ho! Mark, ho!"
"Charco'!"—"Mark, ho!"—Such joy abounds
When he has closed his daily rounds!

The hearth is warm, the fire is bright;
And while his hand, washed clean and white,
Holds Martha's tender hand once more,
His glowing face bends fondly o'er
The crib wherein his darling lies,
And in a coaxing tone he cries,
    "Charco'! charco'!"
And baby with a laugh replies,
    "Ah, go! ah, go!"
"Charco'!"—"Ah, go!"—while at the sounds
The mother's heart with gladness bounds.

Henry Timrod

(1828–1867)

Henry Timrod, "The Poet Laureate of the Confederacy," was born in Charleston, South Carolina. He studied at the University of Georgia and went into law, but gave it up for teaching. He was a war correspondent for the *Charleston Mercury* during the Civil War where he wrote his stirring war verses. Poverty and disease eventually took their toll on Timrod, and he died of consumption at the age of thirty-eight.

AT MAGNOLIA CEMETERY

Sleep sweetly in your humble graves,
  Sleep, martyrs of a fallen cause;
Though yet no marble column craves
  The pilgrim here to pause.

In seeds of laurel in the earth
  The blossom of your fame is blown,
And somewhere, waiting for its birth,
  The shaft is in the stone!

Meanwhile, behalf the tardy years
  Which keep in trust your storied tombs,
Behold! your sisters bring their tears,
  And these memorial blooms.

Small tributes! but your shades will smile
  More proudly on these wreaths to-day,

Than when some cannon-moulded pile
    Shall overlook this bay.

Stoop, angels, hither from the skies!
    There is no holier spot of ground
Than where defeated valor lies,
    By mourning beauty crowned.
                    —*Charleston, 1867*

QUATORZAIN

Most men know love but as a part of life;
They hide it in some corner of the breast,
Even from themselves; and only when they rest
In the brief pauses of that daily strife,
Wherewith the world might else be not so rife,
They draw it forth (as one draws forth a toy
To soothe some ardent kiss-exacting boy)
And hold it up to sister, child, or wife.

Ah me! why may not love and life be one?
Why walk we thus alone, when by our side,
Love, like a visible god, might be our guide?
How would the marts grow noble! and the street,
Worn like a dungeon-floor by weary feet,
Seem then a golden court-way of the Sun!

CHARLESTON

Calm as that second summer which precedes
    The first fall of the snow,
In the broad sunlight of heroic deeds,
    The city bides the foe.

As yet, behind their ramparts, stern and proud,
    Her bolted thunders sleep,—
Dark Sumter, like a battlemented cloud,
    Looms o'er the solemn deep.

No Calpe frowns from lofty cliff or scaur
    To guard the holy strand;

But Moultrie holds in leash her dogs of war
    Above the level sand.

And down the dunes a thousand guns lie couched,
    Unseen, beside the flood,—
Like tigers in some Orient jungle crouched,
    That wait and watch for blood.

Meanwhile, through streets still echoing with trade,
    Walk grave and thoughtful men,
Whose hands may one day wield the patriot's blade
    As lightly as the pen.

And maidens, with such eyes as would grow dim
    Over a bleeding hound,
Seem each one to have caught the strength of him
    Whose sword she sadly bound.

Thus girt without and garrisoned at home,
    Day patient following day,
Old Charleston looks from roof and spire and dome,
    Across her tranquil bay.

Ships, through a hundred foes, from Saxon lands
    And spicy Indian ports,
Bring Saxon steel and iron to her hands,
    And summer to her courts.

But still, along yon dim Atlantic line,
    The only hostile smoke
Creeps like a harmless mist above the brine,
    From some frail floating oak.

Shall the spring dawn, and she, still clad in smiles,
    And with an unscathed brow,
Rest in the strong arms of her palm-crowned isles,
    As fair and free as now?

We know not; in the temple of the Fates
    God has inscribed her doom:
And, all untroubled in her faith, she waits
    The triumph or the tomb.

April, 1863

ETHNOGENESIS

Written During the Meeting of the First Southern
Congress, at Montgomery, February, 1861

I

Hath not the morning dawned with added light?
And shall not evening call another star
Out of the infinite regions of the night,
To mark this day in Heaven? At last, we are
A nation among nations; and the world
Shall soon behold in many a distant port
    Another flag unfurled!
Now, come what may, whose favor need we court?
And, under God, whose thunder need we fear?
    Thank Him who placed us here
Beneath so kind a sky—the very sun
Takes part with us; and on our errands run
All breezes of the ocean; dew and rain
Do noiseless battle for us; and the Year,
And all the gentle daughters in her train,
March in our ranks, and in our service wield
    Long spears of golden grain!
A yellow blossom as her fairy shield,
June flings her azure banner to the wind,
   While in the order of their birth
Her sisters pass, and many an ample field
Grows white beneath their steps, till now, behold,
    Its endless sheets unfold
THE SNOW OF SOUTHERN SUMMERS! Let the earth
Rejoice! beneath those fleeces soft and warm
    Our happy land shall sleep
    In a repose as deep
  As if we lay intrenched behind
Whole leagues of Russian ice and Arctic storm!

II

And what if, mad with wrongs themselves have wrought,
    In their own treachery caught,
    By their own fears made bold,
    And leagued with him of old,
Who long since in the limits of the North

Set up his evil throne, and warred with God—
What if, both mad and blinded in their rage,
Our foes should fling us down their mortal gage,
And with a hostile step profane our sod!
We shall not shrink, my brothers, but go forth
To meet them, marshaled by the Lord of Hosts,
And overshadowed by the mighty ghosts
Of Moultrie and of Eutaw—who shall foil
Auxiliars such as these? Nor these alone,
    But every stock and stone
    Shall help us; but the very soil,
And all the generous wealth it gives to toil,
And all for which we love our noble land,
Shall fight beside, and through us; sea and strand,
    The heart of woman, and her hand,
Tree, fruit, and flower, and every influence,
    Gentle, or grave, or grand;
    The winds in our defence
Shall seem to blow; to us the hills shall lend
    Their firmness and their calm;
And in our stiffened sinews we shall blend
    The strength of pine and palm!

III

Nor would we shun the battle-ground,
    Though weak as we are strong;
Call up the clashing elements around,
    And test the right and wrong!
On one side, creeds that dare to teach
What Christ and Paul refrained to preach;
Codes built upon a broken pledge,
And Charity that whets a poniard's edge;
Fair schemes that leave the neighboring poor
To starve and shiver at the schemer's door,
While in the world's most liberal ranks enrolled,
He turns some vast philanthropy to gold;
Religion, taking every mortal form
But that a pure and Christian faith makes warm,
Where not to vile fanatic passion urged,
Or not in vague philosophies submerged,
Repulsive with all Pharisaic leaven,
And making laws to stay the laws of Heaven!
And on the other, scorn of sordid gain,

Unblemished honor, truth without a stain,
Faith, justice, reverence, charitable wealth,
And, for the poor and humble, laws which give,
Not the mean right to buy the right to live,
        But life, and home, and health!
To doubt the end were want of trust in God,
        Who, if he has decreed
    That we must pass a redder sea
Than that which rang to Miriam's holy glee,
        Will surely raise at need
        A Moses with his rod!

IV

But let our fears—if fears we have—be still,
And turn us to the future! Could we climb
Some mighty Alp, and view the coming time,
The rapturous sight would fill
        Our eyes with happy tears!
Not only for the glories which the years
Shall bring us; not for lands from sea to-sea,
And wealth, and power, and peace, though these shall be;
But for the distant peoples we shall bless,
And the hushed murmurs of a world's distress:
For, to give labor to the poor,
        The whole sad planet o'er,
And save from want and crime the humblest door,
Is one among the many ends for which
        God makes us great and rich!
The hour perchance is not yet wholly ripe
When all shall own it, but the type
Whereby we shall be known in every land
Is that vast gulf which lips our Southern strand,
And through the cold, untempered ocean pours
Its genial streams, that far off Arctic shores
May sometimes catch upon the softened breeze
Strange tropic warmth and hints of summer seas.

Paul Hamilton Hayne

(1830–1886)

Paul Hamilton Hayne was born in Charleston, South Carolina. He became one of an important group of pre–Civil War writers who gathered in Charleston in the 1850s. He graduated from Charleston College and went on to study law. He founded *Russell's Magazine* with fellow poet Henry Timrod and was its editor from 1857 to 1860. Hayne was a colonel in the Confederate Army during the Civil War. His house, including his library, was destroyed in the course of the war. After the fighting ended, Hayne moved to Augusta, Georgia, where he lived the remainder of his life.

PRE-EXISTENCE

While sauntering through the crowded street,
Some half-remembered face I meet,

Albeit upon no mortal shore
That face, methinks, has smiled before.

Lost in a gay and festal throng,
I tremble at some tender song,—

Set to an air whose golden bars
I must have heard in other stars.

In sacred aisles I pause to share
The blessings of a priestly prayer,—

When the whole scene which greets mine eyes
In some strange mode I recognize

As one whose every mystic part
I feel prefigured in my heart.

At sunset, as I calmly stand,
A stranger on an alien strand,

Familiar as my childhood's home
Seems the long stretch of wave and foam

One sails toward me o'er the bay,
And what he comes to do and say

I can foretell. A prescient lore
Springs from some life outlived of yore.

O swift, instinctive, startling gleams
Of deep soul-knowledge! not as *dreams*

For aye ye vaguely dawn and die,
But oft with lightning certainty

Pierce through the dark, oblivious brain,
To make old thoughts and memories plain,

Thoughts which perchance must travel back
Across the wild, bewildering track

Of countless æons; memories far,
High-reaching as yon pallid star,

Unknown, scarce seen, whose flickering grace
Faints on the outmost rings of space!

LOVE SCORNS DEGREES

From *"The mountain of the lovers"*

Love scorns degrees; the low he lifteth high,
The high he draweth down to that fair plain
Whereon, in his divine equality,

Two loving hearts may meet, nor meet in vain;
'Gainst such sweet levelling Custom cries amain,
But o'er its harshest utterance one bland sigh,
Breathed passion-wise, doth mount victorious still,
For Love, earth's lord, must have his lordly will.

A LITTLE WHILE I FAIN
WOULD LINGER YET

A little while (my life is almost set!)
  I fain would pause along the downward way,
  Musing an hour in this sad sunset ray,
While, Sweet! our eyes with tender tears are wet:
A little hour I fain would linger yet.

A little while I fain would linger yet,
  All for love's sake, for love that cannot tire;
  Though fervid youth be dead, with youth's desire,
And hope had faded to a vague regret,
A little while I fain would linger yet.

A little while I fain would linger here:
  Behold! who knows what strange, mysterious bars
  'Twixt souls that love may rise in other stars?
Nor can love deem the face of death is fair:
A little while I still would linger here.

A little while I yearn to hold thee fast,
  Hand locked in hand, and loyal heart to heart;
  (O pitying Christ! those woeful words, "We part!")
So ere the darkness fall, the light be past,
A little while I fain would hold thee fast.

A little while, when light and twilight meet,—
  Behind, our broken years; before, the deep
  Weird wonder of the last unfathomed sleep,—
A little while I still would clasp thee, Sweet,
A little while, when night and twilight meet.

A little while I fain would linger here;
  Behold! who knows what soul-dividing bars
  Earth's faithful loves may part in other stars?

Nor can love deem the face of death is fair:
A little while I still would linger here.

THE MOCKING BIRD

At Night

A golden pallor of voluptuous light
Filled the warm southern night:
The moon, clear orbed, above the sylvan scene
Moved like a stately queen,
So rife with conscious beauty all the while,
What could she do but smile
At her own perfect loveliness below,
Glassed in the tranquil flow
Of crystal fountains and unruffled streams?
Half lost in waking dreams,
As down the loneliest forest dell I strayed,
Lo! from a neighboring glade,
Flashed through the drifts of moonshine, swiftly came
A fairy shape of flame.
It rose in dazzling spirals overhead,
Whence to wild sweetness wed,
Poured marvelous melodies, silvery trill on trill;
The very leaves grew still
On the charmed trees to hearken; while for me,
Heart-trilled to ecstasy,
I followed—followed the bright shape that flew,
Still circling up the blue,
Till as a fountain that has reached its height,
Falls back in sprays of light
Slowly dissolved, so that enrapturing lay,
Divinely melts away
Through tremulous spaces to a music-mist,
Soon by the fitful breeze
How gently kissed
Into remote and tender silences.

IN HARBOR

I think it is over, over
    I think it is over at last;

Voices of foeman and lover,
   The sweet and the bitter, have passed;
Life, like a tempest of ocean,
Hath outblown its ultimate blast:
There's but a faint sobbing seaward
While the calm of the tide deepens leeward,
And behold! like the welcoming quiver
Of heart-pulses throbbed through the river,
   Those lights in the harbor at last,
   The heavenly harbor at last!

I feel it is over! over!
   For the winds and the waters surcease;
Ah, few were the days of the rover
   That smiled in the beauty of peace!
And distant and dim was the omen
That hinted redress or release:—
From the ravage of life, and its riot,
What marvel I yearn for the quiet
   Which bides in the harbor at last,
For the lights, with their welcoming quiver,
That throb through the sanctified river,
   Which girdle the harbor at last,
   This heavenly harbor at last?

Emily Dickinson

(1830–1886)

Emily Dickinson was born in Amherst, Massachusetts. She lived her whole life, and died, in the same house in which she was born. She was an energetic and outgoing young woman, attending Amhurst Academy and Holyoke Female Seminary. A tendency toward reclusiveness began to grow when Dickinson reached her mid-twenties. She began attending almost exclusively to household chores (baking and preserving) and to writing poetry. She sent a sample of her poetry to a well-known man of letters, Thomas Wentworth Higginson, who rejected her first poems but eventually edited posthumous volumes of her work. Dickinson disliked publicity, and it was her self-imposed isolation, rather than her writing, that made her a legend and mystery in her day. She only had a handful of her poems published in minor magazines during her lifetime. Emily Dickinson died of Bright's disease at the age of fifty-five.

THE RAILWAY TRAIN

I like to see it lap the miles,
And lick the valleys up,
And stop to feed itself at tanks;
And then, prodigious, step

Around a pile of mountains,
And, supercilious, peer
In shanties by the sides of roads;
And then a quarry pare

To fit its sides, and crawl between,
Complaining all the while
In horrid, hooting stanza;
Then chase itself down hill

And neigh like Boanerges;
Then, punctual as a star,
Stop—docile and omnipotent—
At its own stable door.

"I DIED FOR BEAUTY"

I died for beauty, but was scarce
Adjusted in the tomb,
When one who died for truth was lain
In an adjoining room.

He questioned softly why I failed?
"For beauty," I replied.
"And I for truth,—the two are one;
We brethren are," he said.

And so, as kinsmen met a night,
We talked between the rooms,
Until the moss had reached our lips,
And covered up our names.

THE CHARIOT

Because I could not stop for Death,
He kindly stopped for me;
The carriage held but just ourselves
And Immortality.

We slowly drove, he knew no haste,
And I had put away
My labor, and my leisure too,
For his civility.

We passed the school where children played,
Their lessons scarcely done;

We passed the fields of gazing grain,
We passed the setting sun.

We paused before a house that seemed
A swelling of the ground;
The roof was scarcely visible,
The cornice but a mound.

Since then 't is centuries; but each
Feels shorter than the day
I first surmised the horses' heads
Were toward eternity.

DYING

I heard a fly buzz when I died;
   The stillness round my form
Was like the stillness in the air
   Between the heaves of storm.

The eyes beside had wrung them dry,
   And breaths were gathering sure
For that last onset, when the king
   Be witnessed in his power.

I willed my keepsakes, signed away
   What portion of me I
Could make assignable,—and then
   There interposed a fly,

With blue, uncertain, stumbling buzz,
   Between the light and me;
And then the windows failed, and then
   I could not see to see.

"YOUR RICHES TAUGHT ME POVERTY"

Your riches taught me poverty.
Myself a millionnaire
In little wealths,—as girls could boast,—
Till broad as Buenos Ayre,

You drifted your dominions
A different Peru;
And I esteemed all poverty,
For life's estate with you.

Of mines I little know, myself,
But just the names of gems,—
The colors of the commonest;
And scarce of diadems

So much that, did I meet the queen,
Her glory I should know:
But this must be a different wealth,
To miss it beggars so.

I'm sure 't is India all day
To those who look on you
Without a stint, without a blame,—
Might I but be the Jew!

I'm sure it is Golconda,
Beyond my power to deem,—
To have a smile for mine each day,
How better than a gem!

At least, it solaces to know
That there exists a gold,
Although I prove it just in time
Its distance to behold!

It's far, far treasure to surmise,
And estimate the pearl
That slipped my simple fingers through
While just a girl at school!

STORM

It sounded as if the streets were running,
And then the streets stood still.
Eclipse was all we could see at the window,
And awe was all we could feel.

By and by the boldest stole out of his covert,
To see if time was there.
Nature was in her beryl apron,
Mixing fresher air.

THE WIND'S VISIT

The wind tapped like a tired man,
And like a host, "Come in,"
I boldly answered; entered then
My residence within

A rapid, footless guest,
To offer whom a chair
Were as impossible as hand
A sofa to the air.

No bone had he to bind him,
His speech was like the push
Of numerous humming-birds at once
From a superior bush.

His countenance a billow,
His fingers, if he pass,
Let go a music, as of tunes
Blown tremulous in glass.

He visited, still flitting;
Then, like a timid man,
Again he tapped—'t was flurriedly—
And I became alone.

SUCCESS

Success is counted sweetest
By those who ne'er succeed.
To comprehend a nectar
Requires sorest need.

Not one of all the purple host
Who took the flag to-day

Can tell the definition,
So clear, of victory,

As he, defeated, dying,
On whose forbidden ear
The distant strains of triumph
Break, agonized and clear.

LIFE'S TRADES

It's such a little thing to weep,
So short a thing to sigh;
And yet by trades the size of these
We men and women die!

"I FELT A FUNERAL IN MY BRAIN"

I felt a funeral in my brain,
And mourners, to and fro,
Kept treading, treading, till it seemed
That sense was breaking through.

And when they all were seated,
A service like a drum
Kept beating, beating, till I thought
My mind was going numb.

And then I heard them lift a box,
And creak across my soul
With those same boots of lead, again.
Then space began to toll

As all the heavens were a bell,
And Being but an ear,
And I and silence some strange race,
Wrecked, solitary, here.

ASPIRATION

We never know how high we are
Till we are called to rise;

And then, if we are true to plan,
　　Our statures touch the skies.

The heroism we recite
　　Would be a daily thing,
Did not ourselves the cubits warp
　　For fear to be a king.

"I HAVE NOT TOLD MY GARDEN YET"

I have not told my garden yet,
Lest that should conquer me;
I have not quite the strength now
To break it to the bee.

I will not name it in the street,
For shops would stare, that I,
So shy, so very ignorant,
Should have the face to die.

The hillsides must not know it,
Where I have rambled so,
Nor tell the loving forests
The day that I shall go,

Nor lisp it at the table,
Nor heedless by the way
Hint that within the riddle
One will walk to-day!

"I'M NOBODY! WHO ARE YOU?"

I'm nobody! Who are you?
Are you nobody, too?
Then there's a pair of us—don't tell!
They'd banish us, you know.

How dreary to be somebody!
How public, like a frog
To tell your name the livelong day
To an admiring bog!

"NOT ANY HIGHER STANDS THE GRAVE"

Not any higher stands the grave
    For heroes than for men;
Not any nearer for the child
    Than numb three-score and ten.

This latest leisure equal lulls
    The beggar and his queen;
Propitiate this democrat
    By summer's gracious mien.

"THE DISTANCE THAT THE DEAD HAVE GONE"

The distance that the dead have gone
    Does not at first appear;
Their coming back seems possible
    For many an ardent year.

And then, that we have followed them
    We more than half suspect,
So intimate have we become
    With their dear retrospect.

"WE NEVER KNOW WE GO"

We never know we go,—when we are going
    We jest and shut the door;
Fate following behind us bolts it,
    And we accost no more.

"SUPERFLUOUS WERE THE SUN"

Superfluous were the sun
    When excellence is dead;
He were superfluous every day,
    For every day is said

That syllable whose faith
  Just saves it from despair,
And whose 'I'll meet you' hesitates
  If love inquire, 'Where?'

Upon his dateless fame
  Our periods may lie,
As stars that drop anonymous
  From an abundant sky.

Edmund Clarence Stedman

(1833–1908)

Edmund Clarence Stedman was born in Hartford, Connecticut. He studied at Yale, worked for the *Tribune* under Horace Greeley, and served as a war correspondent during the Civil War. After the war he became a Wall Street broker and sat on the New York Stock Exchange for more than twenty years.

THE HAND OF LINCOLN

Look on this cast, and know the hand
   That bore a nation in its hold:
From this mute witness understand
   What Lincoln was,—how large of mould.

The man who sped the woodsman's team,
   And deepest sunk the ploughman's share,
And pushed the laden raft astream,
   Of fate before him unaware.

This was the hand that knew to swing
   The axe—since thus would Freedom train
Her son—and made the forest ring,
   And drove the wedge, and toiled amain.

Firm hand, that loftier office took,
   A conscious leader's will obeyed,
And, when men sought his word and look,
   With steadfast might the gathering swayed.

No courtier's, toying with a sword,
   Nor minstrel's, laid across a lute;
A chief's uplifted to the Lord
   When all the kings of earth were mute!

The hand of Anak, sinewed strong,
   The fingers that on greatness clutch;
Yet, lo! the marks their lines along
   Of one who strove and suffered much.

For here in knotted cord and vein
   I trace the varying chart of years;
I know the troubled heart, the strain,
   The weights of Atlas—and the tears.

Again I see the patient brow
   That palm erewhile was wont to press;
And now 't is furrowed deep, and now
   Made smooth with hope and tenderness.

For something of a formless grace
   This moulded outline plays about;
A pitying flame, beyond our trace,
   Breathes like a spirit, in and out,—

The love that cast an aureole
   Round one who, longer to endure,
Called mirth to ease his ceaseless dole,
   Yet kept his nobler purpose sure.

Lo, as I gaze, the statured man,
   Built up from yon large hand, appears:
A type that Nature wills to plan
   But once in all a people's years.

What better than this voiceless cast
   To tell of such a one as he,
Since through its living semblance passed
   The thought that bade a race be free!

WHAT THE WINDS BRING

Which is the Wind that brings the cold?
　The North-Wind, Freddy, and all the snow;
And the sheep will scamper into the fold
　When the North begins to blow.

Which is the Wind that brings the heat?
　The South-Wind, Katy, and corn will grow,
And peaches redden for you to eat,
　When the South begins to blow.

Which is the Wind that brings the rain?
　The East-Wind, Arty; and farmers know
That cows come shivering up the lane
　When the East begins to blow.

Which is the Wind that brings the flowers?
　The West-Wind, Bessy; and soft and low
The birdies sing in the summer hours
　When the West begins to blow.

THE DISCOVERER

　I have a little kinsman
Whose earthly summers are but three,
　And yet a voyager is he
　Greater than Drake or Frobisher,
　Than all their peers together!
　He is a brave discoverer,
　And, far beyond the tether
　Of them who seek the frozen Pole,
Has sailed where the noiseless surges roll.
　Ay, he has travelled whither
　A winged pilot steeréd his bark
　Through the portals of the dark,
　Past hoary Mimir's well and tree,
　　Across the unknown sea.

　Suddenly, in his fair young hour,
　Came one who bore a flower,
　And laid it in his dimpled hand
　　With this command:

· 355 ·

"Henceforth thou art a rover!
Thou must make a voyage far.
Sail beneath the evening star,
And a wondrous land discover."
—With his sweet smile innocent
    Our little kinsman went.

Since that time no word
From the absent has been heard.
    Who can tell
How he fares, or answer well
What the little one has found
Since he left us, outward bound?
Would that he might return!
Then should we learn
From the pricking of his chart
How the skyey roadways part.
Hush! does not the baby this way bring,
    To lay beside this severed curl,
        Some starry offering
Of chrysolite or pearl?
        Ah, no! not so!
We may follow on his track,
    But he comes not back.
    And yet I dare aver
He is a brave discoverer
Of climes his elders do not know.
He has more learning than appears
On the scroll of twice three thousand years,
More than in the groves is taught,
Or from furthest Indies brought;
He knows, perchance, how spirits fare,—

What shapes the angels wear,
What is their guise and speech
In those lands beyond our reach,—
    And his eyes behold
Things that shall never, never be to mortal hearers told

WANTED—A MAN

Back from the trebly crimsoned field
    Terrible words are thunder-tost;

Full of the wrath that will not yield,
  Full of revenge for battles lost!
  Hark to their echo, as it crost
The Capital, making faces wan:
  'End this murderous holocaust;
Abraham Lincoln, give us a MAN!

'Give us a man of God's own mold,
  Born to marshal his fellow-men;
One whose fame is not bought and sold
  At the stroke of a politician's pen;
  Give us the man of thousands ten,
Fit to do as well as to plan;
  Give us a rallying-cry, and then,
Abraham Lincoln, give us a MAN!

'No leader to shirk the boasting foe,
  And to march and countermarch our brave,
Till they fall like ghosts in the marshes low,
  And the swamp-grass covers each nameless grave;
  Nor another, whose fatal banners wave
Aye in Disaster's shameful van;
  Nor another, to bluster, and lie, and rave;—
Abraham Lincoln, give us a MAN!

'Hearts are mourning in the North,
  While the sister rivers seek the main,
Red with our life-blood flowing forth,—
  Who shall gather it up again?
  Though we march to the battle-plain
Firmly as when the strife began,
  Shall all our offering be in vain?—
Abraham Lincoln, give us a MAN!

'Is there never one in all the land,
  One on whose might the cause may lean?
Are all the common ones so grand,
  And all the titled ones so mean?
  What if your failure may have been
In trying to make good bread from bran,
  From worthless metal a weapon keen?—
Abraham Lincoln, find us a MAN!

'O, we will follow him to the death,
  Where the foeman's fiercest columns are!
O, we will use our latest breath,
  Cheering for every sacred star!
  His to marshal us high and far;
Ours to battle, as patriots can
  When a Hero leads the Holy War!—
Abraham Lincoln, give us a MAN!'

KEARNY AT SEVEN PINES

So that soldierly legend is still on its journey,—
  That story of Kearny who knew not to yield!
'Twas the day when with Jameson, fierce Berry, and Birney,
  Against twenty thousand he rallied the field.
Where the red volleys poured, where the clamor rose highest,
  Where the dead lay in clumps through the dwarf oak and pine,
Where the aim from the thicket was surest and nighest,—
  No charge like Phil Kearny's along the whole line.

When the battle went ill, and the bravest were solemn,
  Near the dark Seven Pines, where we still held our ground,
He rode down the length of the withering column,
  And his heart at our war cry leapt up with a bound;
He snuffed, like his charger, the wind of the powder,—
  His sword waved us on and we answered the sign:
Loud our cheer as we rushed, but his laugh rang the louder,
  "There's the devil's own fun, boys, along the whole line!"

How he strode his brown steed! How we saw his blade brighten
  In the one hand still left,—and the reins in his teeth!
He laughed like a boy when the holidays heighten,
  But a soldier's glance shot from his visor beneath.
Up came the reserves to the mellay infernal,
  Asking where to go in,—through the clearing or pine?
"O, anywhere! Forward! 'Tis all the same, Colonel:
  You'll find lovely fighting along the whole line!"

O, evil the black shroud of night at Chantilly,
  That hid him from sight of his brave men and tried!
Foul, foul sped the bullet that clipped the white lily,
  The flower of our knighthood, the whole army's pride!
Yet we dream that he still,—in the shadowy region

Where the dead form their ranks at the wan drummer's sign,—
Rides on, as of old, down the length of his legion,
And the word still is Forward! along the whole line.

PAN IN WALL STREET

A.D. 1867

Just where the Treasury's marble front
　　Looks over Wall Street's mingled nations;
Where Jews and Gentiles most are wont
　　To throng for trade and last quotations;
Where, hour by hour, the rates of gold
　　Outrival, in the ears of people,
The quarter-chimes, serenely tolled
　　From Trinity's undaunted steeple—

Even there I heard a strange, wild strain
　　Sound high above the modern clamor,
Above the cries of greed and gain,
　　The curbstone war, the auction's hammer;
And swift, on Music's misty ways,
　　It led, from all this strife for millions,
To ancient, sweet-do-nothing days
　　Among the kirtle-robed Sicilians.

And as it stilled the multitude,
　　And yet more joyous rose, and shriller,
I saw the minstrel, where he stood
　　At ease against a Doric pillar:
One hand a droning organ played,
　　The other held a Pan's-pipe (fashioned
Like those of old) to lips that made
　　The reeds give out that strain impassioned.

'Twas Pan himself had wandered here
　　A-strolling through this sordid city,
And piping to the civic ear
　　The prelude of some pastoral ditty!
The demigod had crossed the seas—
　　From haunts of shepherd, nymph, and satyr,
And Syracusan times—to these
　　Far shores and twenty centuries later.

A ragged cap was on his head;
    But—hidden thus—there was no doubting
That, all with crispy locks o'erspread,
    His gnarlèd horns were somewhere sprouting;
His club-feet, cased in rusty shoes,
    Were crossed, as on some frieze you see them,
And trousers, patched of divers hues,
    Concealed his crooked shanks beneath them.

He filled the quivering reeds with sound,
    And o'er his mouth their changes shifted,
And with his goat's-eyes looked around
    Where'er the passing current drifted;
And soon, as on Trinacrian hills
    The nymphs and herdsmen ran to hear him,
Even now the tradesmen from their tills,
    With clerks and porters, crowded near him.

The bulls and bears together drew
    From Jauncey Court and New Street Alley,
As erst, if pastorals be true,
    Came beasts from every wooded valley;
The random passers stayed to list—
    A boxer Ægon, rough and merry,
A Broadway Daphnis, on his tryst
    With Nais at the Brooklyn Ferry.

A one-eyed Cyclops halted long
    In tattered cloak of army pattern,
And Galatea joined the throng,—
    A blowsy, apple-vending slattern;
While old Silenus staggered out
    From some new-fangled lunch-house handy,
And bade the piper, with a shout,
    To strike up Yankee Doodle Dandy!

A newsboy and a peanut-girl
    Like little Fauns began to caper:
His hair was all in tangled curl,
    Her tawny legs were bare and taper;
And still the gathering larger grew,
    And gave its pence and crowded nigher,
While aye the shepherd-minstrel blew
    His pipe, and struck the gamut higher.

O heart of Nature, beating still
　　With throbs her vernal passion taught her—
Even here, as on the vine-clad hill,
　　Or by the Arethusan water!
New forms may fold the speech, new lands
　　Arise within these ocean-portals,
But Music waves eternal wands—
　　Enchantress of the souls of mortals!

So thought I,—but among us trod
　　A man in blue, with legal baton,
And scoffed the vagrant demigod,
　　And pushed him from the step I sat on.
Doubting, I mused upon the cry,
　　"Great Pan is dead!"—and all the people
Went on their ways:—and clear and high
　　The quarter sounded from the steeple.

Thomas Bailey Aldrich

(1836–1907)

Thomas Bailey Aldrich was born in Portsmouth, New Hampshire, and in his teens, moved to New York where he made friends with prominent literary figures. At twenty, he was editor of the *Home Journal* and wrote for several other New York journals. It was in 1855 that he had received national recognition for his poem, "The Ballad of Baby Bell." Aldrich moved to Boston and edited the *Atlantic Monthly* from 1881 to 1900.

THE BALLAD OF BABY BELL

Have you not heard the poets tell
How came the dainty Baby Bell
   Into this world of ours?
The gates of heaven were left ajar;
With folded hands and dreamy eyes,
Wandering out of Paradise,
She saw this planet, like a star,
   Hung in the glistening depths of even,—
Its bridges, running to and fro,
O'er which the white-winged angels go,
   Bearing the holy dead to heaven.
She touched a bridge of flowers,—those feet,
So light they did not bend the bells
Of the celestial asphodels!
They fell like dew upon the flowers,
Then all the air grew strangely sweet!
And thus came dainty Baby Bell
   Into this world of ours.

She came and brought delicious May.
　　The swallows built beneath the eaves;
　　Like sunlight in and out the leaves,
The robins went the livelong day;
The lily swung its noiseless bell,
　　And o'er the porch the trembling vine
　　Seemed bursting with its veins of wine.
How sweetly, softly, twilight fell!
Oh, earth was full of singing-birds,
And opening spring-tide flowers,
When the dainty Baby Bell
　　Came to this world of ours!

O Baby, dainty Baby Bell,
How far she grew from day to day!
What woman-nature filled her eyes,
What poetry within them lay!
Those deep and tender twilight eyes,
　　So full of meaning, pure and bright,
　　As if she yet stood in the light
Of those oped gates of Paradise.
And so we loved her more and more;
Ah, never in our hearts before
　　Was love so lovely born:
We felt we had a link between
This real world and that unseen—
　　The land beyond the morn.
And for the love of those dear eyes,
For love of her whom God led forth
(The mother's being ceased on earth
When Baby came from Paradise),—
For love of Him who smote our lives,
　　And woke the chords of joy and pain,
We said, *Dear Christ!*—our hearts bent down
　　Like violets after rain.

And now the orchards, which were white
And red with blossoms when she came,
Were rich in autumn's mellow prime.
The clustered apples burnt like flame,
The soft-cheeked peaches blushed and fell,
The ivory chestnut burst its shell,
The grapes hung purpling in the grange;

And time wrought just as rich a change
  In little Baby Bell.
Her lissome form more perfect grew,
  And in her features we could trace,
  In softened curves, her mother's face!
Her angel-nature ripened too.
We thought her lovely when she came,
But she was holy, saintly now:—
Around her pale angelic brow
We saw a slender ring of flame!

God's hand had taken away the seal
  That held the portals of her speech;
And oft she said a few strange words
  Whose meaning lay beyond our reach.
She never was a child to us,
We never held her being's key,
We could not teach her holy things;
  She was Christ's self in purity.

It came upon us by degrees,
We saw its shadow ere it fell:
The knowledge that our God had sent
His messenger for Baby Bell.
We shuddered with unlanguaged pain,
And all our hopes were changed to fears,
And all our thoughts ran into tears
Like sunshine into rain.
We cried aloud in our belief,
"Oh, smite us gently, gently, God!
Teach us to bend and kiss the rod,
And perfect grow through grief."
Ah, how we loved her, God can tell;
Her heart was folded deep in ours.
Our hearts are broken, Baby Bell!

At last he came, the messenger,
  The messenger from unseen lands:
And what did dainty Baby Bell?
She only crossed her little hands,
She only looked more meek and fair!
We parted back her silken hair,
We wove the roses round her brow,—
White buds, the summer's drifted snow,—

Wrapt her from head to foot in flowers!
And then went dainty Baby Bell
   Out of this world of ours!

FANNIE

Fannie has the sweetest foot
Ever in a gaiter boot!
And the hoyden knows it,
And, of course, she shows it,—
Not the knowledge, but the foot,—
Yet with such a modest grace,
Never seems it out of place,
      Ah, there are not many
         Half so sly, or sad, or mad,
      Or wickeder than Fannie.

Fannie has the blackest hair
   Of any of the village girls;
It does not shower on her neck
   In silken or coquettish curls.
It droops in folds around her brow,
   As clouds, at night, around the moon,
Looped with lilies here and there,
   In many a dangerous festoon.
And Fannie wears a gipsy hat,
Saucily—yes, all of that!
      Ah, there are not many
         Half so sly, or sad, or mad,
      Or wickeder than Fannie.

Fannie wears an open dress—
   Ah! the charming chemisette!
Half concealing, half revealing
   Something far more charming yet.
Fannie drapes her breast with lace,
As one would drape a costly vase
To keep away mischievous flies;
But lace can't keep away one's eyes,
For every time her bosom heaves,
   Ah, it peepeth through it;
Yet Fannie looks the while as if
   Never once she knew it.

Ah, there are not many
    Half so sly, or sad, or mad,
Or innocent as Fannie.

Fannie lays her hand in mine;
    Fannie speaks with *naïveté,*
Fannie kisses me, she does!
    In her own coquettish way.
Then softly speaks and deeply sighs,
With angels nestled in her eyes.
In the merrie month of May,
Fannie swears sincerely
She will be my own, my wife,
And love me dearly, dearly
Ever after all her life.
        Ah, there are not many
            Half so sly, or sad, or mad,
        As my true-hearted Fannie.

AT A READING

The spare Professor, grave and bald,
Began his paper. It was called,
I think, "A brief Historic Glance
At Russia, Germany, and France."
A glance, but to my best belief
'Twas almost anything but brief—
A wide survey, in which the earth
Was seen before mankind had birth;
Strange monsters basked them in the sun,
Behemoth, armored glyptodon,
And in the dawn's unpractised ray
The transient dodo winged its way;
Then, by degrees, through silt and slough,
We reached Berlin—I don't know how.
The good Professor's monotone
Had turned me into senseless stone
Instanter, but that near me sat
Hypatia in her new spring hat,
Blue-eyed, intent, with lips whose bloom
Lighted the heavy-curtained room.
Hypatia—ah, what lovely things
Are fashioned out of eighteen springs!

At first, in sums of this amount,
The blighting winters do not count.
Just as my eyes were growing dim
With heaviness, I saw that slim,
Erect, elastic figure there,
Like a pond-lily taking air.
She looked so fresh, so wise, so neat,
So altogether crisp and sweet,
I quite forgot what Bismarck said,
And why the Emperor shook his head,
And how it was Von Moltke's frown
Cost France another frontier town.
The only facts I took away
From the Professor's theme that day
Were these: a forehead broad and low,
Such as the antique sculptures show;
A chin to Greek perfection true;
Eyes of Astarte's tender blue;
A high complexion without fleck
Or flaw, and curls about her neck.

MEMORY

My mind lets go a thousand things,
Like dates of wars and deaths of kings,
And yet recalls the very hour—
'Twas noon by yonder village tower,
And on the last blue noon in May—
The wind came briskly up this way,
Crisping the brook beside the road;
Then, pausing here, set down its load
Of pine-scents, and shook listlessly
Two petals from that wild-rose tree.

APPARITIONS

At noon of night, and at the night's pale end,
  Such things have chanced to me
As one, by day, would scarcely tell a friend
  For fear of mockery.

Shadows, you say, mirages of the brain!
  I know not, faith, not I.
Is it more strange the dead should walk again
  Than that the quick should die?

FREDERICKSBURG

The increasing moonlight drifts across my bed,
  And on the churchyard by the road, I know,
  It falls as white and noislessly as snow. . . .
'Twas such a night two weary summers fled
The stars as now were waning overhead.
  Listen! again the shrill-lipt bugles blow
  Where the swift currents of the river flow
Past Fredericksburg: far off the heavens are red
With sudden conflagration: on yon height,
  Linstock in hand, the gunners hold their breath:
A signal rocket pierces the dense night,
  Flings its spent stars upon the town beneath:
Hark!—the artillery massing on the right,
  Hark!—the black squadrons wheeling down to death!

GUILIELMUS REX

The folk who lived in Shakespeare's day
And saw that gentle figure pass
By London Bridge, his frequent way—
They little knew what man he was.

The pointed beard, the courteous mien,
The equal port to high and low,
All this they saw or might have seen—
But not the light behind the brow!

The doublet's modest gray or brown,
The slender sword-hilt's plain device,
What sign had these for prince or clown?
Few turned, or none, to scan him twice.

Yet 't was the king of England's kings!
The rest with all their pomps and trains

Are mouldered, half-remembered things—
'T is he alone that lives and reigns!

BATUSCHKA

From yonder gilded minaret
Beside the steel-blue Neva set,
I faintly catch, from time to time,
The sweet, aerial midnight chime—
    "God save the Tsar!"

Above the ravelins and the moats
Of the white citadel it floats;
And men in dungeons far beneath
Listen, and pray, and gnash their teeth—
    "God save the Tsar!"

The soft reiterations sweep
Across the horror of their sleep,
As if some demon in his glee
Were mocking at their misery—
    "God save the Tsar!"

In his Red Palace over there,
Wakeful, he needs must hear the prayer.
How can it drown the broken cries
Wrung from his children's agonies?—
    "God save the Tsar!"

Father they called him from of old—
Batuschka! . . . How his heart is cold!
Wait till a million scourgëd men
Rise in their awful might, and then—
    "God save the Tsar!"

UNGUARDED GATES

Wide open and unguarded stand our gates,
Named of the four winds, North, South, East, and West;
Portals that lead to an enchanted land
Of cities, forests, fields of living gold,
Vast prairies, lordly summits touched with snow,

Majestic rivers sweeping proudly past
The Arab's date palm and the Norseman's pine—
A realm wherein are fruits of every zone,
Airs of all climes, for, lo! throughout the year
The red rose blossoms somewhere—a rich land,
A later Eden planted in the wilds,
With not an inch of earth within its bound
But if a slave's foot press it sets him free.
Here, it is written, Toil shall have its wage,
And Honor honor, and the humblest man
Stand level with the highest in the law.
Of such a land have men in dungeons dreamed,
And with the vision brightening in their eyes
Gone smiling to the fagot and the sword.

Wide open and unguarded stand our gates,
And through them presses a wild, motley throng—
Men from the Volga and the Tartar steppes,
Featureless figures of the Hoang-Ho,
Malayan, Scythian, Teuton, Kelt, and Slav,
Flying the Old World's poverty and scorn;
These bringing with them unknown gods and rites,—
Those, tiger passions, here to stretch their claws.
In street and alley what strange tongues are loud,
Accents of menace alien to our air,
Voices that once the Tower of Babel knew!

O Liberty, white Goddess! is it well
To leave the gates unguarded? On thy breast
Fold Sorrow's children, soothe the hurts of fate.
Lift the downtrodden, but with hand of steel
Stay those who to thy sacred portals come
To waste the gifts of freedom. Have a care
Lest from thy brow the clustered stars be torn
And trampled in the dust. For so of old
The thronging Goth and Vandal trampled Rome,
And where the temples of the Caesars stood
The lean wolf unmolested made her lair.

John Hay

(1838–1905)

John Hay was born in Salem, Indiana, and grew up in Pike County, Illinois, which was the setting for his famous *Pike County Ballads*. Hay graduated from Brown University and was admitted to the bar in Illinois. During the Civil War he served active duty as a colonel and was a private secretary to Abraham Lincoln. After the war he held diplomatic posts in Paris, Vienna, and Madrid. Under President McKinley he served as ambassador to England from 1897 to 1898. When the Spanish-American war broke out Hay was appointed secretary of state.

JIM BLUDSO

Wall, no! I can't tell whar he lives,
    Becase he don't live, you see;
Leastways, he's got out of the habit
    Of livin' like you and me.
Whar have you been for the last three year
    That you haven't heard folks tell
How Jimmy Bludso passed in his checks
    The night of the Prairie Belle?

He weren't no saint,—them engineers
    Is all pretty much alike,—
One wife in Natchez-under-the-Hill
    And another one here, in Pike;
A keerless man in his talk was Jim,
    And an awkward hand in a row,

But he never flunked, and he never lied,—
    I reckon he never knowed how.

And this was all the religion he had,—
    To treat his engine well;
Never be passed on the river;
    To mind the pilot's bell;
And if ever the Prairie Belle took fire,—
    A thousand times he swore,
He'd hold her nozzle agin the bank
    Till the last soul got ashore.

All boats has their day on the Mississip,
    And her day come at last,—
The Movastar was a better boat,
    But the Belle she *wouldn't* be passed.
And so she come tearin' along that night—
    The oldest craft on the line—
With a nigger squat on her safety-valve,
    And her furnace crammed, rosin and pine

The fire bust out as she clared the bar,
    And burnt a hole in the night,
And quick as a flash she turned, and made
    For that willer-bank on the right.
There was runnin' and cursin', but Jim yelled out,
    Over all the infernal roar,
"I'll hold her nozzle agin the bank
    Till the last galoot's ashore."

Through the hot, black breath of the burnin' boat
    Jim Bludso's voice was heard,
And they all had trust in his cussedness,
    And knowed he would keep his word.
And, sure's you're born, they all got off
    Afore the smokestacks fell,—
And Bludso's ghost went up alone
    In the smoke of the Prairie Belle.

He weren't no saint,—but at jedgment
    I'd run my chance with Jim,
'Longside of some pious gentlemen
    That wouldn't shook hands with him.
He seen his duty, a dead-sure thing,—

And went for it thar and then;
And Christ ain't a goin to be too hard
On a man that died for men.

LITTLE BREECHES

I don't go much on religion,
    I never ain't had no show;
But I've got a middlin' tight grip, sir,
    On a handful o' things I know.
I don't pan out on the prophets
    And free-will and that sort of thing—
But I be'lieve in God and the angels,
    Ever sence one night last spring.

I come into town with some turnips,
    And my little Gabe come along—
No four-year-old in the county
    Could beat him for pretty and strong—
Peart and chipper and sassy,
    Always ready to swear and fight—
And I'd larnt him to chaw terbacker
    Jest to keep his milk-teeth white.

The snow come down like a blanket
    As I passed by Taggart's store;
I went in for a jug of molasses
    And left the team at the door.
They scared at something and started—
    I heard one little squall,
And hell-to-split over the prairie!
    Went team, Little Breeches, and all.

Hell-to-split over the prairie!
    I was almost froze with skeer;
But we rousted up some torches,
    And sarched for 'em far and near.
At last we struck hosses and wagon,
    Snowed under a soft white mound,
Upsot, dead beat, but of little Gabe
    No hide nor hair was found.

And here all hope soured on me
    Of my fellow-critter's aid;
I jest flopped down on my marrow-bones,
    Crotch-deep in the snow, and prayed.

  * * * * *

By this, the torches was played out,
    And me and Isrul Parr
Went off for some wood to a sheepfold
    That he said was somewhar thar.

We found it at last, and a little shed
    Where they shut up the lambs at night;
We looked in and seen them huddled thar,
    So warm and sleepy and white;
And thar sot Little Breeches and chirped,
    As peart as ever you see,
"I want a chaw of terbacker,
    And that's what's the matter of me."

How did he git thar? Angels.
    He could never have walked in that storm:
They jest scooped down and toted him
    To whar it was safe and warm.
And I think that saving a little child,
    And fotching him to his own,
Is a derned sight better business
    Than loafing around the Throne.

GOOD AND BAD LUCK

Good Luck is the gayest of all gay girls;
    Long in one place she will not stay:
Back from your brow she strokes the curls,
    Kisses you quick and flies away.

But Madame Bad Luck soberly comes
    And stays—no fancy has she for flitting;
Snatches of true-love songs she hums,
    And sits by your bed, and brings her knitting.

THE ENCHANTED SHIRT

The King was sick. His cheek was red,
 And his eye was clear and bright;
He ate and drank with a kingly zest,
 And peacefully snored at night.

But he said he was sick, and a king should know,
 And doctors came by the score.
They did not cure him. He cut off their heads,
 And sent to the schools for more.

At last two famous doctors came,
 And one was as poor as a rat,—
He had passed his life in studious toil,
 And never found time to grow fat.

The other had never looked in a book;
 His patients gave him no trouble:
If they recovered, they paid him well;
 If they died, their heirs paid double.

Together they looked at the royal tongue,
 As the King on his couch reclined;
In succession they thumped his august chest,
 But no trace of disease could find.

The old sage said, "You're as sound as a nut."
 "Hang him up," roared the King in a gale—
In the ten-knot gale of royal rage;
 The other leech grew a shade pale;

But he pensively rubbed his sagacious nose,
 And thus his prescription ran—
The King will be well, if he sleeps one night
 In the Shirt of a Happy Man.

      *   *   *   *   *

Wide o'er the realm the couriers rode,
 And fast their horses ran,
And many they saw, and to many they spoke,
 But they found no Happy Man.

They found poor men who would fain be rich,
   And rich who thought they were poor;
And men who twisted their waist in stays,
   And women that shorthose wore.

They saw two men by the roadside sit,
   And both bemoaned their lot;
For one had buried his wife, he said,
   And the other one had not.

At last they came to a village gate,
   A beggar lay whistling there;
He whistled, and sang, and laughed, and rolled
   On the grass in the soft June air.

The weary courtiers paused and looked
   At the scamp so blithe and gay;
And one of them said, "Heaven save you, friend!
   You seem to be happy to-day."

"O yes, fair sirs," the rascal laughed,
   And his voice rang free and glad;
"An idle man has so much to do
   That he never has time to be sad."

"This is our man," the courier said;
   "Our luck has lead us aright.
I will give you a hundred ducats, friend,
   For the loan of your shirt to-night."

The merry blackguard lay back on the grass,
   And laughed till his face was black;
"I would do it, God wot," and he roared with the fun,
   "But I haven't a shirt to my back."

     *   *   *   *   *

Each day to the King the reports came in
   Of his unsuccessful spies,
And the sad panorama of human woes
   Passed daily under his eyes.

And he grew ashamed of his useless life,
   And his maladies hatched in gloom;

He opened his windows and let the air
  Of the free heaven into his room.

And out he went in the world, and toiled
  In his own appointed way;
And the people blessed him, the land was glad,
  And the King was well and gay.

DISTICHS

I

Wisely a woman prefers to a lover a man who neglects her.
  This one may love her some day, some day the lover will not.

II

There are three species of creatures who when they seem coming
    are going,
  When they seem going they come: Diplomates, women, and
    crabs.

III

Pleasures too hastily tasted grow sweeter in fond recollection,
  As the pomegranate plucked green ripens far over the sea.

IV

As the meek beasts in the Garden came flocking for Adam to name
    them,
  Men for a title to-day crawl to the feet of a king.

V

What is a first love worth, except to prepare for a second?
  What does the second love bring? Only regret for the first.

VI

Health was wooed by the Romans in groves of the laurel and myrtle.
  Happy and long are the lives brightened by glory and love.

VII

Wine is like rain: when it falls on the mire it but makes it the fouler,
  But when it strikes the good soil wakes it to beauty and bloom.

VIII

Break not the rose; its fragrance and beauty are surely sufficient:
  Resting contented with these, never a thorn shall you feel.

IX

When you break up housekeeping, you learn the extent of your
    treasures;
  Till he begins to reform, no one can number his sins.

X

Maidens! why should you worry in choosing whom you shall
    marry?
  Choose whom you may, you will find you have got somebody
    else.

XI

Unto each man comes a day when his favorite sins all forsake him,
  And he complacently thinks he has forsaken his sins.

XII

Be not too anxious to gain your next-door neighbor's approval:
  Live your own life, and let him strive your approval to gain.

XIII

Who would succeed in the world should be wise in the use of his
    pronouns.
  Utter the You twenty times, where you once utter the I.

XIV

The best loved man or maid in the town would perish with anguish
  Could they hear all that their friends say in the course of a day.

XV

True luck consists not in holding the best of the cards at the table:
  Luckiest he who knows just when to rise and go home.

XVI

Pleasant enough it is to hear the world speak of your virtues;
  But in your secret heart 't is of your faults you are proud.

XVII

Try not to beat back the current, yet be not drowned in its waters;
  Speak with the speech of the world, think with the thoughts of
    the few.

XVIII

Make all good men your well-wishers, and then, in the years' steady
    sifting,
  Some of them turn into friends. Friends are the sunshine of life.

THE ADVANCE GUARD

In the dream of the Northern poets,
    The brave who in battle die
Fight on in shadowy phalanx
    In the field of the upper sky;
And as we read the sounding rhyme,
    The reverent fancy hears
The ghostly ring of the viewless swords
    And the clash of the spectral spears.

We think with imperious questionings
    Of the brothers whom we have lost,
And we strive to track in death's mystery
    The flight of each valiant ghost.
The Northern myth comes back to us,
    And we feel, through our sorrow's night,
That those young souls are striving still
    Somewhere for the truth and light.

It was not their time for rest and sleep;
  Their hearts beat high and strong;
In their fresh veins the blood of youth
  Was singing its hot, sweet song.
The open heaven bent over them,
  Mid flowers their lithe feet trod,
Their lives lay vivid in light, and blest
  By the smiles of women and God.

Again they come! Again I hear
  The tread of that goodly band;
I know the flash of Ellsworth's eye
  And the grasp of his hard, warm hand;
And Putnam, and Shaw, of the lion-heart,
  And an eye like a Boston girl's;
And I see the light of heaven which lay
  On Ulric Dahlgren's curls.

There is no power in the gloom of hell
  To quench those spirits' fire;
There is no power in the bliss of heaven
  To bid them not aspire;
But somewhere in the eternal plan
  That strength, that life survive,
And like the files on Lookout's crest,
  Above death's clouds they strive.

A chosen corps, they are marching on
  In a wider field than ours;
Those bright battalions still fulfill
  The scheme of the heavenly powers;
And high brave thoughts float down to us,
  The echoes of that far fight,
Like the flash of a distant picket's gun
  Through the shades of the severing night.

No fear for them! In our lower field
  Let us keep our arms unstained,
That at last we be worthy to stand with them
  On the shining heights they've gained.
We shall meet and greet in closing ranks
  In Time's declining sun,
When the bugles of God shall sound recall
  And the battle of life be won.

THE LIGHT OF LOVE

Each shining light above us
  Has its own peculiar grace;
But every light of heaven
  Is in my darling's face.

For it is like the sunlight,
  So strong and pure and warm,
That folds all good and happy things,
  And guards from gloom and harm.

And it is like the moonlight,
  So holy and so calm;
The rapt peace of a summer night,
  When soft winds die in balm.

And it is like the starlight;
  For, love her as I may,
She dwells still lofty and serene
  In mystery far away.

WORDS

When violets were springing
  And sunshine filled the day,
And happy birds were singing
  The praises of the May,
A word came to me, blighting
  The beauty of the scene,
And in my heart was winter,
  Though all the trees were green.

Now down the blast go sailing
  The dead leaves, brown and sere;
The forests are bewailing
  The dying of the year;
A word comes to me, lighting
  With rapture all the air,
And in my heart is summer,
  Though all the trees are bare.

THE WHITE FLAG

I sent my love two roses,—one
   As white as driven snow,
And one a blushing royal red,
   A flaming Jacqueminot.

I meant to touch and test my fate;
   That night I should divine,
The moment I should see my love,
   If her true heart were mine.

For if she holds me dear, I said,
   She'll wear my blushing rose;
If not, she'll wear my cold Lamarque,
   As white as winter's snows.

My heart sank when I met her: sure
   I had been overbold,
For on her breast my pale rose lay
   In virgin whiteness cold.

Yet with low words she greeted me,
   With smiles divinely tender;
Upon her cheek the red rose dawned,—
   The white rose meant surrender.

Bret Harte

(1839–1902)

Francis Bret Harte, internationally known novelist and short story writer, was born in Albany, New York, and at the age of eighteen, moved to California. He taught school, worked in a mine and printing office, and edited a newspaper. In 1863 he was appointed secretary of the U.S. branch mint in San Francisco. He was editor of the *Overland Monthly*, the West's important literary magazine, from 1868 to 1870. He moved back to New York in 1871 but left seven years later, this time for good. Harte held consulships in Germany and Scotland after which he moved to London where he lived the last years of his life. He never returned to America.

JOHN BURNS OF GETTYSBURG

Have you heard the story that gossips tell
Of Burns of Gettysburg?—No? Ah, well:
Brief is the glory that hero earns,
Briefer the story of poor John Burns.
He was the fellow who won renown,—
The only man who did n't back down
When the rebels rode through his native town;
But held his own in the fight next day,
When all his townsfolk ran away.
That was in July sixty-three,
The very day that General Lee,
Flower of Southern chivalry,
Baffled and beaten, backward reeled
From a stubborn Meade and a barren field.

I might tell how but the day before
John Burns stood at his cottage door,
Looking down the village street,
Where, in the shade of his peaceful vine,
He heard the low of his gathered kine,
And felt their breath with incense sweet;
Or I might say, when the sunset burned
The old farm gable, he thought it turned
The milk that fell like a babbling flood
Into the milk-pail red as blood!
Or how he fancied the hum of bees
Were bullets buzzing among the trees.
But all such fanciful thoughts as these
Were strange to a practical man like Burns,
Who minded only his own concerns,
Troubled no more by fancies fine
Than one of his calm-eyed, long-tailed kine,—
Quite old-fashioned and matter-of-fact,
Slow to argue, but quick to act.
That was the reason, as some folk say,
He fought so well on that terrible day.

And it was terrible. On the right
Raged for hours the heady fight,
Thundered the battery's double bass,—
Difficult music for men to face;
While on the left—where now the graves
Undulate like the living waves
That all that day unceasing swept
Up to the pits the rebels kept—
Round shot ploughed the upland glades,
Sown with bullets, reaped with blades;
Shattered fences here and there
Tossed their splinters in the air;
The very trees were stripped and bare;
The barns that once held yellow grain
Were heaped with harvests of the slain;
The cattle bellowed on the plain,
The turkeys screamed with might and main,
And brooding barn-fowl left their rest
With strange shells bursting in each nest.

Just where the tide of battle turns,
Erect and lonely stood old John Burns.

How do you think the man was dressed?
He wore an ancient long buff vest,
Yellow as saffron,—but his best;
And buttoned over his manly breast
Was a bright blue coat, with a rolling collar,
And large gilt buttons,—size of a dollar,—
With tails that the country-folk called "swaller."
He wore a broad-brimmed, bell-crowned hat,
White as the locks on which it sat.
Never had such a sight been seen
For forty years on the village green,
Since old John Burns was a country beau,
And went to the "quiltings" long ago.

Close at his elbows all that day,
Veterans of the Peninsula,
Sunburnt and bearded, charged away;
And striplings, downy of lip and chin,—
Clerks that the Home Guard mustered in,—
Glanced, as they passed, at the hat he wore,
Then at the rifle his right hand bore,
And hailed him, from out their youthful lore.
With scraps of a slangy *répertoire:*
"How are you, White Hat?" "Put her through!"
"Your head's level!" and "Bully for you!"
Called him "Daddy,"—begged he'd disclose
The name of the tailor who made his clothes,
And what was the value he set on those;
While Burns, unmindful of jeer and scoff,
Stood there picking the rebels off,—
With his long brown rifle and bell-crown hat,
And the swallow-tails they were laughing at.

'T was but a moment, for that respect
Which clothes all courage their voices checked;
And something the wildest could understand
Spake in the old man's strong right hand,
And his corded throat, and the lurking frown
Of his eyebrows under his old bell-crown;
Until, as they gazed, there crept an awe
Through the ranks in whispers, and some men saw,
In the antique vestments and long white hair,
The Past of the Nation in battle there;
And some of the soldiers since declare

That the gleam of his old white hat afar,
Like the crested plume of the brave Navarre,
That day was their oriflamme of war.

So raged the battle. You know the rest:
How the rebels, beaten and backward pressed,
Broke at the final charge and ran.
At which John Burns—a practical man—
Shouldered his rifle, unbent his brows,
And then went back to his bees and cows.

That is the story of old John Burns;
This is the moral the reader learns:
In fighting the battle, the question 's whether
You'll show a hat that's white, or a feather!

"HOW ARE YOU, SANITARY?"

Down the picket-guarded lane
   Rolled the comfort-laden wain,
Cheered by shouts that shook the plain,
   Soldier-like and merry:
Phrases such as camps may teach,
Sabre-cuts of Saxon speech,
Such as "Bully!" "Them's the peach!"
   "Wade in, Sanitary!"

Right and left the caissons drew
As the car went lumbering through,
Quick succeeding in review
   Squadrons military;
Sunburnt men with beards like frieze,
Smooth-faced boys, and cries like these,—
"U.S. San. Com." "That's the cheese!"
   "Pass in, Sanitary!"

In such cheer it struggled on
Till the battle front was won:
Then the car, its journey done,
   Lo! was stationary;
And where bullets whistling fly
Came the sadder, fainter cry,

"Help us, brothers, ere we die,—
  Save us, Sanitary!"

Such the work. The phantom flies,
Wrapped in battle clouds that rise;
But the brave—whose dying eyes,
  Veiled and visionary,
See the jasper gates swung wide,
See the parted throng outside—
Hears the voice to those who ride:
  "Pass in, Sanitary!"

A SANITARY MESSAGE

Last night, above the whistling wind,
  I heard the welcome rain,—
A fusillade upon the roof,
  A tattoo on the pane:
The keyhole piped; the chimney-top
  A warlike trumpet blew;
Yet, mingling with these sounds of strife,
  A softer voice stole through.

"Give thanks, O brothers!" said the voice,
  "That He who sent the rains
Hath spared your fields the scarlet dew
  That drips from patriot veins:
I've seen the grass on Eastern graves
  In brighter verdure rise;
But, oh! the rain that gave it life
  Sprang first from human eyes.

"I come to wash away no stain
  Upon your wasted lea;
I raise no banners, save the ones
  The forest waves to me:
Upon the mountain side, where Spring
  Her farthest picket sets,
My reveille awakes a host
  Of grassy bayonets.

"I visit every humble roof;
  I mingle with the low

Only upon the highest peaks
    My blessings fall in snow;
Until, in tricklings of the stream
    And drainings of the lea,
My unspent bounty comes at last
    To mingle with the sea."

And thus all night, above the wind,
    I heard the welcome rain,—
A fusillade upon the roof,
    A tattoo on the pane:
The keyhole piped; the chimney-top
    A warlike trumpet blew;
But, mingling with these sound of strife,
    This hymn of peace stole through.

GRIZZLY

Coward,—of heroic size,
In whose lazy muscles lies
Strength we fear and yet despise;
Savage,—whose relentless tusks
Are content with acorn husks;
Robber,—whose exploits ne'er soared
O'er the bee's or squirrel's hoard;
Whiskered chin and feeble nose,
Claws of steel on baby toes,—
Here, in solitude and shade,
Shambling, shuffling plantigrade,
Be thy courses undismayed!

Here, where Nature makes thy bed,
Let thy rude, half-human tread
    Point to hidden Indian springs,
Lost in ferns and fragrant grasses,
    Hovered o'er by timid wings,
Where the wood-duck lightly passes,
Where the wild bee holds her sweets,—
Epicurean retreats,
Fit for thee, and better than
Fearful spoils of dangerous man.
In thy fat-jowled deviltry
Friar Tuck shall live in thee;

Thou mayst levy tithe and dole;
  Thou shalt spread the woodland cheer,
From the pilgrim taking toll;
  Match thy cunning with his fear;
Eat, and drink, and have thy fill;
Yet remain an outlaw still!

COYOTE

Blown out of the prairie in twilight and dew,
Half bold and half timid, yet lazy all through;
Loath ever to leave, and yet fearful to stay,
He limps in the clearing, an outcast in gray.

A shade on the stubble, a ghost by the wall,
Now leaping, now limping, now risking a fall,
Lop-eared and large-jointed, but ever alway
A thoroughly vagabond outcast in gray.

Here, Carlo, old fellow,—he's one of your kind,—
Go, seek him, and bring him in out of the wind.
What! snarling, my Carlo! So even dogs may
Deny their own kin in the outcast in gray.

Well, take what you will—though it be on the sly,
Marauding or begging,—I shall not ask why,
But will call it a dole, just to help on his way
A four-footed friar in orders of gray!

DICKENS IN CAMP

Above the pines the moon was slowly drifting,
  The river sang below;
The dim Sierras, far beyond, uplifting
  Their minarets of snow.

The roaring camp-fire, with rude humor, painted
  The ruddy tints of health
On haggard face and form that drooped and fainted
  In the fierce race for wealth;

Till one arose, and from his pack's scant treasure
   A hoarded volume drew,
And cards were dropped from hands of listless leisure
   To hear the tale anew.

And then, while round them shadows gathered faster,
   And as the firelight fell,
He read aloud the book wherein the Master
   Had writ of "Little Nell."

Perhaps 't was boyish fancy,—for the reader
   Was youngest of them all,—
But, as he read, from clustering pine and cedar
   A silence seemed to fall;

The fir-trees, gathering closer in the shadows,
   Listened in every spray,
While the whole camp with "Nell" on English meadows
   Wandered and lost their way.

And so in mountain solitudes—o'ertaken
   As by some spell divine—
Their cares dropped from them like the needles shaken
   From out the gusty pine.

Lost is that camp and wasted all its fire;
   And he who wrought that spell?
Ah! towering pine and stately Kentish spire,
   Ye have one tale to tell!

Lost is that camp, but let its fragrant story
   Blend with the breath that thrills
With hop-vine's incense all the pensive glory
   That fills the Kentish hills.

And on that grave where English oak and holly
   And laurel wreaths entwine,
Deem it not all a too presumptuous folly,
   This spray of Western pine!

THE AGED STRANGER

An Incident of the War

"I was with Grant"—the stranger said;
    Said the farmer, "Say no more,
But rest thee here at my cottage porch,
    For thy feet are weary and sore."

"I was with Grant"—the stranger said;
    Said the farmer, "Nay, no more,—
I prithee sit at my frugal board,
    And eat of my humble store.

"How fares my boy,—my soldier boy,
    Of the old Ninth Army Corps?
I warrant he bore him gallantly
    In the smoke and the battle's roar!"

"I know him not," said the aged man,
    "And, as I remarked before,
I was with Grant"— "Nay, nay, I know,"
    Said the farmer, "say no more:

"He fell in battle,—I see, alas!
    Thou 'dst smooth these tidings o'er,—
Nay, speak the truth, whatever it be,
    Though it rend my bosom's core.

"How fell he? With his face to the foe,
    Upholding the flag he bore?
Oh, say not that my boy disgraced
    The uniform that he wore!"

"I cannot tell," said the aged man,
    "And should have remarked before,
That I was with Grant,—in Illinois,—
    Some three years before the war."

Then the farmer spake him never a word,
    But beat with his fist full sore
That aged man who had worked for Grant
    Some three years before the war.

"JIM"

Say there! P'r'aps
Some on you chaps
   Might know Jim Wild?
Well,—no offense:
Thar ain't no sense
   In gittin' riled!

Jim was my chum
   Up on the Bar:
That's why I come
   Down from up yar,
Lookin' for Jim.
Thank ye, sir! *You*
Ain't of that crew,—
   Blest if you are!

Money? Not much:
   That ain't my kind;
I ain't no such.
   Rum? I don't mind,
Seein' it's you.

Well, this yer Jim,—
Did you know him?
Jes' 'bout your size;
Same kind of eyes;—
Well, that is strange:
   Why, it's two year
   Since he came here,
Sick, for a change.

Well, here's to us:
   Eh?
The h—— you say!
   Dead?
That little cuss?

What makes you star',
You over thar?
Can't a man drop
's glass in yer shop
But you must r'ar?

It would n't take
    D———d much to break
You and your bar.

        Dead!
Poor—little—Jim!
Why, thar was me,
Jones, and Bob Lee,
Harry and Ben,—
No-account men:
Then to take *him!*

Well, thar— Good-by—
No more, sir—I—
        Eh?
What's that you say?
Why, dern it!—sho!—
No? Yes! By Joe!
        Sold!

Sold! Why, you limb,
You ornery,
        Derned old
Long-legged Jim.

CHIQUITA

Beautiful! Sir, you may say so. Thar is n't her match in the county;
Is thar, old gal,—Chiquita, my darling, my beauty?
Feel of that neck, sir,—thar's velvet! Whoa! steady,—ah, will you,
    you vixen!
Whoa! I say. Jack, trot her out; let the gentleman look at her paces.

Morgan!—she ain't nothing else, and I've got the papers to prove it.
Sired by Chippewa Chief, and twelve hundred dollars won't buy
    her.
Briggs of Tuolumne owned her. Did you know Briggs of Tuo-
    lumme?
Busted hisself in White Pine, and blew out his brains down in
    'Frisco?

Hed n't no savey, hed Briggs. Thar, Jack! that'll do,—quit that
    foolin'!

Nothin' to what she kin do, when she's got her work cut out before
her.
Hosses is hosses, you know, and likewise, too, jockeys is jockeys:
And 't ain't ev'ry man as can ride as knows what a hoss has got in
him.

Know the old ford on the Fork, that nearly got Flanigan's leaders?
Nasty in daylight, you bet, and a mighty rough ford in low water!

Well, it ain't six weeks ago that me and the Jedge and his nevey
Struck for that ford in the night, in the rain, and the water all round
us;
Up to our flanks in the gulch, and Rattlesnake Creek just a-bilin',
Not a plank left in the dam, and nary a bridge on the river.
I had the gray, and the Jedge had his roan, and his nevey, Chiquita;
And after us trundled the rocks jest loosed from the top of the
cañon.

Lickity, lickity, switch, we came to the ford, and Chiquita
Buckled right down to her work, and, afore I could yell to her rider,
Took water jest at the ford, and there was the Jedge and me stand-
ing,
And twelve hundred dollars of hoss-flesh afloat, and a-driftin' to
thunder!

Would ye b'lieve it? That night, that hoss, that 'ar filly, Chiquita,
Walked herself into her stall, and stood there, all quiet and dripping:
Clean as a beaver or rat, with nary a buckle of harness,
Just as she swarm the Fork,—that hoss, that 'ar filly, Chiquita.

That's what I call a hoss! and— What did you say?—Oh, the nevey?
Drownded, I reckon,—leastways, he never kem back to deny it.

Ye see the derned fool had no seat, ye could n't have made him a
rider;
And then, ye know, boys will be boys, and hosses—well, hosses is
hosses!

DOW'S FLAT

(1856)

Dow's Flat. That's its name;
   And I reckon that you
  Are a stranger? The same?
   Well, I thought it was true,—
For thar is n't a man on the river as can't spot the place at first view.

It was called after Dow,—
   Which the same was an ass,—
  And as to the how
   Thet the thing kem to pass,—
Jest tie up your hoss to that buckeye, and sit ye down here in the
      grass.

You see this 'yer Dow
   Hed the worst kind of luck;
  He slipped up somehow
   On each thing thet he struck.
Why, ef he'd a straddled thet fence-rail, the derned thing 'd get up
      and buck.

He mined on the bar
   Till he could n't pay rates;
  He was smashed by a car
   When he tunneled with Bates;
And right on the top of his trouble kem his wife and five kids from
      the States.

It was rough,—mighty rough;
   But the boys they stood by,
  And they brought him the stuff
   For a house, on the sly;
And the old woman,—well, she did washing, and took on when no
      one was nigh.

But this 'yer luck of Dow's
   Was so powerful mean
  That the spring near his house
   Dried right up on the green;
And he sunk forty feet down for water, but nary a drop to be seen.

Then the bar petered out,
  And the boys would n't stay;
And the chills got about,
  And his wife fell away;
But Dow in his well kept a peggin' in his usual ridikilous way.

One day,—it was June,—
  And a year ago, jest—
This Dow kem at noon
  To his work like the rest,
With a shovel and pick on his shoulder, and derringer hid in his
  breast.

He goes to the well,
  And he stands on the brink,
And stops for a spell
  Jest to listen and think:
For the sun in his eyes (jest like this, sir!), you see, kinder made the
  cuss blink.

His two ragged gals
  In the gulch were at play,
And a gownd that was Sal's
  Kinder flapped on a bay:
Not much for a man to be leavin', but his all,—as I've heer'd the
  folks say.

And—That's a peart hoss
  Thet you 've got,—ain't it now?
What might be her cost?
  Eh? Oh!—Well, then, Dow—
Let's see,—well, that forty-foot grave wasn't his, sir, that day,
  anyhow.

For a blow of his pick
  Sorter caved in the side,
And he looked and turned sick,
  Then he trembled and cried.
For you see the dern cuss had struck—"Water?"—Beg your parding,
  young man,—there you lied!

It was *gold*,—in the quartz,
  And it ran all alike;

And I reckon five oughts
　　Was the worth of that strike;
And that house with the coopilow's his'n,—which the same is n't
　　bad for a Pike.

Thet's why it's Dow's Flat;
　　And the thing of it is
That he kinder got that
　　Through sheer contrairiness:
For 't was *water* the derned cuss was seekin', and his luck made him
　　certain to miss.

Thet's so! Thar's your way,
　　To the left of yon tree;
But—a—look h'yur, say?
　　Won't you come up to tea?
No? Well, then the next time you're passin'; and ask after Dow,—
　　and thet's *me*.

PLAIN LANGUAGE FROM TRUTHFUL JAMES
—or—
THE HEATHEN CHINEE

Table Mountain, 1870

Which I wish to remark,
　　And my language is plain,
That for ways that are dark
　　And for tricks that are vain,
The heathen Chinee is peculiar,
　　Which the same I would rise to explain.

Ah Sin was his name;
　　And I shall not deny,
In regard to the same,
　　What that name might imply;
But his smile it was pensive and childlike,
　　As I frequent remarked to Bill Nye.

It was August the third,
　　And quite soft was the skies;
Which it might be inferred
　　That Ah Sin was likewise;

Yet he played it that day upon William
  And me in a way I despise.

Which we had a small game,
  And Ah Sin took a hand:
It was Euchre. The same
  He did not understand;
But he smiled as he sat by the table,
  With the smile that was childlike and bland.

Yet the cards they were stocked
  In a way that I grieve,
And my feelings were shocked
  At the state of Nye's sleeve,
Which was stuffed full of aces and bowers,
  And the same with intent to deceive.

But the hands that were played
  By that heathen Chinee,
And the points that he made,
  Were quite frightful to see,—
Till at last he put down a right bower,
  Which the same Nye had dealt unto me.

Then I looked up at Nye,
  And he gazed upon me;
And he rose with a sigh,
  And said, "Can this be?
We are ruined by Chinese cheap labor,"—
  And he went for that heathen Chinee.

In the scene that ensued
  I did not take a hand,
But the floor it was strewed
  Like the leaves on the strand
With the cards that Ah Sin had been hiding,
  In the game "he did not understand."

In his sleeves, which were long,
  He had twenty-four jacks,—
Which was coming it strong,
  Yet I state but the facts;
And we found on his nails, which were taper,
  What is frequent in tapers,—that's wax.

Which is why I remark,
  And my language is plain,
That for ways that are dark
  And for tricks that are vain,
The heathen Chinee is peculiar,—
  Which the same I am free to maintain.

THE SOCIETY UPON THE STANISLAUS

I reside at Table Mountain, and my name is Truthful James;
I am not up to small deceit or any sinful games;
And I'll tell in simple language what I know about the row
That broke up our Society upon the Stanislow.

But first I would remark, that it is not a proper plan
For any scientific gent to whale his fellow-man,
And, if a member don't agree with his peculiar whim,
To lay for that same member for to "put a head" on him.

Now nothing could be finer or more beautiful to see
Than the first six months' proceedings of that same Society,
Till Brown of Calaveras brought a lot of fossil bones
That he found within a tunnel near the tenement of Jones.

Then Brown he read a paper, and he reconstructed there,
From those same bones, an animal that was extremely rare;
And Jones then asked the Chair for a suspension of the rules,
Till he could prove that those same bones was one of his lost mules.

Then Brown he smiled a bitter smile, and said he was at fault,
It seemed he had been trespassing on Jones's family vault;
He was a most sarcastic man, this quiet Mr. Brown,
And on several occasions he had cleaned out the town.

Now I hold it is not decent for a scientific gent
To say another is an ass,—at least, to all intent;
Nor should the individual who happens to be meant
Reply by heaving rocks at him, to any great extent.

Then Abner Dean of Angel's raised a point of order, when
A chunk of old red sandstone took him in the abdomen,
And he smiled a kind of sickly smile, and curled up on the floor,
And the subsequent proceedings interested him no more.

For, in less time than I write it, every member did engage
In a warfare with the remnants of a palæozoic age;
And the way they heaved those fossils in their anger was a sin,
Till the skull of an old mammoth caved the head of Thompson in.

And this is all I have to say of these improper games,
For I live at Table Mountain, and my name is Truthful James;
And I've told in simple language what I know about the row
That broke up our Society upon the Stanislow.

THE BALLAD OF MR. COOKE

A Legend of the Cliff House, San Francisco

Where the sturdy ocean breeze
Drives the spray of roaring seas,
That the Cliff House balconies
                    Overlook:
There, in spite of rain that balked,
With his sandals duly chalked,
Once upon a tight-rope walked
                    Mr. Cooke.

But the jester's lightsome mien,
And his spangles and his sheen,
All had vanished when the scene
                    He forsook.
Yet in some delusive hope,
In some vague desire to cope,
One still came to view the rope
                    Walked by Cooke.

        *   *   *   *   *

Amid Beauty's bright array,
On that strange eventful day,
Partly hidden from the spray,
                    In a nook,
Stood Florinda Vere de Vere;
Who, with wind-disheveled hair,
And a rapt, distracted air,
                    Gazed on Cooke.

· 400 ·

Then she turned, and quickly cried
To her lover at her side,
While her form with love and pride
                              Wildly shook:
"Clifford Snook! oh, hear me now!
Here I break each plighted vow;
There's but one to whom I bow,
                              And that's Cooke!"

Haughtily that young man spoke:
"I descend from noble folk;
'Seven Oaks,' and then 'Se'nnoak,'
                              Lastly 'Snook,'
Is the way my name I trace.
Shall a youth of noble race
In affairs of love give place
                              To a Cooke?"

"Clifford Snook, I know thy claim
To that lineage and name,
And I think I've read the same
                              In Horne Tooke;
But I swear, by all divine,
Never, never, to be thine,
Till thou canst upon yon line
                              Walk like Cooke."

Though to that gymnastic feat
He no closer might compete
Than to strike a *balance*-sheet
                              In a book;
Yet thenceforward from that day
He his figure would display
In some wild athletic way,
                              After Cooke.

On some household eminence,
On a clothes-line or a fence,
Over ditches, drains, and thence
                              O'er a brook,
He, by high ambition led,
Ever walked and balancèd,

Till the people, wondering, said,
           "How like Cooke!"

Step by step did he proceed,
Nerved by valor, not by greed,
And at last the crowning deed
           Undertook.
Misty was the midnight air,
And the cliff was bleak and bare,
When he came to do and dare,
           Just like Cooke.

Through the darkness, o'er the flow,
Stretched the line where he should go,
Straight across as flies the crow
           Or the rook.
One wild glance around he cast;
Then he faced the ocean blast,
And he strode the cable last
           Touched by Cooke.

Vainly roared the angry seas,
Vainly blew the ocean breeze;
But, alas! the walker's knees
           Had a crook;
And before he reached the rock
Did they both together knock,
And he stumbled with a shock—
           Unlike Cooke!

Downward dropping in the dark,
Like an arrow to its mark,
Or a fish-pole when a shark
           Bites the hook,
Dropped the pole he could not save,
Dropped the walker, and the wave
Swift engulfed the rival brave
           Of J. Cooke!

Came a roar across the sea,
Of sea-lions in their glee,
In a tongue remarkably
           Like Chinook;
And the maddened sea-gull seemed
Still to utter, as he screamed,

"Perish thus the wretch who deemed
                Himself Cooke!"

But on misty moonlit nights
Comes a skeleton in tights,
Walks once more the giddy heights
                He mistook;
And unseen to mortal eyes,
Purged of grosser earthly ties,
Now at last in spirit guise
                Outdoes Cooke.

*   *   *   *   *

Still the sturdy ocean breeze
Sweeps the spray of roaring seas,
Where the Cliff House balconies
                Overlook;
And the maidens in their prime,
Reading of this mournful rhyme,
Weep where, in the olden time,
                Walked J. Cooke.

HER LETTER

I'm sitting alone by the fire,
   Dressed just as I came from the dance,
In a robe even *you* would admire,—
   It cost a cool thousand in France;
I'm be-diamonded out of all reason,
   My hair is done up in a cue:
In short, sir, "the belle of the season"
   Is wasting an hour upon you.

A dozen engagements I've broken:
   I left in the midst of a set;
Likewise a proposal, half spoken,
   That waits—on the stairs—for me yet.
They say he'll be rich,—when he grows up,—
   And then he adores me indeed;
And you, sir, are turning your nose up,
   Three thousand miles off, as you read.

"And how do I like my position?"
  "And what do I think of New York?"
"And now, in my higher ambition,
  With whom do I waltz, flirt, or talk?"
"And is n't it nice to have riches,
  And diamonds and silks, and all that?"
"And are n't they a change to the ditches
  And tunnels of Poverty Flat?"

Well, yes,—if you saw us out driving
  Each day in the Park, four-in-hand,
If you saw poor dear mamma contriving
  To look supernaturally grand,—
If you saw papa's picture, as taken
  By Brady, and tinted at that,—
You'd never suspect he sold bacon
  And flour at Poverty Flat.

And yet, just this moment, when sitting
  In the glare of the grand chandelier,—
In the bustle and glitter befitting
  The "finest *soirée* of the year,"—
In the mists of a *gaze de Chambéry*,
  And the hum of the smallest of talk,—
Somehow, Joe, I thought of the "Ferry,"
  And the dance that we had on "The Fork;"

Of Harrison's barn, with its muster
  Of flags festooned over the wall;
Of the candles that shed their soft lustre
  And tallow on head-dress and shawl;
Of the steps that we took to one fiddle,
  Of the dress of my queer *vis-à-vis;*
And how I once went down the middle
  With the man that shot Sandy McGee;

Of the moon that was quietly sleeping
  On the hill, when the time came to go;
Of the few baby peaks that were peeping
  From under their bedclothes of snow;
Of that ride,—that to me was the rarest;
  Of—the something you said at the gate.
Ah! Joe, then I was n't an heiress
  To "the best-paying lead in the State."

Well, well, it's all past; yet it's funny
    To think, as I stood in the glare
Of fashion and beauty and money,
    That I should be thinking, right there,
Of some one who breasted high water,
    And swam the North Fork, and all that,
Just to dance with old Folinsbee's daughter,
    The Lily of Poverty Flat.

But goodness! what nonsense I'm writing!
    (Mamma says my taste still is low),
Instead of my triumphs reciting,
    I'm spooning on Joseph,—heigh-ho!
And I'm to be "finished" by travel,—
    Whatever's the meaning of that.
Oh, why did papa strike pay gravel
    In drifting on Poverty Flat?

Good-night!—here's the end of my paper;
    Good-night!—if the longitude please,—
For maybe, while wasting my taper,
    Your sun's climbing over the trees.
But know, if you have n't got riches,
    And are poor, dearest Joe, and all that,
That my heart's somewhere there in the ditches,
    And you've struck it,—on Poverty Flat.

HIS ANSWER TO "HER LETTER"

Reported by Truthful James

Being asked by an intimate party,—
    Which the same I would term as a friend,—
Though his health it were vain to call hearty,
    Since the mind to deceit it might lend;
For his arm it was broken quite recent,
    And there's something gone wrong with his lung,—
Which is why it is proper and decent
    I should write what he runs off his tongue.

First, he says, Miss, he's read through your letter
    To the end,—and "the end came too soon;"
That a "slight illness kept him your debtor,"

(Which for weeks he was wild as a loon);
That "his spirits are buoyant as yours is;"
That with you, Miss, he "challenges Fate,"
(Which the language that invalid uses
At times it were vain to relate).

And he says "that the mountains are fairer
For once being held in your thought;"
That each rock "holds a wealth that is rarer
Than ever by gold-seeker sought."
(Which are words he would put in these pages,
By a party not given to guile;
Though the claim not, at date, paying wages,
Might produce in the sinful a smile.)

He remembers the ball at the Ferry,
And the ride, and the gate, and the vow,
And the rose that you gave him,—that very
Same rose he is "treasuring now."
(Which his blanket he's kicked on his trunk, Miss,
And insists on his legs being free;
And his language to me from his bunk, Miss,
Is frequent and painful and free.)

He hopes you are wearing no willows,
But are happy and gay all the while;
That he knows—(which this dodging of pillows
Imparts but small ease to the style,
And the same you will pardon)—he knows, Miss,
That, though parted by many a mile,
"Yet, were *he* lying under the snows, Miss,
They'd melt into tears at your smile."

And "you'll still think of him in your pleasures,
In your brief twilight dreams of the past;
In this green laurel spray that he treasures,—
It was plucked where your parting was last;
In this specimen,—but a small trifle,—
It will do for a pin for your shawl."
(Which, the truth not to wickedly stifle,
Was his last week's "clean up,"—and *his all*.)

He's asleep, which the same might seem strange, Miss,
Were it not that I scorn to deny

That I raised his last dose, for a change, Miss,
  In view that his fever was high;
But he lies there quite peaceful and pensive.
  And now, my respects, Miss, to you;
Which my language, although comprehensive,
  Might seem to be freedom, is true.

For I have a small favor to ask you,
  As concerns a bull-pup, and the same,—
If the duty would not overtask you,—
  You would please to procure for me, *game;*
And send per express to the Flat, Miss,—
  For they say York is famed for the breed,
Which, though words of deceit may be that, Miss,
  I'll trust to your taste, Miss, indeed.

P.S.—Which this same interfering
  Into other folks' way I despise;
Yet if it so be I was hearing
  That it's just empty pockets as lies
Betwixt you and Joseph, it follers
  That, having no family claims,
Here's my pile, which it's six hundred dollars,
  As is *yours*, with respects,
                                    —*Truthful James*

A GREYPORT LEGEND

(1797)

They ran through the streets of the seaport town,
They peered from the decks of the ships that lay;
The cold sea-fog that came whitening down
Was never as cold or white as they.
    "Ho, Starbuck and Pinckney and Tenterden!
    Run for your shallops, gather your men,
      Scatter your boats on the lower bay."

Good cause for fear! In the thick mid-day
The hulk that lay by the rotting pier,
Filled with the children in happy play,
Parted its moorings and drifted clear,

Drifted clear beyond reach or call,—
Thirteen children they were in all,—
   All adrift in the lower bay!

Said a hard-faced skipper, "God help us all!
She will not float till the turning tide!"
Said his wife, "My darling will hear *my* call,
Whether in sea or heaven she bide;"
   And she lifted a quavering voice and high,
   Wild and strange as a sea-bird's cry,
     Till they shuddered and wondered at her side.

The fog drove down on each laboring crew,
Veiled each from each and the sky and shore:
There was not a sound but the breath they drew,
And the lap of water and creak of oar;
   And they felt the breath of the downs, fresh blown
   O'er leagues of clover and cold gray stone,
     But not from the lips that had gone before.

They came no more. But they tell the tale
That, when fogs are thick on the harbor reef,
The mackerel fishers shorten sail—
For the signal they know will bring relief;
   For the voices of children, still at play
   In a phantom hulk that drifts alway
     Through channels whose waters never fail.

It is but a foolish shipman's tale,
A theme for a poet's idle page;
But still, when the mists of Doubt prevail,
And we lie becalmed by the shores of Age,
   We hear from the misty troubled shore
   The voice of the children gone before,
     Drawing the soul to its anchorage.

Joaquin Miller

(1841–1913)

Cincinnatus Hiner Miller was born in Liberty, Indiana. He moved to California, dabbled as a goldminer, worked as an editor and a judge, and lived with Indians. He traveled through Europe and spent the last part of his life in a beautiful house in Oakland, overlooking the San Francisco Bay. Miller lived a flamboyant life-style.

COLUMBUS

Columbus

August 3 and October 12, 1492

Behind him lay the gray Azores,
  Behind the Gates of Hercules;
Before him not the ghost of shores,
  Before him only shoreless seas.
The good mate said: "Now must we pray,
  For lo! the very stars are gone.
Brave Adm'r'l, speak! What shall I say?"
  "Why, say: 'Sail on! sail on! and on!'"

"My men grow mutinous day by day;
  My men grow ghastly, wan and weak."
The stout mate thought of home; a spray
  Of salt wave washed his swarthy cheek.
"What shall I say, brave Adm'r'l, say,
If we sight naught but seas at dawn?"
"Why, you shall say at break of day:
  'Sail on! sail on! sail on! and on!'"

They sailed and sailed, as winds might blow,
    Until at last the blanched mate said:
"Why, now not even God would know
    Should I and all my men fall dead.
These very winds forget their way,
    For God from these dread seas is gone.
Now speak, brave Adm'r'l, speak and say—"
    He said: "Sail on! sail on! and on!"

They sailed. They sailed. Then spake the mate:
    "This mad sea shows his teeth tonight.
He curls his lip, he lies in wait,
    He lifts his teeth as if to bite!
Brave Adm'r'l, say but one good word:
    What shall we do when hope is gone?"
The words leapt like a leaping sword:
    "Sail on! sail on! sail on! and on!"

Then pale and worn, he paced his deck,
    And peered through darkness. Ah, that night
Of all dark nights! And then a speck—
    A light! A light! A light! A light!
It grew, a starlit flag unfurled!
    It grew to be Time's burst of dawn.
He gained a world; he gave that world
    Its grandest lesson: "On! sail on!"

IN MEN WHOM MEN CONDEMN

In men whom men condemn as ill
I find so much of goodness still,
In men whom men pronounce divine
I find so much of sin and blot,
I hesitate to draw the line
Between the two, where God has not.

CROSSING THE PLAINS

What great yoked brutes with briskets low,
With wrinkled necks like buffalo,
With round, brown, liquid, pleading eyes,
That turned so low and sad to you,

That shone like love's eyes soft with tears,
That seemed to plead, and make replies,
The while they bowed their necks and drew
The creaking load; and looked at you.
Their sable briskets swept the ground,
Their cloven feet kept solemn sound.

Two sullen bullocks led the line,
Their great eyes shining bright like wine;
Two sullen captive kings were they,
That had in time held herds at bay,
And even now they crushed the sod
With stolid sense of majesty,
And stately stepped and stately trod,
As if 'twere something still to be
Kings even in captivity.

WILLIAM BROWN OF OREGON

They called him Bill, the hired man,
    But she, her name was Mary Jane,
    The Squire's daughter; and to reign
The belle from Ber-she-be to Dan
Her little game. How lovers rash
    Got mittens at the spelling school!
    How many a mute, inglorious fool
Wrote rhymes and sighed and died—mustache!

This hired man had loved her long,
    Had loved her best and first and last,
    Her very garments as she passed
For him had symphony and song.
So when one day with sudden frown
    She called him "Bill," he raised his head,
    He caught her eye and, faltering, said,
"I love you; and my name is Brown."

She fairly waltzed with rage; she wept;
    You would have thought the house on fire.
    She told her sire, the portly squire,
Then smelt her smelling-salts, and slept.
Poor William did what could be done;
    He swung a pistol on each hip,

He gathered up a great ox-whip,
And drove toward the setting sun.

He crossed the great back-bone of earth,
  He saw the snowy mountains rolled
  Like mighty billows; saw the gold
Of awful sunsets; felt the birth
Of sudden dawn that burst the night
  Like resurrection; saw the face
  Of God and named it boundless space
Ringed round with room and shoreless light.

Her lovers passed. Wolves hunt in packs,
  They sought for bigger game; somehow
  They seemed to see above her brow
The forky sign of turkey tracks.
The teter-board of life goes up,
  The teter-board of life goes down,
  The sweetest face must learn to frown;
The biggest dog has been a pup.

O maidens! pluck not at the air;
  The sweetest flowers I have found
  Grow rather close unto the ground,
And highest places are most bare.
Why, you had better win the grace
  Of our poor cussed Af-ri-can,
  Than win the eyes of every man
In love alone with his own face.

At last she nursed her true desire.
  She sighed, she wept for William Brown,
  She watched the splendid sun go down
Like some great sailing ship on fire,
Then rose and checked her trunk right on;
  And in the cars she lunched and lunched,
  And had her ticket punched and punched,
Until she came to Oregon.

She reached the limit of the lines,
  She wore blue specs upon her nose,
  Wore rather short and manly clothes,
And so set out to reach the mines.
Her pocket held a parasol

Her right hand held a Testament,
  And thus equipped right on she went,
Went water-proof and water-fall.

She saw a miner gazing down,
  Slow stirring something with a spoon;
  "O, tell me true and tell me soon,
What has become of William Brown?"
He looked askance beneath her specs,
  Then stirred his cocktail round and round,
  Then raised his head and sighed profound,
And said, "He's handed in his checks."

Then care fed on her damaged cheek,
  And she grew faint, did Mary Jane,
  And smelt her smelling-salts in vain,
She wandered, weary, worn, and weak.
At last, upon a hill alone,
  She came, and there she sat her down;
  For on that hill there stood a stone.
And, lo! that stone read, "William Brown."

"O William Brown! O William Brown!
  And here you rest at last," she said,
  "With this lone stone above your head,
And forty miles from any town!
I will plant cypress trees, I will,
  And I will build a fence around,
  And I will fertilise the ground
With tears enough to turn a mill."

She went and got a hired man,
  She brought him forty miles from town,
  And in the tall grass squatted down
And bade him build as she should plan.
But cruel cow-boys with their bands
  They saw, and hurriedly they ran
  And told a bearded cattle man
Somebody builded on his lands.

He took his rifle from the rack,
  He girt himself in battle pelt,
  He stuck two pistols in his belt,
And, mounting on his horse's back,

He plunged ahead. But when they showed
   A woman fair, about his eyes
   He pulled his hat, and he likewise
Pulled at his beard, and chewed and chewed.

At last he gat him down and spake:
   "O lady dear, what do you here?"
   "I build a tomb unto my dear,
I plant sweet flowers for his sake."
The bearded man threw his two hands
   Above his head, then brought them down
   And cried, "Oh, I am William Brown,
And this the corner-stone of my lands!"

THAT TEXAN CATTLE MAN

We rode the tawny Texan hills,
   A bearded cattle man and I;
Below us laughed the blossomed rills,
   Above the dappled clouds blew by.
We talked. The topic? Guess. Why, sir,
   Three-fourths of man's whole time he keeps
To talk, to think, to *be* of HER;
   The other fourth he sleeps.

To learn what he might know of love,
   I laughed all constancy to scorn.
"Behold yon happy, changeful dove!
   Behold this day, all storm at morn,
Yet now 't is changed to cloud and sun.
   Yea, all things change—the heart, the head,
Behold on earth there is not one
   That changeth not," I said.

He drew a glass as if to scan
   The plain for steers; raised it and sighed.
He craned his neck, this cattle man,
   Then drove the cork home and replied:
"For twenty years (forgive these tears)—
   For twenty years no word of strife—
I have not known for twenty years
   One folly from my wife."

I looked that Texan in the face—
   That dark-browed, bearded cattle man,
He pulled his beard, then dropped in place
   A broad right hand, all scarred and tan,
And toyed with something shining there
   From out his holster, keen and small.
I was convinced. I did not care
   To argue it at all.

But rest I could not. Know I must
   The story of my Texan guide;
His dauntless love, enduring trust;
   His blessed, immortal bride.
I wondered, marvelled, marvelled much.
   Was she of Texan growth? Was she
Of Saxon blood, that boasted such
   Eternal constancy?

I could not rest until I knew—
   "Now twenty years, my man," said I,
"Is a long time." He turned and drew
   A pistol forth, also a sigh.
" 'Tis twenty years or more," said he,
   "Nay, nay, my honest man, I vow
I do not doubt that this may be;
   But tell, oh! tell me how.

" 'Twould make a poem true and grand;
   All time should note it near and far;
And thy fair, virgin Texan land
   Should stand out like a Winter star.
America should heed. And then
   The doubtful French beyond the sea—
'T would make them truer, nobler men
   To know how this may be."

"It's twenty years or more," urged he,
   "Nay, that I know, good guide of mine;
But lead me where this wife may be,
   And I a pilgrim at a shrine.
And kneeling, as a pilgrim true"—
   He scowling, shouted in my ear;
"I cannot show my wife to you;
   She's dead this twenty year."

WASHINGTON BY THE DELAWARE

The snow was red with patriot blood,
The proud foe tracked the blood-red snow.
The flying patriots crossed the flood
A tattered, shattered band of woe.
Forlorn each barefoot hero stood,
With bare head bended low.

"Let us cross back! Death waits us here:
Recross or die!" the chieftain said.
A famished soldier dropped a tear—
A tear that froze as it was shed:
For oh, his starving babes were dear—
They had but this for bread!

A captain spake: "It cannot be!
These bleeding men, why, what could they?
'Twould be as snowflakes in the sea!"
The worn chief did not heed or say.
He set his firm lips silently,
Then turned aside to pray.

And as he kneeled and prayed to God,
God's finger spun the stars in space;
He spread his banner blue and broad,
He dashed the dead sun's stripes in place,
Till war walked heaven fire shod
And lit the chieftain's face:

Till every soldier's heart was stirred,
Till every sword shook in its sheath—
"Up! up! Face back. But not one word!"
God's flag above; the ice beneath—
They crossed so still, they only heard
The icebergs grind their teeth!

Ho! Hessians, hirelings at meat
While praying patriots hunger so!
Then, bang! Boom! Bang! Death and defeat!
And blood? Ay, blood upon the snow!
Yet not the blood of patriot feet,
But heart's blood of the foe!

O ye who hunger and despair!
O ye who perish for the sun,
Look up and dare, for God is there;
And man can do what man has done!
Think, think of darkling Delaware!
Think, think of Washington!

WESTWARD HO!

What strength! what strife! what rude unrest!
What shocks! what half-shaped armies met!
A mighty nation moving west,
With all its steely sinews set
Against the living forests. Hear
The shouts, the shots of pioneer,
The rended forests, rolling wheels,
As if some half-check'd army reels,
Recoils, redoubles, comes again,
Loud sounding like a hurricane.

O bearded, stalwart, westmost men,
So tower-like, so Gothic built!
A kingdom won without the guilt
Of studied battle, that hath been
Your blood's inheritance. . . . Your heirs
Know not your tombs: the great plowshares
Cleave softly through the mellow loam
Where you have made eternal home,
And set no sign. Your epitaphs
Are writ in furrows. Beauty laughs
While through the green ways wandering
Beside her love, slow gathering
White, starry-hearted May-time blooms
Above your lowly leveled tombs;
And then below the spotted sky
She stops, she leans, she wonders why
The ground is heaved and broken so,
And why the grasses darker grow
And droop and trail like wounded wing.

Yea, Time, the grand old harvester,
Has gather'd you from wood and plain.
We call to you again, again;

The rush and rumble of the car
Comes back in answer. Deep and wide
The wheels of progress have passed on;
The silent pioneer is gone.
His ghost is moving down the trees,
And now we push the memories
Of bluff, bold men who dared and died
In foremost battle, quite aside.

AT THE GRAVE OF WALKER

He lies low in the levelled sand,
Unsheltered from the tropic sun,
And now of all he knew not one
Will speak him fair in that far land.
Perhaps 'twas this that made me seek,
Disguised, his grave one winter-tide;
A weakness for the weaker side,
A siding with the helpless weak.

A palm not far held out a hand,
Hard by a long green bamboo swung,
And bent like some great bow unstrung,
And quivered like a willow wand;
Perched on its fruits that crooked hand,
Beneath a broad banana's leaf,
A bird in rainbow splendor sang
A low, sad song, of tempered grief.

No sod, no sign, no cross nor stone,
But at his side a cactus green
Upheld its lances long and keen;
It stood in sacred sands alone,
Flat-palmed and fierce with lifted spears;
One bloom of crimson crowned its head,
A drop of blood, so bright, so red,
Yet redolent as roses' tears.

In my left hand I held a shell,
All rosy lipped and pearly red;
I laid it by his lowly bed,
For he did love so passing well
The grand songs of the solemn sea.

O shell! sing well, wild, with a will,
When storms blow loud and birds be still,
The wildest sea-song known to thee!

I said some things with folded hands,
Soft whispered in the dim sea-sound,
And eyes held humbly to the ground,
And frail knees sunken in the sands.
He had done more than this for me,
And yet I could not well do more:
I turned me down the olive shore,
And set a sad face to the sea.

THAT GENTLE MAN FROM BOSTON TOWN

An Idyl of Oregon

Two webfoot brothers loved a fair
  Young lady, rich and good to see;
And oh, her black abundant hair!
  And oh, her wondrous witchery!
Her father kept a cattle farm,
These brothers kept her safe from harm:

From harm of cattle on the hill;
  From thick-necked bulls loud bellowing
The livelong morning, loud and shrill,
  And lashing sides like anything;
From roaring bulls that tossed the sand
And pawed the lilies from the land.

There came a third young man. He came
  From far and famous Boston town.
He was not handsome, was not "game,"
  But he could "cook a goose" as brown
As any man that set foot on
The sunlit shores of Oregon.

This Boston man he taught the school,
  Taught gentleness and love alway,
Said love and kindness, as a rule,
  Would ultimately "make it pay."

He was so gentle, kind, that he
Could make a noun and verb agree.

So when one day the brothers grew
    All jealous and did strip to fight,
He gently stood between the two,
    And meekly told them 'twas not right.
"I have a higher, better plan,"
Outspake this gentle Boston man.

"My plan is this: Forget this fray
    About that lily hand of hers;
Go take your guns and hunt all day
    High up yon lofty hill of firs,
And while you hunt, my loving doves,
Why, I will learn which one she loves."

The brothers sat the windy hill,
    Their hair shone yellow, like spun gold,
Their rifles crossed their laps, but still
    They sat and sighed and shook with cold.
Their hearts lay bleeding far below;
Above them gleamed white peaks of snow.

Their hounds lay couching, slim and neat;
    A spotted circle in the grass.
The valley lay beneath their feet;
    They heard the wide-winged eagles pass.
The eagles cleft the clouds above;
Yet what could they but sigh and love?

"If I could die," the elder sighed,
    "My dear young brother here might wed."
"Oh, would to Heaven I had died!"
    The younger sighed, with bended head.
Then each looked each full in the face
And each sprang up and stood in place.

"If I could die,"—the elder spake,—
    "Die by your hand, the world would say
'Twas accident;—and for her sake,
    Dear brother, be it so, I pray."
"Not that!" the younger nobly said;
Then tossed his gun and turned his head.

And fifty paces back he paced!
  And as he paced he drew the ball;
Then sudden stopped and wheeled and faced
  His brother to the death and fall!
Two shots rang wild upon the air!
But lo! the two stood harmless there!

An eagle poised high in the air;
  Far, far below the bellowing
Of bullocks ceased, and everywhere
  Vast silence sat all questioning.
The spotted hounds ran circling round
Their red, wet noses to the ground.

And now each brother came to know
  That each had drawn the deadly ball;
And for that fair girl far below
  Had sought in vain to silent fall.
And then the two did gladly "shake,"
And thus the elder bravely spake:

"Now let us run right hastily
  And tell the kind schoolmaster all!
Yea! yea! and if she choose not me,
  But all on you her favors fall,
This valiant scene, till all life ends,
Dear brother, binds us best of friends."

The hounds sped down, a spotted line,
  The bulls in tall, abundant grass,
Shook back their horns from bloom and vine,
  And trumpeted to see them pass—
They loved so good, they loved so true,
These brothers scarce knew what to do.

They sought the kind schoolmaster out
  As swift as sweeps the light of morn;
They could but love, they could not doubt
  This man so gentle, "in a horn,"
They cried, "Now whose the lily hand—
That lady's of this webfoot land?"

They bowed before that big-nosed man,
  That long-nosed man from Boston town;

They talked as only lovers can,
    They talked, but he could only frown;
And still they talked, and still they plead;
It was as pleading with the dead.

At last this Boston man did speak—
    "Her father has a thousand ceows,
An hundred bulls, all fat and sleek;
    He also had this ample heouse."
The brothers' eyes stuck out thereat,
So far you might have hung your hat.

"I liked the looks of this big heouse—
    My lovely boys, won't you come in?
Her father has a thousand ceows,
    He also had a heap of tin.
The guirl? Oh yes, the guirl, you see—
The guirl, just neow she married me."

Edward Rowland Sill

(1841–1887)

Edward Rowland Sill was born in Windsor, Connecticut, and graduated from Yale in 1861. Poor health forced him to move west where he was a professor of English at the University of California. Sill died in Cleveland, at age forty-five, at the start of a potentially promising poetic career.

OPPORTUNITY

This I beheld, or dreamed it in a dream:—
There spread a cloud of dust along a plain;
And underneath the cloud, or in it, raged
A furious battle, and men yelled, and swords
Shocked upon swords and shields. A prince's banner
Wavered, then staggered backward, hemmed by foes.
A craven hung along the battle's edge,
And thought, "Had I a sword of keener steel—
That blue blade that the king's son bears—but this
Blunt thing—!" he snapt and flung it from his hand,
And lowering crept away and left the field.
Then came the king's son, wounded, sore bestead,
And weaponless, and saw the broken sword,
Hilt-buried in the dry and trodden sand,
And ran and snatched it, and with battle-shout
Lifted afresh he hewed his enemy down,
And saved a great cause that heroic day.

THE DESERTER

Blindest and most frantic prayer,
  Clutching at a senseless boon,
His that begs, in mad despair,
  Death to come;—he comes so soon!

Like a reveler that strains
  Lip and throat to drink it up—
The last ruby that remains,
  One red droplet in the cup,

Like a child that, sullen, mute,
  Sulking spurns, with chin on breast,
Of the Tree of Life the fruit,
  His gift of whom he is the guest,

Outcast on the thither shore,
  Open scorn to him shall give
Souls that heavier burdens bore:
  "See the wretch that dared not live!"

THE PHILOSOPHER

  His wheel of logic whirled and spun all day;
All day he held his system, grinding it
Finer and finer, till 't was fined away.

  But the chance sparks of sense and mother-wit,
Flung out as that wheel-logic spun and whirled,
Kindled the nations, and lit up the world.

LOST LOVE

Bury it, and sift
  Dust upon its light,—
Death must not be left,
  To offend the sight.

Cover the old love—
  Weep not on the mound—

Grass shall grow above,
  Lilies spring around.

Can we fight the law,
  Can our natures change—
Half-way through withdraw—
  Other lives exchange?

You and I must do
  As the world has done,
There is nothing new
  Underneath the sun.

Fill the grave up full—
  Put the dead love by—
Not that men are dull,
  Not that women lie,—

But 't is well and right—
  Safest, you will find—
That the Out of Sight
  Should be Out of Mind.

TEMPTED

Yes, I know what you say:
  Since it cannot be soul to soul,
Be it flesh to flesh, as it may;
  But is Earth the whole?

Shall a man betray the Past
  For all Earth gives?
"But the Past is dead?" At last,
  It is all that lives.

Which were the nobler goal—
  To snatch at the moment's bliss,
Or to swear I will keep my soul
  Clean for her kiss?

TO A MAID DEMURE

Often when the night is come,
With its quiet group at home,
While they broider, knit, or sew,
Read, or chat in voices low,
Suddenly you lift your eyes
With an earnest look, and wise;
But I cannot read their lore,—
Tell me less, or tell me more.

Like a picture in a book,
Pure and peaceful is your look,
Quietly you walk your ways;
Steadfast duty fills the days.
Neither tears nor fierce delights,
Feverish days nor tossing nights,
Any troublous dreams confess,—
Tell me more, or tell me less.

Swift the weeks are on the wing;
Years are brief, and love a thing
Blooming, fading, like a flower;
Wake and seize the little hour.
Give me welcome, or farewell;
Quick! I wait! And who can tell
What to-morrow may befall,—
Love me more, or not at all.

THE CRICKETS IN THE FIELDS

One, or a thousand voices?—filling noon
  With such an undersong and drowsy chant
As sings in ears that waken from a swoon,
  And know not yet which world such murmurs haunt:
  Single, then double beats, reiterant;
Far off and near; one ceaseless, changeless tune.

If bird or breeze awake the dreamy will
  We lose the song, as it had never been;
Then suddenly we find 't is singing still
  And had not ceased. So, friend of mine, within
  My thoughts one underthought, beneath the din

Of life, doth every quiet moment fill.
Thy voice is far, thy face is hid from me,
But day and night are full of dreams of thee.

THE THINGS THAT WILL NOT DIE

What am I glad will stay when I have passed
   From this dear valley of the world, and stand
On yon snow-glimmering peaks, and lingering cast
      From that dim land
   A backward look, and haply stretch my hand,
Regretful, now the wish comes true at last?

Sweet strains of music I am glad will be
   Still wandering down the wind, for men will hear
And think themselves from all their care set free,
      And heaven near
   When summer stars burn very still and clear,
And waves of sound are swelling like the sea.

And it is good to know that overhead
   Blue skies will brighten, and the sun will shine,
And flowers be sweet in many a garden bed,
      And all divine,
   (For are they not, O Father, thoughts of thine?)
Earth's warmth and fragrance shall on men be shed.

And I am glad that Night will always come,
   Hushing all sounds, even the soft-voiced birds,
Putting away all light from her deep dome,
      Until are heard
   In the wide starlight's stillness, unknown words,
That make the heart ache till it finds its home.

And I am glad that neither golden sky,
   Nor violet lights that linger on the hill,
Nor ocean's wistful blue shall satisfy,
      But they shall fill
   With wild unrest and endless longing still,
The soul whose hope beyond them all must lie.

And I rejoice that love shall never seem
   So perfect as it ever was to be,

But endlessly that inner haunting dream
    Each heart shall see
Hinted in every dawn's fresh purity,
Hopelessly shadowed in each sunset's gleam.

And though warm mouths will kiss and hands will cling,
    And thought by silent thought be understood,
I do rejoice that the next hour will bring
    That far off mood,
   That drives one like a lonely child to God,
Who only sees and measures everything.

And it is well that when these feet have pressed
   The outward path from earth, 't will not seem sad
To them that stay; but they who love me best
    Will be most glad
   That such a long unquiet now has had,
At last, a gift of perfect peace and rest.

SPACE

Black, frost-cold distance, sparsely honey-combed
With hollow shells of glimmering golden light;
   Mere amber bubbles floating through the night,
Lit by one centred sparkle, azure-domed,
With circling motes where life hath lodged and roamed.

FORCE

The stars know a secret
   They do not tell;
And morn brings a message
   Hidden well.

There's a blush on the apple,
   A tint on the wing,
And the bright wind whistles,
   And the pulses sting.

Perish dark memories!
   There's light ahead;

This world's for the living;
  Not for the dead.

In the shining city,
  On the loud pave,
The life-tide is running
  Like a leaping wave.

How the stream quickens,
  As noon draws near,
No room for loiterers,
  No time for fear.

Out on the farm lands
  Earth smiles as well;
Gold-crusted grain-fields,
  With sweet, warm smell;

Whir of the reaper,
  Like a giant bee;
Like a Titan cricket,
  Thrilling with glee.

On mart and meadow,
  Pavement or plain;
On azure mountain,
  Or azure main—

Heaven bends in blessing;
  Lost is but won;
Goes the good rain-cloud,
  Comes the good sun!

Only babes whimper,
  And sick men wail,
And faint hearts and feeble hearts,
  And weaklings fail.

Down the great currents
  Let the boat swing;
There was never winter
  But brought the spring.

EVE'S DAUGHTER

I waited in the little sunny room:
   The cool breeze waved the window-lace at play,
The white rose on the porch was all in bloom,
   And out upon the bay
I watched the wheeling sea birds go and come.

"Such an old friend,—she would not make me stay
   While she bound up her hair." I turned, and lo,
Danaë in her shower! and fit to slay
   All a man's hoarded prudence at a blow:
Gold hair, that streamed away
   As round some nymph a sunlit fountain's flow.
   "She would not make me wait"—but well I know
She took a good half hour to loose and lay
   Those locks in dazzling disarrangement so!

Sidney Lanier

(1842–1881)

Sidney Lanier, the "chief of Southern poets," was born into a musical family in Macon, Georgia, and learned to play guitar, piano, flute, and violin. He graduated from Oglethorpe College and during the Civil War served as a private in the Confederate Army; he was taken prisoner while serving as a blockade runner. After the war he moved to Baltimore where he played flute in the Peabody Symphony Orchestra and lectured at John Hopkins University. Lanier died of tuberculosis in the hills of North Carolina.

SONG OF THE CHATTAHOOCHE

Out of the hills of Habersham,
　Down the valleys of Hall,
I hurry amain to reach the plain,
Run the rapid and leap the fall,
Split at the rock and together again,
Accept my bed, or narrow or wide,
And flee from folly on every side
With a lover's pain to attain the plain
　Far from the hills of Habersham,
　Far from the valleys of Hall.

All down the hills of Habersham,
　All through the valleys of Hall,
The rushes cried, *Abide, abide,*
The willful water weeds held me thrall,
The laving laurel turned my tide,
The ferns and the fondling grass said, *Stay,*

The dewberry dipped for to work delay,
And the little reeds sighed, *Abide, abide,*
Here in the hills of Habersham,
Here in the valleys of Hall.

High o'er the hills of Habersham,
Veiling the valleys of Hall,
The hickory told me manifold
Fair tales of shade, the poplar tall
Wrought me her shadowy self to hold,
The chestnut, the oak, the walnut, the pine,
Overleaning, with flickering meaning and sign,
Said, *Pass not, so cold, these manifold*
Deep shades of the hills of Habersham,
These glades in the valleys of Hall.

And oft in the hills of Habersham,
And oft in the valleys of Hall,
The white quartz shone, and the smooth brook-stone
Did bar me of passage with friendly brawl,
And many a luminous jewel lone
—Crystals clear or a-cloud with mist,
Ruby, garnet, and amethyst—
Made lures with the lights of streaming stone
In the clefts of the hills of Habersham,
In the beds of the valleys of Hall.

But oh, not the hills of Habersham,
And oh, not the valleys of Hall
Avail: I am fain for to water the plain.
Downward the voices of Duty call—
Downward, to toil and be mixed with the main,
The dry fields burn, and the mills are to turn,
And a myriad flowers mortally yearn,
And the lordly main from beyond the plain
Calls o'er the hills of Habersham,
Calls through the valleys of Hall.

TAMPA ROBINS

The robin laughed in the orange tree:
"Ho, windy North, a fig for thee:
While breasts are red and wings are bold

And green trees wave us globes of gold,
   Time's scythe shall reap but bliss for me
   —Sunlight, song, and the orange tree.

Burn, golden globes in leafy sky,
My orange planets: crimson I
Will shine and shoot among the spheres
(Blithe meteor that no mortal fears)
   And thrid the heavenly orange tree
   With orbits bright of minstrelsy.

If that I hate wild winter's spite—
The gibbet trees, the world in white,
The sky but gray wind over a grave—
Why should I ache, the season's slave?
   I'll sing from the top of the orange tree,
   Gramercy, winter's tyranny.

I'll south with the sun, and keep my clime;
My wing is king of the summer time;
My breast to the sun his torch shall hold;
And I'll call down through the green and gold,
   Time, take thy scythe, reap bliss for me,
   Bestir thee under the orange tree."
              —Tampa, Florida, 1877

OPPOSITION

Of fret, of dark, of thorn, of chill,
   Complain no more; for these, O heart,
Direct the random of the will
   As rhymes direct the rage of art.

The lute's fixt fret, that runs athwart
   The strain and purpose of the string,
For governace and nice consort
   Doth bar his wilful wavering.

The dark hath many dear avails;
   The dark distils divinist dews;
The dark is rich with nightingales,
   With dreams, and with the heavenly Muse.

Bleeding with thorns of petty strife,
   I'll ease (as lovers do) my smart
With sonnets to my lady Life
   Writ red in issues from the heart.

What grace may lie within the chill
   Of favor frozen fast in scorn!
When Good's a-freeze, we call it Ill!
   This rosy Time is glacier-born.

Of fret, of dark, of thorn, of chill,
   Complain thou not, O heart; for these
Bank-in the current of the will
   To uses, arts, and charities.

THE MARSHES OF GLYNN

Glooms of the live-oaks, beautiful-braided and woven
With intricate shades of the vines that myriad-cloven
   Clamber the forks of the multiform boughs,—
     Emerald twilights,—
     Virginal shy lights,
Wrought of the leaves to allure to the whisper of vows,
When lovers pace timidly down through the green colonnades
Of the dim sweet woods, of the dear dark woods,
   Of the heavenly woods and glades,
That run to the radiant marginal sand-beach within
     The wide sea-marshes of Glynn;—

Beautiful glooms, soft dusks in the noon-day fire,—
Wildwood privacies, closets of lone desire,
Chamber from chamber parted with wavering arras of leaves,—
Cells for the passionate pleasure of prayer to the soul that grieves,
Pure with a sense of the passing of saints through the wood,
Cool for the dutiful weighing of ill with good;—
O braided dusks of the oak and woven shades of the vine,
While the riotous noon-day sun of the June-day long did shine
Ye held me fast in your heart and I held you fast in mine;
But now when the noon is no more, and riot is rest,
And the sun is a-wait at the ponderous gate of the West,
And the slant yellow beam down the wood-aisle doth seem
Like a lane into heaven that leads from a dream,—
Ay, now, when my soul all day hath drunken the soul of the oak,

And my heart is at ease from men, and the wearisome sound of the
    stroke
  Of the scythe of time and the trowel of trade is low,
  And belief overmasters doubt, and I know that I know,
  And my spirit is grown to a lordly great compass within,
That the length and the breadth and the sweep of the marshes of
    Glynn
Will work me no fear like the fear they have wrought me of yore
When length was fatigue, and when breadth was but bitterness sore,
And when terror and shrinking and dreary unnamable pain
Drew over me out of the merciless miles of the plain,—

Oh, now, unafraid, I am fain to face
  The vast sweet visage of space.
To the edge of the wood I am drawn, I am drawn,
Where the gray beach glimmering runs, as a belt of the dawn,
  For a mete and a mark
    To the forest-dark:—
      So:
Affable live-oak, leaning low,—
Thus—with your favor—soft, with a reverent hand
(Not lightly touching your person, Lord of the land!),
Bending your beauty aside, with a step I stand
On the firm-packed sand,
    Free
By a world of marsh that borders a world of sea.

Sinuous southward and sinuous northward the shimmering band
Of the sand-beach fastens the fringe of the marsh to the folds of the
    land.
Inward and outward to northward and southward the beach-lines
    linger and curl
As a silver-wrought garment that clings to and follows the firm
    sweet limbs of a girl.
Vanishing, swerving, evermore curving again into sight,
Softly the sand-beach wavers away to a dim gray looping of light.
And what if behind me to westward the wall of the woods stands
    high?
The world lies east: how ample, the marsh and the sea and the sky!
A league and a league of marsh-grass, waist-high, broad in the blade,
Green, and all of a height, and unflecked with a light or a shade,
Stretch leisurely off, in a pleasant plain,
To the terminal blue of the main.

Oh, what is abroad in the marsh and the terminal sea?
  Somehow my soul seems suddenly free
From the weighing of fate and the sad discussion of sin,
By the length and the breadth and the sweep of the marshes of
  Glynn.

Ye marshes, how candid and simple and nothing-withholding and
  free
Ye publish yourselves to the sky and offer yourselves to the sea!
Tolerant plains, that suffer the sea and the rains and the sun,
Ye spread and span like the catholic man who hath mightily won
God out of knowledge and good out of infinite pain
And sight out of blindness and purity out of a stain.

As the marsh-hen secretly builds on the watery sod,
Behold I will build me a nest on the greatness of God:
I will fly in the greatness of God as the marsh-hen flies
In the freedom that fills all the space 'twixt the marsh and the skies:
By so many roots as the marsh-grass sends in the sod
I will heartily lay me a-hold on the greatness of God:
Oh, like to the greatness of God is the greatness within
The range of the marshes, the liberal marshes of Glynn.

And the sea lends large, as the marsh: lo, out of his plenty the sea
Pours fast: full soon the time of the flood-tide must be:
Look how the grace of the sea doth go
About and about through the intricate channels that flow
  Here and there,
    Everywhere,
Till his waters have flooded the uttermost creeks and the low-lying
  lanes,
And the marsh is meshed with a million veins,
That like as with rosy and silvery essences flow
In the rose-and-silver evening glow.

    Farewell, my lord Sun!
The creeks overflow: a thousand rivulets run
'Twixt the roots of the sod; the blades of the marsh-grass stir;
Passeth a hurrying sound of wings that westward whirr;
Passeth, and all is still; and the currents cease to run;
And the sea and the marsh are one.
How still the plains of the waters be!
The tide in his ecstasy.

The tide is at his highest height:
    And it is night.

And now from the Vast of the Lord will the waters of sleep
Roll in on the souls of men,
But who will reveal to our waking ken
The forms that swim and the shapes that creep
    Under the waters of sleep?
And I would I could know what swimmeth below when the tide comes in
On the length and breadth of the marvelous marshes of Glynn.

EVENING SONG

Look off, dear Love, across the sallow sand,
    And mark yon meeting of the sun and sea,
How long they kiss in sight of all the land.
    Ah! longer, longer, we!

Now in the sea's red vintage melts the sun,
    As Egypt's pearl dissolved in rosy wine,
And Cleopatra night drinks all. 'Tis done,
    Love, lay thy hand in mine.

Come forth, sweet stars, and comfort heaven's heart;
    Glimmer, ye waves, round else unlighted sands.
O night! Divorce our sun and sky apart,
    Never our lips, our hands.

THE STIRRUP-CUP

Death, thou'rt a cordial old and rare:
Look how compounded, with what care,
Time got his wrinkles reaping thee
Sweet herbs from all antiquity.

David to thy distillage went,
Keats, and Gotama excellent,
Omar Khayyám, and Chaucer bright,
And Shakespeare for a king-delight.

Then, Time, let not a drop be spilt:
Hand me the cup whene'er thou wilt;
'Tis thy rich stirrup-cup to me;
I'll drink it down right smilingly.

THE RAVEN DAYS

Our hearths are gone out, and our hearts are broken,
　　And but the ghosts of homes to us remain,
And ghostly eyes and hollow sighs give token
　　From friend to friend of an unspoken pain.

O, Raven Days, dark Raven Days of sorrow,
　　Bring to us, in your whetted ivory beaks,
Some sign out of the far land of To-morrow,
　　Some strip of sea-green dawn, some orange streaks.

Ye float in dusky files, forever croaking—
　　Ye chill our manhood with your dreary shade.
Pale, in the dark, not even God invoking,
　　We lie in chains, too weak to be afraid.

O Raven Days, dark Raven Days of sorrow,
　　Will ever any warm light come again?
Will ever the lit mountains of To-morrow
　　Begin to gleam across the mournful plain?

FROM THE FLATS

　　What heartache—ne'er a hill!
Inexorable, vapid, vague, and chill
The drear sand-levels drain my spirit low.
With one poor word they tell me all they know;
Whereat their stupid tongues, to tease my pain,
Do drawl it o'er again and o'er again.
They hurt my heart with griefs I cannot name:
　　Always the same, the same.

　　Nature hath no surprise,
No ambuscade of beauty 'gainst mine eyes
From brake or lurking dell or deep defile;
No humors, frolic forms—this mile, that mile;

No rich reserves or happy-valley hopes
Beyond the bends of roads, the distant slopes.
Her fancy fails, her wild is all run tame:
    Ever the same, the same.

Oh, might I through these tears
But glimpse some hill my Georgia high uprears,
Where white the quartz and pink the pebble shine,
The hickory heavenward strives, the muscadine
Swings o'er the slope, the oak's far-falling shade
Darkens the dogwood in the bottom glade,
And down the hollow from a ferny nook
    Bright leaps a living brook!

A BALLAD OF TREES AND THE MASTER

Into the woods my Master went,
    Clean forspent, forspent.
Into the woods my Master came,
    Forspent with love and shame.
But the olives they were not blind to Him,
The little gray leaves were kind to Him:
The thorn-tree had a mind to Him
    When into the woods He came.

Out of the woods my Master went,
    And He was well content.
Out of the woods my Master came,
    Content with death and shame.
When Death and Shame would woo Him last,
From under the trees they drew Him last:
'Twas on a tree they slew Him—last
    When out of the woods He came.

James Whitcomb Riley

(1849–1916)

James Whitcomb Riley was born in Greenfield, Indiana. He almost
followed his father's footsteps in law, but, his restless nature forced
him to follow other directions instead. In 1882, while on the staff of
the *Indianapolis Journal,* Riley started writing poems in regional
dialect that earned him the title "the Hoosier poet." These poems
earned Riley a place in American folk literature.

LITTLE ORPHANT ANNIE

Little Orphant Annie's come to our house to stay,
An' wash the cups and saucers up, an' brush the crumbs away,
An' shoo the chickens off the porch, an' dust the hearth, an' sweep,
An' make the fire, an' bake the bread, an' earn her board-an'-keep;
An' all us other children, when the supper things is done,
We set around the kitchen fire an' has the mostest fun
A-list'nin' to the witch-tales 'at Annie tells about,
An' the Gobble-uns 'at gits you
        Ef you
          Don't
            Watch
            Out!

Onc't they was a little boy wouldn't say his pray'rs—
An' when he went to bed at night, away up-stairs,
His mammy heerd him holler, an' his daddy heerd him bawl,
An' when they turn't the kivvers down, he wasn't there at all!
An' they seeked him in the rafter-room, an' cubby-hole, an' press,
An' seeked him up the chimbly flue, an' ever'-wheres, I guess;

But all they ever found was thist his pants an round about!
An' the Gobble-uns'll git you
                    Ef you
                        Don't
                            Watch
                            Out!

WHEN SHE COMES HOME

When she comes home again! A thousand ways
    I fashion, to myself, the tenderness
    Of my glad welcome: I shall tremble, yes;
And touch her, as when first in the old days
I touched her girlish hand, nor dared upraise
    Mine eyes, such was my faint heart's sweet distress.
    Then silence: and the perfume of her dress:
The room will sway a little, and a haze
Cloy eyesight—soul-sight, even—for a space;
    And tears—yes, and the ache here in the throat,
To know that I so ill deserve the place
    Her arms make for me; and the sobbing note
I stay with kisses, ere the tearful face
Again is hidden in the old embrace.

WHEN THE FROST IS ON THE PUNKIN

When the frost is on the punkin and the fodder's in the shock,
And you hear the kyouck and gobble of the struttin' turkey-cock,
And the clackin' of the guineys, and the cluckin' of the hens,
And the rooster's hallylooyer as he tiptoes on the fence;
O it's then's the times a feller is a-feelin' at his best,
With the risin' sun to greet him from a night of peaceful rest,
As he leaves the house, bare-headed, and goes out to feed the stock,
When the frost is on the punkin and the fodder's in the shock.

They's something kindo' hearty-like about the atmosphere,
When the heat of summer's over and the coolin' fall is here—
Of course we miss the flowers, and the blossoms on the trees,
And the mumble of the hummin'-birds and buzzin' of the bees;
But the air's so appetisin'; and the landscape through the haze
Of a crisp and sunny morning of the airly autumn days

Is a pictur that no painter has the colorin' to mock—
When the frost is on the punkin and the fodder's in the shock.

The husky, rusty rustle of the tossels of the corn,
And the raspin' of the tangled leaves, as golden as the morn;
The stubble in the furries—kindo' lonesome-like, but still
A-preachin' sermons to us of the barns they growed to fill;
The strawstack in the medder, and the reaper in the shed;
The hosses in theyr stalls below—the clover overhead!—
O, it sets my heart a-clickin' like the tickin' of a clock,
When the frost is on the punkin and the fodder's in the shock!

A SONG

There is ever a song somewhere, my dear,
    There is ever a something sings always;
There's the song of the lark when the skies are clear,
    And the song of the thrush when the skies are gray.
The sunshine showers across the grain,
    And the bluebird trills in the orchard tree;
And in and out, when the eaves drip rain,
    The swallows are twittering ceaselessly.

There is ever a song somewhere, my dear,
    Be the skies above or dark or fair;
There is ever a song that our hearts may hear—
    There is ever a song somewhere, my dear—
There is ever a song somewhere!

There is ever a song somewhere, my dear,
    In the midnight black or the midday blue;
The robin pipes when the sun is here,
    And the cricket chirrups the whole night through.
The buds may blow and the fruit may grow,
    And the autumn leaves drop crisp and sere;
But whether the sun, or the rain, or the snow,
    There is ever a song somewhere, my dear.

There is ever a song somewhere, my dear,
    Be the skies above or dark or fair;
There is ever a song that our hearts may hear—
    There is ever a song somewhere, my dear,
There is ever a song somewhere!

ON A SPLENDUD MATCH

On the night of the marriage of the foregoin' couple, which shall be nameless here, these lines was ca'mly dashed off in the albun of the happy bride whilse the shivver-ree was goin' on outside the residence.

> He was warned aginst the *womern*—
> She was warned aginst the *man*.—
> And ef that won't make a weddin',
> Wy, they's nothin' else that can!

A TALE OF THE AIRLY DAYS

Oh! tell me a tale of the airly days—
    Of the times as they ust to be;
"Pillar of Fi-er" and "Shakspeare's Plays"
    Is a' most too deep fer me!
I want plane facts, and I want plane words,
    Of the good old-fashioned ways,
When speech run free as the songs of birds
    'Way back in the airly days.

Tell me a tale of the timber-lands—
    Of the old-time pioneers;
Somepin' a pore man understands
    With his feelins's well as ears.
Tell of the old log house,—about
    The loft, and the puncheon floor—
The old fi-er-place, with the crane swung out,
    And the latch-string through the door.

Tell of the things jest as they was—
    They don't need no excuse!—
Don't tech 'em up' like the poets does,
    Tel theyr all too fine fer use!—
Say they was 'leven in the fambily—
    Two beds, and the chist, below,
And the trundle-beds that each helt three,
    And the clock and the old bureau.

Then blow the horn at the old back-door
    Tel the echoes all halloo,
And the children gethers home onc't more,

Jest as they ust to do:
Blow fer Pap tel he hears and comes,
    With Tomps and Elias, too,
A-marchin' home, with the fife and drums
    And the old Red White and Blue!

Blow and blow tel the sound draps low
    As the moan of the whipperwill,
And wake up Mother, and Ruth and Jo,
    All sleepin' at Bethel Hill:
Blow and call tel the faces all
    Shine out in the back-log's blaze,
And the shadders dance on the old hewed wall
    As they did in the airly days.

ON A DEAD BABE

Fly away! thou heavenly one!—
    I do hail thee on thy flight!
Sorrow! thou hath tasted none—
    Perfect joy is yourn by right.
        Fly away! and bear our love
        To thy kith and kin above!

I can tetch thy finger-tips
    Ca'mly, and bresh back the hair
From thy forr'ed with my lips,
    And not leave a teardrop thare.—
        Weep fer *Tomps and Ruth*—and *me*—
        But I cannot weep fer *thee.*

THE HOSS

The hoss he is a splendud beast;
    He is man's friend, as heaven designed,
And, search the world from west to east,
    No honester you'll ever find!

Some calls the hoss "a pore dumb brute,"
    And yit, like Him who died fer you,
I say, as I theyr charge refute,
    " 'Fergive; they know not what they do!' "

No wiser animal makes tracks
   Upon these earthly shores, and hence
Arose the axium, true as facts,
   Extolled by all, as "Good hoss-sense!"

The hoss is strong, and knows his stren'th,—
   You hitch him up a time er two
And lash him, and he'll go his le'nth,
   And kick the dashboard out fer you!

But, treat him allus good and kind,
   And never strike him with a stick,
Ner aggervate him, and you'll find
   He'll never do a hostile trick.

A hoss whose master tends him right
   And worters him with daily care,
Will do your biddin' with delight,
   And act as docile as *you* air.

He'll paw and prance to hear your praise,
   Because he's learnt to love you well;
And, though you can't tell what he says,
   He'll nicker all he wants to tell.

He knows you when you slam the gate
   At early dawn, upon your way
Unto the barn, and snorts elate,
   To git his corn, er oats, er hay.

He knows you, as the orphant knows
   The folks that loves her like theyr own,
And raises her and "finds" her clothes,
   And "schools" her tel a womern-grown!

I claim no hoss will harm a man,
   Ner kick, ner run away, cavort,
Stump-suck, er balk, er "catamaran,"
   Ef you'll jest treat him as you ort.

But when I see the beast abused,
   And clubbed around as I've saw some,
I want to see his owner noosed,
   And jest yanked up like Absolum!

Of course they's differunce in stock,—
    A hoss that has a little yeer,
And slender build, and shaller hock,
    Can beat his shadder, mighty near!

Whilse one that's thick in neck and chist
    And big in leg and full in flank,
That tries to race, I still insist
    He'll have to take the second rank.

And I have jest laid back and laughed,
    And rolled and wallered in the grass
At fairs, to see some heavy-draft
    Lead out at *first*, yit come in *last!*

Each hoss has his appinted place,—
    The heavy hoss should plow the soil;—
The blooded racer, he must race,
    And win big wages fer his toil.

I never bet—ner never wrought
    Upon my feller-man to bet—
And yit, at times, I've often thought
    Of my convictions with regret.

I bless the hoss from hoof to head—
    From head to hoof, and tale to mane!—
I bless the hoss, as I have said,
    From head to hoof, and back again!

I love my God the first of all,
    Then him that perished on the cross;
And next, my wife,—and then I fall
    Down on my knees and love the hoss.

WET-WEATHER TALK

It hain't no use to grumble and complane;
    It's jest as cheap and easy to rejoice;
When God sorts out the weather and sends rain,
    W'y, rain's my choice.

Men giner'ly, to all intents—
   Although they're apt to grumble some—
Puts most theyr trust in Providence,
   And takes things as they come—
      That is, the commonality
      Of men that's lived as long as me
      Has watched the world enugh to learn
      They're not the boss of this concern.

With *some*, of course, it's different—
   I've saw *young* men that knowed it all,
And didn't like the way things went
   On this terrestial ball;—
      But all the same, the rain, some way,
      Rained jest as hard on picnic day;
      Er, when they railly *wanted* it,
      It mayby wouldn't rain a bit!

In this existunce, dry and wet
   Will overtake the best of men—
Some little skift o' clouds'll shet
   The sun off now and then.—
      And maybe, whilse you're wundern who
      You've fool-like lent your umbrell' to,
      And *want* it—out'll pop the sun,
      And you'll be glad you hain't got none!

It aggervates the farmers, too—
   They's too much wet, er too much sun,
Er work, er waitin' round to do
   Before the plowin's done.
      And mayby, like as not, the wheat,
      Jest as it's lookin' hard to beat,
      Will ketch the storm—and jest about
      The time the corn's a-jintin' out.

These-here *cy-clones* a-foolin' round—
   And back'ard crops!—and wind and rain!—
And yit the corn that's wallerd down
   May elbow up again!—
      They hain't no sense, as I can see,
      Fer mortuls, sich as us, to be
      A-faultin' Natchur's wise intents,
      And lockin' horns with Providence!

It hain't no use to grumble and complane;
   Its jest as cheap and easy to rejoice.—
When God sorts out the weather and sends rain,
   W'y, rain's my choice.

TOWN AND COUNTRY

They's a predjudice allus twixt country and town
   Which I wisht in my hart wasent so.
You take *city* people, jest square up and down,
   And theyr mighty good people to know:
And whare's better people a-livin', to-day,
   Than us in the *country?*—Yit good
As both of us is, we're divorsed, you might say,
   And won't compermise when we could!

Now as nigh into town fer yer Pap, ef you please,
   Is the what's called the sooburbs.—Fer thare
You'll at least ketch a whiff of the breeze and a sniff
   Of the breth of wild-flowrs ev'rywhare.
They's room fer the children to play, and grow, too—
   And to roll in the grass, er to climb
Up a tree and rob nests, like they *ortent* to do,
   But they'll do *any*how ev'ry time!

My Son-in-law said, when he lived in the town,
   He jest natchurly pined, night and day,
Fer a sight of the woods, er a acre of ground
   Whare the trees wasent all cleared away!
And he says to me onc't, whilse a-visitin' us
   On the farm, "It's not strange, I declare,
That we can't coax you folks, without raisin' a fuss,
   To come to town, visitin' thare!"

And says I, "Then git back whare you sorto' *belong*—
   And *Madaline*, too,—and yer three
Little children," says I, "that don't know a bird-song,
   Ner a hawk from a chicky-dee-dee!
Git back," I-says-I, "to the blue of the sky
   And the green of the fields, and the shine
Of the sun, with a laugh in yer voice and yer eye
   As harty as Mother's and mine!"

Well—long-and-short of it,—he's compermised *some*—
  He's moved in the sooburbs.—And now
They don't haf to coax, when they want us to come,
  'Cause we turn in and go *anyhow!*
Fer thare—well, they's room fer the songs and purfume
  Of the grove and the old orchurd-ground,
And they's room fer the children out thare, and they's room
  Fer theyr Gran' pap to waller 'em round!

THE CLOVER

Some sings of the lilly, and daisy, and rose,
And the pansies and pinks that the Summertime throws
In the green grassy lap of the medder that lays
Blinkin' up at the skyes through the sunshiney days;
But what is the lilly and all of the rest
Of the flowers, to a man with a hart in his brest
That was dipped brimmin' full of the honey and dew
Of the sweet clover-blossoms his babyhood knew?

I never set eyes on a clover-field now,
Er fool round a stable, er climb in the mow,
But my childhood comes back jest as clear and as plane
As the smell of the clover I'm sniffin' again;
And I wunder away in a bare-footed dream,
Whare I tangle my toes in the blossoms that gleam
With the dew of the dawn of the morning of love
Ere it wept ore the graves that I'm weepin' above.

And so I love clover—it seems like a part
Of the sacerdest sorrows and joys of my hart;
And wherever it blossoms, oh, thare let me bow
And thank the good God as I'm thankin' Him now;
And I pray to Him still fer the stren'th when I die,
To go out in the clover and tell it good-bye,
And lovin'ly nestle my face in its bloom
While my soul slips away on a breth of purfume.

THOUGHTS ON A PORE JOKE

I like fun—and I like jokes
'Bout as well as most o' folks!—

Like my joke, and like my fun;—
But a joke, I'll state right here,
'S got some p'int—er I don't keer
    Fer no joke that haint got none.—
I haint got no use, I'll say,
Fer a *pore* joke, anyway!

F'rinstunce, now, when *some* folks gits
To relyin' on theyr wits,
Ten to one they git too smart
And *spile* it all, right at the start!
    Feller wants to jest go slow
    And do his *thinkin'* first, you know.
'F I can't think up somepin' good,
I set still and chaw my cood!
        'F you *think* nothin'—jest keep on,
        But don't *say* it—er you're gone!

MY FIDDLE

My fiddle?—Well, I kindo' keep her handy, don't you know!
Though I aint so much inclined to tromp the strings and switch the bow
As I was before the timber of my elbows got so dry,
And my fingers was more limber-like and caperish and spry;
    Yit I can plonk and pluck and plink,
        And tune her up and play,
    And jest lean back and laugh and wink
        At ev'ry rainy day!

My playin's only middlin'—tunes I picked up when a boy—
The kindo'-sorto' fiddlin' that the folks calls "cordaroy;"
"The Old Fat Gal," and "Rye-straw," and "My Sailyor's on the Sea,"
Is the old cowtillions *I* "saw" when the ch'ice is left to me;
    And so I plunk and plonk and plink,
        And rosum-up my bow,
    And play the tunes that makes you think
        The devil's in your toe!

I was allus a romancin', do-less boy, to tell the truth,
A-fiddlin' and a-dancin', and a-wastin' of my youth,

And a-actin' and a-cuttin'-up all sorts o' silly pranks
That wasn't worth a button of anybody's thanks!
    But they tell me, when I ust to plink
      And plonk and plunk and play,
    My music seemed to have the kink
      O' drivin' cares away!

That's how this here old fiddle's won my hart's indurin love!
From the strings acrost her middle, to the schreechin' keys above—
From her "apern," over "bridge," and to the ribbon round her
      throat,
She's a wooin', cooin' pigeon, singin' "Love me" ev'ry note!
    And so I pat her neck, and plink
      Her strings with lovin' hands,
    And, list'nin' clos't, I sometimes think
      She kindo' understands!

MY PHILOSOFY

I aint, ner don't p'tend to be,
Must posted on philosofy;
But thare is times, when all alone,
I work out idees of my own.
And of these same thare is a few
I'd like to jest refer to you—
Pervidin' that you don't object
To listen clos't and rickollect.

I allus argy that a man
Who does about the best he can
Is plenty good enugh to suit
This lower mundane institute—
No matter ef his daily walk
Is subject fer his neghbor's talk,
And critic-minds of ev'ry whim
Jest all git up and go fer him!

I knowed a feller onc't that had
The yeller-janders mighty bad,
And each and ev-ry friend he'd meet
Would stop and give him some receet
Fer cuorin' of 'em. But he'd say
He kind o' thought they'd go away

Without no medicin', and boast
That he'd git well without one doste.

He kep' a yellerin'on—and they
Perdictin' that he'd die some day
Before he knowed it! Tuck his bed,
The feller did, and lost his head,
And wundered in his mind a spell—
Then rallied, and, at last, got well;
But ev'ry friend that said he'd die
Went back on him eternally!

Its natchurl enugh, I guess,
When some gits more and some gits less,
Fer them-uns on the slimmest side
To claim it ain't a fare divide;
And I've knowed some to lay and wait,
And git up soon, and set up late,
To ketch some feller they could hate
Fer goin' at a faster gait.

The signs is bad when folks commence
A findin' fault with Providence,
And balkin' 'cause the earth don't shake
At ev'ry prancin' step they take.
No man is great tel he can see
How less than little he would be
Ef stripped to self, and stark and bare
He hung his sign out anywhare.

My doctern is to lay aside
Contensions, and be satisfied:
Jest do your best, and praise er blame
That follers that, counts jest the same.
I've allus noticed grate success
Is mixed with troubles, more er less,
And its the man who does the best
That gits more kicks than all the rest.

A SUMMER'S DAY

The Summer's put the idy in
My head that I'm a boy again;

And all around's so bright and gay
I want to put my team away,
And jest git out whare I can lay
And soak my hide full of the day!
But work is work, and must be done—
Yit, as I work, I have my fun,
Jest fancyin' these furries here
Is childhood's paths onc't more so dear:—
And so I walk through medder-lands,
    And country lanes, and swampy trails
Whare long bullrushes bresh my hands;
    And, tilted on the ridered rails
    Of deadnin' fences, "Old Bob White"
    Whissels his name in high delight,
And whirrs away. I wunder still,
Whichever way a boy's feet will—
Whare trees has fell, with tangled tops
    Whare dead leaves shakes, I stop fer breth,
Heerin' the acorn as it drops—
    H'istin' my chin up still as deth,
And watchin' clos't, with upturned eyes,
The tree whare Mr. Squirrel tries
To hide hisse'f above the limb,
But lets his own tale tell on him.

I wunder on in deeper glooms—
    Git hungry, hearin' female cries
From old farm-houses, whare perfumes
    Of harvest dinners seems to rise
And ta'nt a feller, hart and brane,
With memories he can't explain.

I wunder through the underbresh,
    Whare pig-tracks, pintin' to'rds the crick
Is picked and printed in the fresh
    Black bottom-lands, like wimmern pick
Theyr pie-crusts with a fork, some way,
When bakin' fer camp-meetin' day.

I wunder on and on and on,
Tel my gray hair and beard is gone,
And ev'ry wrinkle on my brow
Is rubbed clean out and shaddered now

With curls as brown and fare and fine
As tenderls of the wild grape-vine
That ust to climb the highest tree
To keep the ripest ones fer me.
I wunder still, and here I am
Wadin' the ford below the dam—
The worter chucklin' round my knee
 At hornet-welt and bramble-scratch,
And me a-slippin' 'crost to see
 Ef Tyner's plums is ripe, and size
The old man's wortermelon-patch,
 With juicy mouth and drouthy eyes.
Then, after sich a day of mirth
And happiness as worlds is wurth—
 So tired that heaven seems nigh about,—
The sweetest tiredness on earth
 Is to git home and flatten out—
So tired you can't lay flat enough,
And sort o' wish that you could spred
Out like molasses on the bed,
And jest drip off the aidges in
The dreams that never comes again.

THE OLD SWIMMIN'-HOLE

Oh! the old swimmin'-hole! whare the crick so still and deep
Looked like a baby-river that was laying half asleep,
And the gurgle of the worter round the drift jest below
Sounded like the laugh of something we onc't ust to know
Before we could remember anything but the eyes
Of the angels lookin' out as we left Paradise;
But the merry days of youth is beyond our controle,
And it's hard to part ferever with the old swimmin'-hole.

Oh! the old swimmin'-hole! In the happy days of yore,
When I ust to lean above it on the old sickamore,
Oh! it showed me a face in its warm sunny tide
That gazed back at me so gay and glorified,
It made me love myself, as I leaped to caress
My shadder smilin' up at me with such tenderness.
But them days is past and gone, and old Time's tuck his toll
From the old man come back to the old swimmin'-hole.

Oh! the old swimmin'-hole! In the long, lazy days
When the hum-drum of school made so many run-a-ways,
How plesant was the jurney down the old dusty lane,
Whare the tracks of our bare feet was all printed so plane
You could tell by the dent of the heel and the sole
They was lots o' fun on hands at the old swimmin'-hole.
But the lost joys is past! Let your tears in sorrow roll
Like the rain that ust to dapple up the old swimmin'-hole.

Thare the bullrushes growed, and the cattails so tall,
And the sunshine and shadder fell over it all;
And it mottled the worter with amber and gold
Tel the glad lillies rocked in the ripples that rolled;
And the snake-feeder's four gauzy wings fluttered by
Like the ghost of a daisy dropped out of the sky,
Or a wownded apple-blossom in the breeze's controle
As it cut acrost some orchurd to'rds the old swimmin'-hole.

Oh! the old swimmin'-hole! When I last saw the place,
The scenes was all changed, like the change in my face;
The bridge of the railroad now crosses the spot
Whare the old divin'-log lays sunk and fergot.
And I stray down the banks whare the trees ust to be—
But never again will theyr shade shelter me!
And I wish in my sorrow I could strip to the soul,
And dive off in my grave like the old swimmin'-hole.

Eugene Field

(1850–1895)

Eugene Field was born in St. Louis, Missouri. His mother died when he was still a child, and he moved to Amherst, Massachusetts, with his sister. Field attended Williams College, Knox College, and the University of Missouri. He traveled in Europe and returned to a journalism career in America where he was a reporter for the *St. Louis Evening Journal* and the *Denver Tribune*. From 1883 to 1895 he was a columnist for the *Chicago Daily News*.

DUTCH LULLABY

Wynken, Blynken, and Nod one night
    Sailed off in a wooden shoe,—
Sailed on a river of misty light
    Into a sea of dew.
"Where are you going, and what do you wish?"
    The old moon asked the three.
"We have come to fish for the herring-fish
    That live in this beautiful sea;
    Nets of silver and gold have we,"
            Said Wynken,
            Blynken,
            And Nod.

The old moon laughed and sung a song,
    As they rocked in the wooden shoe;
And the wind that sped them all night long
    Ruffled the waves of dew;
The little stars were the herring-fish

That lived in the beautiful sea.
"Now cast your nets wherever you wish,
  But never afeard are we!"
So cried the stars to the fishermen three,
      Wynken,
      Blynken,
      And Nod.

All night long their nets they threw
  For the fish in the twinkling foam,
Then down from the sky came the wooden shoe,
  Bringing the fishermen home;
'T was all so pretty a sail, it seemed
  As if it could not be;
And some folk thought 't was a dream they'd dreamed
  Of sailing that beautiful sea;
But I shall name you the fishermen three:
      Wynken,
      Blynken,
      And Nod.

Wynken and Blynken are two little eyes,
  And Nod is a little head,
And the wooden shoe that sailed the skies
  Is a wee one's trundle-bed;
So shut your eyes while Mother sings
  Of wonderful sights that be,
And you shall see the beautiful things
  As you rock on the misty sea
Where the old shoe rocked the fishermen three,—
      Wynken,
      Blynken,
      And Nod.

LITTLE BOY BLUE

The little toy dog is covered with dust,
  But sturdy and stanch he stands;
And the little toy soldier is red with rust,
  And his musket molds in his hands.
Time was when the little toy dog was new
  And the soldier was passing fair,

And that was the time when our Little Boy Blue
Kissed them and put them there.

"Now, don't you go till I come," he said,
"And don't you make any noise!"
So toddling off to his trundle-bed
He dreamed of the pretty toys.
And as he was dreaming, an angel song
Awakened our Little Boy Blue,—
Oh, the years are many, the years are long,
But the little toy friends are true.

Ay, faithful to Little Boy Blue they stand,
Each in the same old place,
Awaiting the touch of a little hand,
The smile of a little face.
And they wonder, as waiting these long years through,
In the dust of that little chair,
What has become of our Little Boy Blue
Since he kissed them and put them there.

THE CLINK OF THE ICE

Notably fond of music, I dote on a sweeter tone
Than ever the harp has uttered or ever the lute has known.
When I wake at five in the morning with a feeling in my head
Suggestive of mild excesses before I retired to bed;
When a small but fierce volcano vexes me sore inside,
And my throat and mouth are furred with a fur that seemeth a buf-
    falo hide,—
How gracious those dews of solace that over my senses fall
At the clink of the ice in the pitcher the boy brings up the hall!

Oh, is it the gaudy ballet, with features I cannot name,
That kindles in virile bosoms that slow but devouring flame?
Or is it the midnight supper, eaten before we retire,
That presently by combustion setteth us all afire?
Or is it the cherry magnum?—nay, I'll not chide the cup
That makes the meekest mortal anxious to whoop things up:
Yet, what the cause soever, relief comes when we call,—
Relief with that rapturous clinkety-clink that clinketh alike for all.

I've dreamt of the fiery furnace that was one vast bulk of flame,
And that I was Abednego a-wallowing in that same;
And I've dreamt I was a crater, possessed of a mad desire
To vomit molten lava, and to snort big gobs of fire;
I've dreamt I was Roman candles and rockets that fizzed and
     screamed,—
In short, I have dreamt the cussedest dreams that ever a human
     dreamed:
But all the red-hot fancies were scattered quick as a wink
When the spirit within that pitcher went clinking its clinkety-clink.

Boy, why so slow in coming with that gracious saving cup?
Oh, haste thee to the succor of the man who is burning up!
See how the ice bobs up and down, as if it wildly strove
To reach its grace to the wretch who feels like a red-hot kitchen
     stove!
The piteous clinks its clinks methinks should thrill you through and
     through:
An erring soul is wanting drink, and he wants it p. d. q.!
And, lo! the honest pitcher, too, falls in so dire a fret
That its pallid form is presently bedewed with a chilly sweat.

May blessings be showered upon the man who first devised this
     drink
That happens along at five A.M. with its rapturous clinkety-clink!
I never have felt the cooling flood go sizzling down my throat
But what I vowed to hymn a hymn to that clinkety-clink devote;
So now, in the prime of my manhood, I polish this lyric gem
For the uses of all good fellows who are thirsty at five A.M.,
But specially for those fellows who have known the pleasing thrall
Of the clink of the ice in the pitcher the boy brings up the hall.

THE DREAMS

Two dreams came down to earth one night
     From the realm of mist and dew;
One was a dream of the old, old days,
     And one was a dream of the new.

One was a dream of a shady lane
     That led to the pickerel pond
Where the willows and rushes bowed themselves
     To the brown old hills beyond.

And the people that peopled the old-time dream
    Were pleasant and fair to see,
And the dreamer he walked with them again
    As often of old walked he.

Oh, cool was the wind in the shady lane
    That tangled his curly hair!
Oh, sweet was the music the robins made
    To the springtime everywhere!

Was it the dew the dream had brought
    From yonder midnight skies,
Or was it tears from the dear, dead years
    That lay in the dreamer's eyes?

The *other* dream ran fast and free,
    As the moon benignly shed
Her golden grace on the smiling face
    In the little trundle-bed.

For 't was a dream of times to come—
    Of the glorious noon of day—
Of the summer that follows the careless spring
    When the child is done with play.

And 't was a dream of the busy world
    Where valorous deeds are done;
Of battles fought in the cause of right,
    And of victories nobly won.

It breathed no breath of the dear old home
    And the quiet joys of youth;
It gave no glimpse of the good old friends
    Or the old-time faith and truth.

But 't was a dream of youthful hopes,
    And fast and free it ran,
And it told to a little sleeping child
    Of a boy become a man!

These were the dreams that came one night
    To earth from yonder sky;
These were the dreams two dreamers dreamed—
    My little boy and I.

And in our hearts my boy and I
   Were glad that it was so;
He loved to dream of days to come,
   And *I* of long ago.

So from our dreams my boy and I
   Unwillingly awoke,
But neither of his precious dream
   Unto the other spoke.

Yet of the love we bore those dreams
   Gave each his tender sign;
For there was triumph in *his* eyes—
   And there were tears in *mine!*

THE DREAM-SHIP

When the world is fast asleep,
   Along the midnight skies—
As though it were a wandering cloud—
   The ghostly dream-ship flies.

An angel stands at the dream-ship's helm,
   An angel stands at the prow,
And an angel stands at the dream-ship's side
   With a rue-wreath on her brow.

The other angels, silver-crowned,
   Pilot and helmsman are,
And the angel with the wreath of rue
   Tosseth the dreams afar.

The dreams they fall on rich and poor;
   They fall on young and old;
And some are dreams of poverty,
   And some are dreams of gold.

And some are dreams that thrill with joy,
   And some that melt to tears;
Some are dreams of the dawn of love,
   And some of the old dead years.

On rich and poor alike they fall,
  Alike on young and old,
Bringing to slumbering earth their joys
  And sorrows manifold.

The friendless youth in them shall do
  The deeds of mighty men,
And drooping age shall feel the grace
  Of buoyant youth again.

The king shall be a beggarman—
  The pauper be a king—
In that revenge or recompense
  The dream-ship dreams do bring.

So ever downward float the dreams
  That are for all and me,
And there is never mortal man
  Can solve that mystery.

But ever onward in its course
  Along the haunted skies—
As though it were a cloud astray—
  The ghostly dream-ship flies.

Two angels with their silver crowns
  Pilot and helmsman are,
And an angel with a wreath of rue
  Tosseth the dreams afar.

THE LITTLE PEACH

A little peach in the orchard grew,
A little peach of emerald hue:
Warmed by the sun, and wet by the dew,
              It grew.

One day, walking the orchard through,
That little peach dawned on the view
Of Johnny Jones and his sister Sue—
              Those two.

Up at the peach a club they threw:
Down from the limb on which it grew,
Fell the little peach of emerald hue—
    Too true!

John took a bite, and Sue took a chew,
And then the trouble began to brew,—
Trouble the doctor couldn't subdue,—
    Paregoric too.

Under the turf where the daisies grew,
They planted John and his sister Sue;
And their little souls to the angels flew—
    Boo-hoo!

But what of the peach of emerald hue,
Warmed by the sun, and wet by the dew?
Ah, well! its mission on earth is through—
    Adieu!

OUR BIGGEST FISH

When in the halcyon days of eld, I was a little tyke,
I used to fish in pickerel ponds for minnows and the like;
And oh, the bitter sadness with which my soul was fraught
When I rambled home at nightfall with the puny string I'd caught!
And, oh, the indignation and the valor I'd display
When I claimed that all the biggest fish I'd caught had got away!

Sometimes it was the rusty hooks, sometimes the fragile lines,
And many times the treacherous reeds would foil my just designs;
But whether hooks or lines or reeds were actually to blame,
I kept right on at losing all the monsters just the same—
I never lost a *little* fish—yes, I am free to say
It always was the *biggest* fish I caught that got away.

And so it was, when later on, I felt ambition pass
From callow minnow joys to nobler greed for pike and bass;
I found it quite convenient, when the beauties would n't bite
And I returned all bootless from the watery chase at night,
To feign a cheery aspect and recount in accents gay
How the biggest fish that I had caught had somehow got away.

And really, fish look bigger than they are before they 're caught—
When the pole is bent into a bow and the slender line is taut,
When a fellow feels his heart rise up like a doughnut in his throat
And he lunges in a frenzy up and down the leaky boat!
Oh, you who 've been a-fishing will indorse me when I say
That it always *is* the biggest fish you catch that gets away!

'T 'is even so in other things—yes, in our greedy eyes
The biggest boon is some elusive, never-captured prize;
We angle for the honors and the sweets of human life—
Like fishermen we brave the seas that roll in endless strife;
And then at last, when all is done and we are spent and gray,
We own the biggest fish we 've caught are those that got away.

I would not have it otherwise; 't is better there should be
Much bigger fish than I have caught a-swimming in the sea;
For now some worthier one than I may angle for that game—
May by his arts entice, entrap, and comprehend the same;
Which, having done, perchance he'll bless the man who's proud to
   say
That the biggest fish he ever caught were those that got away.

THE TWO COFFINS

In yonder old cathedral
  Two lovely coffins lie;
In one, the head of the state lies dead,
  And a singer sleeps hard by.

Once had that King great power
  And proudly ruled the land—
His crown e'en now is on his brow
  And his sword is in his hand.

How sweetly sleeps the singer
  With calmly folded eyes,
And on the breast of the bard at rest
  The harp that he sounded lies.

The castle walls are falling
  And war distracts the land,
But the sword leaps not from that mildewed spot
  There in that dead king's hand.

But with every grace of nature
 There seems to float along—
To cheer again the hearts of men—
 The singer's deathless song.

TO A SOUBRETTE

'Tis years, soubrette, since last we met;
 And yet—ah, yet, how swift and tender
My thoughts go back in time's dull track
 To you, sweet pink of female gender!
I shall not say—though others may—
 That time all human joy enhances;
But the same old thrill comes to me still
 With memories of your songs and dances.

Soubrettish ways these latter days
 Invite my praise, but never get it;
I still am true to yours and you—
 My record's made, I 'll not upset it!
The pranks they play, the things they say—
 I 'd blush to put the like on paper,
And I 'll avow they don't know how
 To dance, so awkwardly they caper!

I used to sit down in the pit
 And see you flit like elf or fairy
Across the stage, and I 'll engage
 No moonbeam sprite was half so airy;
Lo, everywhere about me there
 Were rivals reeking with pomatum,
And if, perchance, they caught your glance
 In song or dance, how did I hate 'em!

At half-past ten came rapture—then
 Of all those men was I most happy,
For bottled beer and royal cheer
 And têtes-à-têtes were on the tapis.
Do you forget, my fair soubrette,
 Those suppers at the Café Rector,—
The cosey nook where we partook
 Of sweeter cheer than fabled nectar?

Oh, happy days, when youth's wild ways
   Knew every phase of harmless folly!
Oh, blissful nights, whose fierce delights
   Defied gaunt-featured Melancholy!
Gone are they all beyond recall,
   And I—a shade, a mere reflection—
Am forced to feed my spirit's greed
   Upon the husks of retrospection!

And lo! to-night, the phantom light,
   That, as a sprite, flits on the fender,
Reveals a face whose girlish grace
   Brings back the feeling, warm and tender;
And, all the while, the old-time smile
   Plays on my visage, grim and wrinkled,—
As though, soubrette, your footfalls yet
   Upon my rusty heart-strings tinkled!

JAPANESE LULLABY

Sleep, little pigeon, and fold your wings,—
   Little blue pigeon with velvet eyes;
Sleep to the singing of mother-bird swinging—
   Swinging the nest where her little one lies.

Away out yonder I see a star,—
   Silvery star with a tinkling song;
To the soft dew falling I hear it calling—
   Calling and tinkling the night along.

In through the window a moonbeam comes,—
   Little gold moonbeam with misty wings;
All silently creeping, it asks, "Is he sleeping—
   Sleeping and dreaming while mother sings?"

Up from the sea there floats the sob
   Of the waves that are breaking upon the shore,
As though they were groaning in anguish, and moaning—
   Bemoaning the ship that shall come no more.

But sleep, little pigeon, and fold your wings,—
   Little blue pigeon with mournful eyes;

Am I not singing?—see, I am swinging—
　　Swinging the nest where my darling lies.

THE TRUTH ABOUT HORACE

It is very aggravating
To hear the solemn prating
Of the fossils who are stating
　　That old Horace was a prude;
When we know that with the ladies
He was always raising Hades,
And with many an escapade his
　　Best productions are imbued.

There's really not much harm in a
Large number of his carmina,
But these people find alarm in a
　　Few records of his acts;
So they'd squelch the muse caloric,
And to students sophomoric
They'd present as metaphoric
　　What old Horace meant for facts.

We have always thought 'em lazy;
Now we adjudge 'em crazy!
Why, Horace was a daisy
　　That was very much alive!
And the wisest of us know him
As his Lydia verses show him,—
Go, read that virile poem,—
　　It is No. 25.

He was a very owl, sir,
And starting out to prowl, sir,
You bet he made Rome howl, sir,
　　Until he filled his date;
With a massic-laden ditty
And a classic maiden pretty,
He painted up the city,
　　And Maecenas paid the freight!

Ella Wheeler Wilcox

(1850–1919)

Ella Wheeler Wilcox was born in Johnstown Center, Wisconsin, and lived much of her life in New York City. She was one of the best-selling poets in the late 1800s. Her volume, *Poems of Passion*, shocked the American public with its unconventionality—her work was considered by many to be erotic and daring. She became, for a time, extremely influential as a poet, but her popularity started to wane in her later years as she explored reincarnation and other such topics, becoming more metaphysical in her writings.

SOLITUDE

Laugh, and the world laughs with you;
   Weep, and you weep alone,
For the sad old earth must borrow its mirth,
   But has trouble enough of its own.
Sing, and the hills will answer;
   Sigh, it is lost on the air,
The echoes bound to a joyful sound,
   But shrink from voicing care.

Rejoice, and men will seek you;
   Grieve, and they turn and go.
They want full measure of all your pleasure,
   But they do not need your woe
Be glad, and your friends are many;
   Be sad, and you lose them all,—
There are none to decline your nectar'd wine,
   But alone you must drink life's gall.

Feast, and your halls are crowded;
    Fast, and the world goes by.
Succeed and give, and it helps you live,
    But no man can help you die.
There is room in the halls of pleasure
    For a large and lordly train,
But one by one we must all file on
    Through the narrow aisles of pain.

THE YEAR OUTGROWS THE SPRING

The year outgrows the spring it thought so sweet
    And clasps the summer with a new delight,
Yet wearied, leaves her languors and her heat
    When cool-browed autumn dawns upon his sight.

The tree outgrows the bud's suggestive grace
    And feels new pride in blossoms fully blown.
But even this to deeper joy gives place
    When bending boughs 'neath blushing burdens groan.

Life's rarest moments are derived from change,
    The heart outgrows old happiness, old grief,
And suns itself in feelings new and strange.
    The most enduring pleasure is but brief.

Our tastes, our needs, are never twice the same.
    Nothing contents us long, however dear.
The spirit in us, like the grosser frame,
    Outgrows the garments which it wore last year.

Change is the watchword of Progression. When
    We tire of well-worn ways, we seek for new.
This restless craving in the souls of men
    Spurs them to climb, and seek the mountain view.

So let who will erect an altar shrine
    To meek-browed Constancy, and sing her praise
Unto enlivening Change I shall build mine,
    Who lends new zest, and interest to my days.

AS BY FIRE

Sometimes I feel so passionate a yearning
For spiritual perfection here below,
This vigorous frame with healthful fervor burning,
   Seems my determined foe.

So actively it makes a stern resistance,
So cruelly sometimes it wages war
Against a wholly spiritual existence
   Which I am striving for.

It interrupts my soul's intense devotions,
Some hope it strangles of divinest birth,
With a swift rush of violent emotions
   Which link me to the earth.

It is as if two mortal foes contended
Within my bosom in a deadly strife,
One for the loftier aims for souls intended,
   One for the earthly life.

And yet I know this very war within me,
Which brings out all my will-power and control;
This very conflict at the last shall win me
   The loved and longed-for goal.

The very fire which seems sometimes so cruel,
Is the white light, that shows me my own strength.
A furnace, fed by the divinest fuel
   It may become at length.

Ah! when in the immoral ranks enlisted,
I sometimes wonder if we shall not find
That not by deeds, but by what we've resisted,
   Our places are assigned.

ART AND HEART

Though critics may bow to art, and I am its own true lover,
It is not art, but heart, which wins the wide world over.

Though smooth be the heartless prayer, no ear in

Heaven will mind it,
And the finest phrase falls dead, if there is no feeling behind it.

Though perfect the player's touch, little if any he sways us,
Unless we feel his heart throb through the music he plays us.

Though the poet may spend his life in skillfully rounding a mea-
sure,
Unless he writes from a full warm heart, he gives us little pleasure.

So is not the speech which tells, but the impulse which goes with
the saying,
And it is not the words of the prayer, but the yearning back of the
praying.

It is not the artist's skill, which into our soul comes stealing
With a joy that is almost pain, but it is the player's feeling.

And it is not the poet's song, though sweeter than sweet bells chim-
ing,
Which thrills us through and through, but the heart which beats
under the rhyming.

And therefore I say again, though I am art's own true lover,
That it is not art, but heart, which wins the wide world over.

LOVE'S COMING

She had looked for his coming as warriors come,
    With the clash of arms and the bugle's call;
But he came instead with a stealthy tread,
    Which she did not hear at all.

She had thought how his armor would blaze in the sun,
    As he rode like a prince to claim his bride:
In the sweet dim light of the falling night
    She found him at her side.

She had dreamed how the gaze of his strange, bold eye
    Would wake her heart to a sudden glow:
She found in his face the familiar grace
    Of a friend she used to know.

She had dreamed how his coming would stir her soul,
  As the ocean is stirred by the wild storm's strife:
He brought her the balm of a heavenly calm,
  And a peace which crowned her life.

SUNSET

I saw the day lean o'er the world's sharp edge,
And peer into night's chasm, dark and damp.
High in his hand he held a blazing lamp,
Then dropped it, and plunged headlong down the ledge.

With lurid splendor that swift paled to gray,
I saw the dim skies suddenly flush bright.
'Twas but the expiring glory of the light
Flung from the hand of the adventurous day.

THE DUET

I was smoking a cigarette;
Maud, my wife, and the tenor McKey,
Were singing together a blithe duet,
And days it were better I should forget
  Came suddenly back to me.
Days when life seemed a gay masque ball,
And to love and be loved was the sum of it all.

As they sang together, the whole scene fled,
The room's rich hangings, the sweet home air,
Stately Maud, with her proud blonde head,
And I seemed to see in her place instead
  A wealth of blue-black hair,
And a face, ah! your face,—yours, Lisette,
A face it were wiser I should forget.

We were back—well, no matter when or where,
But you remember, I know, Lisette,
I saw you, dainty, and debonnaire,
With the very same look that you used to wear
  In the days I should forget.
And your lips, as red as the vintage we quaffed,
Were pearl-edged bumpers of wine when you laughed.

Two small slippers with big rosettes,
Peeped out under your kilt-skirt there,
While we sat smoking our cigarettes
(Oh, I shall be dust when my heart forgets!)
    And singing that selfsame air;
And between the verses for interlude,
I kissed your throat, and your shoulders nude.

You were so full of a subtle fire,
You were so warm and so sweet, Lisette;
You were everything men admire
And there were no fetters to make us tire,
    For you were—a pretty grisette.
But you loved, as only such natures can,
With a love that makes heaven or hell for a man.

*   *   *   *   *

They have ceased singing that old duet,
Stately Maud and the tenor McKey.
"You are burning your coat with your cigarette,
And qu' avez vous, dearest, your lids are wet,"
    Maud says, as she leans o'er me,
And I smile, and lie to her, husband-wise,
"Oh, it is nothing but smoke in my eyes."

AN INSPIRATION

However the battle is ended,
    Though proudly the victor comes
With fluttering flags and prancing nags
    And echoing roll of drums,
Still truth proclaims this motto
    In letters of living light,—
No question is ever settled
    Until it is settled right.

Though the heel of the strong oppressor
    May grind the weak in the dust,
And the voices of fame with one acclaim
    May call him great and just,
Let those who applaud take warning,
    And keep this motto in sight,—

No question is ever settled
  Until it is settled right.

Let those who have failed take courage;
  Tho' the enemy seems to have won,
Tho' his ranks are strong, if he be in the wrong
  The battle is not yet done;
For, sure as the morning follows
  The darkest hour of the night,
No question is ever settled
  Until it is settled right.

O man bowed down with labor!
  O woman young, yet old!
O heart oppressed in the toiler's breast
  And crushed by the power of gold!
Keep on with your weary battle
  Against triumphant might;
No question is ever settled
  Until it is settled right.

THROUGH THE VALLEY

After James Thomson

As I came through the Valley of Despair
  As I came through the valley, on my sight,
  More awful than the darkness of the night,
Shone glimpses of a Past that had been fair,
  And memories of eyes that used to smile,
  And wafts of perfume from a vanished isle,
As I came through the valley.

As I came through the valley I could see,
  As I came through the valley, fair and far,
  As drowning men look up and see a star,
The fading shore of my lost Used-to-be;
  And like an arrow in my heart I heard
  The last sad notes of Hope's expiring bird,
As I came through the valley.

As I came through the valley desolate,
  As I came through the valley, like a beam

Of lurid lightning I beheld a gleam
Of Love's great eyes that now were full of hate.
Dear God! dear God! I could bear all but that;
  But I fell down soul-stricken, dead, thereat,
As I came through the valley.

COMMUNISM

When my blood flows calm as a purling river
When my heart is asleep and my brain has sway,
It is then that I vow we must part forever,
That I will forget you, and put you away
Out of my life, as a dream is banished
Out of the mind when the dreamer awakes;
That I know it will be when the spell has vanished,
Better for both of our sakes.

When the court of the mind is ruled by Reason,
I know it is wiser for us to part;
But Love is a spy who is plotting treason,
In league with that warm, red rebel, the Heart
They whisper to me that the King is cruel,
That his reign is wicked, his law a sin,
And every word they utter is fuel
To the flame that smolders within.

And on nights like this, when my blood runs riot
With the fever of youth and its mad desires,
When my brain in vain bids my heart be quiet,
When my breast seems the center of lava-fires,
Oh, then is the time when most I miss you,
And I swear by the stars and my soul and say
That I will have you, and, hold you, and kiss you,
Though the whole world stands in the way.

And like Communists, as mad, as disloyal,
My fierce emotions roam out of their lair;
They hate King Reason for being royal—
They would fire his castle, and burn him there.
O Love! they would clasp you, and crush you and kill you,
In the insurrection of uncontrol.
Across the miles, does this wild war thrill you
That is raging in my soul?

THE WINDS OF FATE

One ship drives east and another drives west,
With the self-same winds that blow,
   'Tis the set of the sails
   And not the gales
That tell them the way to go.

Like the winds of the sea are the winds of fate,
As we voyage along through life,
   'Tis the set of the soul
   That decides its goal
And not the calm or the strife.

UPON THE SAND

All love that has not friendship for its base,
  Is like a mansion built upon the sand.
Though brave its walls as any in the land,
And its tall turrets lift their heads in grace;
Though skillful and accomplished artists trace
   Most beautiful designs on every hand,
   And gleaming statues in dim niches stand,
And fountains play in some flow'r-hidden place:

Yet, when from the frowning east a sudden gust
   Of adverse fate is blown, or sad rains fall
   Day in, day out, against its yielding wall,
Lo! the fair structure crumbles to the dust.
Love, to endure life's sorrow and earth's woe,
Needs friendship's solid masonwork below.

Ben King

(1857–1894)

Ben King was born in St. Joseph, Michigan, and showed himself to be a musical prodigy at a young age. He became a fine satirist combining piano music with comedy. That King greatly enjoyed writing is made obvious by the fact that a number of his poems were written in a humorous vein and many rely for their effect on clever and amusing plays on words. The poet's reputation was growing when, at age thirty-seven, he was found dead in his hotel room. King's best-known work is a parody titled "If I Should Die."

THE PESSIMIST

Nothing to do but work,
  Nothing to eat but food,
Nothing to wear but clothes,
  To keep one from going nude.

Nothing to breathe but air,
  Quick as a flash 't is gone;
Nowhere to fall but off,
  Nowhere to stand but on.

Nothing to comb but hair,
  Nowhere to sleep but in bed,
Nothing to weep but tears,
  Nothing to bury but dead.

Nothing to sing but songs,
  Ah, well, alas! alack!

Nowhere to go but out,
   Nowhere to come but back.

Nothing to see but sights,
   Nothing to quench but thirst,
Nothing to have but what we've got
   Thus through life we are cursed.

Nothing to strike but a gait;
   Everything moves that goes.
Nothing at all but common sense
   Can ever withstand these woes.

IF I SHOULD DIE

If I should die to-night
And you should come to my cold corpse and say,
Weeping and heartsick o'er my lifeless clay—
   If I should die to-night,
And you should come in deepest grief and woe—
And say: "Here's that ten dollars that I owe,"
   I might arise in my large white cravat
   And say, "What's that?"

If I should die to-night
And you should come to my cold corpse and kneel,
Clasping my bier to show the grief you feel,
   I say, if I should die to-night
And you should come to me, and there and then
Just even hint 'bout payin' me that ten,
   I might arise the while,
   But I'd drop dead again.

THE MERMAID

Sweet mermaid of the incomparable eyes,
Surpassing glimpses of the April skies.
Thy form, ah, maid of the billowy deep!
So rare and fair, but to possess I'd creep
Where the old octopus deep in his briny haunts
Comes forth to feed on anything he wants;
Where mollusks crawl and cuttlefish entwine,

There on crustaceans be content to dine.
What ecstacies in some calcareous valley,
Had I but scales like thee 'tis there we'd dally,
There seek each peak and let no other bliss
Be more enchanting than one salt-sea kiss;
There sit and bask in love, and sigh, and feel
Each other's fins throb, or perhaps we'd steal
To some lone cavern. I suppose you know a
Place where we could pluck the polyzoa,
Or in your boudoir by your mirror there
I'd comb the seaweed from your auburn hair.
But hush! A red-haired mermaid sister comes this way,
And lashing with her tail the wavelets into spray.
Cometh she alone o'er yonder watery pampas?
Oh, no. By Jove! There comes the white hippocampus.

THE COW SLIPS AWAY

The tall pines pine,
The pawpaws pause,
And the bumble-bee bumbles all day;
The eavesdropper drops,
And the grasshopper hops,
While gently the cow slips away.

THAT CAT

The cat that comes to my window sill
When the moon looks cold and the night is still—
He comes in a frenzied state alone
With a tail that stands like a pine tree cone,
And says: "I have finished my evening lark,
And I think I can hear a hound dog bark.
My whiskers are froze 'nd stuck to my chin.
I do wish you 'd git up and let me in."
That cat gits in.

But if in the solitude of the night
He does n't appear to be feeling right,
And rises and stretches and seeks the floor,
And some remote corner he would explore,
And does n't feel satisfied just because

There's no good spot for to sharpen his claws,
And meows and canters uneasy about
Beyond the least shadow of any doubt
      That cat gits out.

SUNRISE

The dim light to the sou'ward
    Is the beacon of the coast,
But the white light to the leeward
    The mariner loves most.
And whether 'tis the dim light
    Or the white light to the lee,
That great big hunk of daylight
    Is light of lights for me.
But what it is of all lights
    That fills my soul with glee,
Is when that hunk of daylight
    Climbs up out of the sea.

APPEARANCES

De man dat wahs de slickest tile
    Doan draw de bigges' check;
De riches' lookin' kin' ob sile
    Doan yiel' de bigges' peck.

De hoss dat 's highes' in de pool
    Doan always win de race,
Kase sometimes he 's a little off,
    An' sometimes held fo' place.

De bulldog wid de orn'ry jaw
    Ain' half so bad to meet
As dat dar yaller mungril cur
    Dat 's layin for yo' meat.

De mooley cow dat hists her leg
    An' makes de milkmaid scream,
Am jes' de bossie cow dat gives
    De riches' kin' ob cream.

De mule dat hab de wicked eye
        Ain' half so bad, now min'—
Look out for dat ole sleepy mule
        Yo' 's walkin' 'roun' behin'.

THE GIRL WITH THE JERSEY

You can sing of the maid
Who, in faultless attire,
Rides out in her curtained coupé;
Her robes are exquisitely fashioned by Worth—
At eve they are décolleté;
But I, I will sing of a maiden more fair,
More innocent, too, I opine;
You can choose from society's crust, if you will,
But the girl with the jersey is mine.

I know her by all that is good, kind and true,
This modest young maiden I name;
I've walked with her, talked with her,
Danced with her, too,
And found that my heart was aflame;
I've written her letters, and small billet-doux,
Revealing my love in each line:
You can drink to your slim, satin-bodiced gazelle,
But the girl with the jersey is mine.

THE TRAMP

He came from where he started
        And was going where he went.
He hadn't had a smell of food,
        Not even had a scent.
He never even muttered once
        Till he began to talk,
And when he left the kitchen door
        He took the garden walk.

He said: "There's no one with me,
        Because I am alone;
I might have scintillated once;
        My clothes have always shone.

I got here 'fore the other ones
    Because I started first:
The reason I look shabby is
    Because I'm dressed the worst."

Then I asked him where he came from—
    This was just before we parted,
And he muttered indistinctly,
    "Oh, I come from where I started!"

THE FLOWERS' BALL

There is an olden story,
    'Tis a legend, so I'm told,
How the flowerets gave a banquet,
    In the ivied days of old;
How the posies gave a party once
    That wound up with a ball,
How they held it in a valley,
    Down in "Flowery Kingdom Hall."

The flowers of every clime were there,
    Of high and low degree,
All with their petals polished,
    In sweet aromatic glee.
They met down in this woodland
    In the soft and ambient air,
Each in its lolling loveliness,
    Exhaled a perfume rare.

An orchestra of Blue Bells
    Sat upon a mossy knoll
And pealed forth gentle music
    That quite captured every soul.
The Holly hocked a pistil
    Just to buy a suit of clothes,
And danced with all the flowerets
    But the modest, blushing Rose.

The Morning Glory shining
    Seemed reflecting all the glow
Of dawn, and took a partner;
    It was young Miss Mistletoe.

Miss Maggie Nolia from the South
  Danced with Forget-me-not;
Sweet William took Miss Pink in tow
  And danced a slow gavotte.

Thus everything went swimmingly
  'Mongst perfumed belles and beaux,
And every floweret reveled save
  The modest, blushing Rose.
Miss Fuchsia sat around and told
  For floral emulation,
That she had actually refused
  To dance with A. Carnation.

The Coxcomb, quite a dandy there,
  Began to pine and mope,
Until he had been introduced
  To young Miss Heliotrope.
Sir Cactus took Miss Lily,
  And he swung her so about
She asked Sweet Pea to Cauliflower
  And put the Cactus out.

Miss Pansy took her Poppy
  And she waltzed him down the line
Till they ran against old Sunflower
  With Miss Honeysuckle Vine.
The others at the party that
  Went whirling through the mazy
Were the Misses Rhodo Dendron,
  Daffodil and little Daisy.

Miss Petunia, Miss Verbena, Violet,
  And sweet Miss Dahlia
Came fashionably late, arrayed
  In very rich regalia.
Miss Begonia, sweet Miss Buttercup,
  Miss Lilac and Miss Clover;
Young Dandelion came in late
  When all the feast was over.

The only flower that sent regrets
  And really could n't come,
Who lived in the four hundred, was

The vain Chrysanthemum.
One floweret at the table
　　Grew quite ill, we must regret,
And every posy wondered, too,
　　Just what Miss Mignonette.

Young Tulip chose Miss Orchid
　　From the first, and did not part
With her until Miss Mary Gold
　　Fell with a Bleeding Heart.
But ah! Miss Rose sat pensively
　　Till every young bud passed her;
When just to fill the last quadrille,
　　The little China Aster.

EVOLUTION

We seem to exist in a hazardous time,
　　Driftin' along here through space;
Nobody knows just when we begun
　　Or how fur we 've gone in the race.
Scientists argy we 're shot from the sun,
　　While others we 're goin' right back,
An' some say we 've allers been here more or less,
　　An' seem to establish the fact.
O' course 'at's somepin' 'at nobody knows,
　　As far as I've read or cun see;
An' them as does know all about the hull scheme,
　　Why, none of 'em never agree.

Now, why I think it 's a perilous time,—
　　What do we know 'bout them spots
Up there on that glorious orb of the day?
　　Smart men has argyed an' lots
Of the brainiest folks has been cypherin' out,
　　An' all sorts of stories has riz
'Bout what the sun 's made of or how it 's composed,
　　An' lots of 'em think that it is.
O' course 'at 's somepin' 'at nobody knows—
　　Nobody under the sun;
Nary a body or bein', I s'pose;
　　Nary a bein' but One.

Take Eva Lution, an' what does she say
  'Bout how we all sprung from a ape?
An' there's the goriller and big chimpanzee,
  Patterned exactly our shape.
An' I've seen some folks, an' I guess so have you,
  An' it ain't none of our bizness neither,
That actually looked like they sprung from a ape,
  An' did n't have fur to spring either.
Course 'at 's somepin 'at every one knows;
  I do n't see how you folks can doubt it;
S'posin' they have some resemblance to us,
  No use in a-writin' about it.

If a feller 'll take a geology book
  An' not go a rushin' long through it,
But jes' sort o' figger the thing out hisself—
  What I mean is: 'ply hisself to it—
He'll see we've dug up folks ten thousand years old,
  Built on a ponderous plan;
Somehow this knocks Mr. Moses all out,
  An' Adam, the biblical man.
O' course 'at 's somepin 'at nobody knows,
  Nobody under the sun;
Nary a body or bein' I s'pose,
  Nary a bein' but One.

THE OWL AND THE CROW

There was an old owl,
  With eyes big and bright,
Who sung in a treetop
  One calm summer night.
And the song that he sung
  I will now sing to you—
"To whit! To whoo, hoo!
  To whit! To whoo, hoo!"

He sang there all night
  Till early next morn,
When a crow came along
  That was looking for corn.
The crow heard him singing,
  "To whit! To whoo, hoo!"

And offered to sing
  A few notes that he knew.

Just then the old owl
  In the treetop so high,
With his classical shape
  And his big staring eye,
Requested the crow,
  In the deepest of scorn,
To sing his old chestnut
  About stealing corn.

"Caw! Caw!" said the crow,
  "Well—my deeds are by light.
I do n't steal young chickens
  And sit up all night,
With dew on my feathers;
  When I break the laws
In looking through cornfields
  It's not without caws."

THE ULTIMATUM

"You can decorate your office
  With a thousand gilded signs,
And have upholstered furniture
  In quaint antique designs;
Have the latest patent telephone
  Where you can yell 'Hello!'
But," said she, "I just made up my mind
  That typewriter must go.

"You can stay down at the office,
  As you have done, after hours;
And, if you are partial to bouquets,
  I'll furnish you with flowers.
You can spring the old club story
  When you come home late, you know,
But, remember, I've made up my mind
  That typewriter must go.

"You can let your bookkeepers lay off
  And see a game of ball;

The office-boy can leave at noon
 Or not show up at all.
There—what is this upon your coat?
 It is n't mine I know.
I think I know a thing or two—
 That typewriter shall go."

Bliss Carman

(1861–1929)

Bliss Carman was born in Fredericton, New Brunswick, Canada, but lived for most of his life in Boston and New York. He was educated at the Universities of New Brunswick and Edinburgh and at Harvard. He took up U.S. residence in 1889, and from 1894 to 1898, he was editor of the *Chap-Book*. Carman was named "poet laureate of Canada" and achieved international recognition for his collaboration with Richard Hovey on the *Songs from Vagabondia*.

A MORE ANCIENT MARINER

The swarthy bee is a buccaneer,
A burly velveted rover,
Who loves the booming wind in his ear
As he sails the seas of clover.

A waif of the goblin pirate crew,
With not a soul to deplore him.
He steers for the open verge of blue
With the filmy world before him.

His flimsy sails abroad on the wind
Are shivered with fairy thunder;
On a line that sings to the light of his wings
He makes for the lands of wonder.

He harries the ports of the Hollyhocks,
And levies on poor Sweetbrier;

He drinks the whitest wine of Phlox,
And the Rose is his desire.

He hangs in the Willows a night and a day;
He rifles the Buckwheat patches;
Then battens his store of pelf galore
Under the tautest hatches.

He woos the Poppy and weds the Peach,
Inveigles Daffodilly,
And then like a tramp abandons each
For the gorgeous Canada Lily.

There's not a soul in the garden world
But wishes the day were shorter,
When Mariner B. puts out to sea
With the wind in the proper quarter.

Or, so they say! But I have my doubts;
For the flowers are only human,
And the valor and gold of a vagrant bold
Were always dear to woman.

He dares to boast, along the coast,
The beauty of Highland Heather,—
How he and she, with night on the sea,
Lay out on the hills together.

He pilfers from every port of the wind,
From April to golden autumn;
But the thieving ways of his mortal days
Are those his mother taught him.

His morals are mixed, but his will is fixed;
He prospers after his kind,
And follows an instinct, compass-sure,
The philosophers call blind.

And that is why, when he comes to die,
He'll have an easier sentence
Than some one I know who thinks just so,
And then leaves room for repentance.

He never could box the compass round;
He doesn't know port from starboard;
But he knows the gates of the Sundown Straits,
Where the choicest goods are harbored.

He never could see the Rule of Three,
But he knows a rule of thumb
Better than Euclid's, better than yours,
Or the teachers' yet to come.

He knows the smell of the hydromel
As if two and two were five;
And hides it away for a year and a day
In his own hexagonal hive.

Out in the day, hap-hazard, alone,
Booms the old vagrant hummer,
With only his whim to pilot him
Through the splendid vast of summer.

He steers and steers on the slant of the gale,
Like the fiend or Vanderdecken;
And there's never an unknown course to sail
But his crazy log can reckon.

He drones along with his rough sea-song
And the throat of a salty tar,
This devil-may-care, till he makes his lair
By the light of a yellow star.

He looks like a gentleman, lives like a lord,
And works like a Trojan hero;
Then loafs all winter upon his hoard,
With the mercury at zero.

HEM AND HAW

Hem and Haw were the sons of sin,
Created to shally and shirk;
Hem lay 'round and Haw looked on
While God did all the work.

Hem was a fogy, and Haw was a prig,
For both had the dull, dull mind;
And whenever they found a thing to do,
They yammered and went it blind.

Hem was the father of bigots and bores;
As the sands of the sea were they.
And Haw was the father of all the tribe
Who criticise to-day.

But God was an artist from the first,
And knew what he was about;
While over his shoulder sneered these two,
And advised him to rub it out.

They prophesied ruin ere man was made:
"Such folly must surely fail!"
And when he was done, "Do you think, my Lord,
He's better without a tail?"

And still in the honest working world,
With posture and hint and smirk,
These sons of the devil are standing by
While Man does all the work.

They balk endeavor and baffle reform,
In the sacred name of law;
And over the quavering voice of Hem
Is the droning voice of Haw.

THE JOYS OF THE ROAD

Now the joys of the road are chiefly these:
A crimson touch on the hard-wood trees;
A vagrant's morning wide and blue,
In early fall, when the wind walks, too;
A shadowy highway cool and brown,
Alluring up and enticing down
From rippled water to dappled swamp,
From purple glory to scarlet pomp;
The outward eye, the quiet will,
And the striding heart from hill to hill;
The tempter apple over the fence;

The cobweb bloom on the yellow quince;
The palish asters along the wood,—
A lyric touch of the solitude;
An open hand, an easy shoe,
And a hope to make the day go through,—
Another to sleep with, and a third
To wake me up at the voice of a bird;
The resonant far-listening morn,
And the hoarse whisper of the corn;
The crickets mourning their comrades lost,
In the night's retreat from the gathering frost;
(Or is it their slogan, plaintive and shrill,
As they beat on their corselets, valiant still?)
A hunger fit for the kings of the sea,
And a loaf of bread for Dickon and me;
A thirst like that of the Thirsty Sword,
And a jug of cider on the board;
An idle noon, a bubbling spring,
The sea in the pine-tops murmuring;
A scrap of gossip at the ferry;
A comrade neither glum nor merry,
Asking nothing, revealing naught,
But minting his words from a fund of thought
A keeper of silence eloquent,
Needy, yet royally well content,
Of the mettled breed, yet abhorring strife,
And full of the mellow juice of life,
A taster of wine, with an eye for a maid,
Never too bold, and never afraid,
Never heart-whole, never heart-sick,
(These are the things I worship in Dick)
No fidget and no reformer, just
A calm observer of ought and must,
A lover of books, but a reader of man,
No cynic and no charlatan,
Who never defers and never demands,
But, smiling, takes the world in his hands,—
Seeing it good as when God first saw
And gave it the weight of his will for law.
And O the joy that is never won,
But follows and follows the journeying sun,
By marsh and tide, by meadow and stream,
A will-o'-the-wind, a light-o'-dream,
Delusion afar, delight anear,

From morrow to morrow, from year to year,
A jack-o'-lantern, a fairy fire,
A dare, a bliss, and a desire!
The racy smell of the forest loam,
When the stealthy, sad-heart leaves go home;
(O leaves, O leaves, I am one with you,
Of the mould and the sun and the wind and the dew!)
The broad gold wake of the afternoon;
The silent fleck of the cold new moon;
The sound of the hollow sea's release
From stormy tumult to starry peace;
With only another league to wend;
And two brown arms at the journey's end!
These are the joys of the open road—
For him who travels without a load.

SPRING SONG

Make me over, mother April,
When the sap begins to stir!
When thy flowery hand delivers
All the mountain-prisoned rivers,
And thy great heart-beats and quivers
To revive the days that were,
Make me over, mother April,
When the sap begins to stir!

Take my dust and all my dreaming,
Count my heart-beats one by one,
Send them where the winters perish;
Then some golden noon recherish
And restore them in the sun,
Flower and scent and dust and dreaming,
With their heart-beats every one!

Set me in the urge and tide-drift
Of the streaming hosts a-wing!
Breast of scarlet, throat of yellow,
Raucous challenge, wooings mellow
Every migrant is my fellow,
Making northward with the spring.
Loose me in the urge and tide-drift
Of the streaming hosts a-wing!

Shrilling pipe or fluting whistle,
In the valleys come again;
Fife of frog and call of tree-toad,
All my brothers, five or three-toed,
With their revel no more vetoed,
Making music in the rain;
Shrilling pipe or fluting whistle,
In the valleys come again.

Make me of thy seed to-morrow,
When the sap begins to stir!
Tawny light-foot, sleepy bruin,
Bright-eyes in the orchard ruin,
Gnarl the good life goes askew in,
Whiskey-jack, or tanager,—
Make me anything to-morrow,
When the sap begins to stir!

Make me even (How do I know?)
Like my friend the gargoyle there;
It may be the heart within him
Swells that doltish hands should pin him
Fixed forever in mid-air.
Make me even sport for swallows,
Like the soaring gargoyle there!

Give me the old clue to follow,
Through the labyrinth of night!
Clod of clay with heart of fire,
Things that burrow and aspire,
With the vanishing desire,
For the perishing delight,—
Only the old clue to follow,
Through the labyrinth of night!

Make me over, mother April,
When the sap begins to stir!
Fashion me from swamp or meadow,
Garden plot or ferny shadow,
Hyacinth or humble burr!
Make me over, mother April,
When the sap begins to stir!

Let me hear the far, low summons,
When the silver winds return;
Rills that run and streams that stammer
Goldenwing with his loud hammer,
Icy brooks that brawl and clamor,
Where the Indian willows burn;
Let me hearken to the calling,
When the silver winds return,

Till recurring and recurring,
Long since wandered and come back,
Like a whim of Grieg's or Gounod's,
This same self, bird, bud, or Bluenose,
Some day I may capture (Who knows?)
Just the one last joy I lack,
Waking to the far new summons,
When the old spring winds come back.

For I have no choice of being,
When the sap begins to climb,—
Strong insistence, sweet intrusion,
Vasts and verges of illusion,—
So I win, to time's confusion,
The one perfect pearl of time,
Joy and joy and joy forever,
Till the sap forgets to climb!

Make me over in the morning
From the rag-bag of the world!
Scraps of dreams and duds of daring,
Home-brought stuff from far sea-faring,
Faded colors once so flaring,
Shreds of banners long since furled!
Hues of ash and glints of glory,
In the rag-bag of the world!

Let me taste the old immortal
Indolence of life once more;
Not recalling nor foreseeing,
Let the great slow joys of being
Well my heart through as of yore!
Let me taste the old immortal
Indolence of life once more!

Give me the old drink of rapture,
The delirium to drain,
All my fellows drank in plenty
At the Three Score Inns and Twenty
From the mountains to the main!
Give me the old drink for rapture,
The delirium to drain!

Only make me over, April,
When the sap begins to stir!
Make me man or make me woman
Make me oaf or ape or human,
Cup of flower or cone of fir;
Make me anything but neuter
When the sap begins to stir!

A ROVER'S SONG

Snowdrift of the mountains,
Spindrift of the sea,
We who down the border
Rove from gloom to glee,—

Snowdrift of the mountains,
Spindrift of the sea,
There be no such gypsies
Over earth as we.

Snowdrift of the mountains,
Spindrift of the sea,
Let us part the treasure
Of the world in three.

Snowdrift of the mountains,
Spindrift of the sea,
You shall keep your kingdoms,
Joscelyn for me!

RESIGNATION

When I am only fit to go to bed,
Or hobble out to sit within the sun,

Ring down the curtain, say the play is done,
And the last petals of the poppy shed!

I do not want to live when I am old,
I have no use for things I cannot love;
And when the day that I am talking of
(Which God forfend!) is come, it will be cold.

But if there is another place than this,
Where all the men will greet me as "Old Man,"
And all the women wrap me in a smile,
Where money is more useless than a kiss,
And good wine is not put beneath the ban,
I will go there and stay a little while.

EARTH'S LYRIC

April. You hearken, my fellow,
Old slumberer down in my heart?
There's a whooping of ice in the rivers:
The sap feels a start.

The snow-melted torrents are brawling;
The hills, orange-misted and blue,
Are touched with the voice of the rainbird
Unsullied and new.

The houses of frost are deserted,
Their slumber is broken and done,
And empty and pale are the portals
Awaiting the sun.

The bands of Arcturus are slackened;
Orion goes forth from his place
On the slopes of the night, leading homeward
His hound from the chase.

The Pleiades weary and follow
The dance of the ghostly dawn;
The revel of silence is over;
Earth's lyric comes on.

A golden flute in the cedars,
A silver pipe in the swales,
And the slow large life of the forest
Wells back and prevails.

A breath of the woodland spirit
Has blown out the bubble of spring
To this tenuous hyaline glory
One touch sets a-wing.

DAISIES

Over the shoulders and slopes of the dune
I saw the white daisies go down to the sea,
A host in the sunshine, an army in June,
The people God sends us to set our heart free.

The bobolinks rallied them up from the dell,
The orioles whistled them out of the wood;
And all of their singing was, "Earth, it is well!"
And all of their dancing was, "Life, thou art good!"

CONCERNING KAVIN

When Kavin comes back from the barber
Although he no longer is young,
One cheek is as soft as his heart,
And the other as smooth as his tongue.

THE FIRST JULEP

I love the lazy Southern spring,
The way she melts around a chap
And lets the great magnolias fling
Their languid petals in his lap.

I love to travel down half-way
And meet her coming up the earth,
With hurdy-gurdy men who play
And make the children dance for mirth.

But best of all I love to steer
For quiet corners not too far,
Where the first juleps reappear
With fresh green mint behind the bar.

P.S. Perhaps you'll think it queer,
But I do not dislike a hint
To let the juleps disappear
And stick my nose into the mint.

WHEN I WAS TWENTY

It was June, and I was twenty.
All my wisdom, poor but plenty,
Never learned Festina lente.
Youth is gone, but whither went he?

Madeline came down the orchard
With a mischief in her eye,
Half demure and half inviting,
Melting, wayward, wistful, shy.

Four bright eyes that found life lovely,
And forgot to wonder why;
Four warm lips at one love-lesson,
Learned by heart so easily.

We gained something of that knowledge
No man ever yet put by,
But his after days of sorrow
Left him nothing but to die.

Madeline went up the orchard,
Down the hurrying world went I;
Now I know love has no morrow,
Happiness no by-and-by.

Youth is gone, but whither went he?
All my wisdom, poor but plenty,
Never learned Festina lente.
It was June and I was twenty.

NANCIBEL

The ghost of a wind came over the hill,
While day for a moment forgot to die,
And stirred the sheaves
Of the millet leaves,
As Nancibel went by.

Out of the lands of Long Ago,
Into the land of By and By,
Faded the gleam
Of a journeying dream,
As Nancibel went by.

A VAGABOND SONG

There is something in the autumn that is native to my blood—
Touch of manner, hint of mood;
And my heart is like a rhyme,
With the yellow and the purple and the crimson keeping time.

The scarlet of the maples can shake me like a cry
Of bugles going by.
And my lonely spirit thrills
To see the frosty asters like a smoke upon the hills.

There is something in October sets the gypsy blood astir;
We must rise and follow her,
When from every hill of flame
She calls and calls each vagabond by name.

IN A COPY OF BROWNING

Browning, old fellow,
Your leaves grow yellow,
Beginning to mellow
As seasons pass.
Your cover is wrinkled,
And stained and sprinkled,
And warped and crinkled
From sleep on the grass.

Is it a wine stain,
Or only a pine stain,
That makes such a fine stain
On your dull blue,—
Got as we numbered
The clouds that lumbered
Southward and slumbered
When day was through?

What is the dear mark
There like an earmark,
Only a tear mark
A woman let fall?—
As bending over
She bade me discover,
"Who *plays* the lover,
He loses all!"

With you for teacher
We learned love's feature
In every creature
That roves or grieves;
When winds were brawling,
Or bird-folk calling,
Or leaf-folk falling,
About our eaves.

No law must straiten
The ways they wait in,
Whose spirits greaten
And hearts aspire.
The world may dwindle,
And summer brindle,
So love but kindle
The soul to fire.

Here many a red line,
Or pencilled headline,
Shows love could wed line
To golden sense;
And something better
Than wisdom's fetter
Has made your letter
Dense to the dense.

No April robin,
Nor clacking bobbin,
Can make of Dobbin
A Pegasus;
But Nature's pleading
To man's unheeding,
Your subtile reading
Made clear to us.

You made us farers
And equal sharers
With homespun wearers
In home-made joys;
You made us princes
No plea convinces
That spirit winces
At dust and noise.

When Fate was nagging,
And days were dragging,
And fancy lagging,
You gave it scope,—
When eaves were drippy,
And pavements slippy,—
From Lippo Lippi
To Evelyn Hope.

When winter's arrow
Pierced to the marrow,
And thought was narrow,
You gave it room;
We guessed the warder
On Roland's border,
And helped to order
The Bishop's Tomb.

When winds were harshish,
And ways were marshish,
We found with Karshish
Escape at need;
Were bold with Waring
In far seafaring,
And strong in sharing
Ben Ezra's creed.

We felt the menace
Of lovers pen us,
Afloat in Venice
Devising fibs;
And little mattered
The rain that pattered,
While Blougram chattered
To Gigadibs.

And we too waited
With heart elated
And breathing bated,
For Pippa's song;
Saw Satan hover,
With wings to cover
Porphyria's lover,
Pompilia's wrong.

Long thoughts were started,
When youth departed
From the half-hearted
Riccardi's bride;
For, saith your fable,
Great Love is able
To slip the cable
And take the tide.

Or truth compels us
With Paracelsus
Till nothing else is
Of worth at all.
Del Sarto's vision
Is our own mission,
And art's ambition
Is God's own call.

Through all the seasons,
You gave us reasons
For splendid treasons
To doubt and fear;
Bade no foot falter,
Though weaklings palter,
And friendships alter
From year to year.

Since first I sought you,
Found you and bought you,
Hugged you and brought you
Home from Cornhill,
While some upbraid you,
And some parade you,
Nine years have made you
My master still.

THE EAVESDROPPER

In a still room at hush of dawn,
  My Love and I lay side by side
And heard the roaming forest wind
  Stir in the paling autumn-tide.

I watched her earth-brown eyes grow glad
  Because the round day was so fair;
While memories of reluctant night
  Lurked in the blue dusk of her hair.

Outside, a yellow maple-tree,
  Shifting upon the silvery blue
With small unnumerable sound,
  Rustled to let the sunlight through.

The livelong day the elvish leaves
  Danced with their shadows on the floor;
And the lost children of the wind
  Went straying homeward by our door.

And all the swarthy afternoon
  We watched the great deliberate sun
Walk through the crimsoned hazy world,
  Counting his hilltops one by one.

Then as the purple twilight came
  And touched the vines along our eaves,
Another Shadow stood without
  And gloomed the dancing of the leaves.

The silence fell on my Love's lips;
  Her great brown eyes were veiled and sad

With pondering some maze of dream,
  Though all the splendid year was glad.

Restless and vague as a gray wind
  Her heart had grown, she knew not why.
But hurrying to the open door,
  Against the verge of western sky

I saw retreating on the hills,
  Looming and sinister and black,
The stealthy figure swift and huge
  Of One who strode and looked not back.

George Santayana

(1863–1952)

George Santayana was born in Madrid, Spain, and came to the United States when he was eight. He studied philosophy at Harvard and stayed on after graduation, long occupying the chair of the philosophy department. Unhappy with America's puritan ethics and commercialism, Santayana returned to Europe in 1912 and lived variously in Oxford, Paris, Spain, and Rome. He never returned to the United States.

"I SOUGHT ON EARTH A GARDEN OF DELIGHT"

I sought on earth a garden of delight,
Or island altar to the Sea and Air,
When gentle music were accounted prayer,
And reason, veiled, performed the happy rite.
My sad youth worshipped at the piteous height
Where God vouchsafed the death of man to share;
His love made mortal sorrow light to bear,
But his deep wounds put joy to shamèd flight.
And though his arms, outstretched upon the tree,
Were beautiful, pleaded my embrace,
My sins were loth to look upon his face.
So came I down from Golgotha to thee,
Eternal Mother; let the sun and sea
Heal me, and keep me in thy dwelling-place.

"HAVE I THE HEART
TO WANDER"

Have I the heart to wander on the earth,
So patient in her everlasting course,
Seeking no prize, but bowing to the force
That gives direction and hath given birth?
Rain tears, sweet Pity, to refresh my dearth,
And plough my sterile bosom, sharp Remorse,
That I grow sick and curse my being's source
If haply one day passes lacking mirth.
Doth the sun therefore burn, that I may bask?
Or do the tirèd earth and tireless sea,
That toil not for their pleasure, toil for me?
Amid the world's long striving, wherefore ask
What reasons were, or what rewards shall be?
The covenant God gave us is a task.

"SWEET ARE THE DAYS"

Sweet are the days we wander with no hope
Along life's labyrinthine trodden way,
With no impatience at the steep's delay,
Nor sorrow at the swift-descended slope.
Why this inane curiosity to grope
In the dim dust for gems' unmeaning ray?
Why this proud piety, that dares to pray
For a world wider than the heaven's cope?
Farewell, my burden! No more will I bear
The foolish load of my fond faith's despair,
But trip the idle race with careless feet.
The crown of olive let another wear;
It is my crown to mock the runner's heat
With gentle wonder and with laughter sweet.

"O WORLD, THOU CHOOSEST
NOT THE BETTER PART!"

O world, thou choosest not the better part!
It is not wisdom to be only wise,
And on the inward vision close the eyes,
But it is wisdom to believe the heart.

Columbus found a world, and had no chart,
Save one that faith deciphered in the skies;
To trust the soul's invincible surmise
Was all his science and his only art.
Our knowledge is a torch of smoky pine
That lights the pathway but one step ahead
Across a void of mystery and dread.
Bid, then, the tender light of faith to shine
By which alone the mortal heart is led
Unto the thinking of the thought divine.

"DREAMT I TODAY THE DREAM OF YESTERNIGHT"

Dreamt I today the dream of yesternight,
Sleep ever feigning one evolving theme,—
Of my two lives which should I call the dream?
Which action vanity? which vision sight?
Some greater waking must pronounce aright,
If aught abideth of the things that seem,
And with both currents swell the flooded stream
Into an ocean infinite of light.
Even such a dream I dream, and know full well
My waking passeth like a midnight spell,
But know not if my dreaming breaketh through
Into the deeps of heaven and of hell.
I know but this of all I would I knew:
Truth is a dream, unless my dream is true.

"MIGHTIER STORMS THAN THIS"

Mightier storms than this are brewed on earth
That pricks the crystal lake with summer showers.
The past hath treasure of sublimer hours,
And God is witness to their changeless worth.
Big is the future with portentous birth
Of battles numberless, and nature's powers
Outdo my dreams of beauty in the flowers,
And top my revels with the demons' mirth.
But thou, glad river that hast reached the plain,
Scarce wak'st the rushes to a slumberous sigh.

The mountains sleep behind thee, and the main
Awaits thee, lulling an eternal pain
With patience; nor doth Phoebe, throned on high,
The mirror of thy placid heart disdain.

"THERE MAY BE CHAOS STILL"

There may be chaos still around the world,
This little world that in my thinking lies;
For mine own bosom is the paradise
Where all my life's fair visions are unfurled.
Within my nature's shell I slumber curled,
Unmindful of the changing outer skies,
Where now, perchance, some new-born Eros flies,
Or some old Cronos from his throne is hurled.
I heed them not; or if the subtle night
Haunt me with deities I never saw,
I soon mine eyelid's drowsy curtain draw
To hide their myriad faces from my sight.
They threat in vain; the whirlwind cannot awe
A happy snow-flake dancing in the flaw.

"AS IN THE MIDST OF BATTLE"

As in the midst of battle there is room
For thoughts of love, and in foul sin for mirth;
As gossips whisper of a trinket's worth
Spied by the death-bed's flickering candle-gloom;
As in the crevices of Caesar's tomb
The sweet herbs flourish on a little earth:
So in this great disaster of our birth
We can be happy, and forget our doom.
For morning, with a ray of tenderest joy
Gilding the iron heaven, hides the truth,
And evening gently woos us to employ
Our grief in idle catches. Such is youth;
Till from that summer's trance we wake, to find
Despair before us, vanity behind.

"A PERFECT LOVE IS
NOURISHED BY DESPAIR"

A perfect love is nourished by despair.
I am thy pupil in the school of pain;
Mine eyes will not reproach thee for disdain,
But thank thy rich disdain for being fair.
Aye! the proud sorrow, the eternal prayer
Thy beauty taught, what shall unteach again?
Hid from my sight, thou livest in my brain;
Fled from my bosom, thou abidest there.
And though they buried thee, and called thee dead,
And told me I should never see thee more,
The violets that grew above thy head
Would waft thy breath and tell thy sweetness o'er,
And every rose thy scattered ashes bred
Would to my sense thy loveliness restore.

" 'TIS LOVE THAT MOVETH
THE CELESTIAL SPHERES"

'Tis love that moveth the celestial spheres
In endless yearning for the Changeless One,
And the stars sing together, as they run
To number the innumerable years.
'Tis love that lifteth through their dewy tears
The roses' beauty to the heedless sun,
And with no hope, nor any guerdon won,
Love leads me on, nor end of love appears.
For the same breath that did awake the flowers,
Making them happy with a joy unknown,
Kindled my light and fixed my spirit's goal;
And the same hand that reined the flying hours
And chained the whirling earth to Phoebus's throne,
In love's eternal orbit keeps the soul.

"AMONG THE MYRIAD VOICES
OF THE SPRING"

Among the myriad voices of the Spring

What were the voice of my supreme desire,
What were my cry amid the vernal choir,
Or my complaint before the gods that sing?
O too late love, O flight on wounded wing,
Infinite hope my lips should not suspire,
Why, when the world is thine, my grief require,
Or mock my dear-bought patience with thy sting!
Though I be mute, the birds will in the boughs
Sing as in every April they have sung,
And, though I die, the incense of heart-vows
Will float to heaven, as when I was young.
But, O ye beauties I must never see,
How great a lover have you lost in me!

ON THE DEATH OF A
METAPHYSICIAN

Unhappy dreamer, who outwinged in flight
The pleasant region of the things I love,
And soared beyond the sunshine, and above
The golden cornfields and the dear and bright
Warmth of the hearth,—blasphemer of delight,
Was your proud bosom not at peace with Jove,
That you sought, thankless for his guarded grove,
The empty horror of abysmal night?
Ah, the thin air is cold above the moon!
I stood and saw you fall, befooled in death,
As, in your numbèd spirit's fatal swoon,
You cried you were a god, or were to be;
I heard with feeble moan your boastful breath
Bubble from depths of the Icarian sea.

CAPE COD

The low sandy beach and the thin scrub pine,
The wide reach of bay and the long sky line,—
    O, I am sick for home!

The salt, salt smell of the thick sea air,
And the smooth round stones that the ebbtides wear,—
    When will the good ship come?

The wretched stumps all charred and burned,
And the deep soft rut where the cartwheel turned,—
    Why is the world so old?

The lapping wave, and the broad gray sky
Where the cawing crows and the slow gulls fly,
    Where are the dead untold?

The thin, slant willows by the flooded bog,
The huge stranded hulk and the floating log,
    Sorrow with life began!

And among the dark pines, and along the flat shore,
O the wind, and the wind, for evermore!
    What will become of man?

"AFTER GREY VIGILS"

After grey vigils, sunshine in the heart;
After long fasting on the journey, food;
After sharp thirst, a draught of perfect good
To flood the soul, and heal her ancient smart.
Joy of my sorrow, never can we part;
Thou broodest o'er me in the haunted wood,
And with new music fill'st the solitude
By but so sweetly being what thou art.
He who hath made thee perfect, makes me blest.
O fiery minister, on mighty wings
Bear me, great love, to mine eternal rest.
Heaven it is to be at peace with things;
Come chaos now, and in a whirlwind's rings
Engulf the planets. I have seen the best.

Richard Hovey

(1864–1900)

Richard Hovey was born in Normal, Illinois. He went to Dartmouth College where he started out studying theology, and then switched to literature. He was a professor of literature at Barnard College and visited Europe from 1891 to 1892. Hovey's reputation rests primarily on his coauthorship, with Bliss Carman, of *Songs from Vagabondia*. Hovey was on the verge of becoming one of America's great poets but was prevented from attaining such stature by an early death.

THE SEA GYPSY

I am fevered with the sunset,
I am fretful with the bay,
For the wander-thirst is on me
And my soul is in Cathay.

There's a schooner in the offing,
With her topsails shot with fire,
And my heart has gone aboard her
For the Islands of Desire.

I must forth again to-morrow!
With the sunset I must be
Hull down on the trail of rapture
In the wonder of the sea.

ISABEL

In her body's perfect sweet
Suppleness and languor meet,—
Arms that move like lapsing billows,
Breasts that Love would make his pillows.
Eyes where vision melts in bliss,
Lips that ripen to a kiss.

Marna with the wind's will,
Daughter of the sea!
Marna of the quick disdain,
Starting at the drean of stain!
At a smile with love aglow,
At a frown a statued woe,
Standing pinnacled in pain
Till a kiss sets free!

Down the world with Marna,
Daughter of the fire!
Marna of the deathless hope,
Still alert to win new scope
Where the wings of life may spread
For a flight unhazarded!
Dreaming of the speech to cope
With the heart's desire!

Marna of the far quest
After the divine!
Striving ever for some goal
Past the blunder-god's control!
Dreaming of potential years
When no day shall dawn in fears!
That's the Marna of my soul,
Wander-bride of mine!

LAURANA'S SONG

For "A Lady of Venice"

Who'll have the crumpled pieces of a heart?
Let him take mine!

Who'll give his whole of passion for a part,
And call't divine?
Who'll have the soiled remainder of desire?
Who'll warm his fingers at a burnt-out fire?
Who'll drink the lees of love, and cast i' the mire
The nobler wine?

Let him come here, and kiss me on the mouth,
And have his will!
Love dead and dry as summer in the South
When winds are still
And all the leafage shrivels in the heat!
Let him come here and linger at my feet
Till he grow weary with the over-sweet,
And die, or kill.

IN A SILENCE

Heart to heart!
And the stillness of night and the moonlight, like hushed breathing
Silently, stealthily moving across thy hair!

O womanly face!
Tender and strong and lucent with infinite feeling,
Shrinking with startled joy, like wind-struck water,
And yet so frank, so unashamed of love!

Ay, for there it is, love—that's the deepest.
Love's not love in the dark.
Light loves wither i' the sun, but Love endureth,
Clothing himself with the light as with a robe.

I would bare my soul to thy sight—
Leave not a secret deep unsearched,
Unrevealing its shame or its glory.
Love without Truth shall die as a soul without God.
A lying love is the love of a day
But the brave and true shall love forever.

Build Love a house;
Let the walls be thick;
Shut him in from the sight of men;
But hide not Love from himself.

PREMONITION

He said, "Good-night, my heart is light,
To-morrow morn at day
We two together in the dew
Shall forth and fare away.

"We shall go down the halls of dawn
To find the doors of joy;
We shall not part again, dear heart."
And he laughed out like a boy.

He turned and strode down the blue road
Against the western sky
Where the last line of sunset glowed
As sullen embers die.

The night reached out her kraken arms
To clutch him as he passed,
And for one sudden moment
My soul shrank back aghast.

THREE OF A KIND

Three of us without a care
In the red September
Tramping down the roads of Maine,
Making merry with the rain,
With the fellow winds a-fare
Where the winds remember.

Three of us with shocking hats,
Tattered and unbarbered,
Happy with the splash of mud,
With the highways in our blood,
Bearing down on Deacon Platt's
Where last year we harbored.

We've come down from Kennebec,
Tramping since last Sunday,
Loping down the coast of Maine,
With the sea for a refrain,

And the maples neck and neck
All the way to Fundy.

Sometimes lodging in an inn,
Cosy as a dormouse—
Sometimes sleeping on a knoll
With no rooftree but the Pole—
Sometimes halely welcomed in
At an old-time farmhouse.

Loafing under ledge and tree,
Leaping over boulders,
Sitting on the pasture bars,
Hail-fellow with storm or stars—
Three of us alive and free,
With unburdened shoulders!

Three of us with hearts like pine
That the lightnings splinter,
Clean of cleave and white of grain—
Three of us afoot again,
With a rapture fresh and fine
As a spring in winter!

All the hills are red and gold;
And the horns of vision
Call across the crackling air
Till we shout back to them there,
Taken captive in the hold
Of their bluff derision.

Spray-salt gusts of ocean blow
From the rocky headlands;
Overhead the wild geese fly,
Honking in the autumn sky;
Black sinister flocks of crow
Settle on the dead lands.

Three of us in love with life,
Roaming like wild cattle,
With the stinging air a-reel
As a warrior might feel
The swift orgasm of the knife
Slay him in mid-battle.

Three of us to march abreast
Down the hills of morrow!
With a clean heart and a few
Friends to clench the spirit to!—
Leave the gods to rule the rest,
And good-by, sorrow!

DISTILLATION

They that eat the uncrushed grape
Walk with steady heels:
Lo, now, how they stare and gape
Where the poet reels!
He has drunk the sheer divine
Concentration of the vine.

EVENING ON THE POTOMAC

The fervid breath of our flushed Southern May
Is sweet upon the city's throat and lips,
As a lover's whose tired arm slips
Listlessly over the shoulder of a queen.

Far away
The river melts in the unseen.
Oh, beautiful Girl-City, how she dips
Her feet in the stream
With a touch that is half a kiss and half a dream!
Her face is very fair,
With flowers for smiles and sunlight in her hair.

My westland flower-town, how serene she is!
Here on this hill from which I look at her,
All is still as if a worshipper
Left at some shrine his offering.

Soft winds kiss
My cheek with a slow lingering.
A luring whisper where the laurels stir
Wiles my heart back to woodland-ward again.

But lo,
Across the sky the sunset couriers run,
And I remain
To watch the imperial pageant of the Sun
Mock me, an impotent Cortez here below,
With splendors of its vaster Mexico.

O Eldorado of the templed clouds!
O golden city of the western sky!
Not like the Spaniard would I storm thy gates;
Not like the babe stretch chubby hands and cry
To have thee for a toy; but far from crowds,
Like my Faun brother in the ferny glen,
Peer from the wood's edge while thy glory waits,
And in the darkening thickets plunge again.

KAVIN AGAIN

It is not anything he says,
It's just his presence and his smile,
The blarney of his silences
That cocker and beguile.

SECRETS

Three secrets that never were said:
The stir of the sap in the spring,
The desire of a man to a maid,
The urge of a poet to sing.

BARNEY McGEE

Barney McGee, there's no end to good luck in you,
Will-o'-the-wisp, with a flicker of Puck in you,
Wild as a bull-pup and all of his pluck in you,—
Let a man tread on your coat and he'll see!—
Eyes like the lakes of Killarney for clarity,
Nose that turns up without any vulgarity,
Smile like a cherub, and hair that is carroty,—
Wow, you're a rarity, Barney McGee!
Mellow as Tarragon,

Prouder than Aragon—
Hardly a paragon,
You will agree—
Here's all that's fine to you!
Books and old wine to you!
Girls be divine to you,
Barney McGee!

Lucky the day when I met you unwittingly,
Dining where vagabonds came and went flittingly.
Here's some *Barbera* to drink it befittingly,
That day at *Silvio's*, Barney McGee!
Many's the time we have quaffed our Chianti there,
Listened to Silvio quoting us Dante there,—
Once more to drink *Nebiolo spumante* there,
How we'd pitch Pommery into the sea!
There where the gang of us
Met ere Rome rang of us,
They had the hang of us
To a degree.
How they would trust to you!
That was but just to you.
Here's o'er their dust to you,
Barney McGee!

Barney McGee, when you're sober you scintillate,
But when you're in drink you're the pride of the intellect;
Divil a one of us ever came in till late,
Once at the bar where you happened to be—
Every eye there like a spoke in you centering,
You with your eloquence, blarney, and bantering—
All Vagabondia shouts at your entering,
King of the Wander-kin, Barney McGee!
There's no satiety
In your society
With the variety
Of your *esprit.*
Here's a long purse to you,
And a great thirst to you!
Fate be no worse to you,
Barney McGee!

Och, and the girls whose poor hearts you deracinate,
Whirl and bewilder and flutter and fascinate!
Faith, it's so killing you are, you assassinate,—
Murder's the word for you, Barney McGee!
Bold when they're sunny and smooth when they're showery,—
Oh, but the style of you, fluent and flowery!

Chesterfield's way, with a touch of the Bowery!
How would they silence you, Barney *machree?*
Naught can your gab allay,
Learned as Rabelais
(You in his abbey lay
Once on the spree).
Here's to the smile of you,
(Oh, but the guile of you!)
And a long while of you,
Barney McGee!

Facile with phrases of length and Latinity,
Like *honorificabilitudinity,*
Where is the maid could resist your vicinity,
Wiled by the impudent grace of your plea?
Then your vivacity and pertinacity
Carry the day with the divil's audacity;
No mere veracity robs your sagacity
Of perspicacity, Barney McGee.
When all is new to them,
What will you do to them?
Will you be true to them?
Who shall decree?
Here's a fair strife to you!
Health and long life to you!
And a great wife to you,
Barney McGee!

Barney McGee, you're the pick of gentility;
Nothing can phase you, you've such a facility;
Nobody ever yet found your utility,—
That is the charm of you, Barney McGee;
Under conditions that others would stammer in,
Still unperturbed as a cat or a Cameron,
Polished as somebody in the Decameron,
Putting the glamour on prince or Pawnee!
In your meanderin',

Love, and philanderin',
Calm as a mandarin
Sipping his tea!
Under the art of you,
Parcel and part of you,
Here's to the heart of you,
Barney McGee!

You who were ever alert to befriend a man,
You who were ever the first to defend a man,
You who had always the money to lend a man,
Down on his luck and hard up for a V!
Sure, you'll be playing a harp in beatitude
(And a quare sight you will be in that attitude)—
Some day, where gratitude seems but a platitude,
You'll find your latitude, Barney McGee.
That's no flim-flam at all,
Frivol or sham at all,
Just the plain—Damn it all,
Have one with me!
Here's luck and more to you!
Friends by the score to you,
True to the core to you,
Barney McGee!

SPEECH AND SILENCE

The words that pass from lip to lip
For souls still out of reach!
A friend for that companionship
That's deeper than all speech!

VAGABONDIA

Off with the fetters
That chafe and restrain!
Off with the chain!
Here Art and Letters,
Music and wine,
And Myrtle and Wanda,
The winsome witches,
Blithely combine.

Here are true riches,
Here is Golconda,
Here are the Indies,
Here we are free—
Free as the wind is,
Free as the sea,
Free!

Houp-la!

What have we
To do with the way
Of the Pharisee?
We go or we stay
At our own sweet will;
We think as we say,
And we say or keep still
At our own sweet will,
At our own sweet will.
Here we are free
To be good or bad,
Sane or mad,
Merry or grim
As the mood may be,—
Free as the whim
Of a spook on a spree,—
Free to be oddities.
Not mere commodities,
Stupid and salable,
Wholly available,
Ranged upon shelves;
Each with his puny form
In the same uniform,
Cramped and disabled;
We are not labelled,
We are ourselves.

Here is the real,
Here the ideal;
Laughable hardship
Met and forgot,
Glory of bardship—
World's bloom and world's blot;
The shock and the jostle,

The mock and the push,
But hearts like the throstle
A-joy in the bush;
Wits that would merrily
Laugh away wrong,
Throats that would verily
Melt Hell in Song.

What though the dimes be
Elusive as rhymes be,
And Bessie, with finger
Uplifted, is warning
That breakfast next morning
(A subject she's scorning)
Is mighty uncertain!
What care we? Linger
A moment to kiss—
No time's amiss
To a vagabond's ardor—
Then finish the larder
And pull down the curtain.

Unless ere the kiss come,
Black Richard or Bliss come,
Or Tom with a flagon,
Or Karl with a jag on—
Then up and after
The joy of the night
With the hounds of laughter
To follow the flight
Of the fox-foot hours
That double and run
Through brakes and bowers
Of folly and fun.
With the comrade heart
For a moment's play,
And the comrade heart
For a heavier day,
And the comrade heart
Forever and aye.

For the joy of wine
Is not for long;
And the joy of song

Is a dream of shine;
But the comrade heart
Shall outlast art
And a woman's love
The fame thereof.
But wine for a sign
Of the love we bring!
And song for an oath
That Love is king!
And both, and both
For his worshipping!

Then up and away
Till the break of day,
With a heart that's merry
And a Tom-and-Jerry,
And a derry-down-derry—
What's that you say,
You highly respectable
Buyers and sellers?
We should be decenter?
Not as we please inter
Custom, frugality,
Use and morality
In the delectable
Depths of wine-cellars?

Midnights of revel,
And noondays of song!
Is it so wrong?
Go to the Devil!

I tell you that we,
While you are smirking
And lying and shirking
Life's duty of duties,
Honest sincerity,
We are in verity
Free!
Free to rejoice

In blisses and beauties!
Free as the voice
Of the wind as it passes!

Free as the bird
In the weft of the grasses!
Free as the word
Of the sun to the sea—
Free!

THE CALL OF THE BUGLES

Bugles!
And the Great Nation thrills and leaps to arms!
Prompt, unconstrained, immediate,
Without misgiving and without debate,
Too calm, too strong for fury or alarms,
The people blossoms armies and puts forth
The splendid summer of its noiseless might;
For the old sap of fight
Mounts up in South and North,
The thrill
That tingled in our veins at Bunker Hill
And brought to bloom July of 'Seventy-Six!
Pine and palmetto mix
With the sequoia of the giant West.

Their ready banners and the hosts of war,
Near and far,
Sudden as dawn,
Innumerable as forests, hear the call
Of the bugles,
The battle birds!
For not alone the brave, the fortunate,
Who first of all
Have put their knapsacks on—
They are the valiant vanguard of the rest!—
Not they alone, but all our millions wait,
Hands on sword,
For the word
That bids them bid the nations know us sons of Fate.

Bugles!
And in my heart a cry,
—Like a dim echo far and mournfully
Blown back to answer them from yesterday!
A soldier's burial!

November hillsides and the falling leaves
Where the Potomac broadens to the tide—
The crisp autumnal silence and the gray
(As of a solemn ritual
Whose congregation glories as it grieves,
Widowed but still a bride)—
The long hills sloping to the wave,
And the lone bugler standing by the grave!

Taps!
The lonely call over the lonely woodlands—
Rising like the soaring of wings,
Like the flight of an eagle—
Taps!
They sound forever in my heart.

From farther still,
The echoes—still the echoes!
The bugles of the dead
Blowing from spectral ranks an answering cry!
The ghostly roll of immaterial drums,
Beating reveille in the camps of dream,
As from far meadows comes,
Over the pathless hill,
The irremeable stream.
I hear the tread
Of the great armies of the Past go by;
I hear,
Across the wide sea wash of years between,
Concord and Valley Forge shout back from the unseen,
And Vicksburg give a cheer.

Our cheer goes back to them, the valiant dead!
Laurels and roses on their graves to-day,
Lilies and laurels over them we lay,
And violets o'er each unforgotten head.
Their honor still with the returning May
Puts on its springtime in our memories,
Nor till the last American with them lies
Shall the young year forget to strew their bed.
Peace to their ashes, sleep and honored rest!
But we—awake!
Ours to remember them with deeds like theirs!
From sea to sea the insistent bugle blares,

The drums will not be still for any sake,
And as an eagle rears his crest,
Defiant, from some tall pine of the North,
And spreads his wings to fly,
The banners of America go forth
Against the clarion sky.
Veteran and volunteer.

They who were comrades of that shadow host,
And the young brood whose veins renew the fires
That burned in their great sires,
Alike we hear
The summons sounding clear
From coast to coast,—
The cry of the bugles,
The battle birds!

* * * * *

Bugles!
The imperious bugles!
Still their call
Soars like an exaltation to the sky.
They call on men to fall,
To die,—
Remembered or forgotten, but a part
Of the great beating of the Nation's heart!
A call to sacrifice!
A call to victory!
Hark, in the Empyrean
The battle birds!
The bugles!

William Vaughn Moody

(1869–1910)

William Vaughn Moody was born in Spencer, Indiana, and, in 1893, graduated from Harvard University. He was highly respected as an assistant professor of English at Harvard and was also a member of the English department at the University of Chicago. Moody was a playwright as well as a poet.

GLOUCESTER MOORS

A mile behind is Gloucester town
Where the fishing fleets put in,
A mile ahead the land dips down
And the woods and farms begin.
Here, where the moors stretch free
In the high blue afternoon,
Are the marching sun and talking sea,
And the racing winds that wheel and flee
On the flying heels of June.

Jill-o'er-the-ground is purple blue,
Blue is the quaker-maid,
The wild geranium holds its dew
Long in the boulder's shade.
Wax-red hangs the cup
From the huckleberry boughs,
In barberry bells the grey moths sup,
Or where the choke-cherry lifts high up
Sweet bowls for their carouse.

Over the shelf of the sandy cove
Beach-peas blossom late.
By corpse and cliff the swallows rove
Each calling to his mate.
Seaward the sea-gulls go,
And the land-birds all are here;
That green-gold flash was a vireo,
And yonder flame where the marsh-flags grow
Was a scarlet tanager.

This earth is not the steadfast place
We landsmen build upon;
From deep to deep she varies pace,
And while she comes is gone.
Beneath my feet I feel
Her smooth bulk heave and dip;
With velvet plunge and soft upreel
She swings and steadies to her keel
Like a gallant, gallant ship.

These summer clouds she sets for sail,
The sun is her masthead light,
She tows the moon like a pinnace frail
Where her phosphor wake churns bright.
Now hid, now looming clear,
On the face of the dangerous blue
The star fleets tack and wheel and veer,
But on, but on does the old earth steer
As if her port she knew.

God, dear God! Does she know her port,
Though she goes so far about?
Or blind astray, does she make her sport
To brazen and chance it out?
I watched when her captains passed:
She were better captainless.
Men in the cabin, before the mast,
But some were reckless and some aghast,
And some sat gorged at mess.

By her battened hatch I leaned and caught
Sounds from the noisome hold,—
Cursing and sighing of souls distraught
And cries too sad to be told.

Then I strove to go down and see;
But they said, "Thou art not of us!"
I turned to those on the deck with me
And cried, "Give help!" But they said, "Let be:
Our ship sails faster thus."

Jill-o'-er-the-ground is purple blue,
Blue is the quaker-maid,
The alder-clump where the brook comes through
Breeds cresses in its shade.
To be out of the moiling street
With its swelter and its sin!
Who has given to me this sweet,
And given my brother dust to eat?
And when will his wage come in?

Scattering wide or blown in ranks,
Yellow and white and brown,
Boats and boats from the fishing banks
Come home to Gloucester town.
There is cash to purse and spend,
There are wives to be embraced,
Hearts to borrow and hearts to lend,
And hearts to take and keep to the end,—
O little sails, make haste!

But thou, vast outbound ship of souls,
What harbor town for thee?
What shapes, when thy arriving tolls,
Shall crowd the banks to see?
Shall all the happy shipmates then
Stand singing brotherly?
Or shall a haggard ruthless few
Warp her over and bring her to,
While the many broken souls of men
Fester down in the slaver's pen,
And nothing to say or do?

ON A SOLDIER FALLEN IN
THE PHILIPPINES

Streets of the roaring town,
Hush for him, hush, be still!

He comes, who was stricken down
Doing the word of our will.
Hush! Let him have his state,
Give him his soldier's crown.
The grists of trade can wait
Their grinding at the mill,
But he cannot wait for his honor, now the trumpet has been blown.
Wreathe pride now for his granite brow, lay love on his breast of
    stone.

Toll! Let the great bells toll
Till the clashing air is dim.
Did we wrong this parted soul?
We will make it up to him.
Toll! Let him never guess
What work we set him to.
Laurel, laurel, yes;
He did what we bade him do.
Praise, and never a whispered hint but the fight he fought was good;
Never a word that the blood on his sword was his country's own
    heart's-blood.

A flag for the soldier's bier
Who dies that his land may live;
O, banners, banners here,
That he doubt not nor misgive!
That he heed not from the tomb
The evil days draw near
When the nation, robed in gloom,
With its faithless past shall strive.
Let him never dream that his bullet's scream went wide of its island
    mark,
Home to the heart of his darling land where she stumbled and
    sinned in the dark.

HARMONICS

This string upon my harp was best beloved:
I thought I knew its secrets through and through;
Till an old man, whose young eyes lightened blue
'Neath his white hair, bent over me and moved
His fingers up and down, and broke the wire
To such a laddered music, rung on rung,

As from the patriarch's pillow skyward sprung
Crowded with wide-flung wings and feet of fire.

O vibrant heart! so metely tuned and strung
That any untaught hand can draw from thee
One clear gold note that makes the tired years young—
What of the time when Love had whispered me
Where slept thy nodes, and my hand pausefully
Gave to the dim harmonics voice and tongue?

ON THE RIVER

The faint stars wake and wonder,
Fade and find heart anew;
Above us and far under
Sphereth the watchful blue.

Silent she sits, outbending,
A wild pathetic grace,
A beauty strange, heart-rending,
Upon her hair and face.

O spirit cries that sever
The cricket's level drone!
O to give o'er endeavor
And let love have its own!

Within the mirrored bushes
There wakes a little stir;
The white-throat moves, and hushes
Her nestlings under her.

Beneath, the lustrous river,
The watchful sky o'erhead.
God, God, that Thou should'st ever
Poison thy children's bread!

AN ODE IN TIME OF HESITATION

After seeing at Boston the statue of Robert
Gould Shaw, killed while storming Fort Wagner,
July 18, 1863, at the head of the first enlisted
Negro regiment, the 54th Massachusetts

I

Before the solemn bronze Saint Gaudens made
To thrill the heedless passer's heart with awe,
And set here in the city's talk and trade
To the good memory of Robert Shaw,
This bright March morn I stand,
And hear the distant spring come up the land;
Knowing that what I hear is not unheard
Of this boy soldier and his negro band,
For all their gaze is fixed so stern ahead,
For all the fatal rhythm of their tread.
The land they died to save from death and shame
Trembles and waits, hearing the spring's great name,
And by her pangs these resolute ghosts are stirred.

II

Through street and mall the tides of people go
Heedless; the trees upon the Common show
No hint of green; but to my listening heart
The still earth doth impart
Assurance of her jubilant emprise,
And it is clear to my long-searching eyes
That love at last has might upon the skies.
The ice is runneled on the little pond;
A telltale patter drips from off the trees;
The air is touched with southland spiceries,
As if but yesterday it tossed the frond
Of pendent mosses where the live-oaks grow
Beyond Virginia and the Carolines,
Or had its will among the fruits and vines
Of aromatic isles asleep beyond
Florida and the Gulf of Mexico.

III

Soon shall the Cape Ann children shout in glee,
Spying the arbutus, spring's dear recluse;
Hill lads at dawn shall hearken the wild goose
Go honking northward over Tennessee;
West from Oswego to Sault Sainte-Marie,
And on to where the Pictured Rocks are hung,
And yonder where, gigantic, willful, young,
Chicago sitteth at the northwest gates,
With restless violent hands and casual tongue
Moulding her mighty fates,
The Lakes shall robe them in ethereal sheen;
And like a larger sea, the vital green
Of springing wheat shall vastly be outflung
Over Dakota and the prairie states.
By desert people immemorial
On Arizonan mesas shall be done
Dim rites unto the thunder and the sun;
Nor shall the primal gods lack sacrifice
More splendid, when the white Sierras call
Unto the Rockies straightway to arise
And dance before the unveiled ark of the year,
Sounding their windy cedars as for shawms,
Unrolling rivers clear
For flutter of broad phylacteries;
While Shasta signals to Alaskan seas
That watch old sluggish glaciers downward creep
To fling their icebergs thundering from the steep,
And Mariposa through the purple calms
Gazes at far Hawaii crowned with palms
Where East and West are met,—
A rich seal on the ocean's bosom set
To say that East and West are twain,
With different loss and gain:
The Lord hath sundered them; let them be sundered yet.

IV

Alas! what sounds are these that come
Sullenly over the Pacific seas,—
Sounds of ignoble battle, striking dumb
The season's half-awakened ecstasies?
Must I be humble, then,

Now when my heart hath need of pride?
Wild love falls on me from these sculptured men;
By loving much the land for which they died
I would be justified.
My spirit was away on pinions wide
To soothe in praise of her its passionate mood
And ease it of its ache of gratitude.
Too sorely heavy is the debt they lay
On me and the companions of my day.
I would remember now
My country's goodliness, make sweet her name.
Alas! what shade art thou
Of sorrow or of blame
Liftest the lyric leafage from her brow,
And pointest a slow finger at her shame?

V

Lies! lies! It cannot be! The wars we wage
Are noble, and our battles still are won
By justice for us, ere we lift the gage.
We have not sold our loftiest heritage.
The proud republic hath not stooped to cheat
And scramble in the market-place of war;
Her forehead weareth yet its solemn star.
Here is her witness: this, her perfect son,
This delicate and proud New England soul
Who leads despisèd men, with just-unshackled feet,
Up the large ways where death and glory meet,
To show all peoples that our shame is done,
That once more we are clean and spirit-whole.

VI

Crouched in the sea fog on the moaning sand
All night he lay, speaking some simple word
From hour to hour to the slow minds that heard,
Holding each poor life gently in his hand
And breathing on the base rejected clay
Till each dark face shone mystical and grand
Against the breaking day;
And lo, the shard the potter cast away
Was grown a fiery chalice crystal-fine
Fulfilled of the divine

Great wine of battle wrath by God's ring-finger stirred.
Then upward, where the shadowy bastion loomed
Huge on the mountain in the wet sea light,
Whence now, and now, infernal flowerage bloomed,
Bloomed, burst, and scattered down its deadly seed,—
They swept, and died like freemen on the height,
Like freemen, and like men of noble breed;
And when the battle fell away at night
By hasty and contemptuous hands were thrust
Obscurely in a common grave with him
The fair-haired keeper of their love and trust.
Now limb doth mingle with dissolvèd limb
In nature's busy old democracy
To flush the mountain laurel when she blows
Sweet by the southern sea,
And heart with crumbled heart climbs in the rose:—
The untaught hearts with the high heart that knew
This mountain fortress for no earthly hold
Of temporal quarrel, but the bastion old
Of spiritual wrong,
Built by an unjust nation sheer and strong,
Expugnable but by a nation's rue
And bowing down before that equal shrine
By all men held divine,
Whereof his band and he were the most holy sign.

VII

O bitter, bitter shade!
Wilt thou not put the scorn
And instant tragic question from thine eyes?
Do thy dark brows yet crave
That swift and angry stave—
Unmeet for this desirous morn—
That I have striven, striven to evade?
Gazing on him, must I not deem they err
Whose careless lips in street and shop aver
As common tidings, deeds to make his cheek
Flush from the bronze, and his dead throat to speak?
Surely some elder singer would arise,
Whose harp hath leave to threaten and to mourn
Above this people when they go astray.
Is Whitman, the strong spirit, overworn?
Has Whittier put his yearning wrath away?

I will not and I dare not yet believe!
Though furtively the sunlight seems to grieve,
And the spring-laden breeze
Out of the gladdening west is sinister
With sounds of nameless battle overseas;
Though when we turn and question in suspense
If these things be indeed after these ways,
And what things are to follow after these,
Our fluent men of place and consequence
Fumble and fill their mouths with hollow phrase,
Or for the end-all of deep arguments
Intone their dull commercial liturgies—
I dare not yet believe! My ears are shut!
I will not hear the thin satiric praise
And muffled laughter of our enemies,
Bidding us never sheathe our valiant sword
Till we have changed our birthright for a gourd
Of wild pulse stolen from a barbarian's hut;
Showing how wise it is to cast away
The symbols of our spiritual sway,
That so our hands with better ease
May wield the driver's whip and grasp the jailer's keys.

VIII

Was it for this our fathers kept the law?
This crown shall crown their struggle and their ruth?
Are we the eagle nation Milton saw
Mewing its mighty youth,
Soon to possess the mountain winds of truth,
And be a swift familiar of the sun
Where aye before God's face his trumpets run?
Or have we but the talons and the maw,
And for the abject likeness of our heart
Shall some less lordly bird be set apart?—
Some gross-billed wader where the swamps are fat?
Some gorger in the sun? Some prowler with the bat?

IX

Ah no!
We have not fallen so.
We are our fathers' sons: let those who lead us know!
'T was only yesterday sick Cuba's cry

Came up the tropic wind, "Now help us, for we die!"
Then Alabama heard,
And rising, pale, to Maine and Idaho
Shouted a burning word.
Proud state with proud impassioned state conferred,
And at the lifting of a hand sprang forth,
East, west, and south, and north,
Beautiful armies. Oh, by the sweet blood and young
Shed on the awful hill slope at San Juan,
By the unforgotten names of eager boys
Who might have tasted girls' love and been stung
With the old mystic joys
And starry griefs, now the spring nights come on,
But that the heart of youth is generous,—
We charge you, ye who lead us,
Breathe on their chivalry no hint of stain!
Turn not their new-world victories to gain!
One least leaf plucked for chaffer from the bays
Of their dear praise,
One jot of their pure conquest put to hire,
The implacable republic will require;
With clamor, in the glare and gaze of noon,
Or subtly, coming as a thief at night,
But surely, very surely, slow or soon
That insult deep we deeply will requite.
Tempt not our weakness, our cupidity!
For save we let the island men go free,
Those baffled and dislaureled ghosts
Will curse us from the lamentable coasts
Where walk the frustrate dead.
The cup of trembling shall be drainèd quite,
Eaten the sour bread of astonishment,
With ashes of the hearth shall be made white
Our hair, and wailing shall be in the tent;
Then on your guiltier head
Shall our intolerable self-disdain
Wreak suddenly its anger and its pain;
For manifest in that disastrous light
We shall discern the right
And do it, tardily.—O ye who lead,
Take heed!
Blindness we may forgive, but baseness we will smite.

FADED PICTURES

Only two patient eyes to stare
Out of the canvas. All the rest—
The warm green gown, the small hands pressed
Light in the lap, the braided hair

That must have made the sweet low brow
So earnest, centuries ago,
When some one saw it change and glow—
All faded! Just the eyes burn now.

I dare say people pass and pass
Before the blistered little frame,
And dingy work without a name
Stuck in behind its square of glass.

But I, well, I left Raphael
Just to come drink these eyes of hers,
To think away the stains and blurs
And make all new again and well.

Only, for tears my head will bow,
Because there on my heart's last wall,
Scarce one tint left to tell it all,
A picture keeps its eyes, somehow.

THE DEPARTURE

I

I sat beside the glassy evening sea,
One foot upon the thin horn of my lyre,
And all its strings of laughter and desire
Crushed in the rank wet grasses heedlessly;
Nor did my dull eyes care to question how
The boat close by had spread its saffron sails,
Nor what might mean the coffers and the bales,
And streaks of new wine on the gilded prow.
Neither was wonder in me when I saw
Fair women step therein, though they were fair
Even to adoration and to awe,
And in the gracious fillets of their hair

Were blossoms from a garden I had known,
Sweet mornings ere the apple buds were blown.

II

One gazed steadfast into the dying west
With lips apart to greet the evening star;
And one with eyes that caught the strife and jar
Of the sea's heart, followed the sunward breast
Of a lone gull; from a slow harp one drew
Blind music like a laugh or like a wail;
And in the uncertain shadow of the sail
One wove a crown of berries and of yew.
Yet even as I said with dull desire,
"All these were mine, and one was mine indeed,"
The smoky music burst into a fire,
And I was left alone in my great need,
One foot upon the thin horn of my lyre
And all its strings crushed in the dripping weed.

THE MENAGERIE

Thank God my brain is not inclined to cut
Such capers every day! I'm just about
Mellow, but then— There goes the tent-flap shut.
Rain 's in the wind. I thought so: every snout
Was twitching when the keeper turned me out.

That screaming parrot makes my blood run cold.
Gabriel's trump! the big bull elephant
Squeals "Rain!" to the parched herd. The monkeys scold,
And jabber that it's rain water they want.
(It makes me sick to see a monkey pant.)

I'll foot it home, to try and make believe
I'm sober. After this I stick to beer,
And drop the circus when the sane folks leave.
A man's a fool to look at things too near:
They look back, and begin to cut up queer.

Beasts do, at any rate; especially
Wild devils caged. They have the coolest way
Of being something else than what you see:

You pass a sleek young zebra nosing hay,
A nylghau looking bored and distingué,—

And think you 've seen a donkey and a bird.
Not on your life! Just glance back, if you dare.
The zebra chews, the nylghau has n't stirred;
But something's happened, Heaven knows what or where,
To freeze your scalp and pompadour your hair.

I'm not precisely an æolian lute
Hung in the wandering winds of sentiment,
But drown me if the ugliest, meanest brute
Grunting and fretting in that sultry tent
Did n't just floor me with embarrassment!

'T was like a thunder-clap from out the clear,—
One minute they were circus beasts, some grand,
Some ugly, some amusing, and some queer:
Rival attractions to the hobo band,
The flying jenny, and the peanut stand.

Next minute they were old hearth-mates of mine!
Lost people, eyeing me with such a stare!
Patient, satiric, devilish, divine;
A gaze of hopeless envy, squalid care,
Hatred, and thwarted love, and dim despair.

Within my blood my ancient kindred spoke,—
Grotesque and monstrous voices, heard afar
Down ocean caves when behemoth awoke,
Or through fern forests roared the plesiosaur
Locked with the giant-bat in ghastly war.

And suddenly, as in a flash of light,
I saw great Nature working out her plan;
Through all her shapes from mastodon to mite
Forever groping, testing, passing on
To find at last the shape and soul of Man.

Till in the fullness of accomplished time,
Comes brother Forepaugh, upon business bent,
Tracks her through frozen and through torrid clime,
And shows us, neatly labeled in a tent,
The stages of her huge experiment;

Blabbing aloud her shy and reticent hours;
Dragging to light her blinking, slothful moods;
Publishing fretful seasons when her powers
Worked wild and sullen in her solitudes,
Or when her mordant laughter shook the woods.

Here, round about me, were her vagrant births;
Sick dreams she had, fierce projects she essayed;
Her qualms, her fiery prides, her crazy mirths;
The troublings of her spirit as she strayed,
Cringed, gloated, mocked, was lordly, was afraid,

On that long road she went to seek mankind;
Here were the darkling coverts that she beat
To find the Hider she was sent to find;
Here the distracted footprints of her feet
Whereby her soul's Desire she came to greet.

But why should they, her botch-work, turn about
And stare disdain at me, her finished job?
Why was the place one vast suspended shout
Of laughter? Why did all the daylight throb
With soundless guffaw and dumb-stricken sob?

Helpless I stood among those awful cages;
The beasts were walking loose, and I was bagged!
I, I, last product of the toiling ages,
Goal of heroic feet that never lagged,—
A little man in trousers, slightly jagged.

Deliver me from such another jury!
The Judgment-day will be a picnic to 't.
Their satire was more dreadful than their fury,
And worst of all was just a kind of brute
Disgust, and giving up, and sinking mute.

Survival of the fittest, adaptation,
And all their other evolution terms,
Seem to omit one small consideration,
To wit, that tumblebugs and angleworms
Have souls: there 's soul in everything that squirms.

And souls are restless, plagued, impatient things,
All dream and unaccountable desire;

Crawling, but pestered with the thought of wings;
Spreading through every inch of earth's old mire
Mystical hanker after something higher.

Wishes *are* horses, as I understand.
I guess a wistful polyp that has strokes
Of feeling faint to gallivant on land
Will come to be a scandal to his folks;
Legs he will sprout, in spite of threats and jokes.

And at the core of every life that crawls
Or runs or flies or swims or vegetates—
Churning the mammoth's heart-blood, in the galls
Of shark and tiger planting gorgeous hates,
Lighting the love of eagles for their mates;

Yes, in the dim brain of the jellied fish
That is and is not living—moved and stirred
From the beginning a mysterious wish,
A vision, a command, a fatal Word:
The name of Man was uttered, and they heard.

Upward along the æons of old war
They sought him: wing and shank-bone, claw and bill
Were fashioned and rejected; wide and far
They roamed the twilight jungles of their will;
But still they sought him, and desired him still.

Man they desired, but mind you, Perfect Man,
The radiant and the loving, yet to be!
I hardly wonder, when they came to scan
The upshot of their strenuosity,
They gazed with mixed emotions upon *me*.

Well, my advice to you is, Face the creatures,
Or spot them sideways with your weather eye,
Just to keep tab on their expansive features;
It is n't pleasant when you 're stepping high
To catch a giraffe smiling on the sly.

If nature made you graceful, don't get gay
Back-to before the hippopotamus;
If meek and godly, find some place to play

Besides right where three mad hyenas fuss:
You may hear language that we won't discuss.

If you 're a sweet thing in a flower-bed hat,
Or her best fellow with your tie tucked in,
Don't squander love's bright springtime girding at
An old chimpanzee with an Irish chin:
There may be hidden meaning in his grin.

PANDORA SONG

I stood within the heart of God;
It seemed a place that I had known:
(I was blood-sister to the clod,
Blood-brother to the stone.)

I found my love and labor there,
My house, my raiment, meat and wine,
My ancient rage, my old despair,—
Yea, all things that were mine.

I saw the spring and summer pass,
The trees grow bare, and winter come;
All was the same as once it was
Upon my hills at home.

Then suddenly in my own heart
I felt God walk and gaze about;
He spoke; his words seemed held apart
With gladness and with doubt.

"Here is my meat and wine," He said,
"My love, my toil, my ancient care;
Here is my cloak, my book, my bed,
And here my old despair.

"Here are my seasons: winter, spring,
Summer the same, and autumn spills
The fruits I look for; everything
As on my heavenly hills."

Edwin Arlington Robinson

(1869–1935)

Edwin Arlington Robinson, certainly the greatest American poet of his generation, was born in the village of Head Tide, Maine, and grew up in Gardiner (Tilbury Town), Maine. He entered Harvard in 1891 but left two years later. In 1899 he moved to New York City where he lived a grim existence. Starving and destitute, he took a job in the subways and remained in the dark until President Theodore Roosevelt read some of his poetry and gave him a clerical position in the Custom House. During the latter part of his life Robinson spent part of each year at the McDowell Colony, a writer's and artist's haven in Peterborough, New Hampshire. He was awarded the Pulitzer Prize for poetry in 1922, 1925, and 1928.

RICHARD CORY

Whenever Richard Cory went down town,
We people on the pavement looked at him:
He was a gentleman from sole to crown,
Clean favored, and imperially slim.

And he was always quietly arrayed,
And he was always human when he talked;
But still he fluttered pulses when he said,
"Good-morning," and he glittered when he walked.

And he was rich—yes, richer than a king—
And admirably schooled in every grace:
In fine, we thought that he was everything
To make us wish that we were in his place.

So on we worked, and waited for the light,
And went without the meat, and cursed the bread;
And Richard Cory, one calm summer night,
Went home and put a bullet through his head.

REUBEN BRIGHT

Because he was a butcher and thereby
Did earn an honest living (and did right),
I would not have you think that Reuben Bright
Was any more a brute than you or I;
For when they told him that his wife must die,
He stared at them, and shook with grief and fright,
And cried like a great baby half that night,
And made the women cry to see him cry.

And after she was dead, and he had paid
The singers and the sexton and the rest,
He packed a lot of things that she had made
Most mournfully away in an old chest
Of hers, and put some chopped-up cedar boughs
In with them, and tore down the slaughter house.

AN OLD STORY

Strange that I did not know him then,
   That friend of mine!
I did not even show him then
   One friendly sign;

But cursed him for the ways he had
   To make me see
My envy of the praise he had
   For praising me.

I would have rid the earth of him
   Once, in my pride. . . .
I never knew the worth of him
   Until he died.

JOHN EVERELDOWN

"Where are you going to-night, to-night,—
    Where are you going, John Evereldown?
There's never the sign of a star in sight,
    Nor a lamp that's nearer than Tilbury Town.
Why do you stare as a dead man might?
Where are you pointing away from the light?
And where are you going to-night, to-night,—
    Where are you going, John Evereldown?"

"Right through the forest, where none can see,
    There's where I'm going, to Tilbury Town.
The men are asleep,—or awake, may be,—
    But the women are calling John Evereldown.
Ever and ever they call for me,
And while they call can a man be free?
So right through the forest, where none can see,
    There's where I'm going, to Tilbury Town."

"But why are you going so late, so late,—
    Why are you going, John Evereldown?
Though the road be smooth and the way be straight,
    There are two long leagues to Tilbury Town.
Come in by the fire, old man, and wait!
Why do you chatter out there by the gate?
And why are you going so late, so late,—
    Why are you going, John Evereldown?"

"I follow the women wherever they call,—
    That's why I'm going to Tilbury Town.
God knows if I pray to be done with it all,
    But God is no friend to John Evereldown.
So the clouds may come and the rain may fall,
The shadows may creep and the dead men crawl,—
But I follow the women wherever they call,
    And that's why I'm going to Tilbury Town."

THE TAVERN

Whenever I go by there nowadays
And look at the rank weeds and the strange grass,
The torn blue curtains and the broken glass,

· 548 ·

I seem to be afraid of the old place;
And something stiffens up and down my face,
For all the world as if I saw the ghost
Of old Ham Amory, the murdered host,
With his dead eyes turned on me all aglaze.

The Tavern has a story, but no man
Can tell us what it is. We only know
That once long after midnight, years ago,
A stranger galloped up from Tilbury Town,
Who brushed, and scared, and all but overran
That skirt-crazed reprobate, John Evereldown.

THE FIELD OF GLORY

War shook the land where Levi dwelt,
And fired the dismal wrath he felt,
That such a doom was ever wrought
As his, to toil while others fought;
To toil, to dream—and still to dream,
With one day barren as another;
To consummate, as it would seem,
The dry despair of his old mother.

Far off one afternoon began
The sound of man destroying man;
And Levi, sick with nameless rage,
Condemned again his heritage,
And sighed for scars that might have come,
And would, if once he could have sundered
Those harsh, inhering claims of home
That held him while he cursed and wondered.

Another day, and then there came,
Rough, bloody, ribald, hungry, lame,
But yet themselves, to Levi's door,
Two remnants of the day before.
They laughed at him and what he sought;
They jeered him, and his painful acre;
But Levi knew that they had fought,
And left their manners to their Maker.

That night, for the grim widow's ears,
With hopes that hid themselves in fears,
He told of arms, and fiery deeds,
Whereat one leaps the while he reads,
And said he'd be no more a clown,
While others drew the breath of battle.—
The mother looked him up and down,
And laughed—a scant laugh with a rattle.

She told him what she found to tell,
And Levi listened, and heard well
Some admonitions of a voice
That left him no cause to rejoice.—
He sought a friend, and found the stars,
And prayed aloud that they should aid him;
But they said not a word of wars,
Or of a reason why God made him.

And who's of this or that estate
We do not wholly calculate,
When baffling shades that shift and cling
Are not without their glimmering;
When even Levi, tired of faith,
Beloved of none, forgot by many,
Dismissed as an inferior wraith,
Reborn may be as great as any.

BALLADE BY THE FIRE

Slowly I smoke and hug my knee,
    The while a witless masquerade
Of things that only children see
    Floats in a mist of light and shade:
    They pass, a flimsy cavalcade,
And with a weak, remindful glow,
    The falling embers break and fade,
As one by one the phantoms go.

Then, with a melancholy glee
    To think where once my fancy strayed,
I muse on what the years may be
    Whose coming tales are all unsaid,
    Till tongs and shovel, snugly laid

Within their shadowed niches, grow
  By grim degrees to pick and spade,
As one by one the phantoms go.

But then, what though the mystic Three
  Around me ply their merry trade?—
And Charon soon may carry me
  Across the gloomy Stygian glade?—
  Be up, my soul; nor be afraid
Of what some unborn year may show;
  But mind your human debts are paid,
As one by one the phantoms go.

Envoy

Life is the game that must be played:
  This truth at least, good friends, we know;
So live and laugh, nor be dismayed
  As one by one the phantoms go.

THE CORRIDOR

It may have been the pride in me for aught
I know, or just a patronizing whim;
But call it freak or fancy, or what not,
I cannot hide that hungry face of him.

I keep a scant half-dozen words he said,
And every now and then I lose his name;
He may be living or he may be dead,
But I must have him with me all the same.

I knew it, and I knew it all along,—
And felt it once or twice, or thought I did;
But only as a glad man feels a song
That sounds around a stranger's coffin lid.

I knew it, and he knew it, I believe,
But silence held us alien to the end;
And I have now no magic to retrieve
That year, to stop that hunger for a friend.

THE CLERKS

I did not think that I should find them there
When I came back again; but there they stood,
As in the days they dreamed of when young blood
Was in their cheeks and women called them fair.
Be sure, they met me with an ancient air,—
And yes, there was a shop-worn brotherhood
About them; but the men were just as good,
And just as human as they ever were.

And you that ache so much to be sublime,
And you that feed yourselves with your descent,
What comes of all your visions and your fears?
Poets and kings are but the clerks of Time,
Tiering the same dull webs of discontent,
Clipping the same sad alnage of the years.

CLIFF KLINGENHAGEN

Cliff Klingenhagen had me in to dine
With him one day; and after soup and meat,
And all the other things there were to eat,
Cliff took two glasses and filled one with wine
And one with wormwood. Then, without a sign
For me to choose at all, he took the draught
Of bitterness himself, and lightly quaffed
It off, and said the other one was mine.

And when I asked him what the deuce he meant
By doing that, he only looked at me
And smiled, and said it was a way of his.
And though I know the fellow, I have spent
Long time a-wondering when I shall be
As happy as Cliff Klingenhagen is.

CHARLES CARVILLE'S EYES

A melancholy face Charles Carville had,
But not so melancholy as it seemed,
When once you knew him, for his mouth redeemed
His insufficient eyes, forever sad:

In them there was no life-glimpse, good or bad,
Nor joy nor passion in them ever gleamed;
His mouth was all of him that ever beamed,
His eyes were sorry, but his mouth was glad.

He never was a fellow that said much,
And half of what he did say was not heard
By many of us: we were out of touch
With all his whims and all his theories
Till he was dead, so those blank eyes of his
Might speak them. Then we heard them, every word.

THE PITY OF THE LEAVES

Vengeful across the cold November moors,
Loud with ancestral shame there came the bleak
Sad wind that shrieked, and answered with a shriek,
Reverberant through lonely corridors.

The old man heard it; and he heard, perforce,
Words out of lips that were no more to speak—
Words of the past that shook the old man's cheek
Like dead, remembered footsteps on old floors.

And then there were the leaves that plagued him so!
The brown, thin leaves that on the stones outside
Skipped with a freezing whisper. Now and then
They stopped, and stayed there—just to let him know
How dead they were; but if the old man cried,
They fluttered off like withered souls of men.

THE STORY OF THE ASHES
AND THE FLAME

No matter why, nor whence, nor when she came,
There was her place. No matter what men said,
No matter what she was; living or dead,
Faithful or not, he loved her all the same.
The story was as old as human shame,
But ever since that lonely night she fled,
With books to blind him, he had only read
The story of the ashes and the flame.

There she was always coming pretty soon
To fool him back, with penitent scared eyes
That had in them the laughter of the moon
For baffled lovers, and to make him think—
Before she gave him time enough to wink—
Her kisses were the keys to Paradise.

BOSTON

My northern pines are good enough for me,
But there's a town my memory uprears—
A town that always like a friend appears,
And always in the sunrise by the sea.
And over it, somehow, there seems to be
A downward flash of something new and fierce,
That ever strives to clear, but never clears
The dimness of a charmed antiquity.

HER EYES

Up from the street and the crowds that went,
   Morning and midnight, to and fro,
Still was the room where his days he spent,
   And the stars were bleak, and the nights were slow.

Year after year, with his dream shut fast,
   He suffered and strove till his eyes were dim,
For the love that his brushes had earned at last,
   And the whole world rang with the praise of him.

But he cloaked his triumph, and searched, instead,
   Till his cheeks were sere and his hairs were gray.
"There are women enough, God knows," he said . . .
   "There are stars enough—when the sun's away."

Then he went back to the same still room
   That had held his dream in the long ago,
When he buried his days in a nameless tomb,
   And the stars were bleak, and the nights were slow.

And a passionate humor seized him there—
   Seized him and held him until there grew

Like life on his canvas, glowing and fair,
  A perilous face—and an angel's too.

Angel and maiden, and all in one,—
  All but the eyes. They were there, but yet
They seemed somehow like a soul half done.
  What was the matter? Did God forget? . . .

But he wrought them at last with a skill so sure
  That her eyes were the eyes of a deathless woman,—
With a gleam of heaven to make them pure,
  And a glimmer of hell to make them human.

God never forgets.—And he worships her
  There in that same still room of his,
For his wife, and his constant arbiter
  Of the world that was and the world that is.

And he wonders yet what her love could be
  To punish him after that strife so grim;
But the longer he lives with her eyes to see,
  The plainer it all comes back to him.

Stephen Crane

(1871–1900)

Stephen Crane was born in Newark, New Jersey. He studied at Lafayette College and Syracuse University, became a journalist at the age of sixteen and was a war correspondent in Cuba and Greece. A prolific writer, he published more than ten books including his best-known work, *The Red Badge of Courage.* His two volumes of poetry feature his unique style of free verse. Crane had an exceptional, though short-lived career; he died of tuberculosis in a Black Forest spa before his thirtieth birthday.

"A MAN SAID TO THE UNIVERSE"

A man said to the universe,
"Sir, I exist!"
"However," replied the universe,
"The fact has not created in me
A sense of obligation."

"I SAW A MAN"

I saw a man pursuing the horizon;
Round and round they sped.
I was disturbed at this;
I accosted the man.
"It is futile," I said,
"You can never"—

"You lie," he cried,
And ran on.

"IN THE DESERT"

In the desert
I saw a creature, naked, bestial,
Who, squatting upon the ground,
Held his heart in his hands,
And ate of it.
I said, "Is it good, friend?"
"It is bitter—bitter," he answered;
"But I like it
Because it is bitter,
And because it is my heart."

WAR IS KIND

Do not weep, maiden, for war is kind.
Because your lover threw wild hands toward the sky
And the affrighted steed ran on alone,
Do not weep.
War is kind.

    Hoarse, booming drums of the regiment,
    Little souls who thirst for fight,
    These men were born to drill and die.
    The unexplained glory flies above them,
    Great is the battle-god, great, and his kingdom—
    A field where a thousand corpses lie.

Do not weep, babe, for war is kind.
Because your father tumbled in the yellow trenches,
Raged at his breast, gulped and died,
Do not weep.
War is kind.

    Swift blazing flag of the regiment,
    Eagle with crest of red and gold,
    These men were born to drill and die.
    Point for them the virtue of slaughter,
    Make plain to them the excellence of killing
    And a field where a thousand corpses lie.

Mother whose heart hung humble as a button
On the bright splendid shroud of your son,

Do not weep.
War is kind.

"IN HEAVEN"

In Heaven,
Some little blades of grass
Stood before God.
"What did you do?"
Then all save one of the little blades
Began eagerly to relate
The merits of their lives.
This one stayed a small way behind,
Ashamed.
Presently, God said,
"And what did you do?"

The little blade answered, "Oh, my Lord,
Memory is bitter to me,
For, if I did good deeds,
I know not of them."
Then God, in all his splendor,
Arose from this throne.
"Oh, best little blade of grass!" he said.

"THE WAYFARER"

The wayfarer,
Perceiving the pathway to truth,
Was struck with astonishment.
It was thickly grown with weeds.
"Ha," he said,
"I see that no one has passed here
In a long time."
Later he saw that each weed
Was a singular knife.
"Well," he mumbled at last,
"Doubtless there are other roads."

"WHEN THE PROPHET"

When the prophet, a complacent fat man,
Arrived at the mountain-top,
He cried: "Woe to my knowledge!
I intended to see good white lands
And bad black lands,
But the scene is grey."

"IN A LONELY PLACE"

In a lonely place,
I encountered a sage
Who sat, all still,
Regarding a newspaper.
He accosted me:
"Sir, what is this?"
Then I saw that I was greater,
Ay, greater than this sage.
I answered him at once,
"Old, old man, it is the wisdom of the age."
The sage looked upon me with admiration.

"ONCE THERE CAME A MAN"

Once there came a man
Who said,
"Range me all men of the world in rows."
And instantly
There was terrific clamour among the people
Against being ranged in rows.
There was a loud quarrel, world-wide.
It endured for ages;
And blood was shed
By those who would not stand in rows,
And by those who pined to stand in rows.
Eventually, the man went to death, weeping.
And those who stayed in bloody scuffle
Knew not the great simplicity.

Paul Laurence Dunbar

(1872–1906)

Paul Laurence Dunbar, the son of former slaves, was born in Dayton, Ohio. He lived in poverty and was working as an elevator boy when he was "discovered" as a poet. Later he took a staff position with the Library of Congress. Eventually he returned to Dayton where he died of tuberculosis. Ten years before the poet's death William Dean Howells said of Dunbar, "I should feel that he had made the strongest claim for the Negro in English literature."

A BANJO SONG

Oh, dere's lots o' keer an' trouble
   In dis world to swaller down;
An' ol' Sorrer's purty lively
   In her way o' gittin' roun'.
Yet dere 's times when I furgit 'em,—
   Aches an' pains an' troubles all,—
An' it 's when I tek at ebenin'
   My ol' banjo f'om de wall.

'Bout de time dat night is fallin'
   An' my daily wu'k is done,
An' above de shady hilltops
   I kin see de settin' sun;
When de quiet, restful shadders
   Is beginnin' jes' to fall,—
Den I take de little banjo
   F'om its place upon de wall.

Den my fam'ly gadders roun' me
  In de fadin' o' de light,
Ez I strike de strings to try 'em
  Ef dey all is tuned er-right.
An' it seems we 're so nigh heaben
  We kin hyeah de angels sing
When de music o' dat banjo
  Sets my cabin all er-ring.

An' my wife an' all de othahs,—
  Male an' female, small an' big,—
Even up to gray-haired granny,
  Seem jes' boun' to do a jig;
'Twell I change de style o' music,
  Change de movement an' de time,
An' de ringin' little banjo
  Plays an ol' hea't-feelin' hime.

An' somehow my th'oat gits choky,
  An' a lump keeps tryin' to rise
Lak it wan'ed to ketch de water
  Dat was flowin' to my eyes;
An' I feel dat I could sorter
  Knock de socks clean off o' sin
Ez I hyeah my po' ol' granny
  Wif huh tremblin' voice jine in.

Den we all th'ow in our voices
  Fu' to he'p de chune out too,
Lak a big camp-meetin' choiry
  Tryin' to sing a mou'nah th'oo.
An' our th'oahts let out de music,
  Sweet an' solemn, loud an' free,
'Twell de raftahs o' my cabin
  Echo wif de melody.

Oh, de music o'de banjo,
  Quick an' deb'lish, solemn, slow,
Is de greates' joy an' solace
  Dat a weary slave kin know!
So jes' let me hyeah it ringin',
  Dough de chune be po' an' rough,
It's a pleasure; an' de pleasures
  O' dis life is few enough.

Now, de blessed little angels
　　Up in heaben, we are told,
Don't do nothin' all dere lifetime
　　'Ceptin' play on ha'ps o' gold.
Now I think heaben 'd be mo' homelike
　　Ef we 'd hyeah some music fall
F'om a real ol'-fashioned banjo,
　　Like dat one upon de wall.

DAWN

An angel, robed in spotless white,
Bent down and kissed the sleeping Night.
Night woke to blush; the sprite was gone.
Men saw the blush and called it Dawn.

THE LAWYERS' WAYS

I've been list'nin' to them lawyers
　　In the court house up the street,
An' I 've come to the conclusion
　　That I'm most completely beat.
Fust one feller riz to argy,
　　An' he boldly waded in
As he dressed the tremblin' pris'ner
　　In a coat o' deep-dyed sin.

Why, he painted him all over
　　In a hue o' blackest crime,
An' he smeared his reputation
　　With the thickest kind o' grime,
Tell I found myself a-wond'rin',
　　In a misty way and dim,
How the Lord had come to fashion
　　Sich an awful man as him.

Then the other lawyer started,
　　An', with brimmin', tearful eyes,
Said his client was a martyr
　　That was brought to sacrifice.
An' he give to that same pris'ner
　　Every blessed human grace,

Tell I saw the light o' virtue
  Fairly shinin' from his face.

Then I own 'at I was puzzled
  How sich things could rightly be;
An' this aggervatin' question
  Seems to keep a-puzzlin' me.
So, will some one please inform me,
  An' this mystery unroll—
How an angel an' a devil
  Can persess the self-same soul?

AFTER THE QUARREL

So we, who 've supped the self-same cup,
  To-night must lay our friendship by;
Your wrath has burned your judgment up,
  Hot breath has blown the ashes high.
You say that you are wronged—ah, well,
  I count that friendship poor, at best
A bauble, a mere bagatelle,
  That cannot stand so slight a test.

I fain would still have been your friend,
  And talked and laughed and loved with you;
But since it must, why, let it end;
  The false but dies, 't is not the true.
So we are favored, you and I,
  Who only want the living truth.
It was not good to nurse the lie;
  'Tis well it died in harmless youth.

I go from you to-night to sleep.
  Why, what's the odds? why should I grieve?
I have no fund of tears to weep
  For happenings that undeceive.
The days shall come, the days shall go
  Just as they came and went before.
The sun shall shine, the streams shall flow
  Though you and I are friends no more.

And in the volume of my years,
  Where all my thoughts and acts shall be,

The page whereon your name appears
   Shall be forever sealed to me.
Not that I hate you over-much,
   'T is less of hate than loved defied;
Howe'er, our hands no more shall touch,
   We'll go our ways, the world is wide.

THE DILETTANTE: A MODERN TYPE

He scribbles some in prose and verse,
   And now and then he prints it;
He paints a little,—gathers some
   Of Nature's gold and mints it.

He plays a little, sings a song,
   Acts tragic rôles, or funny;
He does, because his love is strong,
   But not, oh, not for money!

He studies almost everything
   From social art to science;
A thirsty mind, a flowing spring,
   Demand and swift compliance.

He looms above the sordid crowd—
   At least through friendly lenses;
While his mamma looks pleased and proud,
   And kindly pays expenses.

CONSCIENCE AND REMORSE

"Good-bye," I said to my conscience—
   "Good-bye for aye and aye,"
And I put her hands off harshly,
   And turned my face away;
And conscience smitten sorely
   Returned not from that day.

But a time came when my spirit
   Grew weary of its pace;
And I cried: "Come back, my conscience;
   I long to see thy face."

But conscience cried: "I cannot;
Remorse sits in my place."

THE DESERTED PLANTATION

Oh, de grubbin'-hoe 's a-rustin' in de co'nah,
    An' de plow's a-tumblin' down in de fiel',
While de whippo'will 's a-wailin' lak a mou'nah
    When his stubbo'n hea't is tryin' ha'd to yiel'.

In de furrers whah de co'n was allus wavin',
    Now de weeds is growin' green an' rank an' tall;
An' de swallers roun' de whole place is a-bravin'
    Lak dey thought deir folks had allus owned it all.

An' de big house stan's all quiet lak an' solemn,
    Not a blessed soul in pa'lor, po'ch, er lawn;
Not a guest, ner not a ca'iage lef' to haul 'em,
    Fu' de ones dat tu'ned de latch-string out air gone.

An' de banjo's voice is silent in de qua'ters,
    D' ain't a hymn ner co'n-song ringin' in de air;
But de murmur of a branch's passin' waters
    Is de only soun' dat breks de stillness dere.

Whah 's de da'kies, dem dat used to be a-dancin'
    Evry night befo' de ole cabin do'?
Whah 's de chillun, dem dat used to be a-prancin'
    Er a-rollin' in de san' er on de flo'?

Whah 's ole Uncle Mordecai an' Uncle Aaron?
    Whah 's Aunt Doshy, Sam, an' Kit, an' all de res'?
Whah 's ole Tom de da'ky fiddlah, how's he farin'?
    Whah 's de gals dat used to sing an' dance de bes'?

Gone! not one o' dem is lef' to tell de story;
    Dey have lef' de deah ole place to fall away.
Could n't one o' dem dat seed it in its glory
    Stay to watch it in de hour of decay?

Dey have lef' de ole plantation to de swallers,
    But it hol's in me a lover till de las';

Fu' I fin' hyeah in de memory dat follers
   All dat loved me an' dat I loved in de pas'.

So I'll stay an' watch de deah ole place an' tend it
   Ez I used to in de happy days gone by.
'Twell de othah Mastah thinks it 's time to end it,
   An' calls me to my qua'ters in de sky.

WHEN DE CO'N PONE 'S HOT

Dey is times in life when Nature
   Seems to slip a cog an' go,
Jes' a-rattlin' down creation,
   Lak an ocean's overflow;
When de worl' jes' stahts a-spinnin'
   Lak a picaninny's top,
An' yo' cup o' joy is brimmin'
   'Twell it seems about to slop,
An' you feel jes' lak a racah,
   Dat is trainin' fu' to trot—
When yo' mammy says de blessin'
   An' de co'n pone 's hot.

When you set down at de table,
   Kin' o' weary lak an' sad,
An' you 'se jes' a little tiahed
   An' purhaps a little mad;
How yo' gloom tu'ns into gladness,
   How yo' joy drives out de doubt
When de oven do' is opened,
   An' de smell comes po'in' out;
Why, de 'lectric light o' Heaven
   Seems to settle on de spot,
When yo' mammy says de blessin'
   An' de co'n pone 's hot.

When de cabbage pot is steamin'
   An' de bacon good an' fat,
When de chittlins is a-sputter'n'
   So 's to show you whah dey 's at;
Tek away yo' sody biscuit,
   Tek away yo' cake an' pie,

Fu' de glory time is comin',
    An' it 's 'proachin' mighty nigh,
An' you want to jump an' hollah,
    Dough you know you 'd bettah not,
When yo' mammy says de blessin',
    An' de co'n pone 's hot.

I have hyeahd o' lots o' sermons,
    An' I 've hyeahd o' lots o' prayers,
An' I 've listened to some singin'
    Dat has tuck me up de stairs
Of de Glory-Lan' an' set me
    Jes' below de Mahstah's th'one,
An' have lef' my hea't a-singin'
    In a happy aftah tone;
But dem wu'ds so sweetly murmured
    Seem to tech de softes' spot,
When my mammy says de blessin',
    An' de co'n pone 's hot.

COMPENSATION

Because I had loved so deeply,
    Because I had loved so long,
God in His great compassion
    Gave me the gift of song.

Because I have loved so vainly,
    And sung with such faltering breath,
The Master, in infinite mercy,
    Offers the boon of Death.

THE MASTER-PLAYER

An old, worn harp that had been played
Till all its strings were loose and frayed,
Joy, Hate, and Fear, each one essayed,
To play. But each in turn had found
No sweet responsiveness of sound.

Then Love the Master-Player came
With heaving breast and eyes aflame;

The Harp he took all undismayed,
Smote on its strings, still strange to song,
And brought forth music sweet and strong.

LIFE

A crust of bread and a corner to sleep in,
A minute to smile and an hour to weep in,
A pint of joy to a peck of trouble,
And never a laugh but the moans come double;
       And that is life!

A crust and a corner that love makes precious,
With the smile to warm and the tears to refresh us;
And joy seems sweeter when cares come after,
And a moan is the finest of foils for laughter;
       And that is life!

WHITTIER

Not o'er thy dust let there be spent
The gush of maudlin sentiment;
Such drift as that is not for thee,
Whose life and deeds and songs agree,
Sublime in their simplicity.

Nor shall the sorrowing tear be shed.
O singer sweet, thou art not dead!
In spite of time's malignant chill,
With living fire thy songs shall thrill,
And men shall say, "He liveth still!"

Great poets never die, for Earth
Doth count their lives of too great worth
To loose them from her treasured store;
So shalt thou live for evermore—
Though far thy form from mortal ken—
Deep in the hearts and minds of men.

THE OLD APPLE-TREE

There's a memory keeps a-runnin'
  Through my weary head to-night,
An' I see a picture dancin'
  In the fire-flames' ruddy light;
'T is the picture of an orchard
  Wrapped in autumn's purple haze,
With the tender light about it
  That I loved in other days.
An' a-standin' in a corner
  Once again I seem to see
The verdant leaves an' branches
  Of an old apple-tree.

You perhaps would call it ugly,
  An' I don't know but it 's so,
When you look the tree all over
  Unadorned by memory's glow;
For its boughs are gnarled an' crooked,
  An' its leaves are gettin' thin,
An' the apples of its bearin'
  Would n't fill so large a bin
As they used to. But I tell you,
  When it comes to pleasin' me,
It 's the dearest in the orchard,—
  Is that old apple-tree.

I would hide within its shelter,
  Settlin' in some cosy nook,
Where no calls nor threats could stir me
  From the pages o' my book.
Oh, that quiet, sweet seclusion
  In its fulness passeth words!
It was deeper than the deepest
  That my sanctum now affords.
Why, the jaybirds an' the robins,
  They was hand in glove with me,
As they winked at me an' warbled
  In that old apple-tree.

It was on its sturdy branches
  That in summers long ago
I would tie my swing an' dangle

In contentment to an' fro,
Idly dreamin' childish fancies,
   Buildin' castles in the air,
Makin' o' myself a hero
   Of romances rich an' rare.
I kin shet my eyes an' see it
   Jest as plain as plain kin be,
That same old swing a-danglin'
   To the old apple-tree.

There's a rustic seat beneath it
   That I never kin forget.
It's the place where me an' Hallie—
   Little sweetheart—used to set,
When we'd wander to the orchard
   So 's no listenin' ones could hear
As I whispered sugared nonsense
   Into her little willin' ear.
Now my gray old wife is Hallie,
   An' I'm grayer still than she,
But I'll not forget our courtin'
   'Neath the old apple-tree.

Life for us ain't all been summer,
   But I guess we've had our share
Of its flittin' joys an' pleasures,
   An' a sprinklin' of its care.
Oft the skies have smiled upon us;
   Then again we 've seen 'em frown,
Though our load was ne'er so heavy
   That we longed to lay it down.
But when death does come a-callin',
   This my last request shall be,—
That they'll bury me an' Hallie
   'Neath the old apple-tree.

SIGNS OF THE TIMES

Air a-gittin' cool an' coolah,
   Frost a-comin' in de night,
Hicka' nuts an' wa'nuts fallin',
   Possum keepin' out o' sight.
Tu'key struttin' in de ba'nya'd,

Nary step so proud ez his;
Keep on struttin', Mistah Tu'key,
    Yo' do' know whut time it is.

Cidah press commence a-squeakin'
    Eatin' apples sto'ed away,
Chillun swa'min' 'roun' lak ho'nets,
    Huntin' aigs ermung de hay.
Mistah Tu'key keep on gobblin'
    At de geese a-flyin' souf,
Oomph! dat bird do' know whut's comin';
    Ef he did he 'd shet his mouf.

Pumpkin gittin' good an' yallah
    Mek me open up my eyes;
Seems lak it 's a-lookin' at me
    Jes' a-la-in' dah sayin' "Pies."
Tu'key gobbler 'gwine 'roun' blowin',
    Gwine 'roun' gibbin' sass an' slack;
Keep on talkin', Mistah Tu'key,
    You ain't seed no almanac.

Fa'mer walkin' th'oo de ba'nya'd
    Seein' how things is comin' on,
Sees ef all de fowls is fatt'nin'—
    Good times comin' sho 's you bo'n.
Hyeahs dat tu'key gobbler braggin',
    Den his face break in a smile—
Nebbah min', you sassy rascal,
    He's gwine nab you atter while.

Choppin' suet in de kitchen,
    Stonin' raisins in de hall,
Beef a-cookin' fu' de mince meat,
    Spices groun'—I smell 'em all.
Look hyeah, Tu'key, stop dat gobblin',
    You ain' luned de sense ob feah,
You ol' fool, yo' naik 's in dangah,
    Do' you know Thanksgibbin 's hyeah?

THE OL' TUNES

You kin talk about yer anthems
   An' yer arias an' sich,
An' yer modern choir-singin'
   That you think so awful rich;
But you orter heerd us youngsters
   In the times now far away,
A-singin' o' the ol' tunes
   In the ol'-fashioned way.

There was some of us sung treble
   An' a few of us growled bass,
An' the tide o' song flowed smoothly
   With its 'comp'niment o' grace;
There was spirit in that music,
   An' a kind o' solemn sway,
A-singin' o' the ol' tunes
   In the ol'-fashioned way.

I remember oft o' standin'
   In my homespun pantaloons—
On my face the bronze an' freckles
   O' the suns o' youthful Junes—
Thinkin' that no mortal minstrel
   Ever chanted sich a lay
As the ol' tunes we was singin'
   In the ol'-fashioned way.

The boys 'ud always lead us,
   An' the girls 'ud all chime in,
Till the sweetness o' the singin'
   Robbed the list'nin' soul o' sin;
An' I used to tell the parson
   'T was as good to sing as pray,
When the people sung the ol' tunes
   In the ol'-fashioned way.

How I long ag'in to hear 'em
   Pourin' forth from soul to soul,
With the treble high an' meller,
   An' the bass's mighty roll;
But the times is very diff'rent,
   An' the music heerd to-day

Ain't the singin' o' the ol' tunes
   In the ol'-fashioned way.

Little screechin' by a woman,
   Little squawkin' by a man,
Then the organ's twiddle-twaddle,
   Jest the empty space to span,—
An' ef you should even think it,
   'T is n't proper fur to say
That you want to hear the ol' tunes
   In the ol'-fashioned way.

But I think that some bright mornin',
   When the toils of life air o'er,
An' the sun o' heaven arisin'
   Glads with light the happy shore,
I shall hear the angel chorus,
   In the realms of endless day,
A-singin' o' the ol' tunes
   In the ol'-fashioned way.

SHIPS THAT PASS IN THE NIGHT

Out in the sky the great dark clouds are massing;
   I look far out into the pregnant night,
Where I can hear a solemn booming gun
   And catch the gleaming of a random light,
That tells me that the ship I seek is passing, passing.

My tearful eyes my soul's deep hurt are glassing;
   For I would hail and check that ship of ships.

I stretch my hands imploring, cry aloud,
   My voice falls dead a foot from mine own lips,
And but its ghost doth reach that vessel, passing, passing.

O Earth, O Sky, O Ocean, both surpassing,
   O heart of mine, O soul that dreads the dark!
Is there no hope for me? Is there no way
   That I may sight and check that speeding bark
Which out of sight and sound is passing, passing?

Amy Lowell

(1874–1925)

Amy Lowell, one of the chief poets in the Imagist movement, was born in Brookline, Massachusetts, into a distinguished New England family. James Russell Lowell was a cousin of her grandfather. Her brother served as president of Harvard University. Lowell led an extremely active literary life and produced more than a half-dozen books, including poetry collections and literary criticism. She died of a stroke in 1925 and was awarded a Pulitzer Prize for poetry the following year.

NOSTALGIA

"Through pleasures and palaces"—
Through hotels, and Pullman cars, and steamships . . .

Pink and white camellias
    floating in a crystal bowl,
The sharp smell of firewood,
The scrape and rustle of a dog stretching himself
    on a hardwood floor,
And your voice, reading—reading—
    to the slow ticking of an old brass clock . . .

"Tickets, please!"
And I watch the man in front of me
Fumbling in fourteen pockets,
While the conductor balances his ticket-punch
Between his fingers.

A GIFT

See! I give myself to you, Beloved!
My words are little jars
For you to take and put upon a shelf.
Their shapes are quaint and beautiful,
And they have many pleasant colors and lustres
To recommend them.
Also the scent from them fills the room
With sweetness of flowers and crushed grasses.

When I shall have given you the last one
You will have the whole of me,
But I shall be dead.

A LADY

You are beautiful and faded,
Like an old opera tune
Played upon a harpsichord;
Or like the sun-flooded silks
Of an eighteenth-century boudoir.
In your eyes
Smolder the fallen roses of outlived minutes,
And the perfume of your soul
Is vague and suffusing,
With the pungence of sealed spice jars.
Your half-tones delight me,
And I grow mad with gazing
At your blent colors.

My vigor is a new-minted penny,
Which I cast at your feet.
Gather it up from the dust,
That its sparkle may amuse you.

NIGHT CLOUDS

The white mares of the moon rush along the sky
Beating their golden hoofs upon the glass heavens;

The white mares of the moon are all standing on their hind legs
Pawing at the green porcelain doors of the remote heavens.
Fly, mares!
Strain your utmost,
Scatter the milky dust of stars,
Or the tiger sun will leap upon you and destroy you
With one lick of his vermilion tongue.

Robert Frost

(1874–1963)

Robert Frost was born in San Francisco, California. He went to Dartmouth College, was a co-founder of the Bread Loaf School of English at Middlebury College, and professor of English at Amherst College. In addition to being a college professor, he was a shoemaker and a farmer in New Hampshire. In 1912, when events in his life took a downward turn, Frost sold his farm and moved to England. The next year his first book was published and in 1915 Frost returned to America a famous man. He then settled for good in New Hampshire. Frost was a four-time winner of the Pulitzer Prize for poetry.

WIND AND WINDOW FLOWER

Lovers, forget your love,
    And list to the love of these,
She a window flower,
    And he a winter breeze.

When the frosty window veil
    Was melted down at noon,
And the cagèd yellow bird
    Hung over her in tune,

He marked her through the pane,
    He could not help but mark,
And only passed her by,
    To come again at dark.

He was a winter wind,
　Concerned with ice and snow,
Dead weeds and unmated birds,
　And little love could know.

But he sighed upon the sill,
　He gave the sash a shake,
As witness all within
　Who lay that night awake.

Perchance he half prevailed
　To win her for the flight
From the firelit looking-glass
　And warm stove-window light.

But the flower leaned aside
　And thought of naught to say,
And morning found the breeze
　A hundred miles away.

MOWING

There was never a sound beside the wood but one,
And that was my long scythe whispering to the ground.
What was it it whispered? I knew not well myself;
Perhaps it was something about the heat of the sun,
Something, perhaps, about the lack of sound—
And that was why it whispered and did not speak.
It was no dream of the gift of idle hours,
Or easy gold at the hand of fay or elf:
Anything more than the truth would have seemed too weak
To the earnest love that laid the swale in rows,
Not without feeble-pointed spikes of flowers
(Pale orchises), and scared a bright green snake.
The fact is the sweetest dream that labor knows.
My long scythe whispered and left the hay to make.

WARNING

The day will come when you will cease to know,
　The heart will cease to tell you; sadder yet,

Tho you say o'er and o'er what once you knew,
  You will forget, you will forget.

There is no memory for what is true,
  The heart once silent. Well may you regret,
Cry out upon it, that you have known all
  But to forget, but to forget.

Blame no one but yourself for this, lost soul!
  I feared it would be so that day we met
Long since, and you were changed. And I said then,
  He will forget, he will forget.

PARTING. TO—

I dreamed the setting sun would rise no more.
My spirit fled; nor sought an aimless sun
Whirled madly on through pathless space, and free
Amid a world of worlds enthralled. Ah no!
But deep within a silent solitude
It lingered on. The twilight waned; across
The hills and dark'ning sky the west wind stole,
And broad-cast spread the sun-path gathered gold,
Undying memories of the hopeless dead.
The dew of sadness fell, and far into
The coming night of storm and calm I gazed.
Oh, sadness, who may tell what joy is thine?
A whisper breathed: "What lies unvoiced on earth
Is heaven sung." And gloom crept softly down
With longing deep as everlasting night.

MENDING WALL

Something there is that doesn't love a wall,
That sends the frozen-ground-swell under it,
And spills the upper boulders in the sun,
And makes gaps even two can pass abreast.
The work of hunters is another thing:
I have come after them and made repair
Where they have left not one stone on stone,
But they would have the rabbit out of hiding,
To please the yelping dogs. The gaps I mean,

No one has seen them made or heard them made,
But at spring mending-time we find them there.
I let my neighbor know beyond the hill;
And on a day we meet to walk the line
And set the wall between us once again.
We keep the wall between us as we go.
To each the boulders that have fallen to each.
And some are loaves and some so nearly balls
We have to use a spell to make them balance:
"Stay where you are until our backs are turned!"
We wear our fingers rough with handling them.
Oh, just another kind of outdoor game,
One on a side. It comes to little more:
There where it is we do not need the wall:
He is all pine and I am apple orchard.
My apple trees will never get across
And eat the cones under his pines, I tell him.
He only says, "Good fences make good neighbors."
Spring is the mischief in me, and I wonder
If I could put a notion in his head:
"*Why* do they make good neighbors? Isn't it
Where there are cows? But here there are no cows.
Before I built a wall I'd ask to know
What I was walling in or walling out,
And to whom I was like to give offense.
Something there is that doesn't love a wall,
That wants it down," I could say "Elves" to him,
But it's not elves exactly, and I'd rather
He said it for himself. I see him there
Bringing a stone grasped firmly by the top
In each hand, like an old-stone savage armed.
He moves in darkness as it seems to me,
Not of woods only and the shade of trees.
He will not go behind his father's saying,
And he likes having thought of it so well
He says again, "Good fences make good neighbors."

TWILIGHT

Why am I first in thy so sad regard,
O twilight gazing from I know not where?
I fear myself as one more than I guessed!

· 580 ·

Am I instead of one so very fair?—
That thou art sorrowful and I oppressed?

High in the isolating air,
Over the inattentive moon,
Two birds sail on great wings,
    And vanish soon.
(And they leave the north sky bare!)

The far-felt solitudes that harbor night,
Wake to the singing of the wood-bird's fright.
By invocation, O wide silentness,
Thy spirit and my spirit pass in air!
They are unmemoried consciousness,
    Nor great nor less!
And thou art here and I am everywhere!

THE WOOD-PILE

Out walking in the frozen swamp one grey day
I paused and said, "I will turn back from here.
No, I will go on farther—and we shall see."
The hard snow held me, save where now and then
One foot went down. The view was all in lines
Straight up and down of tall slim trees
Too much alike to mark or name a place by
So as to say for certain I was here
Or somewhere else: I was just far from home.
A small bird flew before me. He was careful
To put a tree between us when he lighted,
And say no word to tell me who he was
Who was so foolish as to think what *he* thought.
He thought that I was after him for a feather—
The white one in his tail; like one who takes
Everything said as personal to himself.
One flight out sideways would have undeceived him.
And then there was a pile of wood for which
I forgot him and let his little fear
Carry him off the way I might have gone,
Without so much as wishing him good-night.
He went behind it to make his last stand.
It was a cord of maple, cut and split
And piled—and measured, four by four by eight.

And not another like it could I see.
No runner tracks in this year's snow looped near it.
And it was older sure than this year's cutting.
Or even last year's or the year's before.
The wood was grey and the bark warping off it
And the pile somewhat sunken. Clematis
Had wound strings round and round it like a bundle.
What held it though on one side was a tree
Still growing, and on one a stake and prop,
These latter about to fall. I thought that only
Someone who lived in turning to fresh tasks
Could so forget his handiwork on which
He spent himself, the labor of his axe,
And leave it there far from a useful fireplace
To warm the frozen swamp as best it could
With the slow smokeless burning of decay.

GOOD HOURS

I had for my winter evening walk—
No one at all with whom to talk,
But I had the cottages in a row
Up to their shining eyes in snow.

And I thought I had the folk within:
I had the sound of a violin;
I had a glimpse through curtain laces
Of youthful forms and youthful faces.

I had such company outward bound.
I went till there were no cottages found.
I turned and repented, but coming back
I saw no window but that was black.

Over the snow my creaking feet
Disturbed the slumbering village street
Like profanation, by your leave,
At ten o'clock of a winter eve.

AFTER APPLE-PICKING

My long two-pointed ladder's sticking through a tree
Toward heaven still,
And there's a barrel that I didn't fill
Beside it, and there may be two or three
Apples I didn't pick upon some bough.
But I am done with apple-picking now.
Essence of winter sleep is on the night,
The scent of apples: I am drowsing off.
I cannot rub the strangeness from my sight
I got from looking through a pane of glass
I skimmed this morning from the drinking trough
And held against the world of hoary grass.
It melted, and I let it fall and break.
But I was well
Upon my way to sleep before it fell,
And I could tell
What form my dreaming was about to take.
Magnified apples appear and disappear,
Stem end and blossom end,
And every fleck of russet showing clear.
My instep arch not only keeps the ache,
It keeps the pressure of a ladder-round
I feel the ladder sway as the boughs bend.
And I keep hearing from the cellar bin
The rumbling sound
Of load on load of apples coming in.
For I have had too much
Of apple-picking: I am overtired
Of the great harvest I myself desired.
There were ten thousand thousand fruit to touch,
Cherish in hand, lift down, and not let fall.
For all
That struck the earth,
No matter if not bruised or spiked with stubble,
Went surely to the cider-apple heap
As of no worth.
One can see what will trouble
This sleep of mine, whatever sleep it is.
Were he not gone,
The woodchuck could say whether it's like his
Long sleep, as I describe its coming on,
Or just some human sleep.

Carl Sandburg

(1878–1967)

Carl Sandburg was born in Galesburg, Illinois, the son of Swedish immigrants. As a teenager he worked on a milkwagon, in a barbershop, a brickyard, and a pottery, as a dishwasher in Denver and Omaha, and as a harvester in Kansas. He also attended Lombard College and served with the military in Puerto Rico. In 1905 he married the daughter of famed photographer Edward Steichen and subsequently made his home on the shores of Lake Michigan and, later, on a farm in North Carolina. Sandburg won a Pulitzer Prize for American history in 1940, the Pulitzer Prize for poetry in 1951, and shared the prize for poetry in 1921.

HAPPINESS

I asked professors who teach the meaning of life to tell me what is
    happiness.
And I went to famous executives who boss the work of thousands of
    men.
They all shook their heads and gave me a smile as though I was try-
    ing to fool with them.
And then one Sunday afternoon I wandered out along the Des-
    plaines river
And I saw a crowd of Hungarians under the trees with their women
    and children and a keg of beer and an accordion.

AIR CIRCUS

Were there too many revolving mirrors?
Did silver and rose lights cross too often?
Riders came crying: Riddle me this.
Riders straddling gold prongs cried and held on while trick planes,
pursuit and combat planes, bombers and helicopters, in a bath of
beacons came dropping flags—
And each rider picked up a revolving mirror?
And each rider twisted in silver and rose?

THREES

I was a boy when I heard three red words a thousand Frenchmen
died in the streets for: Liberty, Equality, Fraternity—I asked why
men die for words.

I was older; men with mustaches, sideburns, lilacs, told me the high
golden words are: Mother, Home, and Heaven—other older men
with face decorations said: God, Duty, Immortality—they sang
these threes slow from deep lungs.

Years ticked off their say-so on the great clocks of doom and damna-
tion, soup and nuts: meteors flashed their say-so: and out of great
Russia came three dusky syllables workmen took guns and went out
to die for: Bread, Peace, Land.

And I met a marine of the U.S.A., a leatherneck with a girl on his
knee for a memory in ports circling the earth and he said: Tell me
how to say three things and I always get by—gimme a plate of ham
and eggs—how much?—and—do you love me, kid?

SOUTHERN PACIFIC

Huntington sleeps in a house six feet long.
Huntington dreams of railroads he built and owned.
Huntington dreams of ten thousand men saying: Yes, sir.

Blithery sleeps in a house six feet long.
Blithery dreams of rails and ties he laid.
Blithery dreams of saying to Huntington: Yes, sir.

Huntington,
Blithery, sleep in houses six feet long.

UNDER A HAT RIM

While the hum and the hurry
Of passing footfalls
Beat in my ear like the restless surf
Of a wind-blown sea,
A soul came to me
Out of the look on a face.

Eyes like a lake
Where a storm-wind roams
Caught me from under
The rim of a hat.
    I thought of a midsea wreck
    and bruised fingers clinging
    to a broken state-room door.

FIRE-LOGS

Nancy Hanks dreams by the fire;
Dreams, and the logs sputter,
And the yellow tongues climb.
Red lines lick their way in flickers.
Oh, sputter, logs.
    Oh, dream, Nancy.
Time now for a beautiful child.
Time now for a tall man to come.

CHICAGO

Hog Butcher for the World,
Tool Maker, Stacker of Wheat,
Player with Railroads and the Nation's Freight Handler;
Stormy, husky, brawling,
City of the Big Shoulders:

They tell me you are wicked and I believe them, for I have seen
your painted women under the gas lamps luring the farm boys.

And they tell me you are crooked and I answer: Yes, it is true I have seen the gunman kill and go free to kill again.

And they tell me you are brutal and my reply is: On the faces of women and children I have seen the marks of wanton hunger.

And having answered so I turn once more to those who sneer at this my city, and I give them back the sneer and say to them:

Come and show me another city and lifted head singing so proud to be alive and coarse and strong and cunning.

Flinging magnetic curses amid the toil of piling job on job, here is a tall bold slugger set vivid against the little soft cities;

Fierce as a dog with tongue lapping for action, cunning as a savage pitted against the wilderness,

    Bareheaded,

    Shoveling,

    Wrecking,

    Planning,

    Building, breaking, rebuilding,

Under the smoke, dust all over his mouth, laughing with white teeth,

Under the terrible burden of destiny laughing as a young man laughs,

Laughing even as an ignorant fighter laughs who has never lost a battle,

Bragging and laughing that under his wrist is the pulse, and under his ribs the heart of the people,

                Laughing!

Laughing the stormy, husky, brawling laughter of Youth, half-naked, sweating, proud to be Hog Butcher, Tool Maker, Stacker of Wheat, Player with Railroads and Freight Handler to the Nation.

Wallace Stevens

(1879–1955)

Wallace Stevens was born in Reading, Pennsylvania. Stevens started writing poetry mostly for his own pleasure. He spent many years as an executive with the Hartford Accident and Indemnity Company, writing poetry in his spare time. Stevens has been critically acclaimed as one of the greatest poets of the twentieth century. Among the numerous poems he wrote, his personal favorite was "The Emperor of Ice Cream," a much-anthologized work.

THE EMPEROR OF ICE-CREAM

Call the roller of big cigars,
The muscular one, and bid him whip
In kitchen cups concupiscent curds.
Let the wenches dawdle in such dress
As they are used to wear, and let the boys
Bring flowers in last month's newspapers.
Let be be finale of seem.
The only emperor is the emperor of ice-cream.

Take from the dresser of deal,
Lacking the three glass knobs, that sheet
On which she embroidered fantails once
And spread it so as to cover her face.
If her horny feet protrude, they come
To show how cold she is, and dumb.
Let the lamp affix its beam.
The only emperor is the emperor of ice-cream.

POETRY IS A DESTRUCTIVE FORCE

That's what misery is,
Nothing to have at heart.
It is to have or nothing.

It is a thing to have,
A lion, an ox in his breast,
To feel it breathing there.

Corazon, stout dog,
Young ox, bow-legged bear,
He tastes its blood, not spit.

He is like a man
In the body of a violent beast.
Its muscles are his own . . .

The lion sleeps in the sun.
Its nose is on its paws.
It can kill a man.

DISILLUSIONMENT OF TEN O'CLOCK

The houses are haunted
By white night-gowns.
None are green,
Or purple with green rings,
Or green with yellow rings,
Or yellow with blue rings.
None of them are strange,
With socks of lace
And beaded ceintures.
People are not going
To dream of baboons and periwinkles.
Only, here and there, an old sailor,
Drunk and asleep in his boots,
Catches tigers
In red weather.

William Carlos Williams

(1883–1963)

William Carlos Williams was born in Rutherford, New Jersey, and was educated in New York and Switzerland. He attended the University of Pennsylvania Medical School, studied pediatrics and, after graduation, took up general practice in his native town. It was at the University of Pennsylvania that Williams met the Imagist poets H. D. and Ezra Pound. In 1909 Williams's first book, *Poems*, was privately published. He won the *Dial* award in 1926 and, in 1950, the National Book Award. In 1952 he was appointed a consultant in poetry to the Library of Congress but was not allowed to serve because he had been accused of allegedly having leftist ideological leanings.

PROLETARIAN PORTRAIT

A big young bareheaded woman
in an apron

Her hair slicked back standing
on the street

One stockinged foot toeing
the sidewalk

Her shoe in her hand. Looking
intently into it

She pulls out the paper insole
to find the nail

That has been hurting her

THE RED WHEELBARROW

so much depends
upon

a red wheel
barrow

glazed with rain
water

beside the white
chickens.

TO A POOR OLD WOMAN

munching a plum on
the street a paper bag
of them in her hand

They taste good to her
They taste good
to her. They taste
good to her

You can see it by
the way she gives herself
to the one half
sucked out in her hand

Comforted
a solace of ripe plums
seeming to fill the air
They taste good to her

ARRIVAL

And yet one arrives somehow,
finds himself loosening the hooks of
her dress
in a strange bedroom—
feels the autumn

dropping its silk and linen leaves
about her ankles.
The tawdry veined body emerges
twisted upon itself
like a winter wind . . . !

NANTUCKET

Flowers through the window
lavender and yellow

changed by white curtains—
Smell of cleanliness—

Sunshine of late afternoon—
On the glass tray

a glass pitcher, the tumbler
turned down, by which

a key is lying—And the
immaculate white bed

Sara Teasdale

(1884–1933)

Sara Teasdale was born and educated in St. Louis, Missouri. After completing her education she traveled overseas, always in the care of a chaperon. Teasdale went often to Chicago, where eventually she was accepted into the *Poetry* magazine circle. She married in 1914 and later moved to New York City, where she lived in seclusion until her suicide in 1933.

WOOD SONG

I heard a woodthrush in the dusk
　　Twirl three notes and make a star:
My heart that walked with bitterness
　　Came back from very far.

Three shining notes were all he had,
　　And yet they made a starry call:
I caught life back against my breast
　　And kissed it, scars and all.

UNDERSTANDING

I understood the rest too well,
　　And all their thoughts have come to be
Clear as grey sea-weed in the swell
　　Of a sunny shallow sea.

But you I never understood,
　　Your spirit's secret hides like gold

Sunk in a Spanish galleon
Ages ago in waters cold.

WISDOM

It was a night of early spring,
  The winter sleep was scarcely broken;
Around us shadows and the wind
  Listened for what was never spoken.

Though half a score of years are gone,
  Spring comes as sharply now as then;
But if we had it all to do
  It would be done the same again.

It was spring that never came,
  But we have lived enough to know
What we have never had, remains:
  It is the things we have that go.

LET IT BE FORGOTTEN

Let it be forgotten as a flower is forgotten,
  Forgotten as a fire that once was singing gold.
Let it be forgotten forever and ever.
  Time is a kind friend, he will make us old.

If any one asks, say it was forgotten
  Long and long ago,
As a flower, as a fire, as a hushed footfall
  In a long forgotten snow.

MORNING SONG

A diamond of a morning
  Waked me an hour too soon;
Dawn had taken in the stars
  And left the faint white moon.

O white moon, you are lonely,
  It is the same with me,
But we have the world to roam over,
  Only the lonely are free.

Ezra Pound

(1885–1972)

Ezra Pound was born in Haily, Idaho. He studied Romance languages at Hamilton College and the University of Pennsylvania where he met poets William Carlos Williams and H. D. In 1908 he left America to live in Europe where he went on to start the Imagist movement with T. E. Hulme, H. D., and Richard Aldington. Pound moved to Italy and became an ardent admirer of Mussolini. In 1939 he returned to America for an antiwar crusade and, on his return to Italy, broadcast his political views to American troops. When the American forces invaded Italy near the end of the war, Pound was taken prisoner and, in 1945, indicted for treason. The following year, after several psychiatrists testified that he was not of sound mind, he was committed to St. Elizabeth's Hospital in Washington, D.C. In 1958 treason charges were withdrawn and Pound was permitted to return to Italy, where he died in 1972.

THE GARRET

Come, let us pity those who are better off than we are.
Come, my friend, and remember
    that the rich have butlers and no friends,
And we have friends and no butlers.
Come, let us pity the married and the unmarried.

Dawn enters with little feet
    like a gilded Pavlova,
And I am near my desire.
Nor has life in it aught better

Than this hour of clear coolness,
the hour of waking together.

PICCADILLY

Beautiful, tragical faces—
Ye that were whole, and are so sunken;
And, O ye vile, ye that might have been loved,
That are so sodden and drunken,
    Who hath forgotten you?

O wistful, fragile faces, few out of many!
The crass, the coarse, the brazen,
God knows I cannot pity them, perhaps, as I should do;
But oh, ye delicate, wistful faces,
    Who hath forgotten you?

THE ENCOUNTER

All the while they were talking the new morality
Her eyes explored me.
And when I arose to go
Her fingers were like the tissue
Of a Japanese paper napkin.

A PACT

I make a pact with you, Walt Whitman—
I have detested you long enough.
I come to you as a grown child
Who has had a pig-headed father;
I am old enough now to make friends.
It was you that broke the new wood,
Now is a time for carving.
We have one sap and one root—
Let there be commerce between us.

William Rose Benét

(1886–1950)

William Rose Benét was born in Fort Hamilton, New York Harbor, and graduated from Yale in 1907. He was the elder brother of poet Stephen Vincent Benét and, in 1932, married poet Elinor Wylie. He was an associate editor of the New York *Post*'s "Literary Review" from 1920 to 1923. He was also an editor of the *Saturday Review of Literature*. Benét was a prolific writer with more than half a dozen volumes of poetry to his credit. He won a Pulitzer Prize for poetry in 1942.

VITAL STATISTICS

The statesmen bicker about the non-essential,
Press for advantage, pick the bones of the dove.
But though atoms of cataclysm are evidential,
In Trieste a boy and a girl are making love.

Legislators indulge in national rabies.
They ponder boundaries and bombs and guns;
But the Polish-Jewish mothers think their babies
As valid as the Bessarabian ones.

Mere men, we call the nations, are growling and warning,
Considering all they can get, not what they can give;
But in Oslo a workman looks up in the early morning
And thanks his God because his wife will live.

THE STRICKEN AVERAGE

Little of brilliance did they write or say.
They bore the battle of living, and were gay.
Little of wealth or fame they left behind.
They were merely honorable, brave, and kind.

ON A DEAD POET

For all they minimize and abrade away,
For all they say and say and still mis-say,
The living bronze has age on age for heirs.
What the detractors have is only theirs.

GATE OF HORN

I saw a man standing
        by a dark sea.
Strange was the word
        he said to me:
"A million scenes are in this scene;
through a million battles I have been."

I saw a man riding
        under a star.
Wild was the cry
        he cried from far.
I saw him come to a glimmering ford
and a myriad shadows beset his sword.

I saw a man questing
        under the moon,
through the unresting
        night of June.
In a myrtle bower I well knew of
he sobbed of the power and the pangs of love.

I saw a man reading
        under a dome
piled with high wisdom
        tome on tome.

The moth that around his candle flew
no more ephemeral was, I knew.

Under the eye
        of the open sky,
on a vast plain
        a man was I.
Before him a burning wheel did run.
He staggered after the rolling sun.

On inner space
        and outer space,
I saw the imprint
        of a face
awful and unparadised
yet with the living eyes of Christ;

the face of God
        with Man made one:
author of being
        and eidolon;
the opener of every door,
every symbol's secret core.

I saw a horseman
        beyond a stream
that roiled and boiled
        with the shapes of dream;
but ere his accost had brought me light,
he spurred and was lost in the wood of night.

JUDGMENT

Down the deep steps of stone, through iron doors,
I entered that red room and saw the rack,
And round the walls I saw them sit in black,
The immutable and urgent councilors.
My heart was clotted with an old remorse,
Despair a vulture fast upon my back.
I saw my body like an empty sack
Tossed disarticulate on grated floors.

But even a wilder wonder at this crime,
Tried in the dungeon of my own grim life,
Woke, as your memory awoke with tune
That crazed the very walls. I stared through Time
Like to a man who stands with smoking knife
Above his dead, and sees the rising moon.

H. D.

(1886–1961)

Hilda Doolittle, known as H. D., was born in Bethlehem, Pennsylvania. In 1904 she entered Bryn Mawr College where she met poet Marianne Moore. During that time she also met poets William Carlos Williams and Ezra Pound. H. D. went abroad in 1911 and helped found the Imagists with Pound. In 1913 she married another Imagist cofounder, Richard Aldington. She lived in England and Switzerland.

LETHE

Nor skin nor hide nor fleece
   Shall cover you,
Nor curtain of crimson nor fine
Shelter of cedar-wood be over you,
   Nor the fir-tree
   Nor the pine.

Nor sight of whin nor gorse
   Nor river-yew,
Nor fragrance of flowering bush,
Nor wailing of reed-bird to waken you,
   Nor of linnet,
   Nor of thrush.

Nor word nor touch nor sight
   Of lover, you
Shall long through the night but for this:
The roll of the full tide to cover you

Without question,
Without kiss.

FLUTE SONG

Little scavenger away,
touch not the door,
beat not the portal down,
cross not the sill,
silent until
my song, bright and shrill,
breathes out its lay.

Little scavenger avaunt,
tempt me with jeer and taunt,
yet you will wait to-day;
for it were surely ill
to mock and shout and revel;
it were more fit to tell
with flutes and calathes,
your mother's praise.

HELEN

All Greece hates
the still eyes in the white face,
the lustre as of olives
where she stands,
and the white hands.

All Greece reviles
the wan face when she smiles,
hating it deeper still
when it grows wan and white,
remembering past enchantments
and past ills.

Greece sees unmoved,
God's daughter, born of love,
the beauty of cool feet
and slenderest knees,
could love indeed the maid,

only if she were laid,
white ash amid funereal cypresses.

Marianne Moore

(1887–1972)

Marianne Moore was born in St. Louis, Missouri, and graduated from Bryn Mawr College in 1909. While at Bryn Mawr she met poets H. D., William Carlos Williams and Ezra Pound. She taught stenography for five years and was also involved with the Imagists. In 1921 Moore became an assistant in the New York Public Library, and from 1925 to 1929 she edited the *Dial*, a highly respected literary journal. Her *Collected Poems*, published in 1951, won her a Pulitzer Prize for poetry.

SILENCE

My father used to say,
"Superior people never make long visits,
have to be shown Longfellow's grave
or the glass flowers at Harvard.
Self-reliant like the cat—
that takes its prey to privacy,
the mouse's limp tail hanging like a shoelace from its mouth—
they sometimes enjoy solitude,
and can be robbed of speech
by speech which has delighted them.
The deepest feeling always shows itself in silence;
not in silence, but restraint."
Nor was he insincere in saying, "Make my house your inn."
Inns are not residences.

NO SWAN SO FINE

"No water so still as the
    dead fountains of Versailles." No swan,
with swart blind look askance
and gondoliering legs, so fine
    as the chintz china one with fawn-
brown eyes and toothed gold
collar on to show whose bird it was.

Lodged in the Louis Fifteenth
    candelabrum-tree of cockscomb-
tinted buttons, dahlias,
sea urchins, and everlastings,
    it perches on the branching foam
of polished sculptured
flowers—at ease and tall. The king is dead.

TO MILITARY PROGRESS

You use your mind
like a millstone to grind
    chaff.
You polish it
and with your warped wit
    laugh

At your torso,
prostrate where the crow
    falls
on such faint hearts
as its god imparts,
    calls

and claps its wings
till the tumult brings
    more
black minute-men
to revive again,
    war

at little cost.
They cry for the lost

head
and seek their prize
till the evening sky's
red.

John Crowe Ransom

(1888–1974)

Born in Pulaski, Tennessee, John Crowe Ransom was one of the founders of the "Fugitives," a group of southern poets. He went to Vanderbilt University and attended Oxford University as a Rhodes Scholar. He went on to become a professor at Vanderbilt and, later, professor of poetry at Kenyon College, where he founded and edited the *Kenyon Review,* still a highly respected literary journal. He retired from teaching in 1958.

PIAZZA PIECE

—I am a gentleman in a dustcoat trying
To make you hear. Your ears are soft and small
And listen to an old man not at all,
They want the young men's whispering and sighing.
But see the roses on your trellis dying
And hear the spectral singing of the moon;
For I must have my lovely lady soon,
I am a gentleman in a dustcoat trying.

—I am a lady young in beauty waiting
Until my truelove comes, and then we kiss.
But what grey man among the vines is this
Whose words are dry and faint as in a dream?
Back from my trellis, Sir, before I scream!
I am a lady young in beauty waiting.

PARTING AT DAWN

If there was a broken whispering by night
It was an image of the coward heart,
But the white dawn assures them how to part—
Stoics are born on the cold glitter of light
And with the morning star lovers take flight.
Say then your parting; and most dry should you drain
Your lips of the wine, your eyes of the frantic rain,
Till these be as the barren anchorite.

And then? O dear Sir, stumbling down the street,
Continue, till you come to wars and wounds;
Beat the air, Madam, till your house-clock sounds;
And if no Lethe flows beneath your casement,
And when ten years have not brought full effacement,
Philosophy was wrong, and you may meet.

BLACKBERRY WINTER

If there be a power of sweetness, let it lie,
For being drunken with steam of Cuban cigars
He takes no pungence from the odor of stars,
And even his music stops on one long sigh.

Still he must sing to his virgin apple tree
Who has not borne him a winey beauty of red;
The silver blooms and bronzy nubs drop dead
But the nonpareil may ripen yet, maybe.

Bestarred is the Daughter of Heaven's house, and cold,
He has seen her often, she sat all night on the hill,
Unseemly the pale youth clambered toward her, till
Untimely the peacock screamed, and he wakened old.

The breath of a girl is music of fall and swell.
Trumpets convolve in the warrior's chambered ear,
But he has listened; none is resounding here,
So much the wars have dwindled since Troy fell.

MORNING

Jane awoke Ralph so gently on one morning
That first, before the true householder Learning
Came back to tenant in the haunted head,
He lay upon his back and let his stare
Penetrate dazedly into the blue air
That swam all round his bed,
And in the blessed silence nothing was said.

Then his eyes travelled through the window
And lit, enchantedly, on such a meadow
Of wings and light and clover,
He would propose to Jane then to go walking
Through the green waves, and to be singing not talking;
Such imps were pranking over
Him helpless lying in bed beneath a cover.

Suddenly he remembered about himself,
His manliness returned entire to Ralph;
The dutiful mills of the brain
Began to whir with their smooth-grinding wheels
And the sly visitors wriggled off like eels;
He rose and was himself again.
Simply another morning, and simply Jane.

T. S. Eliot

(1888–1965)

Thomas Stearns Eliot was born in St. Louis, Missouri. He received his education, in classics, at Harvard, the Sorbonne, and Oxford. At Harvard, he was fortunate to have such teachers as philosopher and poet George Santayana, and Irving Babbitt, the respected literary critic. In 1915, Eliot settled in London, and worked for Lloyds Bank and the publishing firm of Faber & Faber. In 1927 he became a British citizen and later was confirmed in the Church of England. Eliot received the British Order of Merit and in 1948 won the Nobel Prize for literature.

SWEENEY
AMONG THE NIGHTINGALES

ὤμοι, πέπληγμαι καιρίαν πληγὴν ἔσω.

Apeneck Sweeney spreads his knees
Letting his arms hang down to laugh,
The zebra stripes along his jaw
Swelling to maculate giraffe.

The circles of the stormy moon
Slide westward toward the River Plate,
Death and the Raven drift above
And Sweeney guards the hornèd gate.

Gloomy Orion and the Dog
Are veiled; and hushed the shrunken seas;

The person in the Spanish cape
Tries to sit on Sweeney's knees

Slips and pulls the table cloth
Overturns a coffee-cup,
Reorganised upon the floor
She yawns and draws a stocking up;

The silent man in mocha brown
Sprawls at the window-sill and gapes;
The waiter brings in oranges
Bananas figs and hothouse grapes;

The silent vertebrate in brown
Contracts and concentrates, withdraws;
Rachel *née* Rabinovitch
Tears at the grapes with murderous paws;

She and the lady in the cape
Are suspect, thought to be in league;
Therefore the man with heavy eyes
Declines the gambit, shows fatigue,

Leaves the room and reappears
Outside the window, leaning in,
Branches of wistaria
Circumscribe a golden grin;

The host with someone indistinct
Converses at the door apart,
The nightingales are singing near
The Convent of the Sacred Heart,

And sang within the bloody wood
When Agamemnon cried aloud,
And let their liquid siftings fall
To stain the stiff dishonoured shroud.

AUNT HELEN

Miss Helen Slingsby was my maiden aunt,
And lived in a small house near a fashionable square
Cared for by servants to the number of four.

Now when she died there was silence in heaven
And silence at her end of the street.
The shutters were drawn and the undertaker wiped his feet—
He was aware that this sort of thing had occurred before.
The dogs were handsomely provided for,
But shortly afterwards the parrot died too.
The Dresden clock continued ticking on the mantel-piece,
And the footman sat upon the dining-table
Holding the second housemaid on his knees—
Who had always been so careful while her mistress lived.

COUSIN NANCY

Miss Nancy Ellicott
Strode across the hills and broke them,
Rode across the hills and broke them—
The barren New England hills—
Riding to hounds
Over the cow-pasture.

Miss Nancy Ellicott smoked
And danced all the modern dances;
And her aunts were not quite sure how they felt about it,
But they knew that it was modern.

Upon the glazen shelves kept watch
Matthew and Waldo, guardians of the faith,
The army of unalterable law.

Conrad Aiken

(1889–1973)

Conrad Aiken was born in Savannah, Georgia, and was orphaned in childhood when his father committed suicide after killing his mother. Aiken then moved to Massachusetts where he lived with relatives. He attended Harvard where he had such later-famous classmates as T. S. Eliot, Robert Benchley, and Van Wyck Brooks. During his tenure at Harvard he was named class poet. Aiken lived for a time in England and won a Pulitzer Prize for poetry in 1930.

ALL LOVELY THINGS

All lovely things will have an ending,
All lovely things will fade and die,
And youth, that's now so bravely spending,
Will beg a penny by and by.

Fine ladies all are soon forgotten,
And goldenrod is dust when dead,
The sweetest flesh and flowers are rotten
And cobwebs tent the brightest head.

Come back, true love! Sweet youth, return!—
But time goes on, and will, unheeding,
Though hands will reach, and eyes will yearn,
And the wild days set true hearts bleeding.

Come back, true love! Sweet youth, remain!—
But goldenrod and daisies wither,

And over them blows autumn rain,
They pass, they pass, and know not whither.

THE SOUNDING

Blue sky, blue noon, and the secret line if flung:
once more, the Mariner his sounding takes;
from heaven's blue bridge once more the Lead is swung,
and downward through the ethereal Ocean breaks

the divine Plummet and the invisible cord
past sun-drowned Vega, and Orion's Belt.
Now the unfathomed is fathomed with a Word:
Earth, and this City, by their heartbeat felt.

Like a small lightning through the clouds' pale glooms,
at intervals unguessed by the faint sun,
down to this stony reef, the city, comes
that cord, unloosed so soundlessly to run;

and on the bridge that arches the unknown
the Master Mariner, his sounding sure,
carves in the ice: A kingdom overthrown—
man kills his children. But the birds endure.

THE NAMELESS ONES

Pity the nameless, and the unknown, where
bitter in heart they wait on the stonebuilt stair,
bend to a wall, forgotten, the freezing wind
no bitterer than the suburbs of the mind;

who from an iron porch lift sightless eyes,
a moment, hopeless, to inflaming skies;
shrink from the light as quickly as from pain,
twist round a corner, bend to the wall again;

are to be seen leaning against a rail
by ornamental waters where toy yachts sail;
glide down the granite steps, touch foot to float,
hate, and desire, the sunlight on the boat;

explore a sullen alley where ash-cans wait,
symbols of waste and want, at every gate;
emerge in sun to mingle with the crowd,
themselves most silent where the world most loud;

anonymous, furtive, shadows in shadow hidden;
who lurk at the garden's edge like guests unbidden;
stare through the leaves with hate, yet wait to listen
as bandstand music begins to rise and glisten;

the fierce, the solitary, divine of heart,
passionate, present, yet godlike and apart;
who, in the midst of traffic, see a vision;
and, on a park bench, come to a last decision.

MUSIC

The calyx of the oboe breaks,
silver and soft the flower it makes.
And next, beyond, the flute-notes seen
now are white and now are green.

What are these sounds, what daft device,
mocking at flame, mimicking ice?
Musicians, will you never rest
from strange translation of the breast?

The heart, from which all horrors come,
grows like a vine, its gourd a drum;
the living pattern sprawls and climbs
eager to bear all worlds and times:

trilling leaf and tinkling grass
glide into darkness clear as glass;
then the musicians cease to play
and the world is waved away.

Edna St. Vincent Millay

(1892–1950)

Edna St. Vincent Millay was born in Rockland, Maine, and grew up in the coastal town of Camden. She graduated from Vassar College in 1917 and was involved with the Greenwich Village bohemians early in her poetry career. Millay won a Pulitzer Prize for poetry in 1923.

THE PENITENT

I had a little Sorrow,
Born of a little Sin,
I found a room all damp with gloom
And shut us all within;
And "Little Sorrow, weep," said I
"And, Little Sin, pray God to die,
And I upon the floor will lie
    And think how bad I've been!"

Alas for pious planning—
    It mattered not a whit!
As far as gloom went in that room,
    The lamp might have been lit!
My Little Sorrow would not weep,
My Little Sin would go to sleep—
To save my soul I could not keep
    My graceless mind on it!

So up I got in anger,
    And took a book I had,

And put a ribbon on my hair
   To please a passing lad.
And, "One thing there's no getting by—
I've been a wicked girl," said I;
"But if I can't be sorry, why,
   I might as well be glad!"

FEAST

I drank at every vine.
   The last was like the first.
I came upon no wine
   So wonderful as thirst.

I gnawed at every root.
   I ate of every plant.
I came upon no fruit
   So wonderful as want.

Feed the grape and bean
   To the vintner and monger;
I will lie down lean
   With my thirst and my hunger.

AFTERNOON ON A HILL

I will be the gladdest thing
   Under the sun!
I will touch a hundred flowers
   And not pick one.

I will look at cliffs and clouds
   With quiet eyes,
Watch the wind bow down the grass,
   And the grass rise.

And when lights begin to show
   Up from the town,
I will mark which must be mine,
   And then start down!

EBB

I know what my heart is like
    Since your love died:
It is like a hollow ledge
Holding a little pool
    Left there by the tide,
    A little tepid pool,
Drying inward from the edge.

Archibald MacLeish

(1892–1982)

Archibald MacLeish was born in Glencoe, Illinois. He graduated from Yale in 1915, and then graduated first in his class from Harvard Law School. Eventually, however, he gave up his Boston law practice for literature. From 1933 to 1944 MacLeish was with the Library of Congress, eventually becoming the Librarian of Congress. From 1944 to 1945 he was the assistant secretary of state. MacLeish went back to Harvard as Professor of Rhetoric and Oratory, a post he held from 1949 to 1962. He also served as a Simpson Lecturer at Amherst College and as the editor of *Fortune* magazine. He won the Pulitzer Prize for poetry in 1933 and 1953 and won in the drama category in 1959.

GRAZING LOCOMOTIVES

Huge upon the hazy plain
Where bloom the momentary trees,
Where blows immensely round their knees
The grass that fades to air again,

Slow and solemn in the night
Beneath the slender pole by pole
That lifts above their reach each sole
Enormous melon of the light,

Still sweating from the deep ravines
Where rot within the buried wood
The bones of Time that are their food,
   Graze the great machines.

THE RAPE OF THE SWAN

To love love and not its meaning
Hardens the heart in monstrous ways.
No one is ours who has this leaning.
Those whose loyalty is love's betray us.

They are not girls with a girl's softness.
They love not us at all but love.
They have hard and fanatical minds most often.
It is not we but a dream that must cover them.

A woman who loves love cannot give it.
Her part is not to give but take.
Even the great swan by the river—
Her fingers strangle and the feathers break.

THUNDERHEAD

Do not lie there in the darkness silent
Hearing his silence by you in the dark.

That sky could tell you that there must be magic
Waiting as well as working to have miracles—

Thunder in earth for thunder in the air
To bring the flash down and the blinding glimpses.

Rock and loam must smoulder with desire
Before the haycock of the heart is struck on fire.

MOTHER GOOSE'S GARLAND

Around, around the sun we go:
The moon goes round the earth.
We do not die of death:
We die of vertigo.

Dorothy Parker

(1893–1967)

Dorothy Parker was born in West End, New Jersey, and educated at the Blessed Sacred Convent in New York City. She started her writing career with *Vogue* magazine and from 1917 to 1920 she was drama critic for *Vanity Fair*. She also reviewed for *The New Yorker* and *Esquire*. Parker wrote a number of short stories and coauthored at least one play. However, she was most well known for her dry wit and pointedly cynical observations especially regarding love and the relationship between men and women.

RÉSUMÉ

Razors pain you;
Rivers are damp;
Acids stain you;
And drugs cause cramp.
Guns aren't lawful;
Nooses give;
Gas smells awful;
You might as well live.

COMMENT

Oh, life is a glorious cycle of song,
A medley of extemporanea;
And love is a thing that can never go wrong;
And I am Marie of Roumania.

ON BEING A WOMAN

Why is it, when I am in Rome
I'd give an eye to be at home,
But when on native earth I be,
My soul is sick for Italy?

And why with you, my love, my lord,
And I spectacularly bored,
Yet do you up and leave me—then
I scream to have you back again?

SOCIAL NOTE

Lady, lady, should you meet
One whose ways are all discreet,
One who murmurs that his wife
Is the lodestar of his life,
One who keeps assuring you
That he never was untrue,
Never loved another one . . .
Lady, lady, better run!

BOHEMIA

Authors and actors and artists and such
Never know nothing, and never know much.
Sculptors and singers and those of their kidney
Tell their affairs from Seattle to Sydney.
Playwrights and poets and such horses' necks
Start off from anywhere, end up at sex.
Diarists, critics, and similar roe
Never say nothing, and never say no.
People Who Do Things exceed my endurance;
God, for a man that solicits insurance!

e. e. cummings

(1894–1962)

Edward Estlin Cummings was born and raised in Cambridge, Massachusetts. He graduated from Harvard in 1916, and during World War I he served on an ambulance team and was imprisoned by mistake in a French detention camp. In 1920 he was writing poetry and painting in Paris; between 1923 and 1944 he wrote nine volumes of poetry. Cummings won the Dial award for distinguished services to literature in 1925.

"MY SWEET OLD ETCETERA"

my sweet old etcetera
aunt lucy during the recent

war could and what
is more did tell you just
what everybody was fighting

for,
my sister

isabel created hundreds
(and
hundreds) of socks not to
mention shirts fleaproof earwarmers

etcetera wristers etcetera, my
mother hoped that

i would die etcetera
bravely of course my father used
to become hoarse talking about how it was
a privilege and if only he
could meanwhile my

self etcetera lay quietly
in the deep mud et

cetera
(dreaming,
et
    cetera, of
Your smile
eyes knees and of your Etcetera)

"IT REALLY MUST BE NICE"

it really must
be Nice, never to

have no imagination)or never
never to wonder about guys you used to(and them
slim hot queens with dam next to nothing

on)tangoing
(while a feller tries
to hold down the fifty bucks per
job with one foot and rock a

cradle with the other)it Must be
nice never to have no doubts about why you
put the ring
on(and watching her
face grow old and tired to which

you're married and hands get red washing
things and dishes)and to never, never really wonder i
mean about the smell
of babies and how you

know the dam rent's going to and everything and never, never
Never to stand at no window
because i can't sleep(smoking sawdust

cigarettes in the
middle of the night

"MY UNCLE DANIEL"

my uncle
Daniel fought in the civil
war band and can play the triangle
like the devil)my

uncle Frank has done nothing for many
years but fly kites and
when the
string breaks(or something)my uncle Frank breaks into
tears. my uncle Tom

knits and is a kewpie above the ears(but

my uncle Ed
that's
dead from the neck

up is lead all over
Brattle Street by a castrated pup

Stephen Vincent Benét

(1898–1943)

Stephen Vincent Benét, the younger brother of William Rose Benét, was born in Bethlehem, Pennsylvania. He graduated from Yale in 1919 and took graduate courses there, as well as at the Sorbonne. He is best known for his short stories and longer poems such as "John Brown's Body" and "The Devil and Daniel Webster." In 1943 Benét died of a heart malfunction. He was the winner of the Pulitzer Prize for poetry in both 1929 and 1944.

DAYS PASS: MEN PASS

When, like all liberal girls and boys,
We too get rid of sight
—The juggler with his painted toys
The elf and her delight—

In the cool place where jests are few
And there's no time to weep
For all the untamed hearts we knew
Creeping like moths to sleep.

This eagerness that burns us yet
Will rot like summer snow,
And we'll forget as winds forget
When they have ceased to blow.

Oh, we'll grow sleepy, lacking mirth!
But there will still endure

Somewhere, like innocence and earth,
The things you wish made pure.

Wide moonlight on a harvest dew,
White silk, too dear to touch,
These will be you and always you
When I am nothing much.

The flowers with the hardy eyes,
The bread that feeds the gods,
These will be you till Last Assize
When I'm improper sods.

Oh dear immortal, while you can,
Commit one mortal sin.
And let me love you like a man
Till Judgment Day comes in!

NOMENCLATURE

Some people have names like pitchforks, some people have names
    like cakes,
Names full of sizzling esses like a family quarrel of snakes,
Names black as a cat, vermilion as the cockscomb-hat of a fool—
But your name is a green, small garden, a rush asleep in a pool.

When God looked at the diffident cherubs and dropped them out of
    the sky,
He named them like Adam's animals, while Mary and Eve stood by,
The poor things huddled before him in scared little naked flocks
—And he gave you a name like sunlight, and clover, and hollyhocks.

For your mouth with its puzzled jesting, for your hair like a dark
    soft bird,
Shy humor and dainty walking, sweet laughter and subtle word,
As a fairy walks with a mushroom to keep the rain from its things
You carry your name forever, like a scepter alive with wings.

Neither change nor despair shall touch it nor the seasons make it
    uncouth,
It will burn like an Autumn maple when your proud age talks to
    your youth,

Wise child, clean friend, adoration, light arrow of God, white flame,
I would break my body to pieces to call you once by your name!

UNFAMILIAR QUARTET

The concert-hall creaked like a full-dress shirt
As the happy audience hugged its musical smart,
And waited to be titillatingly hurt
By the pelting of the over-ripe fruit of Art.

The violin wept its sugar, the saxophone
Howled like a mandrake raped by a lightning-stroke,
The cello gave a blond and stomachy groan—
And then the hard bugle spoke.

Sewing a wound together with brazen stitches,
Stitching a bronze device on the rotten skin,
And calling the elegant audience sons of bitches,
It ceased, and the sons of bitches
Applauded the violin.

GHOSTS OF A LUNATIC ASYLUM

Here, where men's eyes were empty and as bright
As the blank windows set in glaring brick,
When the wind strengthens from the sea—and night
Drops like a fog and makes the breath come thick;

By the deserted paths, the vacant halls,
One may see figures, twisted shades and lean,
Like the mad shapes that crawl an Indian screen,
Or paunchy smears you find on prison walls.

Turn the knob gently! There's the Thumbless Man,
Still weaving glass and silk into a dream,
Although the wall shows through him—and the Khan
Journeys Cathay beside a paper stream.

A Rabbit Woman chitters by the door—
—Chilly the grave-smell comes from the turned sod—
Come—lift the curtain—and be cold before
The silence of the eight men who were God!

Ogden Nash

(1902–1971)

Ogden Nash was born in Rye, New York. Nash was—and still is considered—the "king of humor" among American poets. He attended Harvard and worked in book publishing at Doubleday and Company. He spent many productive years writing for, and working on the editorial staff of, *The New Yorker*.

OLD MEN

People expect old men to die,
They do not really mourn old men.
Old men are different. People look
At them with eyes that wonder when . . .
People watch with unshocked eyes . . .
But the old men know when an old man dies.

THE FISH

The fish, when he's exposed to air,
Can show no trace of savoir faire,
But in the sea regains his balance
And exploits all his manly talents.
The chastest of the vertebrates,
He never even sees his mates,
But when they've finished, he appears
And O.K.'s all their bright ideas.

SONG OF THE OPEN ROAD

I think that I shall never see
A billboard lovely as a tree.
Indeed, unless the billboards fall
I'll never see a tree at all.

Theodore Roethke

(1908–1963)

Theodore Roethke was born and raised in Saginaw, Michigan, and studied at the University of Michigan and Harvard. He taught at Lafayette College, Bennington College, Pennsylvania State College, and the University of Washington. Roethke won Guggenheim Fellowships in 1946 and 1950, a Pulitzer Prize for poetry in 1954, a Bollingen Prize in 1958, and the Edna St. Vincent Millay Prize in 1959. He died in 1963 at the height of his creative powers.

THE SLOTH

In moving-slow he has no Peer.
You ask him something in his Ear,
He thinks about it for a Year;

And, then, before he says a Word
There, upside down (unlike a Bird),
He will assume that you have Heard—

A most Ex-as-per-at-ing Lug.
But should you call his manner Smug,
He'll sigh and give his Branch a Hug;

Then off again to Sleep he goes,
Still swaying gently by his Toes,
And you just *know* he knows he knows.

ROOT CELLAR

Nothing would sleep in that cellar, dank as a ditch,
Bulbs broke out of boxes hunting for chinks in the dark,
Shoots dangled and drooped,
Lolling obscenely from mildewed crates,
Hung down long yellow evil necks, like tropical snakes.
And what a congress of stinks!—
Roots ripe as old bait,
Pulpy stems, rank, silo-rich,
Leaf-mold, manure, lime, piled against slippery planks.
Nothing would give up life:
Even the dirt kept breathing a small breath.

MY PAPA'S WALTZ

The whiskey on your breath
Could make a small boy dizzy;
But I hung on like death:
Such waltzing was not easy.

We romped until the pans
Slid from the kitchen shelf;
My mother's countenance
Could not unfrown itself.

The hand that held my wrist
Was battered on one knuckle;
At every step you missed
My right ear scraped a buckle.

You beat time on my head
With a palm caked hard by dirt,
Then waltzed me off to bed
Still clinging to your shirt.

John Updike

(b. 1932)

John Updike was born in Shillington, Pennsylvania, was graduated from Harvard in 1954, and studied at the Ruskin School of Drawing and Fine Art at Oxford. Updike was, for a while, on the staff of *The New Yorker* to which he still contributes a steady flow of short stories, poems, and humor. Today, he is one of America's most popular novelists. In 1982 he won the American Book Award and the Book Critics Circle Award for his novel *Rabbit Is Rich.*

THE SHORT DAYS

I like the way, in winter, cars
Ignite beneath the lingering stars
And, with a cough or two, unpark,
And roar to work still in the dark.

Like some great father, slugabed,
Whose children crack the dawn with play,
The sun retains a heavy head
Behind the hill, and stalls the day.

Then red rims gild the gutter-spouts;
The streetlamp pales; the milk-truck fades;
And housewives—husbands gone—wash doubts
Down sinks and raise the glowing shades.

The cars are gone, they will return
When headlights in a new night burn;

Between long drinks of Acheron
The thirst of broad day has begun.

3 A.M.

By the brilliant ramp
of a ceaseless garage

the eye like a piece of newspaper
staring from a collage

records on a yellowing
gridwork of nerve

"policemen move on feet of glue,
sailors stick to the curb."

MOSQUITO

On the fine wire of her whine she walked,
Unseen in the ominous bedroom dark.
A traitor to her camouflage, she talked
A thirsty blue streak distinct as a spark.

I was to her a fragrant lake of blood
From which she had to sip a drop or die.
A reservoir, a lavish field of food,
I lay awake, unconscious of my size.

We seemed fair-matched opponents. Soft she dropped
Down like an anchor on her thread of song.
Her nose sank thankfully in; then I slapped
At the sting on my arm, cunning and strong.

A cunning, strong Gargantua, I struck
This lover pinned in the feast of my flesh,
Lulled by my blood, relaxed, half-sated, stuck
Engrossed in the gross rivers of myself.

Success! Without a cry the creature died,
Became a fleck of fluff upon the sheet.

The small welt of remorse subsides as side
By side we, murderer and murdered, sleep.

AGATHA CHRISTIE
AND BEATRIX POTTER

Many-volumed authoresses
In capacious country dresses,
Full of cheerful art and nearly
Perfect craft, we love you dearly.

You know the hedgerow, stile, and barrow,
Have sniffed the cabbage, leek, and marrow,
Have heard the prim postmistress snicker,
And spied out murder in the vicar.

You've drawn the berry-beaded brambles
Where Mrs. Tiggy-Winkle rambles,
And mapped the attics in the village
Where mice plot alibis and pillage.

God bless you, girls, for in these places
You give us cozy scares and chases
That end with innocence acquitted—
Except for Cotton-tail, who did it.

BENDIX

This porthole overlooks a sea
Forever falling from the sky,
The water inextricably
Involved with buttons, suds, and dye.

Like bits of shrapnel, shards of foam
Fly heavenward; a bedsheet heaves,
A stocking wrestles with a comb,
And cotton angels wave their sleeves.

The boiling purgatorial tide
Revolves our dreary shorts and slips,
While Mother coolly bakes beside
Her little jugged apocalypse.

II
The Poems and Songs
of America

Patriotism and Courage

THE STAR-SPANGLED BANNER

O say, can you see, by the dawn's early light,
    What so proudly we hailed at the twilight's last gleaming—
Whose broad stripes and bright stars, through the clouds of the
    fight,
    O'er the ramparts we watched were so gallantly streaming!
And the rocket's red glare, the bombs bursting in air,
Gave proof through the night that our flag was still there;
O! say, does that star-spangled banner yet wave
O'er the land of the free, and the home of the brave?

On that shore dimly seen through the mists of the deep,
    Where the foe's haughty host in dread silence reposes,
What is that which the breeze, o'er the towering steep,
    As it fitfully blows, now conceals, now discloses?
Now it catches the gleam of the morning's first beam,
In full glory reflected now shines on the stream;
'Tis the star-spangled banner; O long may it wave
O'er the land of the free, and the home of the brave!

And where is that band who so vauntingly swore
    That the havoc of war and the battle's confusion
A home and a country should leave us no more?
    Their blood has washed out their foul footsteps' pollution.
No refuge could save the hireling and slave
From the terror of flight, or the gloom of the grave;
And the star-spangled banner in triumph doth wave
O'er the land of the free, and the home of the brave.

O! thus be it ever, when freemen shall stand
    Between their loved homes and the war's desolation!
Blest with victory and peace, may the heav'n-rescued land
    Praise the power that hath made and preserved us a nation.
Then conquer we must, when our cause it is just,
And this be our motto,—*"In God is our trust:"*

And the star-spangled banner in triumph shall wave
O'er the land of the free, and the home of the brave.
                                  —*Francis Scott Key*

HAIL COLUMBIA

Hail, Columbia! happy land!
Hail, ye heroes! heaven-born band!
  Who fought and bled in Freedom's cause,
  Who fought and bled in Freedom's cause,

And when the storm of war was gone,
Enjoyed the peace your valor won.
  Let independence be our boast,
  Ever mindful what it cost;
  Ever grateful for the prize,
  Let its altar reach the skies.

     Firm, united, let us be,
     Rallying round our Liberty;
     As a band of brothers joined,
     Peace and safety we shall find.

Immortal patriots! rise once more:
Defend your rights, defend your shore:
  Let no rude foe, with impious hand,
  Let no rude foe, with impious hand,
Invade the shrine where sacred lies
Of toil and blood and well-earned prize.
  While offering peace sincere and just,
  In Heaven we place a manly trust,
  That truth and justice will prevail,
  And every scheme of bondage fail.

     Firm, united, let us be,
     Rallying round our Liberty;
     As a band of brothers joined,
     Peace and safety we shall find.

Sound, sound, the trump of Fame!
Let WASHINGTON'S great name
  Ring through the world with loud applause,
  Ring through the world with loud applause;

Let every clime to Freedom dear,
Listen with a joyful ear.
　　With equal skill, and godlike power,
　　He governed in the fearful hour
Of horrid war: or guides, with ease,
The happier times of honest peace.

　　　　Firm, united, let us be,
　　　　Rallying round our Liberty;
　　　　As a band of brothers joined,
　　　　Peace and safety we shall find.

Behold the chief who now commands,
Once more to serve his country, stands—
　　The rock on which the storm will beat,
　　The rock on which the storm will beat;
But, armed in virtue firm and true,
His hopes are fixed on Heaven and you.
　　When hope was sinking in dismay,
　　And glooms obscured Columbia's day,
　　His steady mind, from changes free,
　　Resolved on death or liberty.

　　　　Firm, united, let us be,
　　　　Rallying round our Liberty;
　　　　As a band of brothers joined,
　　　　Peace and safety we shall find.
　　　　　　　　　　　—*Joseph Hopkinson*

AMERICA

　　My country, 'tis of thee,
　　Sweet land of liberty,
　　　　Of thee I sing;
　　Land where my fathers died,
　　Land of the pilgrims' pride,
　　From every mountain side
　　　　Let freedom ring.

　　My native country, thee,
　　Land of the noble free,—
　　　　Thy name I love;
　　I love thy rocks and rills,

Thy woods and templed hills;
My heart with rapture thrills
　　Like that above.

Let music swell the breeze,
And ring from all the trees,
　　Sweet freedom's song!
Let mortal tongues awake,
Let all that breathe partake,
Let rocks their silence break,—
　　The sound prolong.

Our fathers' God, to Thee,
Author of liberty,
　　To Thee I sing;
Long may our land be bright
With freedom's holy light;
Protect us by thy might,
　　Great God our King.
　　　　—*Samuel Francis Smith*

YANKEE DOODLE

Yankee Doodle went to town
　Riding on a pony,
Stuck a feather in his cap
　And called it "macaroni."

　　Yankee Doodle, keep it up,
　　Yankee Doodle, dandy,
　　Mind the music and the step,
　　And with the girls be handy.

Father and I went down to camp,
　Along with Captain Gooding,
And there we saw the men and boys,
　As thick as hasting pudding.

And there we see a thousand men,
　As rich as 'Squire David;
And what they wasted every day,
　I wish it could be saved.

And there was Captain Washington
  Upon a slapping stallion,
A-giving orders to his men;
  I guess there was a million.

And then the feathers on
  They look'd so very fine, ah!
I wanted peskily to get
  To give to my Jemima.

And there I see a swamping gun,
  Large as a log of maple,
Upon a mighty little cart,
  A load for father's cattle.

And every time they fired it off,
  It took a horn of powder,
It made a noise like father's gun,
  Only a nation louder.

And there I see a little keg,
  Its heads all made of leather,
They knock'd upon'it with little sticks,
  To call the folks together.

And Captain Davis had a gun,
  He kind of clapped his hand on't,
And stuck a crooked stabbing iron
  Upon the little end on't.

The troopers, too, would gallop up
  And fire right in our faces;
It scared me almost half to death
  To see them run such races.

It scared me so, I hooked it off,
  Nor stopped, as I remember,
Nor turned about till I got home,
  Locked up in mother's chamber.
                            —*Anonymous*

THE BATTLE OF THE KEGS

Gallants attend, and hear a friend
  Trill forth harmonious ditty;
Strange things I'll tell, which late befell
  In Philadelphia city.

'Twas early day, as Poets say,
  Just when the sun was rising;
A soldier stood on a log of wood
  And saw a sight surprising.

As in a maze he stood to gaze,
  The truth can't be deny'd, Sir;
He spy'd a score of kegs, or more,
  Come floating down the tide, Sir.

A sailor too, in jerkin blue,
  This strange appearance viewing,
First damn'd his eyes in great surprize,
  Then said—"Some mischief's brewing:

"These kegs now hold the rebels bold
  Pack'd up like pickl'd herring,
And they're come down t'attack the town
  In this new way of ferrying."

The soldier flew, the sailor too,
  And scar'd almost to death, Sir,
Wore out their shoes to spread the news,
  And ran 'til out of breath, Sir.

Now up and down throughout the town
  Most frantic scenes were acted;
And some ran here and others there,
  Like men almost distracted.

Some fire cry'd, which some deny'd,
  But said the earth had quaked;
And girls and boys, with hideous noise,
  Ran thro' the streets half naked.

Sir William he, snug as a flea,
  Lay all this time a snoring;

Nor dreamt of harm, as he lay warm
   In bed with Mrs. *Loring.*

Now in a fright he starts upright,
   Awak'd by such a clatter;
First rubs his eyes, then boldly cries,
   "For God's sake, what's the matter?"

At his bed side he then espy'd
   Sir Erskine at command, Sir;
Upon one foot he had one boot
   And t'other in his hand, Sir.

"Arise, arise," *Sir Erskine* cries,
   "The rebels—more's the pity!
Without a boat, are all afloat
   And rang'd before the city.

"The motley crew, in vessels new,
   With Satan for their guide, Sir,
Pack'd up in bags, and wooden kegs,
   Come driving down the tide, Sir.

"Therefore prepare for bloody war,
   These kegs must be all routed,
Or surely we despis'd shall be,
   And British valour doubted."

The royal band now ready stand,
   All rang'd in dread array, Sir,
On every slip, in every ship,
   For to begin the fray, Sir.

The cannons roar from shore to shore,
   The small arms make a rattle;
Since wars began I'm sure no man
   E'er saw so strange a battle.

The *rebel* dales—the *rebel* vales,
   With *rebel* trees surrounded;
The distant woods, the hills and floods,
   With *rebel* echoes sounded.

The fish below swam to and fro,
   Attack'd from ev'ry quarter;
Why sure, thought they, the De'il's to pay
   'Mong folks above the water.

The kegs, 'tis said, tho' strongly made
   Of *rebel* staves and hoops, Sir,
Could not oppose their pow'rful foes,
   The conqu'ring British troops, Sir.

From morn to night these men of might
   Display'd amazing courage;
And when the sun was fairly down,
   Retir'd to sup their porridge.

One hundred men, with each a pen
   Or more, upon my word, Sir,
It is most true, would be too few
   Their valour to record, Sir.

Such feats did they perform that day
   Against these wicked kegs, Sir,
That years to come, *if they get home,*
   They'll make their boasts and brag, Sir.
               —*Francis Hopkinson*

GOD SAVE THE PLOUGH

See,—how the shining share
Maketh earth's bosom fair,
   Crowning her brow,—
Bread in its furrow springs,
Health and repose it brings,
Treasures unknown to kings,
   God save the plough!

Look to the warrior's blade,
While o'er the tented glade,
   Hate breathes his vow,—
Strife its unsheathing wakes,
Love at its lightning quakes,
Weeping and wo it makes,
   God save the plough!

Ships o'er the deep may ride,
Storms wreck their banner'd pride,
    Waves whelm their prow,
But the well-loaded wain
Garnereth the golden grain,
Gladdening the household train,
    God save the plough!

Who are the truly great?
Minions of pomp and state,
    Where the crowd bow?
Give us hard hands and free,
Culturers of field and tree,
Best friends of liberty—
    God save the plough!
        —*Lydia Huntley Sigourney*

BATTLE-HYMN OF THE REPUBLIC

Mine eyes have seen the glory of the coming of the Lord:
He is trampling out the vintage where the grapes of wrath are
    stored;
He hath loosed the fateful lightning of his terrible swift sword:
    His truth is marching on.

I have seen Him in the watch-fires of a hundred circling camps;
They have builded Him an altar in the evening dews and damps;
I can read His righteous sentence by the dim and flaring lamps.
    His day is marching on.

I have read a fiery gospel, writ in burnished rows of steel:
"As ye deal with my contemners, so with you my grace shall deal;
Let the Hero, born of woman, crush the serpent with his heel,
    Since God is marching on."

He has sounded forth the trumpet that shall never call retreat;
He is sifting out the hearts of men before his judgment-seat:
Oh! be swift, my soul, to answer Him! be jubilant, my feet!
    Our God is marching on.

In the beauty of the lilies Christ was born across the sea,
With a glory in his bosom that transfigures you and me:

As he died to make men holy, let us die to make men free,
While God is marching on.

—Julia Ward Howe

WARREN'S ADDRESS TO
THE AMERICAN SOLDIERS

Stand! the ground's your own, my braves!
Will ye give it up to slaves?
Will ye look for greener graves?
   Hope ye mercy still?
What's the mercy despots feel?
Hear it in that battle peal!
Read it on yon briskling steel!
   Ask it,—ye who will.

Fear ye foes who kill for hire?
Will ye to your homes retire?
Look behind you! they're a-fire!
   And, before you, see
Who have done it!—From the vale
On they come!—And will ye quail?—
Leaden rain and iron hail
   Let their welcome be!

In the God of battles trust!
Die we may,—and die we must;
But, O, where can dust to dust
   Be consigned so well,
As where Heaven its dews shall shed
On the martyred patriot's bed,
And the rocks shall raise their head,
   Of his deeds to tell!

—John Pierpont

ALL QUIET ALONG THE POTOMAC

"All quiet along the Potomac," they say,
  "Except now and then a stray picket
Is shot, as he walks on his beat to and fro,
  By a rifleman hid in the thicket.
'Tis nothing—a private or two now and then

Will not count in the news of the battle;
Not an officer lost—only one of the men,
  Moaning out, all alone, the death rattle."

All quiet along the Potomac to-night,
  Where the soldiers lie peacefully dreaming;
Their tents in the rays of the clear autumn moon,
  Or the light of the watch fire, are gleaming.
A tremulous sigh of the gentle night wind
  Through the forest leaves softly is creeping;
While stars up above, with their glittering eyes,
  Keep guard, for the army is sleeping.

There's only the sound of the lone sentry's tread,
  As he tramps from the rock to the fountain,
And thinks of the two in the low trundle-bed
  Far away in the cot on the mountain
His musket falls slack; his face, dark and grim
  Grows gentle with memories tender,
As he mutters a prayer for the children asleep,
  For their mother; may Heaven defend her!

The moon seems to shine just as brightly as then,
  That night, when the love yet unspoken
Leaped up to his lips—when low-murmured vows
  Were pledged to be ever unbroken.
Then drawing his sleeve roughly over his eyes,
  He dashes off tears that are welling,
And gathers his gun closer up to its place,
  As if to keep down the heart-swelling.

He passes the fountain, the blasted pine tree,
  The footstep is lagging and weary;
Yet onward he goes, through the broad belt of light,
  Toward the shade of the forest so dreary.
Hark! was it the night wind that rustled the leaves?
  Was it moonlight so wondrously flashing?
It looked like a rifle . . . "Ha! Mary, good-by!"
  The red life-blood is ebbing and plashing.

All quiet along the Potomac to-night;
  No sound save the rush of the river;

While soft falls the dew on the face of the dead—
  The picket's off duty forever!
—Ethel Lynn Beers

LITTLE GIFFEN OF TENNESSEE

Out of the focal and foremost fire,
Out of the hospital walls as dire;
Smitten of grape-shot and gangrene,
(Eighteenth battle, and he sixteen!)
Specter! such as you seldom see,
Little Giffen, of Tennessee!

"Take him and welcome!" the surgeons said;
Little the doctor can help the dead!
So we took him; and brought him where
The balm was sweet in the summer air;
And we laid him down on a wholesome bed,—
Utter Lazarus, heel to head!

And we watched the war with abated breath,—
Skeleton Boy against skeleton Death.
Months of torture, how many such?
Weary weeks of the stick and crutch;
And still a glint of the steel-blue eye
Told of a spirit that wouldn't die,

And didn't. Nay, more! in death's despite
The crippled skeleton "learned to write."
"Dear mother," at first, of course; and then
"Dear captain," inquiring about the men.
Captain's answer: "Of eighty-and-five,
Giffen and I are left alive."

Word of gloom from the war, one day;
Johnston pressed at the front, they say.
Little Giffen was up and away;
A tear—his first—as he bade good-by,
Dimmed the glint of his steel-blue eye.
"I'll write, if spared!" There was news of the fight;
But none of Giffen.—He did not write.

I sometimes fancy that, were I king
Of the princely Knights of the Golden Ring,
With the song of the minstrel in mine ear,
And the tender legend that trembles here,
I'd give the best on his bended knee,
The whitest soul of my chivalry,
For "Little Giffen," of Tennessee.
                    —*Francis O. Ticknor*

THE HIGH TIDE AT GETTYSBURG

A cloud possessed the hollow field,
The gathering battle's smoky shield.
Athwart the gloom the lightning flashed,
And through the cloud some horsemen dashed,
And from the heights the thunder pealed.

Then at the brief command of Lee
Moved out that matchless infantry,
With Pickett leading grandly down,
To rush against the roaring crown
Of those dread heights of destiny.

Far heard above the angry guns
A cry across the tumult runs,—
The voice that rang through Shiloh's woods
And Chickamauga's solitudes,
The fierce South cheering on her sons!

Ah, how the withering tempest blew
Against the front of Pettigrew!
A Khamsin wind that scorched and singed
Like that infernal flame that fringed
The British squares at Waterloo!

A thousand fell where Kemper led;
A thousand died where Garnett bled:
In blinding flame and strangling smoke
The remnant through the batteries broke
And crossed the works with Armistead.

"Once more in Glory's van with me!"
Virginia cried to Tennessee;

"We two together, come what may,
Shall stand upon these works to-day!"
(The reddest day in history.)

Brave Tennessee! In reckless way
Virginia heard her comrade say:
"Close round this rent and riddled rag!"
What time she set her battle flag
Amid the guns of Doubleday.

But who shall break the guards that wait
Before the awful face of Fate?
The tattered standards of the South
Were shriveled at the cannon's mouth,
And all her hope were desolate.

In vain the Tennesseean set
His breast against the bayonet!
In vain Virginia charged and raged,
A tigress in her wrath uncaged,
Till all the hill was red and wet!

Above the bayonets, mixed and crossed,
Men saw a gray, gigantic ghost
Receding through the battle cloud,
And heard across the tempest loud
The death cry of a nation lost!

The brave went down! Without disgrace
They leaped to Ruin's red embrace.
They only heard Fame's thunders wake,
And saw the dazzling sunburst break
In smiles on Glory's bloody face!

They fell, who lifted up a hand
And bade the sun in heaven to stand!
They smote and fell, who set the bars
Against the progress of the stars,
And stayed the march of Motherland!

They stood, who saw the future come
On through the fight's delirium!
They smote and stood, who held the hope

Of nations on that slippery slope
Amid the cheers of Christendom.

God lives! He forged the iron will
That clutched and held that trembling hill.
God lives and reigns! He built and lent
The heights for Freedom's battlement
Where floats her flag in triumph still!

Fold up the banners! Smelt the guns!
Love rules. Her gentler purpose runs.
A mighty mother turns in tears
The pages of her battle years,
Lamenting all her fallen sons!
                    —*Will Henry Thompson*

THE BIVOUAC OF THE DEAD

The muffled drum's sad roll has beat
    The soldier's last tattoo;
No more on Life's parade shall meet
    That brave and fallen few.
On Fame's eternal camping-ground
    Their silent tents are spread,
And Glory guards, with solemn round,
    The bivouac of the dead.

No rumor of the foe's advance
    Now swells upon the wind;
No troubled thought at midnight haunts
    Of loved ones left behind;
No vision of the morrow's strife
    The warrior's dream alarms;
No braying horn nor screaming fife
    At dawn shall call to arms.

Their shivered swords are red with rust,
    Their plumëd heads are bowed;
Their haughty banner, trailed in dust,
    Is now their martial shroud.
And plenteous funeral tears have washed
    The red stains from each brow,

And the proud forms, by battle gashed,
  Are free from anguish now.

The neighing troop, the flashing blade,
  The bugle's stirring blast,
The charge, the dreadful cannonade,
  The din and shout, are past;
Nor war's wild note nor glory's peal
  Shall thrill with fierce delight
Those breasts that nevermore may feel
  The rapture of the fight.

Like the fierce northern hurricane
  That sweeps his great plateau,
Flushed with the triumph yet to gain,
  Came down the serried foe.
Who heard the thunder of the fray
  Break o'er the field beneath,
Knew well the watchword of that day
  Was "Victory or Death."

Long had the doubtful conflict raged
  O'er all that stricken plain,
For never fiercer fight had waged
  The vengeful blood of Spain;
And still the storm of battle blew,
  Still swelled the gory tide;
Not long, our stout old chieftain knew,
  Such odds his strength could bide.

'Twas in that hour his stern command
  Called to a martyr's grave
The flower of his beloved land,
  The nation's flag to save.
By rivers of their father's gore
  His first-born laurels grew,
And well he deemed the sons would pour
  Their lives for glory too.

Full many a norther's breath has swept
  O'er Angostura's plain,
And long the pitying sky has wept
  Above its mouldered slain.
The raven's scream, or eagle's flight

Or shepherd's pensive lay,
Alone awakes each sullen height
    That frowned o'er that dread fray.

Sons of the Dark and Bloody Ground,
    Ye must not slumber there,
Where stranger steps and tongues resound
    Along the heedless air.
Your own proud land's heroic soil
    Shall be your fitter grave:
She claims from war his richest spoil—
    The ashes of her brave.

Thus 'neath their parent turf they rest,
    Far from the gory field,
Borne to a Spartan mother's breast
    On many a bloody shield;
The sunshine of their native sky
    Smiles sadly on them here,
And kindred eyes and hearts watch by
    The heroes' sepulcher.

Rest on, embalmed and sainted dead!
    Dear as the blood ye gave;
No impious footstep here shall tread
    The herbage of your grave;
Nor shall your glory be forgot
    While Fame her record keeps,
Or Honor points the hallowed spot
    Where Valor proudly sleeps.

Yon marble minstrel's voiceless stone
    In deathless song shall tell,
When many a vanished age hath flown,
    The story how ye fell;
Nor wreck, nor change, nor winter's blight,
    Nor time's remorseless doom,
Shall dim one ray of glory's light
    That gilds your deathless tomb.
                                    —*Theodore O'Hara*

THE FIGHTING RACE

"Read out the names!" and Burke sat back,
  And Kelly drooped his head,
While Shea—they call him Scholar Jack—
  Went down the list of the dead.
Officers, seamen, gunners, marines,
  The crews of the gig and yawl,
The bearded man and the lad in his teens,
  Carpenters, coal-passers—all.
Then, knocking the ashes from out his pipe,
  Said Burke in an offhand way:
"We're all in that dead man's list, by Cripe!
  Kelly and Burke and Shea."
"Well, here's to the Maine, and I'm sorry for Spain,"
  Said Kelly and Burke and Shea.

"Wherever there's Kellys there's trouble," said Burke,
  "Wherever fighting's the game,
Or a spice of danger in grown man's work,"
  Said Kelly, "you'll find my name."
"And do we fall short," said Burke, getting mad,
  "When it's touch and go for life?"
Said Shea, "It's thirty-odd years, bedad,
  Since I charged to drum and fife
Up Marye's Heights, and my old canteen
  Stopped a rebel ball on its way.
There were blossoms of blood on our sprigs of green—
  Kelly and Burke and Shea—
And the dead didn't brag." "Well, here's to the flag!"
  Said Kelly and Burke and Shea.

"I wish 'twas in Ireland, for there's the place,"
  Said Burke, "that we'd die by right,
In the cradle of our soldier race,
  After one good standup fight.
My grandfather fell on Vinegar Hill,
  And fighting was not his trade;
But his rusty pike's in the cabin still,
  With Hessian blood on the blade."
"Aye, aye," said Kelly, "the pikes were great
  When the word was 'clear the way!'
We were thick on the roll in ninety-eight—
  Kelly and Burke and Shea."

"Well, here's to the pike and the sword and the like!"
   Said Kelly and Burke and Shea.

And Shea, the scholar, with rising joy,
   Said, "We were at Ramillies.
We left our bones at Fontenoy
   And up in the Pyrenees.
Before Dunkirk, on Landen's plain,
   Cremona, Lille and Ghent,
We're all over Austria, France and Spain,
   Wherever they pitched a tent.
We've died for England from Waterloo
   To Egypt and Dargai;
And still there's enough for a corps or a crew,
   Kelly and Burke and Shea."
"Well, here's to good honest fighting blood!"
   Said Kelly and Burke and Shea.

"Oh, the fighting races don't die out,
   If they seldom die in bed,
For love is first in their hearts, no doubt,"
   Said Burke; then Kelly said:
"When Michael, the Irish Archangel, stands,
   The angel with the sword,
And the battle dead from a hundred lands
   Are ranged in one big horde,
Our line, that for Gabriel's trumpet waits,
   Will stretch three deep that day,
From Jehoshaphat to the Golden Gates—
   Kelly and Burke and Shea."
"Well, here's thank God for the race and the sod!"
   Said Kelly and Burke and Shea.

                    —*Joseph I. C. Clarke*

MONTEREY

We were not many—we who stood
   Before the iron sleet that day—
Yet many a gallant spirit would
Give half his years if he then could
   Have been with us at Monterey.

Now here, now there, the shot, it hailed
  In deadly drifts of fiery spray,
Yet not a single soldier quailed
When wounded comrades round them wailed
  Their dying shout at Monterey.

And on—still on our column kept
  Through walls of flame its withering way;
Where fell the dead, the living stept,
Still charging on the guns which swept
  The slippery streets of Monterey.

The foe himself recoiled aghast,
  When, striking where he strongest lay,
We swooped his flanking batteries past,
And braving full their murderous blast,
  Stormed home the towers of Monterey.

Our banners on those turrets wave,
  And there our evening bugles play;
Where orange boughs above their grave
Keep green the memory of the brave
  Who fought and fell at Monterey.

We are not many—we who pressed
  Beside the brave who fell that day;
But who of us has not confessed
He'd rather share their warrior rest,
  Than not have been at Monterey?
            —*Charles Fenno Hoffman*

MY MARYLAND

The despot's heel is on thy shore,
        Maryland!
His torch is at thy temple door,
        Maryland!
Avenge the patriotic gore
That flecked the streets of Baltimore,
And be the battle-queen of yore,
        Maryland! my Maryland!

Hark to an exiled son's appeal,
    Maryland!
My Mother State, to thee I kneel,
    Maryland!
For life and death, for woe and weal,
Thy peerless chivalry reveal,
And gird thy beauteous limbs with steel,
    Maryland! my Maryland!

Thou wilt not cower in the dust,
    Maryland!
Thy beaming sword shall never rust,
    Maryland!
Remember Carroll's sacred trust,
Remember Howard's warlike thrust,
And all thy slumberers with the just,
    Maryland! my Maryland!

Come! for thy shield is bright and strong,
    Maryland!
Come! for thy dalliance does thee wrong,
    Maryland!
Come to thine own heroic throng
Stalking with Liberty along,
And chant thy dauntless slogan-song,
    Maryland! my Maryland!

I see the blush upon thy cheek,
    Maryland!
For thou wast ever bravely meek,
    Maryland!
But lo! there surges forth a shriek,
From hill to hill, from creek to creek,
Potomac calls to Chesapeake,
    Maryland, my Maryland!

Thou wilt not yield the Vandal toll,
    Maryland!
Thou wilt not crook to his control,
    Maryland!
Better the fire upon thee roll,
Better the shot, the blade, the bowl,
Than crucifixion of the soul,
    Maryland! my Maryland!

I hear the distant thunder-hum,
 Maryland!
The old Line's bugle, fife and drum,
 Maryland!
She is not dead, nor deaf, nor dumb;
Huzza! she spurns the Northern scum!
She breathes! She burns! She'll come!
 She'll come!
 Maryland, my Maryland!
 —*James Ryder Randall*

THE BLUE AND THE GRAY

By the flow of the inland river,
 Whence the fleets of iron have fled,
Where the blades of the grave-grass quiver,
 Asleep are the ranks of the dead:—
 Under the sod and the dew,
 Waiting the Judgment Day:—
 Under the one, the Blue;
 Under the other, the Gray.

These in the robings of glory,
 Those in the gloom of defeat,
All with the battle-blood gory,
 In the dusk of eternity meet:
 Under the sod and the dew,
 Waiting the Judgment Day:—
 Under the laurel, the Blue;
 Under the willow, the Gray.

From the silence of sorrowful hours
 The desolate mourners go,
Lovingly laden with flowers,
 Alike for the friend and the foe:—
 Under the sod and the dew,
 Waiting the Judgment Day:—
 Under the roses, the Blue;
 Under the lilies, the Gray.

So, with an equal splendor
 The morning sun-rays fall,
With a touch impartially tender,

On the blossoms blooming for all:—
    Under the sod and the dew,
        Waiting the Judgment Day:—
    Broidered with gold, the Blue;
        Mellowed with gold, the Gray.

So, when the summer calleth,
    On forest and field of grain,
With an equal murmur falleth
    The cooling drip of the rain:—
        Under the sod and the dew,
            Waiting the Judgment Day:—
        Wet with the rain, the Blue;
            Wet with the rain, the Gray.

Sadly, but not with upbraiding,
    The generous deed was done.
In the storms of the years that are fading
    No braver battle was won:
        Under the sod and the dew,
            Waiting the Judgment Day:—
        Under the blossoms, the Blue;
            Under the garlands, the Gray.

No more shall the war-cry sever,
    Or the winding rivers be red:
They banish our anger forever
    When they laurel the graves of our dead!
        Under the sod and the dew,
            Waiting the Judgment Day:—
        Love and tears for the Blue;
            Tears and love for the Gray.
                    —*Francis Miles Finch*

THE CONQUERED BANNER

Furl that Banner, for 'tis weary;
Round its staff 'tis drooping dreary:
    Furl it, fold it,—it is best;
For there's not a man to wave it,
And there's not a sword to save it,
And there's not one left to lave it
In the blood which heroes gave it,

And its foes now scorn and brave it:
    Furl it, hide it,—let it rest!

Take that Banner down! 'tis tattered;
Broken is its staff and shattered;
And the valiant hosts are scattered,
    Over whom it floated high.
Oh, 'tis hard for us to fold it,
Hard to think there's none to hold it,
Hard that those who once unrolled it
    Now must furl it with a sigh!

Furl that Banner—furl it sadly!
Once ten thousands hailed it gladly,
And ten thousands wildly, madly,
    Swore it should forever wave;
Swore that foeman's sword should never
Hearts like theirs entwined dissever,
Till that flag should float forever
    O'er their freedom or their grave!

Furl it! for the hands that grasped it,
And the hearts that fondly clasped it,
    Cold and dead are lying low;
And that Banner—it is trailing,
While around it sounds the wailing
    Of its people in their woe.

For, though conquered, they adore it,—
Love the cold, dead hands that bore it,
    Weep for those who fell before it,
Pardon those who trailed and tore it;
And oh, wildly they deplore it,
    Now to furl and fold it so!

Furl that Banner! True, 'tis gory,
Yet 'tis wreathed around with glory,
And 'twill live in song and story
    Though its folds are in the dust!
For its fame on brightest pages,
Penned by poets and by sages,
Shall go sounding down the ages—
    Furl its folds though now we must.

Furl that Banner, softly, slowly!
Treat it gently—it is holy,
    For it droops above the dead.
Touch it not—unfold it never;
Let it droop there, furled forever,—
    For its people's hopes are fled!
              —*Abram J. Ryan*

TIPPECANOE AND TYLER TOO

Oh! what has caused this great commotion,
Our country through?
It is the ball that's rolling on,
For Tippecanoe and Tyler too,

> *For Tippecanoe and Tyler too,*
> *And with them, we'll beat little Van,*
> *Van, Van, Van, oh! he's a used up man!*
> *And with them we'll beat little Van.*

Like the working of mighty waters,
On it will go;
And in its course will clear the way
For Tippecanoe and Tyler too,

The Bay State boys turned out in thousands,
Not long ago,
And at Bunker Hill, they set their seals
For Tippecanoe and Tyler too, etc.

Now you hear the Van-jacks talking,
Things look quite blue,
For all the world seems turning round
For Tippecanoe and Tyler too, etc.

Let them talk about hard cider,
And Log Cabins too,
It will only help to speed the ball,
For Tippecanoe and Tyler too, etc.

His latch-string hangs outside the door,
And never is pulled in,

For it always was the custom of
Old Tippecanoe and Tyler too, etc.

See the spoilsmen and leg treasurers,
All in a stew,
For well they know they stand no chance
With Tippecanoe and Tyler too, etc.

Little Marty's days are numbered,
And out he must go,
For in his place we'll put the good
Old Tippecanoe and Tyler too, etc.
—*Alexander Coffman Ross*

BONNIE BLUE FLAG

We are a band of brothers, and native to the soil,
Fighting for the property we gained by honest toil;
And when our rights were threatened, the cry rose near and far,
Hurrah! for the Bonnie Blue Flag that bears a single star.

Hurrah! hurrah! for Southern rights hurrah!
Hurrah for the Bonnie Blue Flag that bears a single star.

First, gallant South Carolina so nobly made the stand,
Then came Alabama, who took her by the hand;
Next quickly Mississippi, Georgia and Florida,
All raised on high the Bonnie Blue Flag that bears a single star.

And here's to brave Virginia! the old Dominion State
That with the young Confederacy at length has linked her fate;
Impelled by her example, now other states prepare
To hoist on high the Bonnie Blue Flag that bears a single star.

Then here's to our Confederacy, for strong we are and brave,
Like patriots of old, we'll fight our heritage to save;
And rather than submit to shame, to die we would prefer,
So cheer for the Bonnie Blue Flag that bears a single star.
—*Harry McCarthy*

DIXIE

I wish I was in de land ob cotton,
Old times dar am not forgotten,
Look away! Look away! Look away! Dixie Land.
In Dixie Land whar I was born in
Early on one frosty mornin',
Look away! Look away! Look away! Dixie Land.

Den I wish I was in Dixie, Hooray! Hooray!
In Dixie Land I'll take my stand,
To lib and die in Dixie!
Away, away, away down South in Dixie!
Away, away, away down South in Dixie!

Old Missus marry Will de Weaber,
Willium was a gay deceaber,
Look away! Look away! Look away! Dixie Land.
But when he put his arm around 'er,
He smiled as fierce as a forty-pounder,
Look away! Look away! Look away! Dixie Land.

His face was sharp as a butcher's cleaber,
But dat did not seem to greab 'er,
Look away! Look away! Look away! Dixie Land.
Old Missus acted the foolish part,
And died for a man dat broke her heart,
Look away! Look away! Look away! Dixie Land.

Now here's a health to the next old Missus,
And all de gals dat want to kiss us,
Look away! Look away! Look away! Dixie Land.
But if you want to drive 'way sorrow,
Come and hear dis song tomorrow,
Look away! Look away! Look away! Dixie Land.

Dar's buckwheat cakes an' Ingen batter
Makes you fat or a little fatter,
Look away! Look away! Look away! Dixie Land.
Den hoe it down an' scratch your grabble,
To Dixie's land I'm bound to trabble,
Look away! Look away! Look away! Dixie Land.
—*Daniel Emmett*

THE BATTLE-CRY OF FREEDOM

Yes, we'll rally round the flag, boys, we'll rally once again,
Shouting the battle-cry of Freedom;
We will rally from the hillside, we'll gather from the plain,
Shouting the battle-cry of Freedom.

The Union forever, Hurrah! boys, Hurrah!
Down with the traitor,
Up with the stars;
While we rally round the flag, boys,
Rally once again,
Shouting the battle-cry of freedom.

We are springing to the call of our brothers gone before,
Shouting the battle-cry of Freedom;
And we'll fill the vacant ranks with a million free men more,
Shouting the battle-cry of Freedom.

—*George F. Root*

America's Heartbeat: Home and Sentiment

THE HOUSE BY THE SIDE OF THE ROAD

There are hermit souls that live withdrawn
    In the place of their self-content,
There are souls like stars, that dwell apart,
    In a fellowless firmament;
There are pioneer souls that blaze their paths
    Where highways never ran—
But let me live by the side of the road
    And be a friend to man.

Let me live in a house by the side of the road
    Where the race of men go by—
The men who are good and the men who are bad,
    As good and as bad as I.
I would not sit in the scorner's seat
    Nor hurl the cynic's ban—
Let me live in a house by the side of the road
    And be a friend to man.

I see from my house by the side of the road,
    By the side of the highway of life,
The men who press with the ardor of hope,
    The men who are faint with the strife,
But I turn not away from their smiles nor their tears,
    Both parts of an infinite plan—
Let me live in a house by the side of the road
    And be a friend to man.

I know there are brook-gladdened meadows ahead,
    And mountains of wearisome height;
That the road passes on through the long afternoon
    And stretches away to the night.
And still I rejoice when the travellers rejoice
    And weep with the strangers that moan,

Nor live in my house by the side of the road
   Like a man who dwells alone.

Let me live in my house by the side of the road,
   Where the race of men go by—
They are good, they are bad, they are weak, they are
    strong,
   Wise, foolish—so am I.
Then why should I sit in the scorner's seat,
   Or hurl the cynic's ban?
Let me live in my house by the side of the road
   And be a friend to man.

—Sam Walter Foss

WHEN THE GREAT GRAY SHIPS COME IN

New York Harbor, August 20, 1898

To eastward ringing, to westward winging, o'er mapless miles of
   sea,
On winds and tides the gospel rides that the furthermost isles are
   free,
And the furthermost isles make answer, harbor, and height, and hill,
Breaker and beach cry each to each, " 'Tis the Mother who calls! Be
   still!"
Mother! new-found, beloved, and strong to hold from harm,
Stretching to these across the seas the shield of her sovereign arm,
Who summoned the guns of her sailor sons, who bade her navies
   roam,
Who calls again to the leagues of main, and who calls them this time
   home!

And the great gray ships are silent, and the weary watchers rest,
The black cloud dies in the August skies, and deep in the golden
   west
Invisible hands are limning a glory of crimson bars,
And far above is the wonder of a myriad wakened stars!
Peace! As the tidings silence the strenuous cannonade,
Peace at last! Is the bugle blast the length of the long blockade,
And eyes of vigil weary are lit with the glad release,
From ship to ship and from lip to lip it is "Peace! Thank God for
   peace."

Ah, in the sweet hereafter Columbia still shall show
The sons of these who swept the seas how she bade them rise and
    go,—
How, when the stirring summons smote on her children's ear,
South and North at the call stood forth, and the whole land an-
    swered, "Here!"
For the soul of the soldier's story and the heart of the sailor's song
Are all of those who meet their foes as right should meet with
    wrong,
Who fight their guns till the foeman runs, and then, on the decks
    they trod,
Brave faces raise, and give the praise to the grace of their country's
    God!

Yes, it is good to battle, and good to be strong and free,
To carry the hearts of the people to the uttermost ends of sea,
To see the day steal up the bay where the enemy lies in wait,
To run your ship to the harbor's lip and sink her across the strait:—
But better the golden evening when the ships round heads for home,
And the long gray miles slip swiftly past in a swirl of seething foam,
And the people wait at the haven's gate to greet the men who win!
Thank God for peace! Thank God for peace, when the great gray
    ships come in!

—Guy Wetmore Carryl

MY OLD KENTUCKY HOME, GOOD NIGHT

The sun shines bright in the old Kentucky home;
    'Tis summer, the darkies are gay;
The corn-top's ripe, and the meadow's in the bloom,
    While the birds make music all the day.
The young folks roll on the little cabin floor,
    All merry, all happy and bright;
By-'n'-by hard times comes a-knocking at the door:—
    Then my old Kentucky home, good night!
      Weep no more, my lady,
      O, weep no more to-day!
We will sing one song for the old Kentucky home,
    For the old Kentucky home, far away.

They hunt no more for the possum and the coon,
    On the meadow, the hill, and the shore;

They sing no more by the glimmer of the moon,
   On the bench by the old cabin door.
The day goes by like a shadow o'er the heart,
   With sorrow, where all was delight;
The time has come when the darkies have to part:—
   Then my old Kentucky home, good night!

The head must bow, and the back will have to bend,
   Wherever the darky may go;
A few more days, and the trouble all will end,
   In the field where the sugar canes grow.
A few more days for to tote the weary load,
   No matter, 'twill never be light;
A few more days till we totter on the road:—
   Then my old Kentucky home, good night!
      Weep no more, my lady,
      O, weep no more to-day!
   We will sing one song for the old Kentucky home,
      For the old Kentucky home, far away.
                    —*Stephen Collins Foster*

HOME, SWEET HOME

'Mid pleasures and palaces though we may roam,
Be it ever so humble, there's no place like home!
A charm from the skies seems to hallow us there,
Which, seek through the world, is ne'er met with elsewhere.
      Home, home, sweet, sweet home!
      There's no place like home!

An exile from home, splendor dazzles in vain!
Oh, give me my lowly thatched cottage again!
The birds singing gayly that came at my call:—
Oh, give me sweet peace of mind, dearer than all!
      Home, home, sweet, sweet home!
      There's no place like home!

To thee I'll return, overburdened with care;
The heart's dearest solace will smile on me there;
No more from the cottage again will I roam;
Be it ever so humble, there's no place like home.

Home! Home! sweet, sweet Home!
There's no place like Home! there's no place like Home!
—*John Howard Payne*

SIX O'CLOCK

Now burst above the city's cold twilight
The piercing whistles and the tower-clocks:
For day is done. Along the frozen docks
The workmen set their ragged shirts aright.
Thro' factory doors a stream of dingy light
Follows the scrimmage as it quickly flocks
To hut and home among the snow's gray blocks.—
I love you, human labourers. Good-night!
Good-night to all the blackened arms that ache!
Good-night to every sick and sweated brow,
To the poor girl that strength and love forsake,
To the poor boy who can no more! I vow
The victim soon shall shudder at the stake
And fall in blood: we bring him even now.
—*Trumbull Stickney*

OLD FOLKS AT HOME

'Way down upon de Swanee ribber,
Far, far away,
Dere's where my heart is turning ebber,
Dere's where de old folks stay.
All up and down de whole creation,
Sadly I roam,
Still longing for de old plantation,
And for de old folks at home.

> *All de world am sad and dreary,*
> *Ebry where I roam,*
> *Oh! Darkies how my heart grows weary,*
> *Far from de old folks at home.*

All round de little farm I wandered
When I was young,
Den many happy days I squandered,
Many de songs I sung.

When I was playing wid my brudder
Happy was I.
Oh! Take me to my kind old mudder,
Dere let me live and die.

One little hut among de bushes,
One dat I love,
Still sadly to my memory rushes,
No matter where I rove.
When will I see de bees a humming
All round de comb?
When will I hear de banjo tumming
Down in my good old home?
—*Stephen Collins Foster*

THE OLD OAKEN BUCKET

How dear to this heart are the scenes of my childhood,
   When fond recollection presents them to view!
The orchard, the meadow, the deep-tangled wild wood,
   And every loved spot which my infancy knew!
The wide-spreading pond, and the mill that stood by it,
   The bridge, and the rock where the cataract fell,
The cot of my father, the dairy house nigh it,
   And e'en the rude bucket that hung in the well—
The old oaken bucket, the iron-bound bucket,
The moss-covered bucket which hung in the well.

That moss-covered vessel I hailed as a treasure,
   For often at noon, when returned from the field,
I found it the source of an exquisite pleasure,
   The purest and sweetest that nature can yield.
How ardent I seized it, with hands that were glowing,
   And quick to the white-pebbled bottom it fell;
Then soon, with the emblem of truth overflowing,
   And dripping with coolness, it rose from the well—
The old oaken bucket, the iron-bound bucket,
The moss-covered bucket arose from the well.

How sweet from the green mossy brim to receive it,
   As poised on the curb it inclined to my lips!
Not a full blushing goblet could tempt me to leave it,
   The brightest that beauty or revelry sips.

And now, far removed from the loved habitation,
   The tear of regret will intrusively swell,
As fancy reverts to my father's plantation,
   And sighs for the bucket that hangs in the well—
The old oaken bucket, the iron-bound bucket,
The moss-covered bucket that hangs in the well!
                —*Samuel Woodworth*

Humor and Parodies

HOW A GIRL WAS TOO RECKLESS OF GRAMMAR

Matilda Maud Mackenzie frankly hadn't any chin,
Her hands were rough, her feet she turned invariably in;
   Her general form was German,
     By which I mean that you
   Her waist could not determine
     Within a foot or two.
And not only did she stammer,
But she used the kind of grammar
   That is called, for sake of euphony, askew.

From what I say about her, don't imagine I desire
A prejudice against this worthy creature to inspire.
   She was willing, she was active,
     She was sober, she was kind,
   But she *never* looked attractive
     And she *hadn't* any mind.
I knew her more than slightly,
And I treated her politely
   When I met her, but of course I wasn't blind!

Matilda Maud Mackenzie had a habit that was droll,
She spent her morning seated on a rock or on a knoll,
   And threw with much composure
     A smallish rubber ball
   At an inoffensive osier
     By a little waterfall;
But Matilda's way of throwing
Was like other people's mowing,
   And she never hit the willow-tree at all!

One day as Miss Mackenzie with uncommon ardour tried
To hit the mark, the missile flew exceptionally wide,
   And, before her eyes astounded,

On a fallen maple's trunk
Ricochetted and rebounded
In the rivulet, and sunk!
Matilda, greatly frightened,
In her grammar unenlightened,
Remarked, "Well now I ast yer, who'd 'er thunk?"

But what a marvel followed! From the pool at once there rose
A frog, the sphere of rubber balanced deftly on his nose.
He beheld her fright and frenzy
And, her panic to dispel,
On his knee by Miss Mackenzie
He obsequiously fell.
With quite as much decorum
As a speaker in a forum
He started in his history to tell.

"Fair maid," he said, "I beg you do not hesitate or wince,
If you'll promise that you'll wed me, I'll at once become a
    prince;
For a fairy, old and vicious,
An enchantment round me spun!"
Then he looked up, unsuspicious,
And he saw what he had won,
And in terms of sad reproach, he
Made some comments, *sotto voce,*
(Which the publishers have bidden me to shun!)

Matilda Maud Mackenzie said, as if she meant to scold;
"I *never!* Why, you forward thing! Now, ain't you awful
    bold!"
Just a glance he paused to give her,
And his head was seen to clutch,
Then he darted to the river,
And he dived to beat the Dutch!
While the wrathful maiden panted
"I don't think he was enchanted!"
(And he really didn't look it overmuch!)

The Moral

In one's language one conservative should be;
Speech is silver and it never should be free!
—*Guy Wetmore Carryl*

BALLAD OF THE CANAL

We were crowded in the cabin,
   Not a soul had room to sleep;
It was midnight on the waters,
   And the banks were very steep.

'Tis a fearful thing when sleeping
   To be startled by the shock,
And to hear the rattling trumpet
   Thunder, "Coming to a lock!"

So we shuddered there in silence,
   For the stoutest berth was shook,
While the wooden gates were opened
   And the mate talked with the cook.

And as thus we lay in darkness,
   Each one wishing we were there,
"We are through!" the captain shouted,
   And he sat down on a chair.

And his little daughter whispered,
   Thinking that he ought to know,
"Isn't travelling by canal-boats
   Just as safe as it is slow?"

Then he kissed the little maiden,
   And with better cheer we spoke,
And we trotted into Pittsburg,
   When the morn looked through the smoke.
                 —*Phoebe Cary*

THE IDEAL HUSBAND TO HIS WIFE

We've lived for forty years, dear wife,
   And walked together side by side,
And you to-day are just as dear
   As when you were my bride.
I've tried to make life glad for you,
   One long, sweet honeymoon of joy,
A dream of marital content,
   Without the least alloy.

I've smoothed all boulders from our path,
    That we in peace might toil along,
By always hastening to admit
    That I was right and you were wrong.

No mad diversity of creed
    Has ever sundered me from thee;
For I permit you evermore
    To borrow your ideas of me.
And thus it is, through weal or woe,
    Our love forevermore endures;
For I permit that you should take
    My views and creeds, and make them yours.
And thus I let you have my way,
    And thus in peace we toil along,
For I am willing to admit
    That I am right and you are wrong.

And when our matrimonial skiff
    Strikes snags in love's meandering stream,
I lift our shallop from the rocks,
    And float as in a placid dream.
And well I know our marriage bliss
    While life shall last will never cease;
For I shall always let thee do,
    In generous love, just what I please.
Peace comes, and discord flies away,
    Love's bright day follows hatred's night;
For I am ready to admit
    That you are wrong and I am right.
                              —*Sam Walter Foss*

THE AHKOOND OF SWAT

"The Ahkoond of Swat is dead."
London Papers of Jan. 22, 1878

What, what, what,
        What's the news from Swat?
        Sad news,
        Bad news,
Comes by the cable led
Through the Indian Ocean's bed,

Through the Persian Gulf, the Red
Sea and the Med-
Iterranean—he's dead;
The Ahkoond is dead!

For the Ahkoond I mourn,
    Who wouldn't?
He strove to disregard the message stern,
    But he Ahkoodn't.
Dead, dead, dead:
    (Sorrow, Swats!)
Swats wha hae wi' Ahkoond bled,
Swats whom he hath often led
Onward to a gory bed,
    Or to victory,
      As the case might be.
        Sorrow, Swats!
Tears shed,
    Shed tears like water.
Your great Ahkoond is dead!
    That Swats the matter!

Mourn, city of Swat,
Your great Ahkoond is not,
But laid 'mid worms to rot.
His mortal part alone, his soul was caught
    (Because he was a good Ahkoond)
    Up to the bosom of Mahound.
Though earthly walls his frame surround
(Forever hallowed by the ground!)

And skeptics mock the lowly mound
And say "He's now of no Ahkoond!"
    His soul is in the skies—
The azure skies that bend above his loved
    Metropolis of Swat.
  He sees with larger, other eyes,
  Athwart all earthly mysteries—
    He knows what's Swat.

Let Swat bury the great Ahkoond
    With a noise of mourning and of lamentation!
Let Swat bury the great Ahkoond

With the noise of the mourning of the Swattish nation!
Fallen is at length
Its tower of strength;
Its sun is dimmed ere it had nooned;
Dead lies the great Ahkoond,
The great Ahkoond of Swat
Is not!

—George Thomas Lanigan

CLEMENTINE

In a cavern in a canyon, excavating for a mine,
Dwelt a miner, forty-niner, and his daughter, Clementine.

Oh, my darling, oh, my darling, oh, my darling Clementine,
You are lost and gone forever, dreadful sorry, Clementine.

Light she was and like a fairy, and her shoes were number nine,
Herring boxes without topses, sandals were for Clementine.

Drove her ducklings to the water, every morning just at nine,
Hit her foot against a splinter, fell into the foaming brine.

Ruby lips above the water, blowing bubbles soft and fine,
Alas, for me! I was no swimmer, so I lost my Clementine.

In a churchyard, near the canyon, where the myrtle doth entwine,
There grow roses and other posies fertilized by Clementine.

Then the miner, forty-niner, soon began to droop and pine,
Thought he ought to join his daughter, now he's with his Clem-
entine.

In my dreams she still doth haunt me, robed in garments soaked in
brine,
Though in life I used to kiss her, now she's dead, I draw the line.

—Anonymous

THE ZEALLESS XYLOGRAPHER

Dedicated to the End of the Dictionary

A xylographer started to cross the sea
  By means of a Xanthic Xebec;
But, alas! he sighed for the Zuyder Zee,
  And feared he was in for a wreck.
He tried to smile, but all in vain,
  Because of a Zygomatic pain;
And as for singing, his cheeriest tone
  Reminded him of a Xylophone—
Or else, when the pain would sharper grow,
  His notes were as keen as a Zuffolo.
And so it is likely he did not find
  On board Xenodochy to his mind.
The fare was poor, and he was sure
  Xerofphagy he could not endure;
Zoöphagous surely he was, I aver,
  This dainty and starving Xylographer.
Xylophagous truly he could not be—
  No sickly vegetarian he!
He'd have blubbered like any old Zeuglodon
  Had Xerophthalmia not come on.
And the end of it was he never again
  In a Xanthic Xebec went sailing the main.
                    —*Mary Mapes Dodge*

HANS BREITMANN'S PARTY

Hans Breitmann gife a barty;
  Dey had biano-blayin':
I felled in lofe mit a Merican frau,
  Her name was Madilda Yane.
She hat haar as prown ash a pretzel,
  Her eyes vas himmel-plue,
Und ven dey looket indo mine,
  Dey shplit mine heart in two.

Hans Breitmann gife a barty:
  I vent dere, you'll pe pound.
I valtzet mit Madilda Yane
  Und vent shpinnen round und round.

De pootiest Fräulein in de house,
　She vayed 'pout dwo hoondred pound,
Und efery dime she gife a shoomp
　She make de vindows sound.

Hans Breitmann gife a barty:
　I dells you it cost him dear.
Dey rolled in more ash sefen kecks
　Of foost-rate Lager Beer,
Und venefer dey knocks de shpicket in
　De Deutschers gifes a cheer.
I dinks dat so vine a barty
　Nefer coon to a het dis year.

Hans Breitmann gife a barty:
　Dere all vas Souse und Brouse;
Ven de sopper comed in, de gompany
　Did make demselfs to house.
Dey ate das Brot und Gensy broost,
　De Bratwurst und Braten fine,
Und vash der Abendessen down
　Mit four parrels of Neckarwein.

Hans Breitmann gife a barty.
　We all cot troonk ash bigs.
I poot mine mout to a parrel of bier,
　Und emptied it oop mit a schwigs.
Und denn I gissed Madilda Yane
　Und she shlog me on de kop,
Und de gompany fited mit daple-lecks
　Dill be coonshtable made oos shtop.

Hans Breitmann gife a barty—
　Where ish dat barty now!
Where ish de lofely golden cloud
　Dat float on de moundain's prow?
Where ish de himmelstrahlende Stern—
　De shtar of de shpirit's light?
All goned afay mit de Lager Beer—
　Afay in de Ewigkeit!
　　　　　—Charles Godfrey Leland

THE FOUR NIGHTS' DRUNK

The first night when I come home, drunk as I could be,
I found this horse in the stable, where my horse ought to be.
   "Come here, little wifey! Explain yourself to me:
   Why is there a horse in the stable, where my horse ought to be?"
   "Why, you durn fool, you blame fool, can't you plainly see?
   It's only a milk cow my momma give to me."
Now, I been living in this here world forty years and more,
And I never seen a milk cow with a saddle on before.

The second night when I come home, drunk as I could be,
I found a coat in the closet, where my coat ought to be.
   "Come here, little wifey! Explain yourself to me:
   Why is there a coat in the closet, where my coat ought to be?"
   "Why, you durn fool, you blame fool, can't you plainly see?
   It's only a coverlet my momma give to me."
Now, I been living in this here world forty years and more,
And I never seen a coverlet with buttons on before.

The third night when I come home, drunk as I could be,
I found a hat hanging on the rack, where my hat ought to be.
   "Come here, little wifey! Explain yourself to me:
   Why is there a hat hanging on the rack, where my hat ought to
     be?"
   "Why, you durn fool, you blame fool, can't you plainly see?
   It's only a chamberpot my momma give to me."
Now, I been living in this here world forty years and more,
And I never seen a J. B. Stetson chamberpot before.

The fourth night when I come home, drunk as I could be,
I found a head lying on the bed, where my head ought to be.
   "Come here, little wifey! Explain yourself to me:
   Why is there a head lying on the bed, where my head ought to
     be?"
   "Why, you durn fool, you blame fool, can't you plainly see?
   It's only a cabbage head my momma give to me."
Now, I been living in this here world forty years and more,
And I never seen a cabbage head with a mustache on before.

—Anonymous

THE CONSTANT CANNIBAL MAIDEN

Far, oh, far is the Mango island,
    Far, oh, far is the tropical sea—
Palms a-slant and the hills a-smile, and
    A cannibal maiden a-waiting for me.

I've been deceived by a damsel Spanish,
    And Indian maidens both red and brown,
A black-eyed Turk and a blue-eyed Danish,
    And a Puritan lassie of Salem town.

For the Puritan Prue she sets in the offing,
    A-castin' 'er eyes at a tall marine,
And the Spanish minx is the wust at scoffing
    Of all of the wimmin I ever seen.

But the cannibal maid is a simple creetur,
    With a habit of gazin' over the sea,
A-hopin' in vain for the day I'll meet 'er,
    And constant and faithful a-yearnin' for me.

Me Turkish sweetheart she played me double—
    Eloped with the Sultan Harum In-Deed,
And the Danish damsel she made me trouble
    When she ups and married an oblong Swede.

But there's truth in the heart of the maiden o' Mango,
    Though her cheeks is black like the kiln-baked cork,
As she sets in the shade o' the whingo-whango,
    A-waitin' for me—with a knife and fork.
                    —*Wallace Irwin*

THE DAY IS DONE

The day is done, and darkness
    From the wing of night is loosed,
As a feather is wafted downward,
    From a chicken going to roost.

I see the lights of the baker,
    Gleam through the rain and mist,

And a feeling of sadness comes o'er me,
　　That I cannot well resist.

A feeling of sadness and longing
　　That is not like being sick,
And resembles sorrow only
　　As a brickbat resembles a brick.

Come, get for me some supper,—
　　A good and regular meal—
That shall soothe this restless feeling,
　　And banish the pain I feel.

Not from the pastry bakers,
　　Not from the shops for cake;
I wouldn't give a farthing
　　For all that they can make.

For, like the soup at dinner,
　　Such things would but suggest
Some dishes more substantial,
　　And to-night I want the best.

Go to some honest butcher,
　　Whose beef is fresh and nice,
As any they have in the city
　　And get a liberal slice.

Such things through days of labor,
　　And nights devoid of ease,
For sad and desperate feelings,
　　Are wonderful remedies.

They have an astonishing power
　　To aid and reinforce,
And come like the "finally, brethren,"
　　That follows a long discourse.

Then get me a tender sirloin
　　From off the bench or hook,
And lend to its sterling goodness
　　The science of the cook.

And the night shall be filled with comfort,
And the cares with which it begun
Shall fold up their blankets like Indians,
And silently cut and run.

—*Phoebe Cary*

ROY BEAN

Cowboys, come and hear a story of Roy Bean in all his glory,
"All the law West of the Pecos," was his line:
You must let our ponies take us, to a town on Lower Pecos
Where the High Bridge spans the cañon thin and fine.

He was born one day near Toyah where he learned to be a lawyer
And a teacher and a barber for his fare,
He was cook and old shoe mender, sometimes preacher and bar-
   tender:
It cost two bits to have him cut your hair.

He was certain sure a hustler and considerable a rustler
And at mixing up an egg nog he was grand.
He was lively, he was merry, he could drink a Tom and Jerry,
On occasion at a round-up took a hand.

You may find the story funny, but once he had no money
Which for him was not so very strange and rare,
And he went to help Pap Wyndid but he got so absent-minded,
Then he put his RB brand on old Pap's steer.

Now Pap was right smart angry so Roy Bean went down to Langtry
Where he opened up an office and a store.
There he'd sell you drinks or buttons or another rancher's muttons,
Though the latter made the other feller sore.

Once there came from Austin city a young dude reputed witty,
Out of Bean he thought he'd quickly take a rise:
And he got frisky as he up and called for whiskey
And he said to Bean, "Now hurry, damn your eyes."

On the counter threw ten dollars and it very quickly follers
That the bar-keep took full nine and gave back one,
Then the stranger give a holler as he viewed his single dollar,
And at that commenced the merriment and fun.

For the dude he slammed the table just as hard as he was able,
That the price of whiskey was too high he swore.
Said Roy Bean, "Cause of your fussin' and your most outrageous
    cussin'
You are fined the other dollar by the law.

—Anonymous

THE CHAPERON

I take my chaperon to the play—
    She thinks she's taking me.
And the gilded youth who owns the box,
    A proud young man is he;
But how would his young heart be hurt
    If he could only know
    That not for his sweet sake I go
    Nor yet to see the trifling show;
But to see my chaperon flirt.

Her eyes beneath her snowy hair
    They sparkle young as mine;
There's scarce a wrinkle in her hand
    So delicate and fine.
And when my chaperon is seen,
    They come from everywhere—
    The dear old boys with silvery hair,
    With old-time grace and old-time air,
To greet their old-time queen.

They bow as my young Midas here
    Will never learn to bow
(The dancing masters do not teach
    That gracious reverence now);
With voices quavering just a bit,
    They play their old parts through,
    They talk of folk who used to woo,
    Of hearts that broke in 'fifty-two—
Now none the worse for it.

And as those aged crickets chirp
    I watch my chaperon's face,
And see the dear old features take

A new and tender grace;
And in her happy eyes I see
     Her youth awakening bright,
     With all its hope, desire, delight—
     Ah, me! I wish that I were quite
As young—as young as she!
                    —*Henry Cuyler Bunner*

Nature: Land and Sea

A LIFE ON THE OCEAN WAVE

A life on the ocean wave,
  A home on the rolling deep,
Where the scattered waters rave,
  And the winds their revels keep!
Like an eagle caged, I pine
  On this dull, unchanging shore:
Oh! give me the flashing brine,
  The spray and the tempest's roar!

Once more on the deck I stand
  Of my own swift-gliding craft:
Set sail! farewell to the land!
  The gale follows fair abaft.
We shoot through the sparkling foam
  Like an ocean bird set free;—
Like the ocean bird, our home
  We'll find far out on the sea.

The land is no longer in view,
  The clouds have begun to frown;
But with a stout vessel and crew,
  We'll say, Let the storm come down!
And the song of our hearts shall be,
  While the winds and the waters rave,
A home on the rolling sea!
  A life on the ocean wave!
                    —*Epes Sargent*

WIND AND WAVE

O when I hear at sea
  The water on our lee,
I fancy that I hear the wind
  That combs my hemlock tree:

But when beneath that tree
   I listen eagerly,
I seem to hear the rushing wave
   I heard far out at sea.
     —Charles Warren Stoddard

IN THE PAST

There lies a somnolent lake
Under a noiseless sky,
Where never the mornings break
Nor the evenings die.

Mad flakes of colour
Whirl on its even face
Iridescent and streaked with pallour;
And, warding the silent place,

The rocks rise sheer and gray
From the sedgeless brink to the sky
Dull-lit with the light of pale half-day
Thro' a void space and dry.

And the hours lag dead in the air
With a sense of coming eternity
To the heart of the lonely boatman there:
That boatman am I,

I, in my lonely boat,
A waif on the somnolent lake,
Watching the colours creep and float
With the sinuous track of a snake.

Now I lean o'er the side
And lazy shades in the water see,
Lapped in the sweep of a sluggish tide
Crawled in from the living sea;

And next I fix mine eyes,
So long that the heart declines,
On the changeless face of the open skies
Where no star shines;

And now to the rocks I turn,
To the rocks, around
That lie like walls of a circling urn
Wherein lie bound

The waters that feel my powerless strength
And meet my homeless oar
Labouring over their ashen length
Never to find a shore.

But the gleam still skims
At times on the somnolent lake,
And a light there is that swims
With the whirl of a snake;

And tho' dead be the hour i' the air,
And dayless the sky,
The heart is alive of the boatman there:
That boatman am I.

—Trumbull Stickney

SPORT

Somewhere, in deeps
  Of tangled ripening wheat,
A little prairie-chicken cries—
Lost from its fellows, it pleads and weeps.
Meanwhile, stained and mangled,
  With dust-filled eyes,
The unreplying mother lies
Limp and bloody at the sportsman's feet.

—Hamlin Garland

FIREFLIES

I saw, one sultry night above a swamp,
The darkness throbbing with their golden pomp!
And long my dazzled sight did they entrance
With the weird chaos of their dizzy dance!
Quicker than yellow leaves, when gales despoil,
Quivered the brilliance of their mute turmoil,
Within whose light was intricately blent

Perpetual rise, perpetual descent.
As though their scintillant flickerings had met
At the vague meshes of some airy net!
And now mysteriously I seemed to guess,
While watching their tumultuous loveliness,
What fervor of deep passion strangely thrives
In the warm richness of these tropic lives,
Whose wings can never tremble but they show
These hearts of living fire that beat below!
                              —*Edgar Fawcett*

TWILIGHT AT SEA

The twilight hours like birds flew by,
    As lightly and as free;
Ten thousand stars were in the sky,
    Ten thousand on the sea;
For every wave, with dimpled face,
    That leaped upon the air,
Had caught a star in its embrace
    And held it trembling there.
                              —*Amelia B. Welby*

AN OPIUM FANTASY

Soft hangs the opiate in the brain,
    And lulling soothes the edge of pain,
Till harshest sound, far off or near,
    Sings floating in its mellow sphere.

What wakes me from my heavy dream?
    Or am I still asleep?
Those long and soft vibrations seem
    A slumberous charm to keep.

The graceful play, a moment stopt,
    Distance again unrolls,
Like silver balls, that, softly dropt,
    Ring into golden bowls.

I question of the poppies red,
    The fairy flaunting band,

While I, a weed with drooping head,
  Within their phalanx stand:—

"Some airy one, with scarlet cap,
  The name unfold to me
Of this new minstrel who can lap
  Sleep in his melody!"

Bright grew their scarlet-kerchief'd heads,
  As freshening winds had blown,
And from their gently-swaying beds
  They sang in undertone:—

"Oh he is but a little owl,
  The smallest of his kin,
Who sits beneath the midnight's cowl
  And makes this airy din."

"Deceitful tongues of fiery tints!
  Far more than this ye know,
That he is your enchanted prince
  Doom'd as an owl to go;—

"Nor his fond play for years hath stopt,
  But nightly he unrolls
His silver balls, that, softly dropt,
  Ring into golden bowls."
                    —*Maria White Lowell*

WILD HONEY

Where hints of racy sap and gum
Out of the old dark forest come;

Where birds their beaks like hammers wield,
And pith is pierced and bark is peeled;

Where the green walnut's outer rind
Gives precious bitterness to the wind;

There lurks the sweet creative power,
As lurks the honey in the flower.

In winter's bud that bursts in spring,
In nut of autumn's ripening,

In acrid bulb beneath the mold,
Sleeps the elixir, strong and old,

That Rosicrucians sought in vain,—
Life that renews itself again!

What bottled perfume is so good
As fragrance of split tulip-wood?

What fabled drink of God or muse
Was rich as purple mulberry juice?

And what school-polished gem of thought
Is like the rune from Nature caught?

He is a poet strong and true
Who loves wild thyme and honey-dew;

And like a brown bee works and sings
With morning freshness on his wings,

And a gold burden on his thighs,—
The pollen-dust of centuries!
                    —*Maurice Thompson*

Religious and Spiritual

O LITTLE TOWN OF BETHLEHEM

O little town of Bethlehem!
  How still we see thee lie;
Above thy deep and dreamless sleep
  The silent stars go by;
Yet in thy dark streets shineth
  The everlasting Light;
The hopes and fears of all the years
  Are met in thee to-night.

For Christ is born of Mary,
  And gathered all above,
While mortals sleep, the angels keep
  Their watch of wondering love.
O morning stars, together
  Proclaim the holy birth!
And praises sing to God the King
  And peace to men on earth.

How silently, how silently,
  The wondrous gift is given!
So God imparts to human hearts
  The blessings of His heaven.
No ear may hear His coming,
  But in this world of sin,
Where meek souls will receive Him still,
  The dear Christ enters in.

O holy Child of Bethlehem!
  Descend to us, we pray;
Cast out our sin, and enter in,
  Be born in us to-day.
We hear the Christmas angels
  The great glad tidings tell;

Oh, come to us, abide with us,
Our Lord Emmanuel!
—*Phillips Brooks*

HARPS HUNG UP IN BABYLON

The harps hung up in Babylon,
Their loosened strings rang on, sang on,
And cast their murmurs forth upon
The roll and roar of Babylon:
'*Forget me, Lord, if I forget*
Jerusalem for Babylon,
If I forget the vision set
High as the head of Lebanon
Is lifted over Syria yet,
If I forget and bow me down
To brutish gods of Babylon."

Two rivers to each other run
In the very midst of Babylon,
And swifter than their current fleets
The restless river of the sweets
Of Babylon, of Babylon,
And Babylon's towers smite the sky,
But higher reeks to God most high
The smoke of her iniquity:
"*But oh, betwixt the green and blue*
To walk the hills that once we knew
When you were pure and I was true,"—
So rang the harps in Babylon—
"*Or ere along the roads of stone*
Had led us captive one by one
The subtle gods of Babylon."

The harps hung up in Babylon
Hung silent till the prophet dawn,
When Judah's feet the highway burned
Back to the holy hills returned,
And shook their dust on Babylon.
In Zion's halls the wild harps rang,
To Zion's walls their smitten clang,
And lo! of Babylon they sang,
They only sang of Babylon:

"Jehovah, round whose throne of awe
The vassal stars their orbits draw
Within the circle of Thy law,
Canst thou make nothing what is done,
Or cause Thy servant to be one
That has not been in Babylon,
That has not known the power and pain
Of life poured out like driven rain?
I will go down and find again
My soul that's lost in Babylon."
                          —Arthur Colton

THE SONG OF A HEATHEN

Sojourning in Galilee, A. D. 32

If Jesus Christ is a man—
    And only a man—I say
That of all mankind I cleave to him,
    And to him will I cleave alway.

If Jesus Christ is a God—
    And the only God—I swear
I will follow Him through heaven and hell,
    The earth, the sea, and the air!
                    —Richard Watson Gilder

FROM GREENLAND'S ICY MOUNTAINS

From Greenland's icy mountains,
From India's coral strand,
Where Africa's sunny fountains
Roll down their golden sand,—
From many an ancient river,
From many a palmy plain,
They call us to deliver
Their land from error's chain.

What though the spicy breezes
Blow soft o'er Ceylon's isle;
Though every prospect pleases,
And only man is vile;

In vain with lavish kindness
The gifts of God are strown;
The heathen, in his blindness,
Bows down to wood and stone.

Shall we, whose souls are lighted
With wisdom from on high,
Shall we, to men benighted,
The lamp of life deny?
Salvation, oh, salvation!
The joyful sound proclaim,
Till earth's remotest nation
Has learned Messiah's name.

Waft, waft, ye winds, His story,
And you, ye waters, roll,
Till, like a sea of glory,
It spreads from pole to pole;
Till o'er our ransomed nature
The Lamb for sinner's slain,
Redeemer, King, Creator,
In bliss returns to reign.
                    —*Reginald Heber*
        (*Music by Lowell Mason*)

GO DOWN MOSES

Go down, Moses
'Way down in Egypt land,
Tell ole Pharaoh,
To let my people go.

When Israel was in Egypt's land;
Let my people go,
Oppressed so hard they could not stand,
Let my people go.

"Thus spoke the Lord," bold Moses said;
Let my people go,
If not I'll smite your first born dead,
Let my people go.
                    —*Spiritual*

SWING LOW SWEET CHARIOT

Swing low sweet chariot,
Comin' for to carry me home,
Swing low sweet chariot,
Comin' for to carry me home.

I looked over Jordan, an' what did I see,
Comin' for to carry me home,
A band of angels comin' after me,
Comin' for to carry me home.

If you get-a dere befo' I do,
Comin' for to carry me home,
Tell all my friends I'm comin' too,
Comin' for to carry me home.

—Spiritual

Native American Poetry

CALLING ONE'S OWN

Ojibwa

Awake! flower of the forest, sky-treading bird of the prairie.
Awake! awake! wonderful fawn-eyed One.
When you look upon me I am satisfied; as flowers that drink dew.
The breath of your mouth is the fragrance of flowers in the morn-
    ing,
Your breath is their fragrance at evening in the moon-of-fading-leaf.
Do not the red streams of my veins run toward you
As forest-streams to the sun in the moon of bright nights?
When you are beside me my heart sings; a branch it is, dancing,
Dancing before the Wind-spirit in the moon of strawberries.
When you frown upon me, beloved, my heart grows dark—
A shining river the shadows of clouds darken,
Then with your smiles comes the sun and makes to look like gold
Furrows the cold wind drew in the water's face.
Myself! behold me! blood of my beating heart.
Earth smiles—the waters smile—even the sky-of-clouds smiles—
    but I,
I lose the way of smiling when you are not near,
Awake! awake! my beloved.
                    —*Translated by Charles Fenno Hoffman*

THE CHILD IS INTRODUCED
TO THE COSMOS AT BIRTH

Omaha

Ho! Ye Sun, Moon, Stars, all ye that move in the heavens,
    I bid you hear me!

Into your midst has come a new life.
 Consent ye, I implore!
Make its path smooth, that it may reach the brow of the first hill!

Ho! Ye Winds, Clouds, Rain, Mist, all ye that move in the air,
 I bid you hear me!
Into your midst has come a new life.
 Consent ye, I implore!

Make its path smooth, that it may reach the brow of the second hill!
Ho! Ye Hills, Valleys, Rivers, Lakes, Trees, Grasses, all ye of the
  earth,
 I bid you hear me!
Into your midst has come a new life.
 Consent ye, I implore!
Make its path smooth, that it may reach the brow of the third hill!
Ho! Ye Birds, great and small, that fly in the air,
Ho! Ye Animals, great and small, that dwell in the forest,
Ho! Ye insects that creep among the grasses and burrow in the
  ground—
 I bid you hear me!
Into your midst has come a new life.
 Consent ye, I implore!
Make its path smooth, that it may reach the brow of the fourth hill!

Ho! All ye of the heavens, all ye of the air, all ye of the earth:
 I bid you all to hear me!
Into your midst has come a new life.
 Consent ye, consent ye all, I implore!
Make its path smooth—then shall it travel beyond the four hills!
                    —*Translated by Alice Fletcher*

MAGPIE SONG

Navajo

The Magpie! The Magpie! Here underneath
In the white of his wings are the footsteps of morning.
It dawns! It dawns!
                    —*Translated by Washington Matthews*

SONGS IN THE GARDEN
OF THE HOUSE GOD

Navajo

I

Truly in the East
The white bean
And the great corn-plant
Are tied with the white lightning.
Listen! rain approaches!
The voice of the bluebird is heard.
Truly in the East
The white bean
And the great squash
Are tied with the rainbow,
Listen! rain approaches!
The voice of the bluebird is heard.

II

From the top of the great corn-plant the water gurgles, I hear it;
Around the roots the water foams, I hear it;
Around the roots of the plants it foams, I hear it;
From their tops the water foams, I hear it.

III

The corn grows up. The waters of the dark clouds drop, drop.
The rain descends. The waters from the corn leaves drop, drop.
The rain descends. The waters from the plants drop, drop.
The corn grows up. The waters of the dark mists drop, drop.

IV

Shall I cull this fruit of the great cornplant?
Shall you break it? Shall I break it?
Shall I break it? Shall you break it?
Shall I? Shall you?
Shall I cull this fruit of the great squash vine?
Shall you pick it up? Shall I pick it up?

Shall I pick it up? Shall you pick it up?
Shall I? Shall you?
—*Translated by Washington Matthews*

RAIN SONG OF THE GIANT SOCIETY

Sia

We, the Ancient Ones,
Who ascended from the middle of the world below,
Our medicine is precious,
It is as our hearts precious to us,
Arrow of lightning
Come to us
Echo.
Spruce of the north
And all your people;
Your thoughts come to us.
Who is it?
White floating clouds.
May your thoughts come to us
And all your people,
May their thoughts come to us.
Who is it?
Clouds like the plains,
May your thoughts come to us.
Who is it?
Arrow of lightning,
May your thoughts come to us.
Who is it?
Earth horizon
And all your people,
May your thoughts come to us.
        —*Translated by Matilda Coxe Stevenson*

Miscellaneous

THE WAY TO ARCADY

Oh, what's the way to Arcady,
* To Arcady, to Arcady;*
Oh, what's the way to Arcady,
* Where all the leaves are merry?*

Oh, what's the way to Arcady?
The spring is rustling in the tree,—
The tree the wind is blowing through,—
  It sets the blossoms flickering white.
I knew not skies could burn so blue
  Nor any breezes blow so light.
They blow an old-time way for me,
Across the world to Arcady.

Oh, what's the way to Arcady?
Sir Poet, with the rusty coat,
Quit mocking of the song bird's note.
How have you heart for any tune,
You with the wayworn russet shoon?
Your scrip, a-swinging by your side,
Gapes with a gaunt mouth hungry-wide.
I'll brim it well with pieces red,
If you will tell the way to tread.

Oh, I am bound for Arcady,
And if you but keep pace with me
You tread the way to Arcady.

And where away lies Arcady,
And how long yet may the journey be?

Ah, that (quoth he) *I do not know:*
Across the clover and the snow—
Across the frost, across the flowers—
Through summer seconds and winter hours,

I've trod the way my whole life long,
   And know not now where it may be;
My guide is but the stir to song,
That tells me I cannot go wrong,
   Or clear or dark the pathway be
   Upon the road to Arcady.

But how shall I do who cannot sing?
   I was wont to sing, once on a time,—
There is never an echo now to ring
   Remembrance back to the trick of rhyme.

'Tis strange you cannot sing (quoth he),—
The folk all sing in Arcady.

But how may he find Arcady
Who hath nor youth nor melody?

What, know you not, old man (quoth he),—
   Your hair is white, your face is wise,—
   That Love must kiss that Mortal's eyes
Who hopes to see fair Arcady?
No gold can buy you entrance there;
But beggared Love may all go bare—
No wisdom won with weariness;
But Love goes in with Folly's dress—
No fame that wit could ever win;
But only Love may lead Love in
   To Arcady, to Arcady.

Ah, woe is me, through all my days
   Wisdom and wealth I both have got,
And fame and name, and great men's praise;
   But Love, ah Love! I have it not.
There was a time, when life was new—
   But far away, and half forgot—
I only know her eyes were blue;
   But Love—I fear I knew it not.
We did not wed, for lack of gold,
And she is dead, and I am old.
All things have come since then to me,
Save Love, ah Love! and Arcady.

Ah, then I fear we part (quoth he),—
My way's for Love and Arcady.

But you, you fare alone, like me;
    The gray is likewise in your hair.
    What love have you to lead you there,
To Arcady, to Arcady?

Ah, no, not lonely do I fare;
    My true companion's Memory.
With Love he fills the Springtime air;
    With Love he clothes the Winter tree.
Oh, past this poor horizon's bound
    My song goes straight to one who stands,—
Her face all gladdening at the sound,—
    To lead me to the Spring-green lands,
To wander with enlacing hands.
The songs within my breast that stir
Are all of her, are all of her.
My maid is dead long years (quoth he),—
She waits for me in Arcady.

Oh, yon's the way to Arcady,
    To Arcady, to Arcady;
Oh, yon's the way to Arcady,
    Where all the leaves are merry.
                        —*Henry Cuyler Bunner*

BEN BOLT

Don't you remember sweet Alice, Ben Bolt,—
    Sweet Alice whose hair was so brown,
Who wept with delight when you gave her a smile,
    And trembled with fear at your frown?
In the old church yard in the valley, Ben Bolt,
    In a corner obscure and alone,
They have fitted a slab of the granite so gray,
    And Alice lies under the stone.

Under the hickory tree, Ben Bolt,
    Which stood at the foot of the hill,
Together we've lain in the noonday shade,
    And listened to Appleton's mill.
The mill wheel has fallen to pieces, Ben Bolt,
    The rafters have tumbled in,

And a quiet which crawls round the walls as you gaze
  Has followed the olden din.

Do you mind of the cabin of logs, Ben Bolt,
  At the edge of the pathless wood,
And the button-ball tree with its motley limbs,
  Which nigh by the doorstep stood?
The cabin to ruin has gone, Ben Bolt,
  The tree you would seek for in vain;
And where once the lords of the forest waved
  Are grass and the golden grain.

And don't you remember the school, Ben Bolt,
  With the master so cruel and grim,
And the shaded nook in the running brook
  Where the children went to swim?
Grass grows on the master's grave, Ben Bolt,
  The spring of the brook is dry,
And of all the boys who were schoolmates then
  There are only you and I.

There is change in the things I loved, Ben Bolt,
  They have changed from the old to the new;
But I feel in the deeps of my spirit the truth,
  There never was change in you.
Twelvemonths twenty have past, Ben Bolt,
  Since first we were friends—yet I hail
Your presence a blessing, your friendship a truth,
  Ben Bolt of the salt-sea gale.
                              —*Thomas Dunn English*

THE CAMPTOWN RACES

De Camptown ladies sing dis song
  Doo dah! doo dah!
De Camptown racetrack five miles long
  Oh! doo dah day!
I come down dah wid my hat caved in
  Doo dah! doo dah!
I go back home wid a pocket full of tin
  Oh! doo dah day!

Gwine to run all night!
Gwine to run all day!
I'll bet my money on de bobtail nag,
Somebody bet on de bay.

De long tail filly, and de big black hoss
  Doo dah! doo dah!
Dey fly de track, and dey both cut across
  Oh! doo dah day!
De blind hoss sticken in a big mud hole
  Doo dah! doo dah!
Can't touch bottom wid a ten foot pole
  Oh! doo dah day!

Old muley cow come on to de track
  Doo dah! doo dah!
De bobtail fling her ober his back
  Oh! doo dah day!
Den fly along like a railroad car
  Doo dah! doo dah!
Runnin' a race wid a shootin' star
  Oh! doo dah day!

See dem flyin' on a ten mile heat
  Doo dah! doo dah!
Round de race track, den repeat
  Oh! doo dah day!
I win my money on de bobtail nag
  Doo dah! doo dah!
I keep my money in an old tow bag
  Oh! doo dah day!

                —*Stephen Collins Foster*

FLORENCE VANE

I loved thee long and dearly,
  Florence Vane;
My life's bright dream and early
  Hath come again;

I renew in my fond vision
  My heart's dear pain,

My hope, and thy derision,
　　Florence Vane.

The ruin lone and hoary,
　　The ruin old,
Where thou didst mark my story,
　　At even told,—
That spot—the hues Elysian
　　Of sky and plain—
I treasure in my vision,
　　Florence Vane.

Thou wast lovelier than the roses
　　In their prime;
Thy voice excelled the closes
　　Of sweetest rhyme;
Thy heart was as a river
　　Without a main.
Would I had loved thee never,
　　Florence Vane!

But, fairest, coldest wonder!
　　Thy glorious clay
Lieth the green sod under,—
　　Alas the day!
And it boots not to remember
　　Thy disdain,—
To quicken love's pale ember,
　　Florence Vane.

The lilies of the valley
　　By young graves weep,
The pansies love to dally
　　Where maidens sleep;

May their bloom, in beauty vying,
　　Never wane
Where thine earthly part is lying,
　　Florence Vane!
　　　　　—*Philip Pendleton Cooke*

THE BARON'S LAST BANQUET

O'er a low couch the setting sun had thrown its latest ray,
Where in his last strong agony a dying warrior lay,
The stern old Baron Rudiger, whose frame had ne'er been bent
By wasting pain, till time and toil its iron strength had spent.

"They come around me here, and say my days of life are o'er,
That I shall mount my noble steed and lead my band no more;
They come, and to my beard they dare to tell me now, that I,
Their own liege lord and master born,—that I, ha! ha! must die.

"And what is death? I've dared him oft before the Paynim spear,—
Think ye he's entered at my gate, has come to seek me here?
I've met him, faced him, scorned him, when the fight was raging
      hot,—
I'll try his might—I'll brave his power; defy, and fear him not.

"Ho! sound the tocsin from my tower, and fire the culverin,—
Bid each retainer arm with speed,—call every vassal in,
Up with my banner on the wall,—the banquet board prepare;
Throw wide the portal of my hall, and bring my armor there!"

An hundred hands were busy then—the banquet forth was
      spread—
And rung the heavy oaken floor with many a martial tread,
While from the rich, dark tracery along the vaulted wall,
Lights gleamed on harness, plume, and spear, o'er the proud old
      Gothic hall.

Fast hurrying through the outer gate the mailed retainers poured,
On through the portal's frowning arch, and thronged around the
      board.
While at its head, within his dark, carved oaken chair of state,
Armed cap-a-pie, stern Rudiger, with girded falchion, sate.

"Fill every beaker up, my men, pour forth the cheering wine;
There's life and strength in every drop,—thanksgiving to the vine!
Are ye all there, my vassals true?—mine eyes are waxing dim;
Fill round, my tried and fearless ones, each goblet to the brim.

"You're there, but yet I see ye not. Draw forth each trusty sword
And let me hear your faithful steel clash once around my board;

I hear it faintly:—Louder yet!—What clogs my heavy breath?
Up all, and shout for Rudiger, 'Defiance unto Death!' "

Bowl rang to bowl—steel clanged to steel—and rose a deafening cry
That made the torches flare around, and shook the flags on high:—
"Ho! cravens, do ye fear him?—Slaves, traitors! have ye flown?
Ho! cowards, have ye left me to meet him here alone!

"But I defy him:—let him come!" Down rang the massy cup,
While from its sheath the ready blade came flashing halfway up;
And with the black and heavy plumes scarce trembling on his head,
There in his dark, carved oaken chair Old Rudiger sat,—dead.
                                        —*Albert Gorton Greene*

JEANIE WITH THE LIGHT BROWN HAIR

I dream of Jeanie with the light brown hair,
Borne, like a vapor, on the summer air;
I see her tripping where the bright streams play,
Happy as the daisies that dance on her way.
Many were the wild notes her merry voice would pour,
Many were the blithe birds that warbled them o'er:
Oh! I dream of Jeanie with the light brown hair,
Floating, like a vapor, on the soft summer air.

I long for Jeanie with the day-dawn smile,
Radiant in gladness, warm with winning guile;
I hear her melodies, like joys gone by,
Sighing 'round my heart over the fond hopes that die:
Sighing like the night wind and sobbing like the rain,
Wail for the lost one that comes not again:
Oh! I long for Jeanie and my heart bows low,
Nevermore to find her where the bright waters flow.

I sigh for Jeanie, but her light form strayed
Far from the fond hearts 'round her native glade;
Her smiles have vanished and her sweet songs flown,
Flitting like the dreams that have cheered us and gone.
Now the nodding wild flowers may wither on the shore
While her gentle fingers will cull them no more:
Oh! I sigh for Jeanie with the light brown hair,
Floating, like a vapor, on the soft summer air.
                                        —*Stephen Collins Foster*

ROCK ME TO SLEEP, MOTHER

Backward, turn backward, O Time, in your flight,
Make me a child again just for tonight!
Mother, come back from the echoless shore,
Take me again to your heart as of yore;
Kiss from my forehead the furrows of care,
Smooth the few silver threads out of my hair;
Over my slumbers your loving watch keep;
Rock me to sleep, mother, rock me to sleep.

Clasped to your heart in a loving embrace,
With your light lashes just sweeping my face,
Never hereafter to wake or to weep;
Rock me to sleep, mother, rock me to sleep.

Tired of the hollow, the base, the untrue,
Mother, O mother, my heart calls for you!
Many a summer the grass has grown green,
Blossomed and faded our faces between;
Yet with strong yearning and passionate pain,
Long I tonight for your presence again;
Come from the silence so long and so deep;
Rock me to sleep, mother, rock me to sleep.

Over my heart, in the days that are flown,
No love like mother-love ever has shone;
No other worship abides and endures,—
Faithful, unselfish, and patient like yours;
None like a mother can charm away pain
From the sick soul and the world-weary brain;
Slumber's soft calms over my heavy lids creep;
Rock me to sleep, mother, rock me to sleep.

Come, let your brown hair, just lighted with gold,
Fall on your shoulders again as of old;
Let it fall over my forehead tonight,
Shading my faint eyes away from the light;
For with its sunny-edged shadows once more
Haply will throng the sweet visions of yore;
Lovingly, softly its bright billows sweep;
Rock me to sleep, mother, rock me to sleep.

—Elizabeth Chase Akers

SONNETS

To Edgar Allan Poe

On our lone pathway bloomed no earthly hopes:
Sorrow and death were near us, as we stood
Where the dim forest, from the upland slopes,
Swept darkly to the sea. The enchanted wood
Thrilled as by some foreboding terror stirred;
And as the waves broke on the lonely shore,
In their low monotone, methought I heard
A solemn voice that sighed, "Ye meet no more."
There, while the level sunbeams seemed to burn
Through the long aisles of red, autumnal gloom—
Where stately, storied cenotaphs inurn
Sweet human hopes, too fair on Earth to bloom—
Was the bud reaped, whose petals pure and cold
Sleep on my heart till Heaven the flower unfold.

If thy sad heart, pining for human love,
In its earth solitude grew dark with fear,
Lest the high Sun of Heaven itself should prove
Powerless to save from that phantasmal sphere
Wherein thy spirit wandered,—if the flowers
That pressed around thy feet, seemed but to bloom
In lone Gethsemanes, through starless hours,
When all who loved had left thee to thy doom,—
Oh, yet believe that, in that hollow vale
Where thy soul lingers, waiting to attain
So much of Heaven's sweet grace as shall avail
To lift its burden of remorseful pain,
My soul shall meet thee, and its Heaven forego
Till God's great love, on both, one hope, one Heaven bestow.
—Sarah Helen Whitman

THE OLD ARM-CHAIR

I love it, I love it, and who shall dare
To chide me for loving that old arm-chair?
I've treasured it long as a holy prize;
I've bedewed it with tears, and embalmed it with sighs;
'Tis bound by a thousand bands to my heart,
Not a tie will break, not a link will start.

Would ye learn the spell? a mother sat there,
And a sacred thing is that old arm-chair.

In childhood's hour I lingered near
The hallowed seat with listening ear;
And gentle words that mother would give,
To fit me to die, and teach me to live.
She told me shame would never betide,
With truth for my creed, and God for my guide;
She taught me to lisp my earliest prayer,
As I knelt beside that old arm-chair.

I sat and watched her many a day,
When her eye grew dim and her locks were gray;
And I almost worshipped her when she smiled,
And turned from her Bible to bless her child.
Years rolled on but the last one sped,
My Idol was shattered, my earth-star fled:
I learned how much the heart can bear,
When I saw her die in that old arm-chair.

'Tis past, 'tis past, but I gaze on it now
With quivering breath and throbbing brow;
'Twas there she nursed me, 'twas there she died;
And memory flows with lava tide.
Say it is folly, and deem me weak,
While the scalding drops start down my cheek;
But I love it, I love it, and cannot tear
My soul from a mother's old arm-chair.

—*Eliza Cook*

ROCKED IN THE CRADLE
OF THE DEEP

Rock'd in the cradle of the deep,
I lay me down in peace to sleep.
Secure I rest upon the wave,
For thou, Oh! Lord, hast pow'r to save.
I know thou wilt not slight my call,
For thou dost mark the sparrow's fall;
And calm and peaceful is my sleep . . .
Rocked in the cradle of the deep,

And calm and peaceful is my sleep . . .
Rocked in the cradle of the deep.

And such the trust that still were mine
When stormy winds swept o'er the brine,
Or tho' the tempest's fiery breath
Roused me from sleep to wreck and death.
In ocean cave still safe with Thee,
The germ of immortality;
And calm and peaceful is my sleep . . .
Rocked in the cradle of the deep,
And calm and peaceful is my sleep . . .
Rocked in the cradle of the deep.

—*Emma Willard*

OH! SUSANNA

I come from Alabama,
Wid my banjo on my knee,
I'm g'wan to Louisiana,
My true love for to see.
It rain'd all night the day I left,
The weather it was dry;
The sun so hot I froze to death;
Susanna, don't you cry.

Oh! Susanna,
Don't you cry for me,
I come from Alabama
Wid my banjo on my knee.

I jumped aboard de telegraph,
And trabbeled down de ribber,
De lectric fluid magnified,
And killed five hundred nigger;
De bullgine bust, de horse run off,
I really thought I'd die;
I shut my eyes to hold my breath;
Susanna, don't you cry.

I had a dream de udder night,
When eb'ryting was still;
I thought I saw Susanna,

A coming down de hill;
De buckwheat-cake was in her mouth,
De tear was in her eye;
Says I, I'm coming from de South,
Susanna, don't you cry.

I soon will be in New Orleans,
And den I'll look all round,
And when I find Susanna,
I'll fall upon the ground.
But if I do not find her,
Dis darkey'l surely die;
And when I'm dead and buried,
Susanna, don't you cry.
                    —*Stephen Collins Foster*

CASEY AT THE BAT

It looked extremely rocky for the Mudville nine that day,
The score stood four to six with but an inning left to play.
And so, when Cooney died at first, and Burrows did the same,
A pallor wreathed the features of the patrons of the game.
A straggling few got up to go, leaving there the rest,
With that hope which springs eternal within the human breast.
For they thought if only Casey could get a whack at that,
They'd put up even money with Casey at the bat.
But Flynn preceded Casey, and likewise so did Blake,
And the former was a pudding and the latter was a fake;
So on that stricken multitude a death-like silence sat,
For there seemed but little chance of Casey's getting to the bat.
But Flynn let drive a single to the wonderment of all,
And the much despisèd Blakey tore the cover off the ball,
And when the dust had lifted and they saw what had occurred,
There was Blakey safe on second, and Flynn a-hugging third.
Then from the gladdened multitude went up a joyous yell,
It bounded from the mountain top and rattled in the dell,
It struck upon the hillside, and rebounded on the flat,
For Casey, mighty Casey, was advancing to the bat.
There was ease in Casey's manner as he stepped into his place,
There was pride in Casey's bearing and a smile on Casey's face,
And when responding to the cheers he lightly doffed his hat,
No stranger in the crowd could doubt, 'twas Casey at the bat.
Ten thousand eyes were on him as he rubbed his hands with dirt,

Five thousand tongues applauded as he wiped them on his shirt;
And while the writhing pitcher ground the ball into his hip—
Defiance gleamed from Casey's eye—a sneer curled Casey's lip.
And now the leather-covered sphere came hurtling through the air,
And Casey stood a-watching it in haughty grandeur there;
Close by the sturdy batsman the ball unheeded sped—
"That hain't my style," said Casey—"Strike one," the Umpire said.
From the bleachers black with people there rose a sullen roar,
Like the beating of the storm waves on a stern and distant shore,
"Kill him! kill the Umpire!" shouted some one from the stand—
And it's likely they'd have done it had not Casey raised his hand.
With a smile of Christian charity great Casey's visage shone,
He stilled the rising tumult and he bade the game go on;
He signalled to the pitcher and again the spheroid flew,
But Casey still ignored it and the Umpire said "Strike two."
"Fraud!" yelled the maddened thousands, and the echo answered
    "Fraud,"
But one scornful look from Casey and the audience was awed;
They saw his face grow stern and cold; they saw his muscles strain,
And they knew that Casey would not let that ball go by again.
The sneer is gone from Casey's lip; his teeth are clenched with hate,
He pounds with cruel violence his bat upon the plate;
And now the pitcher holds the ball, and now he lets it go,
And now the air is shattered by the force of Casey's blow.
Oh! somewhere in this favored land the sun is shining bright,
The band is playing somewhere, and somewhere hearts are light,
And somewhere men are laughing, and somewhere children shout;
But there is no joy in Mudville—mighty Casey has "Struck Out."

—*Ernest Lawrence Thayer*

THE MAN WITH THE HOE

Written After Seeing Millet's World-Famous Painting

Bowed by the weight of centuries he leans
Upon his hoe and gazes on the ground,
The emptiness of ages in his face,
And on his back the burden of the world.
Who made him dead to rapture and despair,
A thing that grieves not and that never hopes,
Stolid and stunned, a brother to the ox?
Who loosened and let down this brutal jaw?

Now motionless, with lifted face,
    And small hands on her bosom crossed.

And now with flashing eyes she springs:—
    Her whole bright figure raised in air,
As if her soul had spread its wings:
    And poised her one wild instant there!

She spoke not—but, so richly fraught
    With language are her glance and smile,
That, when the curtain fell, I thought
    She had been talking all the while.
                    —*Frances Sargeant Osgood*

OPPORTUNITY

Master of human destinies am I.
Fame, love, and fortune on my footsteps wait,
Cities and fields I walk; I penetrate
Deserts and seas remote, and, passing by
Hovel, and mart, and palace, soon or late
I knock unbidden, once at every gate!
If sleeping, wake—if feasting, rise before
I turn away. It is the hour of fate,
And they who follow me reach every state
Mortals desire, and conquer every foe
Save death; but those who doubt or hesitate,
Condemned to failure, penury and woe,
Seek me in vain and uselessly implore—
I answer not, and I return no more.
                    —*John James Ingalls*

WAITING

Serene I fold my hands and wait,
    Nor care for wind, nor tide, nor sea.
I rave no more 'gainst time or fate,
    For lo! my own shall come to me.

I stay my haste, I make delays,
    For what avails this eager pace?

I stand amid the eternal ways,
  And what is mine shall know my face.

Asleep, awake, by night or day,
  The friends I seek are seeking me;
No wind can drive my bark astray,
  Nor change the tide of destiny.

What matter if I stand alone?
  I wait with joy the coming years;
My heart shall reap where it hath sown,
  And garner up its fruit of tears.

The waters know their own and draw
  The brook that springs in yonder height;
So flows the good with equal law
  Unto the soul of pure delight.

The stars come nightly to the sky;
  The tidal wave unto the sea;
Nor time, nor space, nor deep, nor high,
  Can keep my own away from me.
                    —*John Burroughs*

SALLY IN OUR ALLEY

Of all the girls that are so smart,
  There's none like Pretty Sally;
She is the darling of my heart,
  And lives in our alley.
There's ne'er a lady in the land
  That's half so sweet as Sally;
She is the darling of my heart,
  And lives in our alley.

Her father he makes cabbage-nets,
  And through the streets does cry them;
Her mother she sells laces long
  To such as please to buy them:
But sure such folk can have no part
  In such a girl as Sally;
She is the darling of my heart,
  And lives in our alley.

When she is by, I leave my work,
  I love her so sincerely;
My master comes, like any Turk,
  And bangs me most severely:
But let him bang, long as he will,
  I'll bear it all for Sally;
She is the darling of my heart,
  And lives in our alley.

Of all the days are in the week,
  I dearly love but one day,
And that's the day that comes betwixt
  A Saturday and Monday;
For then I'm dressed, all in my best,
  To walk abroad with Sally;
She is the darling of my heart,
  And lives in our alley.

My master carries me to church,
  And often am I blamed,
Because I leave him in the lurch,
  Soon as the text is named:
I leave the church in sermon time,
  And slink away to Sally;
She is the darling of my heart,
  And lives in our alley.

When Christmas comes about again,
  Oh, then I shall have money;
I'll hoard it up and, box and all,
  I'll give it to my honey;
Oh, would it were ten thousand pounds,
  I'd give it all to Sally;
For she's the darling of my heart,
  And lives in our alley.

My master, and the neighbors all,
  Make game of me and Sally,
And but for her I'd better be
  A slave, and row a galley:
But when my seven long years are out,
  Oh, then I'll marry Sally,

And then how happily we'll live—
  But not in our alley.
                       —*Henry Carey*

HEREDITY

That swollen paunch you are doomed to bear
Your gluttonous grandsire used to wear:
That tongue, at once so light and dull,
Wagged in your grandam's empty skull;
That leering of the sensual eye
Your father, when he came to die,
Left yours alone: and that cheap flirt,
Your mother, gave you from the dirt
The simper which she used upon
So many men ere he was won.

Your vanity and greed and lust
Are each your portion from the dust
Of those that died, and from the tomb
Made you what you must needs become.
I do not hold you aught to blame
For sin at second hand, and shame:
Evil could but from evil spring;
And yet, away, you charnel thing!
             —*William Dean Howells*

MY LIFE IS LIKE THE
SUMMER ROSE

My life is like the summer rose,
  That opens to the morning sky,
But, ere the shades of evening close,
  Is scattered on the ground—to die!
Yet on the rose's humble bed
The sweetest dews of night are shed,
As if she wept the waste to see—
But none shall weep a tear for me!

My life is like the autumn leaf
  That trembles in the moon's pale ray:
Its hold is frail—its date is brief,

Restless—and soon to pass away!
Yet, ere that leaf shall fall and fade,
The parent tree will mourn its shade,
The winds bewail the leafless tree—
But none shall breathe a sigh for me!

My life is like the prints, which feet
   Have left on Tampa's desert strand;
Soon as the rising tide shall beat,
   All trace will vanish from the sand;
Yet, as if grieving to efface
All vestige of the human race,
On that lone shore loud moans the sea—
But none, alas! shall mourn for me!
        —*Richard Henry Wilde*

WEARYIN' FOR YOU

Jest a-wearyin' for you,
All the time a-feelin' blue;
Wishin' for you, wondering when
You'll be comin' home agen;
Restless—don't know what to do—
   Jest a-wearyin' for you.

Keep a-mopin' day by day;
Dull—in everybody's way.
Folks they smile and pass along,
Wonderin' what on earth is wrong;
'Twouldn't help 'em if they knew—
   Jest a-wearyin' for you.

Room's so lonesome, with your chair
Empty by the fireplace there;
Jest can't stand the sight of it;
Go out doors and roam a bit;
But the woods is lonesome, too—
   Jest a-wearyin' for you.

Comes the wind with soft caress
Like the rustlin' of your dress;
Blossoms fallin' to the ground
Softly like your footsteps sound;

Violets like your eyes so blue,—
  Jest a-wearyin' for you.

Mornin' comes. The birds awake
(Use to sing so for your sake;)
But there's sadness in the notes
That come thrillin' from their throats!
Seem to feel your absence, too—
  Jest a-wearyin' for you.

Evenin' falls. I miss you more
When the dark gloom's in the door;
Seems jest like you orter be
There to open it for me!
Latch goes tinklin'—thrills me through;
  Sets me wearyin' for you.

Jest a-wearyin' for you!
All the time a-feelin' blue!
Wishin' for you—wonderin' when
You'll be comin' home agen.
Restless—don't know what to do—
  Jest a-wearyin' for you.
                    —*Frank L. Stanton*

CHILD LABOR

No fledgling feeds the fatherbird,
  No chicken feeds the hen,
No kitten mouses for the cat—
  This glory is for men.

We are the wisest, strongest race:
  Long may our praise be sung—
The only animal alive
  That lives upon its young!
                —*Charlotte Perkins Gilman*

A VISIT FROM ST. NICHOLAS

'Twas the night before Christmas, when all through the house
Not a creature was stirring, not even a mouse;

The stockings were hung by the chimney with care,
In hopes that St. Nicholas soon would be there;
The children were nestled all snug in their beds,
While visions of sugar plums danced in their heads;
And mamma in her 'kerchief, and I in my cap,
Had just settled our brains for a long winter's nap,
When out on the lawn there arose such a clatter,
I sprang from the bed to see what was the matter.
Away to the window I flew like a flash,
Tore open the shutters and threw up the sash.
The moon on the breast of the new-fallen snow
Gave the luster of midday to objects below,
When, what to my wondering eyes should appear,
But a miniature sleigh, and eight tiny reindeer,
With a little old driver, so lively and quick,
I knew in a moment it must be St. Nick.
More rapid than eagles his coursers they came,
And he whistled, and shouted, and called them by name;
"Now, *Dasher!* now, *Dancer!* now, *Prancer* and *Vixen!*
On, *Comet!* on, *Cupid!* on, *Donder* and *Blitzen!*
To the top of the porch! to the top of the wall!
Now dash away! dash away! dash away all!"
As dry leaves that before the wild hurricane fly,
When they meet with an obstacle, mount to the sky;
So up to the house top the coursers they flew,
With the sleigh full of toys, and St. Nicholas, too.
And then, in a twinkling, I heard on the roof
The prancing and pawing of each little hoof.
As I drew in my head, and was turning around,
Down the chimney St. Nicholas came with a bound.
He was dressed all in fur, from his head to his foot,
And his clothes were all tarnished with ashes and soot;
A bundle of toys he had flung on his back,
And he looked like a pedler just opening his pack.
His eyes—how they twinkled! his dimples how merry!
His cheeks were like roses, his nose like a cherry!
His droll little mouth was drawn up like a bow,
And the beard of his chin was as white as the snow;
The stump of a pipe he held tight in his teeth,
And the smoke it encircled his head like a wreath;
He had a broad face and a little round belly,
That shook when he laughed like a bowlful of jelly.
He was chubby and plump, a right jolly old elf,
And I laughed when I saw him, in spite of myself;

A wink of his eye and a twist of his head,
Soon gave me to know I had nothing to dread;
He spoke not a word, but went straight to his work,
And filled all the stockings; then turned with a jerk,
And laying his finger aside of his nose,
And giving a nod, up the chimney he rose;
He sprang to his sleigh, to his team gave a whistle,
And away they all flew like the down of a thistle.
But I heard him exclaim, ere he drove out of sight,
"Happy Christmas to all, and to all a good night."
—*Clement Clarke Moore*

Index